THE
AUCKLAND
REGIMENT

Officers of the Original Auckland Infantry Battalion, Epsom, 1914.

The Auckland Regiment

being an account of the doings on Active Service of the First, Second and Third Battalions of the Auckland Regiment

by

2/LIEUT. O. E. BURTON, M.M.
Medaille d'Honneur

MCMXXII

Whitcombe & Tombs Ltd., Auckland
Wellington, Christchurch, Dunedin, New Zealand
Melbourne and London

W. & T. Lᵀᴰ·

PRESS OF
WHITCOMBE & TOMBS LTD.
AUCKLAND, N.Z.

"*I have seen with the eyes of God. I have seen the naked souls of men stripped of circumstance. Rank and reputation, wealth and poverty, knowledge and ignorance, manners and uncouthness, these I saw not. I saw the naked souls of men. I saw who were slaves, and who were free; who were beasts, and who men; who were contemptible, and who honourable. I have seen with the eyes of God. I have seen the vanity of the temporal, and the glory of the eternal. . . . . I have understood the victory of the Cross. 'O, Death, where is thy sting?'*"

Donald Hankey, " A Student in Arms."

Foreword

WHILE the New Zealand Division was still in France, in 1918, it was decided that preliminary steps should be taken to compile the histories of the different units of which the Division was composed. In August, 1918, a Divisional Order was issued directing the senior officer in each Regiment or analogous formation to make proposals for the commencement of this undertaking, and the method of effecting it. The rapid progress of the war during the autumn of 1918, and the quick demobilisation which followed the Armistice, prevented the idea being executed as originally intended. No steps were therefore taken towards writing the history till the Division had returned to New Zealand, and much time, and, what was still more important, the opportunity of collecting valuable material had then been lost.

At a conference of senior officers held in Wellington in November, 1919, it was resolved that the histories of the different formations should be written, financial provision being made from the accumulated canteen funds of units. For the Auckland Regiment, Lieut-Colonel S. S. Allen was appointed to nominate and convene a committee to control the writing and publication of its history. The following Committee was accordingly convened:—

    Colonel A. Plugge, C.M.G.
    Lieut.-Colonel S. S. Allen, C.M.G., D.S.O.
    Lieut.-Colonel R. C. Allen, D.S.O.
    Lieut.-Colonel F. L.-G. West.
    Major J. G. Coates, M.C., M.P.

and by it the necessary arrangements have been made.

The committee commissioned 2nd Lieutenant O. E. Burton, M.M., to write the History. Mr. Burton's personal connection with the Regiment was extensive, he having joined with the Fourth Reinforcements, and having had almost unbroken ser-

Foreword

vice in the field down to the Armistice. The narrative has been entirely in his hands, the manuscript being submitted to the Committee for correction of such inaccuracies as to facts as were within the members' own knowledge. The colloquial style, anecdotes and personal views expressed throughout the book may serve to give an insight into the mentality and general viewpoint of the average soldier, which a more matter-of-fact record of places, names and events would have failed to provide, and will compensate to some extent for the lack of detailed reference to the tactical phases of the operations and the relations of the regimental units to larger formations which a strictly military history should no doubt provide. These can, however, be found by the student in the excellent histories of the New Zealand Division as a whole which have already appeared. It must not be assumed, however, that the writer's personal views, as expressed in the book, are also those of the members of the Committee.

It is believed that substantial accuracy has been obtained in all names and dates in this book, especially in the appendices. Some errors probably have occurred, and the Committee will be grateful for notes of any corrections that should be made. The thanks of the Committee are due to Lieut.-Colonel N. W. B. B. Thoms, D.S.O., M.C., and Major E. Puttick, D.S.O., for their assistance in preparing the maps. The maps have all been drawn by Major Puttick, who has been kind enough to give a very great deal of time and trouble to their preparation.

Author's Foreword

My very pleasant task has at last been completed, and soon the History of the Auckland Regiment will be published. That it will be widely read I feel certain—not because of any merit in the book, but because so many of us loved the old Regiment, and look back with pleasure on the many happy days we spent together. They were rough and dangerous times, but they were made bright by the fine friends we met at every turn. For most of us the wartime will always remain the most vivid and interesting part of our lives.

It may seem strange that I, who am a pacifist, should write a war history. Yet surely one can be quite consistent and do so. Whatever one thinks of war and the causes of war, it is undoubtedly true that in battle the finest sides of human character develop themselves. Valour, self-sacrifice, steadfastness, devotion to duty, gentleness and brotherliness are all great virtues. They shone pre-eminently in those days when Life and Death were the stakes we played for. It is fitting that the boys who are now growing up to manhood should never forget that these are the things which should always characterise the New Zealander. If the story of the Auckland Regiment will serve to set some sort of standard of manhood for the boys of Auckland, I will feel that the writing of it has not been altogether in vain.

I do not suppose that a single member of the Regiment will be satisfied with the book, and many will disapprove quite violently. Critics will please remember two things: First, that I am not John Masefield, and second, that they themselves are probably amongst the number who sent me neither information nor suggestions. It would have taken me years to have hunted up everyone, and so to have amassed the immense amount of detail which one should really have for a book of this nature. Incidentally, writing a book is not

Author's Foreword

as easy as one might think. If anyone has doubts, let him try himself.

Many names have been mentioned. In my judgment, and from the evidence at my disposal, they seemed the most worthy. The main trouble came not with the names put in, but with those left out. I know that many first rate men have been missed, and some will feel disappointed at not getting the mention they so thoroughly deserve. They have been omitted simply because my information has not been as full as I wish it had been. If a second edition of this book should ever be required, perhaps everything can be put right; for I will carefully file all criticisms, suggestions, information, etc., which I know will pour in upon me—AFTER publication.

My thanks are due to all who have assisted me either by the loan of diaries or by giving up their time for personal interviews; also to the Regimental Committee, who have very carefully read all manuscripts, and whose advice and suggestions have been most helpful.

I hope that, if nothing more, this book may serve to quicken old memories and help many of you to live over again the great days when we marched and fought, bivouacked and billeted in Egypt, Gallipoli, France and Flanders.

With best wishes to all my old comrades—better ones a man could never want!

ORMOND BURTON.

Contents

		PAGE
I.—Alexandra Park		1
II.—The Voyage		4
III.—Zeitoun Camp		10
IV.—The Haven of Lemnos		21
V.—The Battle of the Landing		25
VI.—Cape Helles		35
VII.—Quinn's Post		40
VIII.—Anzac Life		46
IX.—June and July		50
X.—The August Fighting—Sari Bair		54
XI.—Rhododendron Spur		66
XII.—Lemnos		69
XIII.—The Last Six Weeks		72
XIV.—The Evacuation		77
XV.—Egypt		82
XVI.—France		90
XVII.—Armentières		93
XVIII.—The Battle of the Somme		104
XIX.—The Winter of 1916-17		118
XX.—Le Bizet—Ploegsteert—Hill 63		129
XXI.—Messines		140
XXII.—The Aftermath of Battle		153
XXIII.—Ypres		165
XXIV.—The Winter in the Salient		182
XXV.—Mailly-Maillet		194
XXVI.—Holding the Line		207
XXVII.—To Bapaume!—Rossignol Wood, Grevillers, Bapaume, Bancourt		220

Contents

	PAGE
XXVIII.—SEPTEMBER	242
XXIX.—WELSH RIDGE—CRÊVECŒUR—RUMILLY—LE QUESNOY	248
XXX.—GERMANY	261
XXXI.—HOME	264
APPENDICES—	
"A" BADGES, PATCHES AND NUMBERS	265
"B" CHRONOLOGY	267
"C" HONOURS AND AWARDS	274
"D" CASUALTY LISTS	282

List of Maps

	FACING PAGE
Suez Canal Zone	16
Anzac	40
Armentières—Fleurbaix	96
North of France—Belgium—The Rhine	96
First Battle of the Somme, 1916	104
Messines, Hill 63—Ploegsteert, Warneton	136
Ypres	168
Gravenstafel—Abraham Heights	168
Hebutérne	200
Somme Area	200
Bapaume—Bancourt	232
Le Quesnoy	248
Crêvecœur	248
Selle River	248

List of Illustrations

	FACING PAGE
Officers of Original Auckland Infantry Battalion, Epsom, 1914	Frontispiece
Private J. Crighton, V.C.	
Sergeant Samuel Forsyth, V.C.	33
Lieutenant R. Judson, V.C., D.C.M., M.M.	48
Brigadier-General R. Young, C.B., C.M.G., D.S.O.	65
Brigadier-General C. H. J. Brown, D.S.O.	80
Colonel A. Plugge, C.M.G.	113
Lieutenant-Colonel W. W. Alderman, C.M.G., D.S.O.	128
Lieutenant-Colonel S. S. Allen, C.M.G., D.S.O.	145
Lieutenant-Colonel R. C. Allen, D.S.O.	160
Lieutenant-Colonel D. B. Blair, D.S.O., M.C.	177
Lieutenant-Colonel A. G. McKenzie, D.S.O.	190

Private J. Crighton, V.C.

I.

Alexandra Park

"For all we have and are,
For all our children's fate
Stand up, and take the war,
The Hun is at the gate!"
—Kipling.

In the first three days of August, 1914, there were hopes, fears, doubtings, but an ever-increasing undercurrent of certainty that war would come.

The Germans crossed the Belgian Frontier. The word came. It was War.

Kitchener accepted the offer of a New Zealand Expeditionary Force, and mobilisation commenced at once. On August 11, Alexandra Park was opened as a military camp, and the Auckland Infantry Battalion was formed.

It was decided that the four Military Districts into which New Zealand had been divided under the Territorial scheme should each provide a Regiment of Infantry, composed of one battalion, and thus form the New Zealand Infantry Brigade, consisting of the Auckland, Wellington, Canterbury, and Otago Battalions. The Infantry Brigade, together with a Brigade of Mounted Rifles, Artillery, and Divisional Troops formed the original N.Z.E.F.

In the Auckland District there were in existence four Infantry Regiments: the 3rd (Auckland), 6th (Hauraki), 15th (North Auckland), and 16th (Waikato). Each of these Regiments provided a Company, and also certain specialists, to form the Battalion for service overseas. The four companies of the Battalion thus formed retained the names and badges of the Territorial Regiments from which they were drawn. The organisation and commands were as follow:—

Commanding Officer: Lieut.-Colonel Plugge
Second-in-Command: Major Harrowell
Adjutant: Capt. Alderman

The Auckland Regiment

Machine-gun Officer: Capt. Wallingford
Asst.-Machine-gun Officer: Lieut. Fraser
Quartermaster: Capt. Graham
Transport Officer: Lieut. Morgan
Medical Officers (attached): Dr. Purchas, Dr. Craig
Chaplain: Rev. Clarkson

3rd (Auckland) Company—
  Officer Commanding: Major Dawson
  Second-in-Command: Capt. Price
  Platoon Commanders: Lieuts. Macfarlane, Woolley, West, and Carpenter

6th (Hauraki) Company—
  Officer Commanding: Major Stuckey
  Second-in-Command: Capt. Sinel
  Platoon Commanders: Lieuts. Morpeth, Algie, Flower, and Dodson

15th (North Auckland) Company—
  Officer Commanding: Major Bayly
  Second-in-Command: Captain Bartlett
  Platoon Commanders: Lieuts. Screaton, Steadman, McClelland, and Weir

16th (Waikato) Company—
  Officer Commanding: Capt. MacDonald
  Platoon Commanders: Lieuts. Allen, Peake, Westmacott, and Baddeley

In Alexandra Park men shed their civilian clothes and received that weird and wonderful collection of odds and ends that are so essential for the making of the perfect soldier. They learned that the Battalion was composed of four companies, to wit, the 3rd (Auckland), the 6th (Hauraki), the 15th (North Auckland), and the 16th (Waikato), all presided over by Battalion Headquarters, where lived the Colonel, the Adjutant, the Doctor, and other all-important people. They learned, too, that a company consisted of four platoons, and that each platoon was subdivided into four sections. A man got to know his own section, the majority of his platoon, a certain number in the company, and, beyond this again, a few

Alexandra Park

notorieties scattered over the Battalion. Discipline was much talked of by all the authorities. It was a magic thing, by virtue of which the war was to be won. It consisted largely in the clicking of heels at stated times, the rapid casting of the eyes to the right or the left, and the saluting at all times of passing Authority. Certain other forms, ceremonies and formulæ were also much bound up with this all-important matter, particularly the constant shining of brass buttons. Shining buttons were almost as important as salutes and the clicking of heels, and would cause much confusion in the ranks of the Hun. For the rest, they learned to form fours, to march reasonably, and to make the proper connection between rifle and bayonet. The most exciting experience was the march to Manurewa—some fifteen miles. The distance was accomplished in good style, and the Battalion then bivouacked for the night in an open field. It was a wet night, and cold. The majority walked about, shivering and miserable, but heroically stuck it out. Half-a-dozen of the fainter-hearted—or longer-headed—took refuge in a neighbouring farm-house. Their conduct excited much indignation at the time, so seriously were all set on the business of developing discipline; but it would be interesting to know what the subsequent war-history of the erring six was like. Khaki was found to have a very potent influence over the youth and beauty of Auckland town, which was very satisfying, and just as it should be. The food was excellent. Training was not too hard. There was a reasonable amount of leave, and all things were going well, except the fact that the war was hurrying on, and unless the "Heads" hurried up, the Auckland Battalion would arrive too late for the fun. It was certainly consoling to know that the *S.S. Waimana*, otherwise *His Majesty's New Zealand Troopship No. 12*, was being fitted out; but yet the weeks were passing, and the "Herald" and "Star" were every day announcing such a startling and brilliant succession of victories that surely the downfall of the Kaiser could be expected at any time.

II.

The Voyage

> "*Wandering spirits seeking lands unknown,
>   Such were our fathers, stout hearts unafraid.
> Have we been faithless leaving homes they made
>   With their life's blood cementing every stone?
> Nay, ... Their restless spirit bade
>   Us fight with those whose homeland was their own.*"
>
> —Capt. James Sprent, A.I.F.,
> In the Anzac Book.

On the evening of September 22nd, the men carrying the greater part of their baggage, marched down to the boat, and were allotted their quarters. Next day an immense crowd assembled in the Domain to farewell the Auckland Battalion and the details who had been with them in the Epsom camp. The men marched through a great throng to the wharf. Merry raillery, handshakes, kisses, and tears, and then the people were shut off by the wharf gates. There was little delay, and just as the transport pulled away the gates were opened, and the crowd came running down to wave a last farewell. North Head was passed, Rangitoto, Tiri, the waters of the Hauraki Gulf, and then the vessel turned northward. About midnight she was in the vicinity of Cape Brett. All was running smoothly when suddenly there was a startled exclamation: "Bli' me, Bill, the blanky moon's turning round!" Whatever might be the moon's intention, there was no doubt that the *Waimana* was turning. To the complete and utter surprise of every man awake, she went round in a circle and headed south. At dawn she was off Rangitoto, and the sound sleepers, upon waking and seeing the familiar outline, rubbed their eyes in amazement.

"What have you come back for?" signalled Fort Cautley.

"It was too dark outside," wagged back a signaller, "so we have come back for the *Torch*."

As a matter of fact, they had returned because the *Pyramus*, scouting well ahead, had come into contact with the German Pacific Fleet.

The Voyage

For the next fortnight the Battalion lived on board the boat. The short experience at sea had shown up several defects in the internal arrangements, which were rectified. The men landed every day for training, and, of course, had opportunities of saying good-byes all over again.

On October 11th, the *Waimana* left once more—this time for Wellington—where the whole of the Expeditionary Force assembled.

At dawn, October 16th, 1914, the escorting warships moved out, with the transports following in file. Hobart was the first port of call, and here everyone was landed for a route march, which developed into a very fine affair. Varying opinions were expressed about the beauty of the town, but there was no doubt about the kindness of the people, or the heartiness of their welcome. They thronged round the marching men, walking beside them, breaking into the ranks, and pressing on everyone gifts of the famous Tasmanian apples, cigarettes, and bunches of flowers. It was the greatest burst of spontaneous welcome the New Zealanders ever received, with the exception, perhaps, of the march through Verviers, in liberated Belgium.

At Albany, the A.I.F. greeted the N.Z.E.F. with much cheering, and then on November 1st the whole great fleet put to sea. The columns of ships covered many miles, and from the deck of the *Waimana,* bringing up the rear, the foremost boat could be located only by the streamer of smoke above the horizon. In the Indian Ocean the weather soon became unbearably hot, and all sorts of wonderful costumes made their appearance. There was little to do but swelter. The sea was a sea of glass, beautifully calm, and of the deepest, most lovely blue imaginable. There was no swell, and the ship moved surely and steadily, with just a fleck of white foam ahead, and the long wake behind. The chief occupation of all hands was to invent and circulate rumours. News consisted of scanty scraps of wireless. With nothing to do all day except lounge round the decks, eat, sleep, smoke, and yarn, it was the most natural thing in the world for the intellectuals to

The Auckland Regiment

"shatter the sorry schemes of things entire, and build anew nearer to the heart's desire." The sea was filled with German cruisers, great fights were won and lost. Impossible dishes were served up for next day's dinner. Notable personages of the Regiment had their careers discussed in detail, and would probably have been somewhat alarmed to have got "the full strength" of their hectic past. The destination of the fleet was a question of perennial interest. India and garrison duty, Egypt, France, England and South Africa all had stout champions and a well-reasoned case. South Africa had, for a while, a very great hold on popular imagination, so great a hold, indeed, that Major Dawson was able to work a very fine hoax. A notice appeared that "A mobile column, commanded by Major Dawson, will be landed at Durban for operations against the rebels in South Africa. Basuto ponies will be provided." Then followed a list of certain officers of the force, and an invitation for volunteers to apply. There was a rush to join, and the orderly room was bombarded with queries. The conquest and pacification of South Africa, however, was for other hands.

A typhoid inoculation at this time was by no means a rumour. It gave the Medical Staff a busy day, and the troops a new topic of conversation. Legalists discovered that this inoculation, being a surgical operation, could not be performed without the consent of the individual. Military authority, apparently, could not be enforced on this point, and pressure only could be brought to bear. The great mass of commonsense people submitted without a murmur, but a few cranks held out, and were ultimately sent back to New Zealand.

The days passed happily enough, without any great event. Lights were never shown, and the closest watch was kept. The *Waimana* was running a double risk—from the enemy and from the ship in line ahead. The *Ruapehu* was a somewhat erratic performer, and was always liable to indulge in little freaks of wayward fancy, whenever her steering gear took a spell off.

At 6.30 on the morning of the 9th, the flagship *Mel-*

The Voyage

bourne was signalling to the *Sydney,* which steered away towards Cocos Island. The *Ibuki* tore round the head of the convoy, flags flying, smoke belching from her funnels, and took up station on the exposed flank. There was something doing all right, and excitement rose high. At 9.30 news came that the action had commenced. Two hours later the Colonel came out with a message form: "*Emden* beached and done for." At once the ship was transformed into a raving, cheering crowd of excitables. For the next few days an emanation of joy hung over the fleet.

Crossing the line the fun was fast and furious. Major Dawson represented His Most Marine Highness, while Lieut. Woolley was the brazen hussy, his bouncing bride. Due notice was given of the Royal visit, and all arangements made. A big canvas bath was set up, and to see that no unauthorised duckings took place before the appointed time, Sergt.-Major King, the Provost-Sergeant, personally mounted guard. He, in all his glory, was too much of a temptation, and certain of the onlookers of the baser sort tipped him "up-and-over." In he went, authority, dignity, uniform and all, with a fine splash. The Padre, the Rev. Clarkson, was taking photos of the gay scene. His spotless raiment was suddenly spoilt by a well-aimed bucket of greasy water. History records that he immediately, in no very muffled tones, swore a good loud swear. Majors, captains, rank and file, all went the same way. Conscientious objectors were summarily dealt with. The bandmaster took refuge in his cabin, and locked the door. This was promptly screwed off its hinges; but he repelled the attackers with his drawn sword. It was a clear case for a barrage, and he was finally overwhelmed by a concentration of three fire-hoses. By this time pandemonium had broken loose, and for two hours a good-natured but very boisterous mob held sway. "McAndrew's Put-Away-Brigade" were very prominent. The cooks kept up a very heavy fire of water on all passers-by. It was a wild day, and everyone at the close was tired and happy.

Colombo was reached, and a little later, the victorious

The Auckland Regiment

Sydney steamed in through the breakwater, her decks covered with wounded Germans. There was no cheering, for fear of "hurting the feelings of the captive enemy." This was perhaps straining the idea of chivalry to a beaten foe rather far; yet the crew of the *Emden* had fought bravely, and had done their duty to the uttermost.

It seemed for a while that very few would be allowed on shore, but Colonel Plugge very dexterously managed to misunderstand the orders issued, with the result that everyone went off. Despite thick woollen clothes and a sweltering sun, the few hours on shore made a splendid break. For the majority, it was their first introduction to the wonders of the Magic East. No sooner were the men ashore than they were assailed by a crowd of long-robed skirmishers: "Flowers, master! Cigarettes, master! Master, look here! Rickshaw, master!" Driven off once, they returned with the pertinacity of hungry flies. Everyone was out to push his wares with the rich Colonials, and many were successful beyond their hopes. It was the only chance of sending back Christmas presents to the home folks. Silks, embroidery, beads, curios, ivory elephants, postcards, and odds and ends of all sorts had a great sale. Everyone had a most interesting wander round—past splendid club-houses, green fields and fine parks, through Buddhist temples and the bizarre native quarters. Last, but not least, often first and foremost, the best hotels were thronged with a multitude seeking for the luxury of a civilised dinner.

Colombo, with all its tropical beauty, its quaint picturesque people, its gorgeous sunsets, and its indescribable charm, was away down behind the horizon, and the *Waimana* was ploughing steadily across the Arabian Sea. Past the barren sunscorched rock of Aden, through the Red Sea, past the Twelve Apostles, leaving Mecca on the one hand and Suakim on the other, until Sinai loomed up in the distance, and passing up the Gulf, the transports came to Suez and cast anchor. All doubts as to destination were quickly satisfied. The N.Z.E.F. was to disembark at Alexandria, and to go into camp outside Cairo, where the training would be completed.

The Voyage

Turks had been reported in the vicinity of the Canal, so the bridge was fortified with flour-bags, and machine-guns were mounted. All on board were hoping that the enemy would be polite, and put himself up as a target. However, he was otherwise engaged, and the Battalion's thirst for blood was perforce unassuaged. It was an interesting trip, with the gleaming yellow desert stretching away as far as the eye could see, the blue waters of Lake Timsah, and the posts of Indian troops guarding the strip of water, who cheered shrilly as the boats passed. One incident occurred at Port Said that will not readily be forgotten. A French man-of-war, the *Henri IV,* lying at anchor, was cheered by the passing troopships. The Frenchmen lined up on deck and sang the "Marseillaise" with a thrill of passion and an abandonment which made a deep impression. New Zealanders were just commencing to feel the first stirring of the profound realisation of nationality which was to be theirs, as afterwards they marched from one field of glory to another; and this spontaneous outburst of French sentiment moved all hearts.

III.

Zeitoun Camp and the Canal

"*For physical beauty and nobility of bearing, they surpassed any men I have ever seen. They walked and looked like the kings in old poems.*"
—John Masefield.

At dawn on December 3rd, before the morning mists had lifted, the masts and spars of innumerable vessels were seen above the horizon, then the brown line of the breakwater, and as the sun gained power, the gleaming white and yellow buildings of Alexandria came into view. The *Waimana* was berthed, and preparations for disembarkation at once commenced. Much was done during the day, and in the evening general leave was granted. What a night it was! The holds afterwards were full of excited men, everyone talking at the top of his voice. No one listened to anyone else. Everyone was too full of his own experiences—and so the babel flowed on. In one evening they had seen Aladdin's cave, the Forty Thieves, and the houris of the Thousand and One Nights; veiled women, and others whose draperies were of the most diaphanous sort; French, Greeks, Russians, and Italians, with the brown-skinned Egyptians and the black Nubians from the South—all these they had seen, and the spell of Egypt had taken hold of them. They were lured by the sensuous, riotous beauty of the land. They were repelled by the sordidness of the vice, and the bare hideousness which peered out from beneath the most wonderful superficial loveliness. Land of Egypt—Egypt land! And so the talk went on, confused and wild, until all at last fell asleep.

The Battalion entrained for Cairo, and for many hours were running through the Nile Delta; past the reedy shores of Lake Mariotis, where the fisher-folk were mending their nets, and then—

Zeitoun Camp

*"Through fields of barley and of rye
That clothed the wold and touched the sky,
And through the fields the road ran by"—*

to the palaces and minarets of ancient Cairo. For great distances the highway ran parallel to the railroad. From the very dawn of history, this has always been a greatly travelled way. Moses the Hebrew, the hoplites of Alexander, the legions of Rome, the hosts of the Saracens, Napoleon and the Army of Egypt, all have tramped this dusty road. Great captains, mighty leaders, great conquerors, they and their marching men came and went, and still the rich land brings forth its teeming abundance; still the patient "fellaheen" plough with the ancient share which was known to their forefathers—men of a hundred generations back; in the same fashion they guide the running water into the rightful channels, and three times a year gather in the harvests. Every yard of that journey was crammed with interest. Strings of loaded camels passed in stately fashion with contemptuous jerkings of their heads, little donkeys ambled along quite happily under appalling loads, goats and geese were driven here and there, the quaint oxen marched steadily round and round, turning the waterwheels, and yoked up with the heavy wooden yokes drawing the ploughs and the rough native carts. The black and white robes of the men and women, the occasional red worn by the children, contrasted strongly with the green fields and the brown dusty road. Here and there the train would stop at some palm-fringed station, and at once the carriages were besieged by an eager throng selling tomatoes, "orangies," and "eggs-a-cook." Teh-el-Baroud, otherwise "To-Hell-by-Road," was passed, and many another small town and clustering village, until late in the afternoon the outskirts of Cairo were reached, and very shortly afterwards the Aucklanders were detraining at Helmieh station, Zeitoun. A short march, and the Battalion reached its camping ground and made preparations to bivouac for the night on the desert sand.

Fatigue parties were busily unloading the train, assisted by a motley crowd of natives, who did not realise for quite a long

The Auckland Regiment

while that they were engaged on a labour of love. They demanded immediate payment, and were told to send in their claims to the British Government, who would surely recompense them well. Abdul, Said, Mohammed and Co. were distinctly dubious about the prospect of any payment to be expected from the representatives of His Britannic Majesty, and loudly proclaimed a desire for "piastres" in the hand, rather than Treasury notes in the future. They became clamorous and a nuisance, whereupon the newly-arrived infidels brushed them aside, and, commandeering their carts, set to work loading and driving. "Oh Allah, what could poor righteous men, followers of the Prophet, do with these mad infidels?" It was quite clear that the poor, righteous men could do nothing, except look on disconsolately, hoping that the mad infidels would be graciously disposed and return the animals and the carts when all the stores were shifted. "Kismet! so are the true believers afflicted in this world by the sons of pigs!" In the meanwhile, the infidels unloaded the train, and enjoyed themselves immensely handling the strange beasts and old-fashioned vehicles.

In two or three days time the camp was completed, and then training commenced in earnest. Hard training it was, too. Imperial men with the Battalion reckoned it was harder than anything they had ever done with British troops. Platoon, company and battalion drill, musketry, extended order work, attack, defence, trench digging, tactical schemes, night bivouacs, and above all, route marching with full packs up, hardened the splendid material into a magnificent regiment, perfectly trained for war. A few of the weaker ones broke under the strain, but the majority throve on the hard work.

Seven o'clock in the morning, the companies fell in, swung away out past the Water Towers, marched, fought, dug and drilled for six or seven hours. The day's work over, all were free to do as they pleased. Heliopolis, the wonderful new tourist resort, was close at hand, and from there the electric railway ran straight into Cairo. Every afternoon and evening

Zeitoun Camp

the city was crowded with high-spirited men looking for fun and finding it.

From the Citadel one could see the whole city spread out before one's gaze, and not the city only, but away back to the blue horizon from which emerged the silver streak running through a strip of vegetation, which was like a veritable Garden of the Lord. Within the walls of the fortress itself were two fine mosques, the Blue and the White, one of them marked by a shot from a cannon of Napoleon. In the city was the great museum of Egyptian antiquities, the Zoo, and the old slave market, now only a mouldering ruin. Bands played in the Ez-be-kieh Gardens. The streets were thronged with people of all kindreds, and tribes and tongues. Places of amusement abounded, and ranged in quality from such resorts of wealth as Shepheard's and the Continental, to cheap and smelly cafés selling fire-water guaranteed to send a man mad in as short a time as anything on earth. Astonished Staff Officers, with red tabs, gold braid, and eye-glasses found themselves rubbing shoulders with democratic but wealthy young Colonials in resorts which had never been so desecrated before. The keepers of booths in the native bazaars did a roaring trade in curios and trinkets. Hotel and restaurant keepers had a "fearful" satisfaction in reaping their rich harvests of "piastres" and "pounds Egyptian"; but it was a precarious kind of satisfaction, for Allah only knew what the mad Australians and New Zealanders might do next. The Kursaal and the Wassah District were thronged with sight-seers. Much of Cairo was a festering sink of iniquity, repellant and yet terribly attractive. There was not a man in the Battalion, however wild he might run at times, who did not thank God that his own womenfolk were not like the horrible harpies who infested the gorgeous Eastern city. Auckland Town, Whangarei and Hamilton might be slow and drab compared with this continental gaiety, but they were clean and good.

After the hard day's training and the evening of sight-seeing and pleasure-seeking, the tired men slept soundly. In the cool of the early morning, before the sun had gained power,

The Auckland Regiment

native boys were round the camp chanting dismally "the very good news, Earl Roberts dead," "Timez Egypt—very good news to-morrow!" The paper was hastily scanned; there was a rush for breakfast, supplemented with "eggs-a-cook" when the finances were holding well, then "fall in" and march away to Fort Auckland and the day's work. At every halt or spell the sellers of "oringies" emerged from the sands of the desert to do business with the thirsty troops. Sometimes they got more than they bargained for, sometimes less. "Very beeg, very sweet, very good, three for one piastre." It was a very dangerous occupation for the "niggers," for the temper of their patrons was of a very variable nature, and quite uncertain. One day they might even give "backsheesh," but next day, if funds were low, they would insist on receiving the same, and any altercation usually ended in the merchant of "oringies" being up-ended and relieved of his burden of juicy fruit. Then a hilarious group of Aucklanders ate stolen fruit, while a gibbering, indignant "heap of blackness" fled far out on to the desert, calling on Allah to avenge his wrongs.

The Battalion was very smart in those days; buttons, belts and boots were just as fine as fine could be. Pride was taken in smart drill, but, above all, in guard mounting. This was a very great ceremony. As soon as the Battalion came in from the day's work, each section seized upon their representative and arrayed him in the section's best tunic, trousers, and equipment. He was surveyed from every point of view, polished and repolished. The best rifle, the best bayonet was his. The Guard were "fallen in" and after a very careful inspection the best man was picked out. He had the "stick"—in other words, purely nominal duties for the next twenty-four hours. So keen was the competition that it was often impossible to allot the coveted "stick" on appearance only. All were so good that there was no "best," and to choose finally, military questions were asked. The relief was carried out in great state before a large assemblage of officers, N.C.O.'s, men, bootblacks, and stray vendors of merchandise. Some of the small boys were immensely impressed with the drill, and learnt large

Zeitoun Camp

sections of the manual of military training by heart. Half-a-dozen or so of them, carefully trained by some of the men, acquired a facility in giving orders that would have done credit to a Guards' sergeant-major.

The Annexation of Egypt passed off quietly enough, although the students of El-Azhar, where the Nationalist spirit was strong, murmured a little. To impress the populace with the might and power of the British rule, the Australian and New Zealand troops marched right through the city. The natives displayed no enthusiasm, but any wild thoughts of a rising were speedily given up. The Battalion took part in this march.

Life was good, as life always is when men are as fit as men were in those days; yet an undercurrent of restlessness moved the force. They might be "Bill Massey's Tourists," but sight-seeing, even in the most wonderful land on earth, was not what they had come for. Garrison duty was all very well, but the tide of national feeling was commencing to rise, and New Zealanders felt that they could do more to win the war than keep down a timorous and subject populace. Pleasures commenced to pall, and training became tiresome. The glamour was wearing off from this land of sand and sin. For the first time the fed-up feeling was becoming really strong. Birdwood's thirty thousand were spoiling for a fight. There was bravery in the air.

It was the 25th January, and the companies were seated around the mess tables after the day's work. As always, there were rumours to discuss—there always had been rumours, and probably there always would be. The officers came round to give orders. At first no one was taking any particular notice. It would be just the usual routine of training. But, then, what orders were these? The Battalion would entrain for the Canal! In two minutes the whole atmosphere had become electrical; not a murmur was heard, all was energy and bustle, packing up and getting ready. The camp was in a ferment. "Ball cartridge!" It was handled lovingly, almost reverently. "Field dressings!" So it was to be real war, with wounds and sudden death for some.

The Auckland Regiment

The stores were served out and the bayonets sharpened. There is scarcely anything which will bring the morale of good fighting-men up to the last pitch as this sharpening of bayonets. The work was done, and now the whole camp was seething with excitement. Never before and never after was there such a spontaneous burst of enthusiasm. The band was playing and marching around. Men were cheering, singing, shouting, rushing round here and there, shaking hands with friends and enemies. The accumulated rubbish of the weeks in camp, the superfluous stuff that could not be carried, was blazing on the bonfires. The "niggers" came round, looking for a rich harvest of "backsheesh," and were immediately commandeered and tossed in blankets, one or two at a time. They fled howling, pursued by roars of wild laughter. So the fun went on till the small hours of the morning, and even then the men could not sleep, but talked and talked of the prospect of fighting.

The Battalion fell in next morning with full packs up, ready to move to the entraining point. Colonel Plugge made a little speech. "Men, there is just one thing I want to say to you. I know it is not necessary; yet I want to say it. It is probable that we shall be scrapping within the next twenty-four hours from now. Play the game. Let Auckland and New Zealand be proud of you. This order is not for nothing. That's all." The trains carrying the New Zealand Infantry Brigade moved out from Helmieh, past Zag-a-Zig and Tel-el-Kebir, and so to Ismalia, where a bivouac was formed on the desert sand. The New Zealand Brigade was to be held in reserve to the Indian troops, and to continue training. The weather was getting hotter and hotter, and training was a very strenuous business. The Turks were known to be only about eight miles from the Canal bank, and in consequence there was great excitement when platoons from the various companies were detailed for "out-post" and "trench duties." Those detailed to man the post at El-Ferdan, Battery Post, Ismalia Ferry, Toussoum, and Serapæum marched off in high spirits, reached their trenches after hard slogging through soft sand, settled

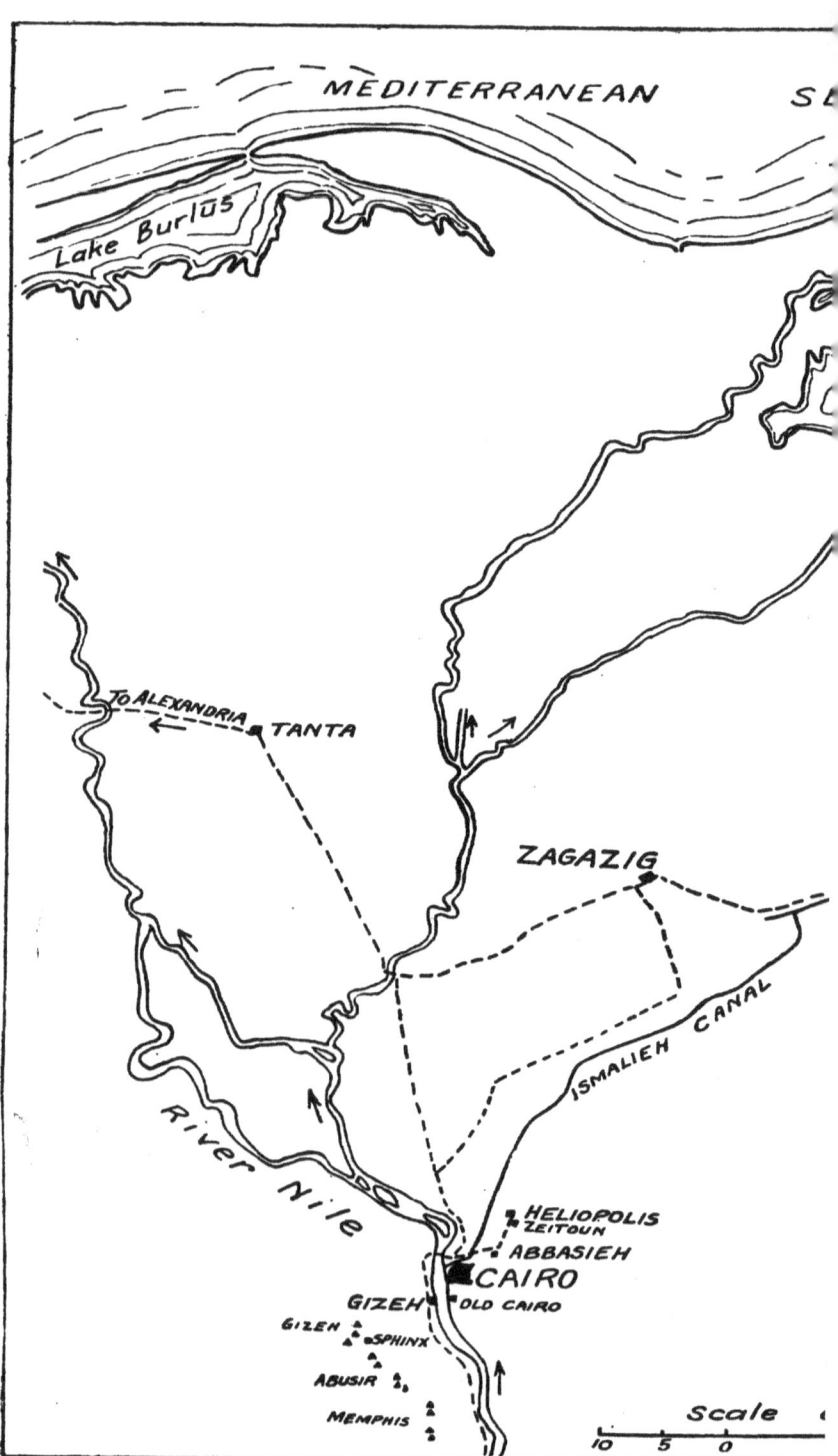

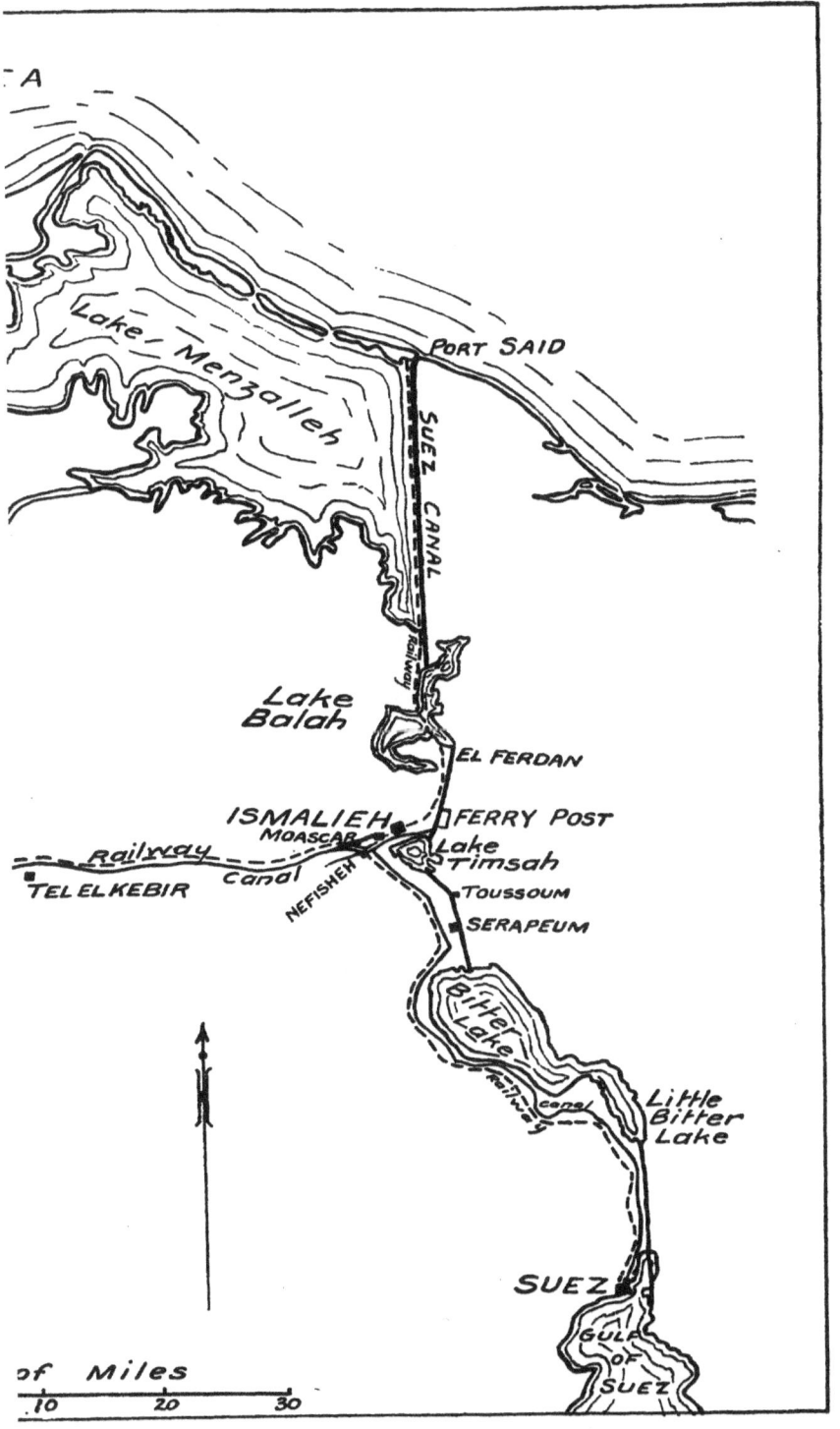

SUEZ CANAL ZONE

Zeitoun Camp

down and prayed fervently that the Turks would appear before the next relief occurred. Indian troops were about in great numbers, and were intensely keen on shooting someone or getting prisoners. They were not over particular whom they went after, evidently believing it was better to be safe than sorry; so they opened up one night on an Auckland party moving out to an outpost. Fortunately no harm was done. An Indian picquet also achieved the distinction of capturing Captain Wallingford, Lieutenant Weir and Dr. Craig, who had been out on a reconnoitring expedition on the chance of having a shot at any wandering Turks they might come across. A shell burst near a platoon of the 3rd Company under Lieut. Woolley. They broke and ran toward the explosion, to gather up the heated bits of metal, and arrived in camp very excited after their baptism of fire. El Ferdan had been shelled. Windows had been broken. There were shot holes in the buildings, bullets and shrapnel pellets lying around. This surely looked like war. However, the Aucklanders were to win no glory on this occasion, although one little party approaching a post at night thought for a brief moment that they had found a chance of distinguishing themselves. They filed through the darkness until they were within challenging distance. The corporal gave the pre-arranged signal. Silence still! What had happened? The Turks must have crept in and butchered the garrison. Very well! They must be driven out. Bayonets were fixed. The section drew up silently, and then charged heroically in. The post was empty. Needless to say, it was some time before that section heard the last of their little exploit. The Turks' attack of February 3rd failed utterly, and, in consequence, the danger to the Canal rapidly faded away. The New Zealanders were kept on a while longer. Training went on as usual, and the main diversion was swimming in Lake Timsah or in the Canal itself. It was the ambition of many to swim from Africa to Asia; while if a ship went past everyone handy stripped off and joined in the joyous scramble for tins of milk, butter, and cigarettes which were thrown over by the passengers.

The Auckland Regiment

On February 26th the Battalion returned to Zeitoun. Amongst themselves the Infantry admitted that there had been little risk and no glory, but the Mounteds and the reinforcements were not permitted to hold this view for an instant. Especially as regards the reinforcements the Canal Battle was of the very greatest importance in maintaining the prestige of the Main Body. Reinforcements were novelties in those days, and as many of them had attained a certain amount of *esprit-de-corps* in Trentham, it was very necessary to reduce them to a fitting state of humility. The logic of a man who had seen a shell burst was irrefutable, and the reinforcement had nothing with which to counter this tremendous fact.

The camp was established once more on the same spot. The old routine was recommenced, a little harder if anything, but it was a welcome change to be back again in Cairo amidst the great bustle of life and the changing scenes of the gay city. Needless to say, the ranks of the Battalion were full of first-class athletes; and so when the Artillery sent in a challenge to play Rugby football, there was not the slightest difficulty in picking a very fine team. The Auckland representatives were Fitzgerald, Les. Hill, Roy Lambert, McGeehan, Fox, Jock McKenzie, Moki, Fordyce, Savory, Frank McKenzie, Ted Lambert, Smith, Gasparich, and two others.

Two great games resulted, the first ending in a draw, neither side scoring, and the second in a win for Auckland, six to three. Never in all its history had the Egyptian Railway Ground seen such struggles.

The weather grew hotter and hotter. The "fellaheen" struggled with a plague of locusts that a wind brought out of the desert, while the troops were plagued with a great thirst. It was not that the springs of water dried up, but that the wet canteen refused to sell more than one bottle of beer to a man. As a special concession, it was announced that if a written order was produced, signed by an officer, a further quantity of liquor as per order could be purchased. The promotions that took place in the Battalion were astonishing. All pieces of paper with writing on were the same to the Greeks who

Zeitoun Camp

were running the bar, so everyone was happy until the matter came to the ears of the Higher Command.

In the course of the training, Auckland carried out an attack with real guns firing real shells overhead, a mimic battle, in which the danger was approximately the same as in the Battle of the Canal. The Artillery kept their heads well, and, allowing a wide margin, inflicted no casualties. During this period, Captain Alderman was promoted Major, and took command of the 16th Company. Captain Price became Adjutant, and Sergeant Frater of the Machine Guns received his commission. At last the training had reached such a stage that it was impossible to do more to improve the magnificent physical fitness of every member of the unit. The Battalion could march twenty-five miles in the day carrying out tactical schemes, and all this with every man carrying full equipment and pack.

Cairo once more ceased to satisfy. The "very good guide, sir," who showed as a testimonial a document from "Billjim" of Australia to the effect that, "This guide is no good at all, give him a kick," was apt to get a good measure of bootleather, but very few "piastres." Even those cheerful young street Arabs, the boot-blacks, who clamoured loudly for the privilege of cleaning "Mr. McKenzie's boots*a*," were not met with the same good temper as formerly. As for the food— it was stew, stew, stew, and ever more stew. The 15th Company even went so far as to hold a public meeting for the abolition of stews. The spirit of restlessness once more grew and increased. When would the fighting start? They had waited for six months, and still there was nothing but the eternal monotony of training. The witchery and mystery of the East began to lose its novelty and charm. There were great deeds doing in the West. The Old Army was dying magnificently to save Europe. The Territorials had fought their first fight. The Canadians had a day of glory in Flanders, but for the New Zealanders it was marching until their souls were sick of marching; training until they were surfeited with training, and still their day did not come. Training, training, always

The Auckland Regiment

training and more training, while the world was ringing with the deeds of the "thin khaki line" which barred the road to Calais. Would orders never come? Was the Battalion destined to be a permanent garrison in this land of heat and flies, sand-storms and smells? Training, everlastingly training, and then at last a growing rumour of an open beach with hills behind and forts said to be impregnable, and beyond these again the prize of Victory. The Mediterranean Expeditionary Force was formed, and Sir Ian Hamilton assumed command. It was scarcely a year before that the Aucklanders had cheered the great fighter to the echo at Hautapu Camp. There was no man living they would sooner have followed on the great adventure which lay before them. Sir Ian held a review out on the desert, and the thirty thousand of the A.N.Z.A.C. marched past him. Everyone knew that the time was now close at hand.

On Good Friday occurred the "Battle of the Wassah," in which certain of the Battalion rendered valiant service. The battle was partly a thanksgiving, partly a protest against the current price of sundry filthy liquors, partly an endeavour to suppress the detested Red Caps, and partly a very riotous bit of real good fun carried a little too far. The inevitable result was the stopping of all leave, which in its turn resulted in the cinema catching fire and the canteen being raided. There was such a superabundance of high spirits that steam simply had to be let off somewhere.

Then, at last, after another weary week of waiting, definite orders came. There was a last rush to Mr. Oatts' Y.M.C.A. tent to write letters home. Kits were packed. The tents were struck, and in high good humour the Battalion entrained at the great "Gare de Caire," and so to Alexandria and the waiting transport.

"Imshi Yallah—Mafeesh Felous!"

IV.

The Haven of Lemnos

"Baited like eagles, having newly bathed."
—Shakespeare.

The Auckland Battalion embarked on the *Lutzow,* a captured German liner, which afterwards made two terrible trips to Alexandria with men desperately wounded, numbers of whom died because there were not the men or the facilities to care for them properly. This dark and terrible side of war was little in the minds of the magnificently trained volunteers who filed up her gangways and rank by rank took up their quarters on the iron decks. At last they, too, were going to war. Greatly elated, they crowded to the rails as the transport slowly steamed through the forest of masts which crowded the harbour, and made for the breakwater and the open sea. They cheered and were cheered. The band was playing. Merry jests flew round. So the harbour was passed, and they, too, had finished with all pleasant and beautiful things. The stately buildings of Alexandria, the tall masts of the ships sank below the horizon, and the *Lutzow* ploughed on through the blue waters of the Mediterranean.

The food was of very poor quality, bully-beef, biscuits, cheese and tea; and by way of variety tea, cheese, biscuits and bully. The iron decks were hard to sleep on. Iron, having no resiliency about it, does not in any way conform itself to the outstanding features of the human body. Moreover, it grows cold of nights. One wag put it rather neatly writing home to his people. "Dear Mother, we are living on iron rations, sleeping on iron decks, and we are commanded by a fellow called *Ian Hamilton.*" Physical comfort and poor food were, however, small things, for now the "Isles of Greece" were on the right hand and the left. Past Patmos, and many another famous place, the ship swept on through the Ægean, while the men sharpened their bayonets and received their orders.

The Auckland Regiment

April 15th, and the *Lutzow* was running up towards the port of Mudros, which harbour had been selected as the main base of the venture for which the Mediterranean Expeditionary Force had been called into being. A great, commodious haven it was, ringed on all sides by green hills, and with room for a great armada to swing at anchor. Through the booms, past the picquet boat, round a spit of land, and the vessel passed to her anchorage.

Never in all her history had Great Britain brought together such an assemblage of ships. There were battleships, cruisers, destroyers and submarines of the British Navy; auxiliary cruisers, Channel picquet boats, tugs, river boats, oil tanks, water tanks, colliers, store ships, quaint French men-of-war of peculiar construction, the Russian "Packet-of-Woodbines," and then row after row of transports crowded with fighting-men. Atlantic liners, battered tramps, boats of the Cunard line and the Castle Company were moored with the vessels of the Nord-Deutscher Lloyd, with Hamburg and Bremen boats, and with Turkish and Egyptian vessels, which in former times plied through the Straits and the Sea of Marmora. The *Gaby Deslys*, a tiny tug, buzzed busily around the harbour. The *Ark Royal* sent up her seaplanes and sometimes the yellow sausage-shaped captive balloon. The *Queen Elizabeth*, super-dreadnought, magnificent, majestic, lay in state, surrounded by ships of lesser name.

Day by day the concentration grew larger and larger. A great transport steamed in with five thousand French soldiers aboard. Battalions of the 29th Division, battalions of English Territorials, Indian troops, Australians, New Zealanders, all came to swell the muster. Here lay the Argonauts before they sailed away for the stormy Euxine and the dark wood of the War God, where hung the Golden Fleece. Here came Agamemnon and his Greeks before they fought the ten years' fight for Troy. Those ancient Greeks live for ever in immortal story, but they were not taller or stronger men, more beautiful in body, higher of heart, or of a more splendid daring than these young unblooded troops who had assembled from the

The Haven of Lemnos

ends of the earth, "to attempt the well-nigh impossible." On board the *Lutzow*, as on board every transport of the fleet, the men were straining at the leash. Cramped in their narrow quarters, with little to do, they were overflowing with energy. Trained to the uttermost perfection of physical fitness, their superb vitality demanded expression, and found none. Above everything, they desired the day of battle and the test of arms. They were impatient, restless, almost bursting with a fierce discontent. Day after day they fell in on the iron decks, with full equipment and packs, clambered down the swaying "Jacob's ladders," and pulled into the shore—then pulled back again to the transport and the weary, monotonous waiting.

At last, on the 23rd April, there was a movement among the transports. All the next day ships were moving to their stations. Now all men knew that the hour had come. There was no more discontent. The *Lutzow* moved to the outer harbour. The decks were crowded with men, all desirous of greeting their fellow adventurers. Now on the eve of battle, there was a great thrill in the hearts of all. Rejoicing in the full strength of their youth, trained until it was impossible for them to be harder, longing for their baptism of fire and the opportunity of doing some feat of arms which would place them on a level with the heroes of Mons, the Marne and Ypres, they had waited with eagerness and desire for this time to come. Now they were on the threshold of great happenings. The Colonel and his officers were high up on the bridge deck. The men were massed along the rails. As the transport passed through the line of shipping, the band played the national anthems of all the nations represented by the men, who cheered and counter-cheered. The hundred thousand men crowded on the transports were exultant and exulting.

On the evening of the 24th, the *Queen Elizabeth* steamed majestically out and away; then another great grey shape, and another, and another, and then the transports, line after line. There was a swell of cheering from the Australians and New Zealanders, for at last they, too, were moving out on the heroes' track, and for them, also, the great adventure had

The Auckland Regiment

begun. It was a happy evening on board the *Lutzow*. The officers spent their last night in the mess joyfully. The sergeants had a particularly merry time, although supper was only the inevitable cheese, biscuits and tea. There were no gloomy forebodings. They might have been going to a picnic, judging by the high spirits shown by all that gallant company. At one o'clock the ship slipped quietly through the boom, and with all lights screened, followed out on the track which for the next nine months was to be so often travelled.

V.

The Battle of the Landing

*"The herdman wandering by the lonely rills,
Marks where they lie on the scarred mountain flanks,
Remembering that mild morning when the hills
Shook to the roar of guns, and those wild Franks
Surged upward from the sea."*
—L.L. in the "Anzac Book."

The sea was full of ships gliding through the darkness toward the Turkish coast. There was quietness now, after the singing and the jollification of the early part of the evening. Some were playing "two-up," a few were sleeping, but the majority were peering into the darkness for the first sign of land. Two o'clock, three o'clock, half-past three, a quarter to four—it must be very near dawn now! The *Lutzow* was running dead slow, just making headway. Of a sudden there was a faint crackle of rifle-fire, the blanketed report of a great gun, and the Battle of the Landing had commenced. Dawn came quickly, and with the full light of day the sounds of conflict swelled into a great rattle and roar. In towards Anzac Cove the transports were rapidly disembarking their men, warships were firing broadside after broadside, tugs and launches towing the barges to the shore. Straight ahead was the rugged mass of Sari Bair, Hill 971, brown and green in the morning mist, brown, green and gleaming yellow as the rising sun shone on the bare cliffs, which stood out in vivid contrast to the blue sea lapping on the pebble beach below. Eager eyes strained shoreward, but little could be seen of the conflict raging so fiercely on the slopes and up the gullies, except the fleecy puffs of drifting smoke from the Turkish shrapnel.

Breakfast was a hurried meal. The last details were soon fixed up, and the Battalion waited eagerly for its turn to come. A passing destroyer megaphoned over that there was "no news in particular, but blowing the b——s to hell." An over-

The Auckland Regiment

turned boat drifted slowly past. The destroyers stood right in and pounded Gaba Tepe Point, smothering it with bursting shell and drifting smoke.

At half-past eight the tows pulled alongside for the Aucklanders, who were to be the first New Zealanders to land. The companies, drawn up on their respective decks, at once commenced to file down the ladders and take their places in the barges. Rifles were loaded. It was the real thing this time; bloody equipment beneath the thwarts of one barge was ample evidence of the fact. Once away from the shelter of the ship, and the danger zone was entered. Bullets wheened overhead, plonked in the water on either side, or struck the boats. Skinner, singer of comic songs, was hit, and so had the honour of being the first battle casualty of the Regiment. There was no excitement. Everyone was cool and quiet, but terribly determined to do his best. There was a thrill of exalted feeling running through the hearts of all. It was an honour to be leading the New Zealanders into battle, and, come whatever chance, New Zealand should be proud of this day's doings. And now the tows were close in-shore! The Colonel leaped into the water, waist deep, and led the way. The men followed across the pebbly beach and the little strip of level ground to the shelter of the hill, and there formed up. Packs were thrown off, and then orders came to move round to the left and reinforce the Australians, who were being hard pushed on top of the great cliff they had won. The Battalion had crossed the spur running down to Ari-Burnu point, and the 3rd Company, crossing Mule Gully, was about to climb the steep hill-side, when fresh orders arrived. It was now the centre which showed signs of breaking, and where help was most urgently needed. There was nothing for it now but to turn about, 16th Waikatos leading, and make by the shortest cut for the threatened point. The Colonel stopped a flying fragment in the wrist; but there was not much harm done, and he carried on. The new route lay over the Plateau, and it was here things started to get busy. Once above the crest-line, across the level, and descending the slope towards Shrapnel

The Battle of the Landing

Valley, men commenced to fall. "Whizz-bang," and a sergeant-major rolled into the scrub with a bullet in his lung. The shrapnel was taking its toll—and the snipers. The rough ground, the thick growth of stunted ilex, the enemy fire, were all disorganising the line. The natural impetuosity of some, the physical strength of others, carried them on ahead. From this time the Battalion as such ceased to exist. In small groups the men passed German Officers' Tent and the sentry guarding the land-mine, broke into the valley, and pushed eagerly towards the fighting in front.

Shrapnel Valley was the main line of direction along which the advance had taken place. It is one of the most famous of all the Gallipoli names. In few of the highways of war have so many died as in this very terrible one. It was accurately marked on the Turkish artillery maps, and their guns ranged every yard of it. It was open to snipers and machine-gun fire. In places the Turks had contested it desperately, and all the way up the dry water-course there was a tangle of Australian and Turkish dead. From the firing-line the wounded were straggling down, making by the best way to the beach, weary, bloodstained, but very exultant. The stretcher-bearers passed backward and forward, doing all they could for the desperately wounded and dying, who were lying here, there and everywhere amongst the tangled scrub and in all the little patches of dead ground.

The Aucklanders streamed upwards, losing men, but nothing daunted. The fire became hotter and hotter. In ones and twos they dodged and ducked forward, and rushed breathless into the firing-line. Generally speaking, the 6th were on the left, towards Walker's, the 16th round Pope's, the 3rd were fighting near Quinn's, and the 15th about Courtenay's and even further to the right. Men of the different companies were, however, scattered everywhere. The advance had reached its furthest limit. The Turks were counter-attacking in overpowering numbers. They were resolute to drive the invaders back into the sea, but the stubborn Australians and the Aucklanders, inextricably mixed together, refused

The Auckland Regiment

to give ground. There was no longer any question of battalion or company command. The natural leaders of men, officers, N.C.O.'s, or privates, took control of whatever men they found to hand, and built up a firing-line for their immediate front. All the valleys and the mountains were full of Turks. Slowly they welled up against the A.N.Z.A.C. lines. The pressure became very intense, but they were held—held by rifle fire and bayonet charge.

Roy Lambert was amongst the foremost. Outdistancing all others, he reached the firing-line in a place swept by enemy fire. Dead and dying were all around, and the living dared not move. He ventured. Three bullets found their mark, and he was dead. Few men were so much beloved, and in a few hours his death was being mourned all through the N.Z.E.F. Donald Lane was wounded in the arm, but pressed on, gathered a little group round him and was hit again in the thigh. The Turks were pressing in. He rose, wounded as he was, to lead a counter-attack with the bayonet, and as he did so received his death-wound. Somewhere over the crest from Quinn's was an old dry water-course full of men, making a desperate stand. Two hundred yards away the Turks were entrenched, and pouring in a very heavy fusillade. Men were going down fast when the enemy field guns picked up the range, and the shrapnel turned the place into a death-trap. There was nothing for it but to get back over the crest. Many fell, but the survivors lined up and shot down all who tried to follow over. At night they brought in their wounded. Major Dawson was a great inspiration to all hereabouts. Lieut. Richardson was dying, shot through and through while tying up a wounded man. Sergt.-Major Rogers went ashore to "win his commission and a Victoria Cross." As he lay dying in the valley, he raised himself on his elbow and spoke to the men passing up: "Don't let them beat you boys! Don't let them beat you!" Bradley was doing splendid work with the Australians. Lawson, the fine scout, was killed. Warden, short, thickset, with clean-cut features, no great soldier on the parade-ground, a quiet and unassuming man, was stalking

The Battle of the Landing

snipers. That evening he had seven identification discs, and from that time on he was Wallingford's right-hand man. Somewhere up on the right flank of the Sphinx, all was going wrong. An officer, very splendid on the drill-ground, was finding a bloody battlefield not to his liking. There was hesitation, weakness, no fine example, a dribble of men going back with the officer at their head, when Corporal Reid, the machine-gunner, put down his gun, opened fire, and rallied a few men round him. One brave example was enough, and so the position was held. Lieut Frater, terribly wounded, insisted on walking out, and died down by the beach. All through the afternoon the Turks pressed on the thinning line, creeping up through the scrub, cutting off small parties, sniping, machine-gunning, crawling out on the exposed flanks, enfilading the torn ranks, and all the time their terrible shrapnel pelted and tore. Smoke, dust, heat, the air whining, singing, trembling, with the screeching shells and the flying fragments, rifle barrels red hot with constant firing, dead and dying all around—this was war. The silent, crumpled figures were hit time and time again. Men with desperate wounds crawled back towards the valley and the stretcher-bearers. There were cries for doctors, bearers, water; confused orders went up and down the line, and all the time the little pile of cartridge cases beside each man grew larger and larger. Ammunition was taken from the dead—and water. Still the pressure was kept up, and it seemed as though very soon things would be desperate. Officers went down fast. Major Stuckey fell, and Lieutenants Flower, Dodson, and Allen. Major Alderman was wounded, Lieutenants Peake, Woolley, Morpeth, were all down.

Still the line held! Jack, Fordyce, Bridson, Revington-Jones, Gardner, all the picked machine-gunners showed their worth that day holding back the Turk. Lieut. Carpenter, "not quite up to the standard" for Duntroon, was a brave leader of brave men. Captain Bartlett was doing great things on the right, and with him fought Lieut. Steadman, Sergeant-Majors Moncrieff and Fletcher. And now at the hardest pinch, *Queen Lizzie* was lying off the shore, she and other grey boats, and the thunder of their guns was sweet music to the hard-pressed men. The fifteen-inch shells were crashing into the Turkish positions. Shrubs, earth, men, rifles, went upward in clouds of black smoke. Oh! *Queen Lizzie! Queen Lizzie!* you were loved that day, idolised that day—a terror to the Turks, but salvation to the reeling line.

Now was the test of manhood! Everywhere the born leaders and the fine fighting men were coming to the front. Tuck and Forrest went side by side up the hill, Fox, McCready, Jock McKenzie, Frank McKenzie, Tilsley, Hall-Jones, Seddon, Tom Gordon, Yorke, Brown, Roberts, Sergt.-Major Partridge, Melville, Tribe, and many other gallant men fought there as staunchly and bravely as they fought again and again on many a stricken field.

Away down in Artillery Lane, Dr. Craig and his devoted little band, Wishart, Shewring, Stacey, and Hill, were doing splendid work. It was a heart-breaking sight; wounded men lying about in hundreds, and no provision made for them. The great-hearted doctor, most unselfish and bravest of men, toiled on without rest or thought of danger, all day and all through the night, and far into the next day. On the beach, Wallingford was sending up new men, collecting stragglers, cursing, threatening, cajoling, encouraging by all means and any means, and bringing order out of chaos. Here was a man who knew his job, who knew his own mind, and could act with decision and determination.

A great horde of Turks hastily marched from Bulair, from Maidos, from Helles, massed on the higher ground and prepared for a counter-attack, that should sweep the attackers back into the sea before darkness gave them an opportunity to consolidate and bring up reinforcements. Nine battleships opened on them with great guns. The heather slopes, purple in the setting sun, were smothered with bursting shell. The vivid flames of the tremendous explosions lit up the dark hillside. The twilight deepened. Night fell on the battlefield, and the line was safe. The men of Anzac were tired and overwrought. They were new to scenes of blood, and all grieved

The Battle of the Landing

for the dear friends who had died that day. There was bitter anger against the Turk, a new sense of brotherhood between Australians and New Zealanders, and something else, also—a thrill of triumphant, exulting feeling—Australia and New Zealand had made good. An order from Sir Ian Hamilton was passed along: "Comrades, I am proud of you; hold on, reinforcements are coming." The words of praise from such a man were as strong wine. All nerved themselves to the task of holding on against every attempt to break through.

For a short while there was quietness and a certain respite. Under cover of the darkness, the work of consolidation went on. Shallow trenches were scraped out, better positions occupied, a certain amount of water and ammunition carried up. The poor wounded, who had lain all day in positions where rescue was impossible, were brought in. Padre Taylor, officially of the Canterbury Regiment, but actually the friend and helper of all who were in trouble, was burying Auckland dead in No-Man's Land, carrying the stricken back to the doctors, passing the ready jest amongst the watchers in the line and those toiling up the steep paths with their heavy loads—"in Christ's name, for Christ's sake."

It was a wild and terrible night. The Turks were moving in the scrub in great numbers, but they also were tired. The resolute defence of the Australasians and the gunfire of the fleet had cost them many thousands of their best men. Urged on from behind, they came on without dash or resolution. Heavy rifle firing commenced. All through the night it rattled along from Fisherman's Hut to Gabe Tepe Point, sometimes dying away and then swelling up again in fury. Often it was wild, aimless, misdirected; but yet it served the purpose. The Turk did not pass, and yet all night he could have smashed through at any point if his resolution had been screwed to a higher pitch. Once disaster was imminent. An Australian colonel was leading his men out of a key position, when Wallingford met him, and in the darkness, pretending that he himself was General Walker, ordered him back. The Australian obeyed. A shower of rain had made everything wet, damp, and miserable; yet the work never ceased. Fresh battalions of Australians, the last half of Canterbury, Wellington and Otago, were landing; the guns were coming ashore and being man-handled up steep slopes into position. Stores of all sorts were piled along the beach. Dawn came at last. For a while the shooting was good, until the enemy took cover. The first twenty-four hours fighting had led to a very great disorganisation. Brigades and battalions and companies were inextricably mixed up. This had been unavoidable; but it was necessary to straighten them out as speedily as possible. The Auckland Battalion was placed in reserve, and ordered to concentrate on Plugge's Plateau, an eminence which covered the actual landing place at Anzac Cove. In response to the order, men commenced to arrive from midday Monday, and kept dribbling in for the next two or three days. It was a rather joyful reunion. Certainly, many fine men had gone under, and many more were on the hospital boats; yet it was a surprise to find so great a number left. The Plateau was a very important tactical feature which the Aucklanders were to fortify. For the next four days they were busily employed digging and carrying. Here on Plugge's Plateau the Battalion learned that the difference between "fighting" and "resting" meant that in the latter case there was more work to be done. "Resting" meant hard toil with the pick and shovel, varied by carrying loads of bully-beef, biscuits and ammunition long distances over steep tracks. Trench-digging was a very laborious business. The sun-baked clay was often as hard as rock, and digging in the ordinary sense was quite impossible. One man picked, while another stood by prepared to shovel out the loose earth. The first making of a trench entailed much labour, but once made, there was little else to be done. "Revetting" and "duck-boarding" were quite unnecessary, and even sand-bags were only occasionally used. Saps twelve feet deep, with perpendicular sides, stood stiffly, with no appreciable slipping. The absolutely dryness of the soil not only saved great work draining, but also enabled trenches to be dug to any convenient depth. By the time the task was finished, the stragglers had

Sergeant Samuel Forsyth, V.C.

The Battle of the Landing

come in from all parts of the line, and the Battalion was once more an organised unit. Five officers and seventy-three men had been killed, while nine officers and two hundred and eleven men were evacuated wounded. The loss was heavy enough, but still there were many left, and every one was high of heart, intensely proud of the great feat of arms performed by the Australasian troops, and very eager for the chance "to get some of their own back." For days they had been shot at by the Turkish riflemen from the trenches, by Turkish snipers hidden here and there in cracks and crevices amongst the scrub-covered hills, by field guns from both flanks. They were longing to get amongst the enemy with the cold steel. Very few had been fortunate to meet them hand-to-hand, although nearly all had done some good shooting, even if it was only at Turkish voices somewhere ahead in the darkness. Seddon and Purchas, indeed, had been somewhat more fortunate. Getting in with some Australians, they had stiffened up a portion of the line. In the night, unknown to the two Aucklanders, who were sleeping, the Australians withdrew. A Turkish patrol blundered in right on top of Seddon. This was a rude awakening, but the Turk must have received a bigger shock when he was smitten on the head with a pick handle and then bayoneted with his own bayonet.

On the afternoon of the 27th, Wallingford greatly distinguished himself. The position above Walker's was obscure, doubtful and dangerous. Arriving on the scene, he found that the casualties had been very heavy, that the Turks had obtained complete superiority of fire and were apparently massing, ready to storm over the disheartened few who were still holding on. No one was in charge. In perilous times the boldest measures are always the best. Wallingford saw that to attack, to get on the offensive, was the only thing that could save the situation. He told the men around that he was going forward. It seemed certain death, but he made the venture, not knowing whether any would follow. Twenty yards forward, thirty yards—and the Turkish fire was very hot—forward still, and then down in a little patch of partially "dead" ground. Here, between the lines was a machine-gun. It was jammed and out of order; belt and spare parts were lying around in confusion. The crew had been killed, with the exception of Preston, who, wounded as he was, stayed by his gun, although he could not put it to rights. For the master gunner it was but a moment's work, and the gun was rattling away. "Rat-tat-tat, rat-tat-tat," and the Turks who were a moment ago insolently showing themselves were shot down. For hours Wallingford and Preston held on, despite every effort of the Turks to dislodge them. The deadly rifle of the great marksman, and the still more deadly bursts of machine-gun fire made short work of any venturesome Turks who dared to show themselves. Their fire slackened. Then the worn-out men behind took fresh courage, and came round the machine-gun. The position was once more secure. It was characteristic of Captain Wallingford that his next business was to get the wounded clear. With the exception of Dr. Craig, no man was ever keener on salvaging the poor broken sufferers on the battlefield than this fighting soldier, of whom it is literally true to say that, like Saul of old, "he had slain his thousands." In those early critical days the fiery enthusiasm, the tireless energy, the stark valour of this man were invaluable. It was he "who gave us the courage."

On May 1st the Aucklanders left the Plateau and climbed the steep track to Walker's Ridge. The next day they were to have been in support to an attack, but at the last moment the operation was cancelled. Half the Battalion then moved to Pope's Hill under Colonel Plugge, while the remainder with Major Harrowell stayed on in the support position. Two days afterwards, orders were received by the Battalion to rendezvous at Brighton Pier, prior to embarking for Cape Helles. The New Zealand Infantry, with a brigade of Australians, were to take part in the general assault on the Achi Baba position, which it was hoped would place the southern key of the Dardanelles in our hands. In the movements of these last few days, four men had been killed, and Captain Price, Lieut. Bodley and twenty-eight men wounded.

VI.

Cape Helles

*"Horror it is, and carnage; yet are both
Part of the price of peace."*
—"Anzac Book."

On the evening of May 5th, after dusk, the men crowded on board the lighters and were towed out to the destroyers and minesweepers, which were to carry them to the southern sector. During the embarkation Brian Willis was fatally hit, but there was no other mishap, except that, in the darkness, some of the lighters were lost and drifted round in the cold for a couple of hours. Finally everyone was packed on board. The sailors were full of admiration for the Anzac soldiers, and displayed their admiration in most practical fashion by giving up dinner and rum issue to their guests. It was a kindness that was very much appreciated by the tired, overwrought men, who had carried on for the last ten days with little sleep and nothing except bully-beef and biscuits to eat.

The Brigade landed, close to the stranded *River Clyde,* on the beach below Seddul Bahr, and marched inland for about a mile. It was a great change after Anzac. There was room to move. The 29th Division had swept in for several miles, and all the level ground, the green fields, the cultivated orchards stretching right up to the slopes of Achi Baba were held by the British. The roads were good. Transport of all sorts was moving. Englishmen, Scotchmen, Frenchmen, Senegalese, Sikhs, Australians, New Zealanders, gave Helles a cosmopolitan character. Here, too, were the guns, seventy-fives, eighteen-pounders, howitzers—guns in numbers not thought of at Anzac. The land seemed a good land, in every way desirable after the experiences of the last ten days. Surely, with all the guns and the easy, level country, it must be a good war in these parts.

The Auckland Regiment

That night the Battalion dug shelter trenches, for there were many enemy shells flying round. The ground was wet, and it was not possible to go far without reaching water. The night was cold and miserable, and many spent it walking about in an attempt to keep warm. Next morning, loaded with extra ammunition, the New Zealanders marched across to the Gully Ravine. As far as Auckland was concerned, the route taken was not the most direct, and the Colonel was more than suspected of having lost his way, a crime which, in the eyes of an Infantry Battalion marching with full pack up, is the crime of crimes. The New Zealanders were now in close support to the 29th Division, which had been fighting desperately to move forward in the direction of Krithia Village.

On the morning of the 8th, orders were issued for the New Zealand Brigade to pass through the British Regulars, and advance towards the village. There was bungled staff work somewhere, with the result that, instead of the New Zealanders taking up their battle stations during the night, dawn found them a long way in the rear. This added several hundred yards to the open ground which had to be crossed under fire, and also took away any advantage which might have been gained by a swift attack unheralded by an obvious concentration under the very eyes of the enemy. Wellington were on the left connecting up with the 29th Division, Auckland in the centre, and Canterbury on the right linking up with the Australians. Otago were in reserve. The Aucklanders moved up along a winding creek bed, just deep enough to give shelter. This brought them within a couple of hundred yards of the main front line, which had to be reached across country. This distance was covered by platoon rushes. Here Lieut. Steadman was killed, and several casualties occurred. There was also a certain amount of confusion, and when everyone had crowded into the British fire-trench, the companies were found to be intermingled to a considerable extent. Very few had a clear idea as to what was to be done, or what really were the objectives—except that a general advance was to be made on Achi Baba.

Cape Helles

Immediately in front the ground sloped away for a little distance; then came a field of beautiful wild flowers, and then a gentle scrub-covered slope rising to a crest-line in the middle distance. Beyond this again was the hump of Achi Baba. To the right front was a clump of pine trees. There was no visible sign of the enemy. The Colonel came along: "Well, boys, the orders are to go ahead, and we have got to carry them out." The Regulars were not encouraging. "What! You are going to cross the Daisy Patch—God help you!" They had tried the day before, with no success. "Yes, of course we are going!" and on the signal every man of the first line was over the parapet and down the slope. Then the hail of Turkish fire smote them. Riflemen and machine-gunners from the stunted pines on the right poured in a hell of fire. The enemy batteries back on Achi Baba picked up the range and swept the ground with shrapnel. Not a man of the first wave faltered, most of them went down, but a few crossed the little field, and in the scrub beyond formed up some sort of a firing-line. The second wave came on, and were shot down to the last man. A third wave tried to cross, but it seemed as though all the Turkish fire was converging on them, and the pleasant field of daisies was full of agony. Yet men got across somehow, somewhere —dashing a few yards from shallow cover to shallow cover, crawling inches at a time, changing direction slightly. Turks in front took their toll, and then before the gleaming bayonets reached them, vanished back through the scrub. The Daisy Patch itself was a tangle of Auckland dead and wounded. Even when all who could had crossed, it was swept by a hellish fire, and many a poor wretch was hit again and again. The officers were leading very bravely, but they were nearly all shot down. Lieutenants Carpenter, Screaton, Morgan, and Graham Reid were killed. Major Dawson was badly hit. Lieutenants West, Macfarlane, who had led the first rush, Fletcher, Weir, McDonald, Fraser, Westmacott and Baddiley were wounded. Without exception they had been a great example to their men.

Dr. Craig, back in the front line, was binding up the

The Auckland Regiment

wounded in the comparative safety of the trench. From beyond the parapet came the moaning of scores of men lying helpless in their agony. The garrison tried to keep him back, but he would not remain. "How do you think I can stay here and listen to those poor fellows moaning?" So he went over the top, he and Stacey with him, and crawled round bandaging wounds, easing some poor sufferer into a more comfortable position, giving a drink of water to those suffering the torments of thirst. It was a morning of heroic rescues and attempts at rescue. Heald was killed trying to bring in Blyth Macfarlane. Cowan bravely rescued Corporal Campbell. Sergt.-Major Leach and Savory were very forward in rescue work. One poor fellow lying in a terribly exposed position was crying for help, and the Doctor, with Donaldson and Dalziel, two volunteers, made a dash out to him. It seemed a miracle that they reached him, but they did, got him on to the stretcher, and were almost back to cover before one of them was hit. As they lowered the stretcher over the parapet the Doctor was hit in the thigh, but Stacey dragged him in. In the meanwhile, Major Harrowell, Captains Sinel and Bartlett, had worked something like two hundred men across, and had got them into a shallow drain. Tilsley and Gasparich had been doing great work here. The clump of pines was outflanked by the Canterbury advance, and the fire from that flank slackened somewhat. Some three hundred yards had been won, but the crest was still four hundred yards away. Breathless, exhausted, disorganised, the attack rested for the time being.

Another attack was ordered. At five o'clock the whole line from sea to sea was to sweep forward. The ships lying off the coast shelled the ridge with fury. The roar swelled into pandemonium. Every gun, great and small, was firing as rapidly as the toiling gunners could serve it. The crest seemed lifted in pieces. It was shrouded in the drifting battle smoke. Once more the Aucklanders were sent forward. It seemed as though the Turks must surely have been blasted from their secure positions. But no! Scarcely had the line of bayonets moved out when the hellish machine-gun fire burst out in greater fury.

Cape Helles

The whole air was full of screaming missiles. Death fell everywhere—death and bloody wounds! The line went on for a hundred yards, then another hundred, little knots of desperate men crawled further. Captain Sinel, Tilsley, McCready, Gasparich, the McKenzies, Tribe, Melville and some thirty others reached a place just below the crest. Flesh and blood could do no more. The Colonel, Major Harrowell, Captain Bartlett, the brave commander of the 15th, were all wounded. The survivors scraped out little hollows, and lay still until nightfall. At nine o'clock an unauthorised order was passed along, and the exhausted remnant fell back on the line which had been won by the first charge in the morning. Captain Sinel had nothing to do with this order, but in the darkness and confusion it was obeyed.

The Battalion was in a terrible state; cut to pieces, disorganised, utterly spent, it was no longer an effective fighting unit, and so was withdrawn, its place being taken by the Otago companies. The remnant concentrated down on the beach under Capt. Sinel. There had been over four hundred casualties, and the residue of the third reinforcement only brought the Battalion up to half strength. Lieut.-Col. Young was appointed to the command.

Two days afterwards the remainder of the Brigade was withdrawn, and for another week the New Zealanders were in reserve, doing fatigues of one sort and another, mainly making roads. It was comparatively quiet, although the big guns from the Asiatic coast accounted for a certain number of casualties—Auckland losing another forty men.

On the 19th May, the Brigade embarked on minesweepers and were carried back to Anzac. Major Bayly was killed by a stray bullet from off the shore. Before daylight on the 20th the men had landed, and the Aucklanders went into reserve at Rest Gully.

VII.

Quinn's Post

*"Ever the day, with its . . . death from the loop-holes around;
Ever the night, with its coffinless corpse to be laid in the ground."*
—"Defence of Lucknow."—Tennyson.

Rest Gully was a typical "bivvy" camp, leading from Monash. It was one of the numerous pieces of dead ground scattered about amongst the hills, which afforded comparatively good shelter from the shrapnel fire. Originally the slopes had been thickly covered with the dwarfed prickly scrub so common at Anzac, but in the last month this had been very much trodden down. Paths had been worn everywhere through it and "bivvies" constructed, giving that peculiar chequered appearance so common to all the places where men lived at Anzac. "Bivvies" were dwellings of a very primitive nature. Their main functions were to give a protective bank between the occupants and the nearest Turkish sniper or field-gun, to keep out the sun by day and the dew by night. The usual method of construction was to cut a face in the bank, level off the floor and the sides, salvage a couple of oil-sheets, and with salvaged bayonets (of which there were any number) pin these over to form a roof. As far as furnishings were concerned, a happy young couple made it their business to secure as many sandbags as possible from the nearest Engineers' dump, a cut-down tin of some sort for a bath, and one or more petrol tins in which to store water. The home was now complete. The permanent residents—the lice and the flies—took up their abode without further ceremony, while the casual boarders, such as soldiers and centipedes, strayed in as occasion offered.

The Battalion's first night in Rest Gully was disturbed by a great racket from the hills above. The Turks attacked in masses all along the line, but were shot down in hundreds by the N.Z.M.R., who were manning the trenches. The repulse

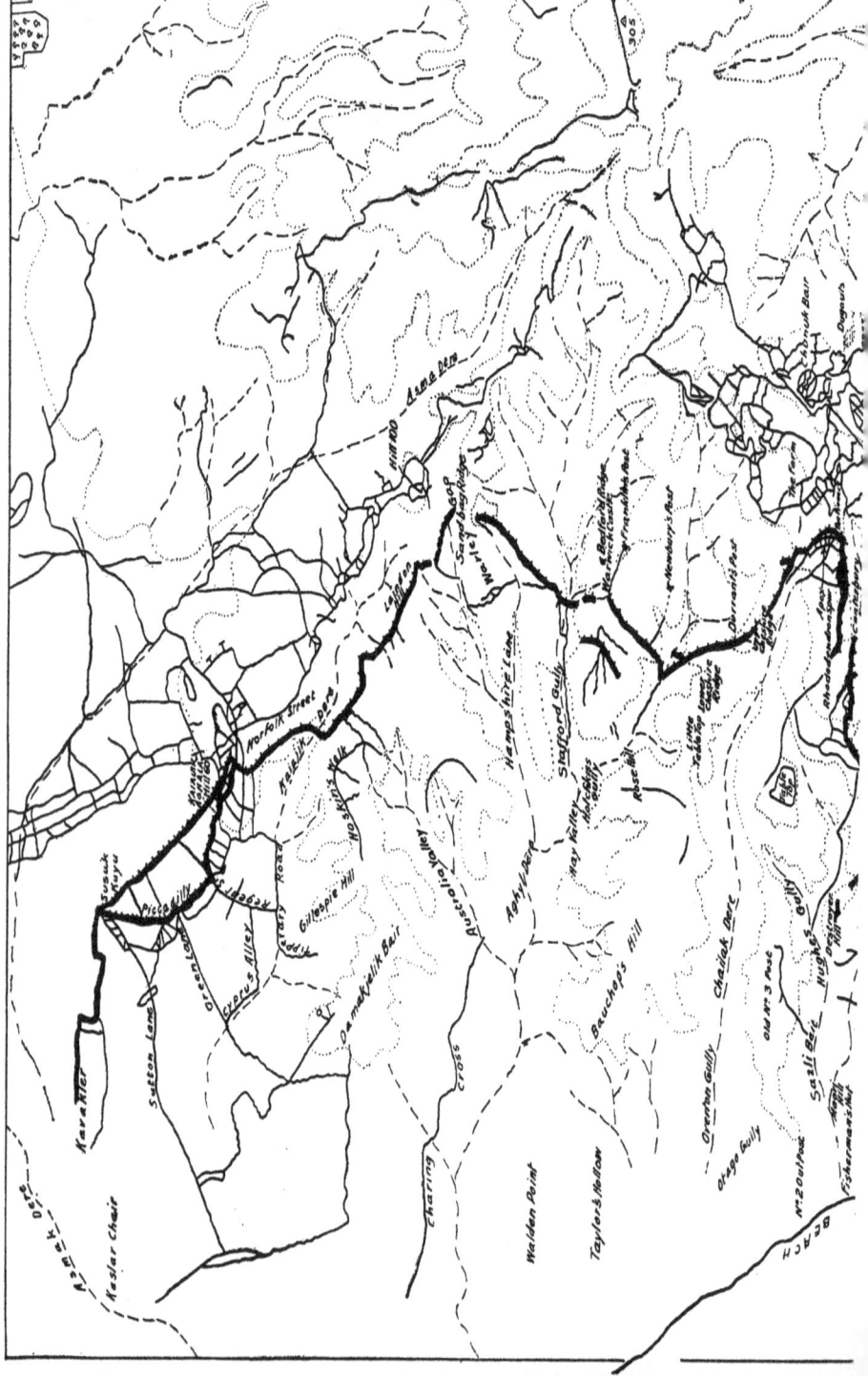

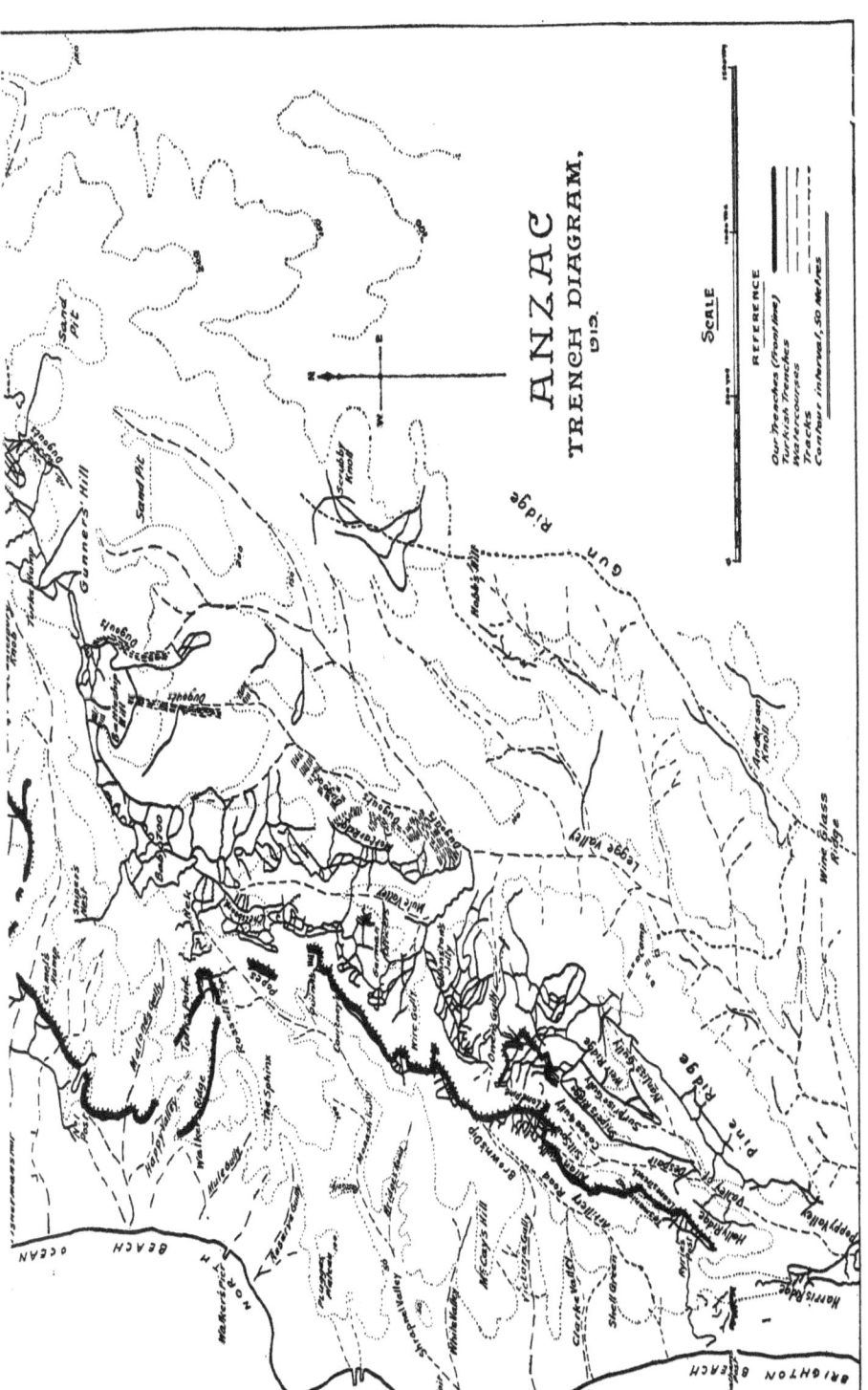

Quinn's Post

was of such a bloody nature that the enemy asked for and obtained an armistice on May 24th for the purpose of burying the dead. Firing ceased at 7.30 a.m., and the demarkation parties, commencing from the right, marked off a line down the centre of No-Man's-Land. Auckland supplied a detail of fifty men for the terrible task of burying. Next day the *Triumph* was sunk in full view of the watchers from the shore.

June 2nd the Battalion went into Quinn's Post.

What the "Dead Man" was at Verdun and "Delville Wood" on the Somme, Quinn's Post was at Anzac. The ridge on which it was placed covered Monash Gully and Shrapnel Valley. Quinn's had at all costs to be held, for if it fell the vital artery of the Anzac position would be cut. The day of the landing the first rush had gone well beyond the crest, but the attackers had been compelled to fall back until there was nothing behind them but the steep cliff falling down to Monash. With their backs to the wall, the Australians and the Aucklanders had fought back the Turks. In succeeding days, New Zealand Engineers had sapped through to the forward slope and built a firing-line with a better field of fire. So close were front and support lines that the earth from the parados of one was touching the parapet of the second. Tunnels were dug from trench to trench to make the passage secure. In places these tunnels were sapped through dead bodies. The Post was noisome and pestilent. Loathsome and terrible vermin crawled about. The winds blew perpetually from the Turkish trenches across No-Man's Land, where lay the unburied dead. The air was poisoned with the disgusting stench. The Turks had pressed close up. At the nearest point their trench was only fifteen yards away. Neither side would budge an inch. We held on for dear life—the Turks to retain a vantage point from which they might strike a blow at the heart. In the first two months attack and counter-attack succeeded one another with bewildering rapidity. Once the Turks rushed the front line, but were bombed out after a bloody struggle. On other occasions their front line was lost, and only by desperate efforts could they restore the position. A mine explosion would blow the

The Auckland Regiment

whole post down into Monash—so they mined. But mine was met with counter-mine. Fifteen yards from trench to trench! During the day every inch of parapet was watched by the snipers of both sides. A second's exposure was instant death. Men stood to all day, bayonets fixed, bombs ready, watching through the periscopes for the slightest movement. A bomb flies up from the enemy post. It is seen in the air. The nearest man runs to the spot and throws an overcoat over it as it touches the ground. Everyone rushes madly away, throws himself flat on the ground, feet toward the coming explosion, and waits with set teeth for the ear-splitting crash. It comes—a blast of devilish noise, a cloud of smoke, dust and flying splinters. The owner of the coat investigates the tatters and finds a plug of priceless tobacco has been ruined. "Damn the ———;" and then before the words are out of his mouth there is a shout of warning and another explosion. Now the jam-tin bombs packed with explosive, old nails, odds and ends of various sorts are flying back in retaliation. For ten minutes the air is full of smoke and noise. There is a scream from the Turkish line: "Allah! Allah!" Quietness again! But there is a very still figure to be carried out to the little cemetery behind the hill, and a couple of others to be helped down the steep track to the dressing station. It is all in the day's work. The trench is straightened up, more bombs brought in, and some bloody equipment passed out. It is dusk. Between the lights is the most dangerous time, and every man is standing-to. Darkness falls. The sentries are up on the fire-step, rifles ready, peering out into the night. Fifteen yards away the Turks are keeping the same anxious vigil. At any moment may come a shower of bombs or a rush of men. At any moment a mine may be sprung and the whole post blown out. The night passes slowly. Every now and again a burst of machine-gun fire sweeps the parapet or crackles overhead. The double report of a Mauser rings clear and sharp, a bullet whistles past, or perchance finds lodgment in heart or brain. Dawn comes at last—another anxious hour—then "stand-down," the rum issue, and breakfast.

Quinn's Post

The Turks who manned Quinn's Post were all picked volunteers, every man of whom was promoted corporal. They were men whom it was a great honour to meet.

From June 2nd to 9th the Aucklanders held Quinn's. The first evening five rounds rapid caused a great and harmless retaliation. On the night of the 5th-6th it was decided to carry out an offensive operation against the Turks in the trenches opposite. The Auckland and Canterbury Battalions were ordered to supply fifty volunteers each for the task. The Auckland men were Lieut. Vear, Hall-Jones, Frank McKenzie, Jock McKenzie, Carlaw, Tilsley, Holland, Black, Coutts *(other names unobtainable)*.

Lieut.-Colonel Brown, then of Canterbury, afterwards of 2/Auckland, was in command of the post and of the whole operation. It goes without saying, therefore, that the preliminary preparations were of the most thorough character. Every man knew precisely what he had to do. All needful material was on the spot. Very quietly the parties of assault filed into the line. Bayonets were fixed and magazines charged. Supports were ready to take over the fire-trench immediately the attacking parties had gone over. Carrying parties were standing by with loads of sand-bags, picks, shovels, bombs, and everything necessary for consolidation.

It is eleven o'clock. The batteries from Plugge's Plateau and Walker's Ridge are firing on the Turk communication sap. The howitzers on Ari Burnu Point join in; so does the little Japanese mortar and a Mountain Battery. In so many seconds the Aucklanders on the left reach the enemy parapet. The loopholes blaze with fire and the bombs come over. The attackers, pressing in, poke their rifles over and fire somewhat at random, with no effect. Then Frank McKenzie hurls a bomb far into the trench. Three loopholes are silent. Another bomb, and another; the fire slackens now, and the left assault party go in with the bayonet. For the first time here is opportunity. At the Landing, at Helles, their mates were shot down helplessly, and never a Turk would come within reach of the cold steel. But now, "a—a—ah," the old primitive blood lust

The Auckland Regiment

is only thinly buried after all. The Turks are beaten. Their trench is a death-trap. Into it! Into it! "Kill the ——." The McKenzies, Tilsley, Holland, Black, Melville, Coutts—they are all into the trench, stabbing, shooting, bayonets red with blood. Thirty Turks surrender, and are sent back. Fifty more are dead, and their bodies thrown out of the trench form a rough parapet in front. The carrying parties rush over with filled sand-bags. The Turkish bags are torn from the old parapet and changed over. On the extreme left men work feverishly on the block. It is completed, and two riflemen fire continuously down the dark trench to keep back any of the enemy trying to work up into bombing range. Three Turks emerge from a dug-out and make a desperate attack on those they find nearest. They are very brave men, and die fighting rather than surrender. By two o'clock the work is all complete, and if things have gone well elsewhere, the position will be held. However, it is not to be; for the Australians have failed at Steele's Post, and from there comes an enfilade of machine-gun fire. The Turks are reinforced. Their picked bombing parties are attacking up every communication sap. Dawn breaks, and with the clear light the enfilade from Steele's becomes more deadly. Tilsley endeavours to build up a barrier of sand-bags, but the bags are blown from his hands by bursting bombs. Nevertheless he perseveres until wounded. Frank McKenzie is wounded in the leg, but carries on as cool as if on parade. Men are falling fast. The bombs rain in. There is no chance of stopping the enfilade. The raiders are driven back step by step. Now they are holding only thirty yards of captured line. At nine o'clock came the order to retire. The remnant withdrew through the newly-dug communication trench, and the great raid was over.

There remained but to count the cost. It was heavy enough. Eight killed, forty-eight wounded, and ten missing, as far as Auckland were concerned. Lieut. Vear was wounded, and also Lieut.-Colonel Brown, who for this operation was awarded the D.S.O. The Turkish loss was very much heavier, and a heavy blow was struck at their morale.

Quinn's Post

On June 7th-8th another sortie was made, with the object of recovering certain material abandoned in the enemy line. It was a complete failure. The loss of Colonel Brown was very much felt. Orders were changed at the last moment. It was impossible to feel the same confidence in the command. So many of the best leaders had gone down, and men were feeling the strain. The Turkish trench was reached, but the attack was driven off with loss to the attackers of Lieut. Corbett and six men killed, Lieut. Topham and twenty-five wounded, and six missing.

Next day the Battalion was relieved and moved down into local reserve in Monash Gully. Here the Fourth Reinforcements, consisting of fifty officers and two hundred and ninety-three other ranks, joined up.

VIII.

Anzac Life

> "*Whilst seated one day in my dugout,*
> *Weary and ill at ease,*
> *I saw a gunner carefully*
> *Scanning his sunburnt knees.*
> *I asked him why he was searching,*
> *And what he was looking for?*
> *But his only reply was a long-drawn sigh,*
> *As he quietly killed one more.*"
> —"Anzac Book."

"Suffering from toothache, owing to the slurring of a fat and sleek dentist who stays at home in comfort and sends the soldier to eat hard biscuits."

Biscuits! Army biscuits! What a part they took in the daily routine.—the carrying of them, the eating of them, the cursing of them. Crawling from their earthy dens at the dawning of the day, men devoured biscuit porridge. They ate their meat, not with thankfulness, but with biscuits. They lengthened out the taste of jam with biscuits. Biscuits were pounded to powder, boiled with bully, stewed in stews, fried as fritters.

Consider the hardness of them. Think of the struggle and strain the crushing and crunching as the two molars wrestled with some rocky fragment. Think of the momentary elation during the fleeting seconds, when it seemed that the molars would triumphantly scrunch through every stratum of the thrice-hardened rock. Try to imagine the agony of mind and body as the almost victorious grinder missed its footing, slipped and snapped hard upon its mate, while the elusive biscuit rasped and scraped upon bruised and tender gums. Plates cracked. Teeth broke and splintered. The finest gold crown weakened, wobbled, and finally shrivelled under the terrific strain of masticating Puntly and Chalmers' No. 5's.

They had the delicious succulency of ground granite, or the savoury toothsomeness of powdered marble, with a delicate flavouring of ferro-concrete and just a dash of scraped iron

Anzac Life

railings. The choicest dishes of civilised life, baked or boiled, stewed or steamed, fried, frizzled, roasted or toasted, have no taste like to that of Army biscuits. It is a debatable question, indeed, as to whether they had any taste at all. If it be granted that they did possess the faculty of stimulating the peripheral extremities of a soldier's taste-buds, then it must also be conceded that the stimulation was of an unpleasant sort. The soldier's feeling, apart from the joy, the pride and the satisfaction at his completed achievement in transferring a whole biscuit from his outer to his inner man without undue accident or loss of teeth was one of pain and disappointment.

Apricot jam was another infliction—that and a detestable mixture known as Deakin's marmalade. "Apricot again!" Why on earth there was not more variety no one knows. One explanation given was that in the clear liquid it was impossible for drowned flies to masquerade as black currants. This is quite the line of reasoning that would appeal to the type of mind responsible for the selection of the supplies sent to Gallipoli, and is therefore quite likely correct. The crowning atrocity, however, as far as food was concerned, was bully-beef of the Fray Bentos variety. If General Birdwood was the soul of Anzac, then bully-beef was its "flesh and body." Bully was always in evidence. It came ashore at the first landing, and remained even after the evacuation. On the beach the A.S.C. made palatial residences of it; in the front line whole boxes were used for parapet building. It was salt, stringy and unpalatable. The only recommendation it had was that some kinds were not as bad as others, and that sometimes the less bad kinds were served out.

There was never any lack of food on Gallipoli. The trouble was that the abundant supplies were of the wrong sort. Meagre supplies of fresh meat, bread, vegetables and milk did commence to come ashore, but never in sufficient quantities. Of cheese and fat bacon there was never any lack. The cheese was utterly useless, but the bacon was very useful as fuel, and, after being rendered down, to make "slushlights." Tinned fruit, fresh vegetables, and tinned milk should have been sup-

The Auckland Regiment

plied in great quantities. The elimination of waste would amply have repaid all the extra expense.

Day by day the sun grew hotter and hotter. At midday it burned down blazingly, scorchingly hot. With the heat came the flies—a very venomous lot of brutes, the lineal descendants of those which plagued the unrighteous Pharoah. Flies formed a staple part of the Anzac's diet. They shared his meals, drowned themselves in his tea, and in massed formation rushed his apricot jam, refusing to be driven off with blows and curses. It was no use slaying them by thousands, for they returned in tens of thousands. They bit like young scorpions. Their only redeeming virtue was that they slept well at night. The lice, beasts of prey of a most voracious and ferocious nature, did not sleep, and the chillier breezes of the night seemed only to spur them on to greater efforts. They refused to die, except under great pressure. They throve exceedingly on Keating's Powder, sent by anxious mothers in Auckland. The flies were the light cavalry, the lice the heavy armed infantry. They moved slowly, but surely. They could not fly but they could crawl, and they always "got there." They were imbued with a certain cold, passionless persistence. The next generation was always in readiness to carry on fighting the good fight in which the generation before had perished. The grandparents were done to death at dawn. The parents were suppressed at midday, the children were massacred in "the evening hate," but the next generation was attacking fiercely by midnight.

Water was at a premium. Dust, heat, flies, vermin, thirst, bad food, the terrible stench of the unburied dead, and then a new experience—the frightful monotony of war. It may seem almost inconceivable to the ordinary civilian that a dangerous life is not necessarily an exciting one. Danger becomes part of the atmosphere. It is not something that can be guarded against. It does not interfere with the hours of waking or sleeping, of rest or of labour. Men were sniped at breakfast, sniped on working parties, sniped while bathing, sniped during the watches of the night, or just as they stood down. Shrapnel

Lieut. R. Judson, V.C., D.C.M., M.M.

Anzac Life

burst at all times and in all places. These dangers could not be avoided. They were exceedingly annoying, but as a general rule not exciting. After the fierce rush of the first battles life was quieter, and a daily routine was established. Soon nothing was new, nothing was interesting, nothing was profitable. The bully-beef was always salt, the biscuits like armour-plate. Nothing mattered. One thing was just as bad as another, and nothing could be worse than some of the things that had gone before. Men became surfeited with experience. Life was a dreadful and barren existence. The strain and weariness of life reacted upon the mental tone. The bad food, the tropical heat, the smell, the flies wore down the physical condition. Then came the spectre of disease. Many men went down in June with diarrhœa, dysentery and enteric. In July they were going down in scores.

Hell was to be an infantryman at Anzac; Heaven was just two miles away, a great white ship with yellow funnel, green band and great Red Cross. Fortunate was he who "landed a buckshee" or ran up sufficient temperature to impress the doctor. For him were stored up all delights, clean white sheets, dainty foods, rest, ministering angels to care for him. Dreams of paradise were of the smells from mother's cooking stove and of fair girls in clean clothes far away in New Zealand.

Men quickly became most dilapidated and disreputable scarecrows. The fewer clothes, the fewer lice to sort out; and so, as there were no girls to "swank up" for, clothes lost their ornamental and acquired value. In the blazing heat little covering was required, and what little was worn was purely a matter for the individual concerned. The Battalion had landed in "Tommy Caps," but these were by this time replaced either by Australian felts, khaki sun helmets, or the New Zealand issue belonging to unfortunate members of the reinforcement drafts. The upper part of the body was clothed in an identity disc. A pair of trousers very raggedly shortened, and boots completed the outfit. For the rest, a very decent coat of sunburn sufficed to complete the picture. Men bathing showed fine impressionist studies in brown, black, and white.

IX.

June and July

*"Heat like the mouth of a hell, or a deluge of cataract skies,
Stench of old offal decaying, and infinite torment of flies."*
—"Defence of Lucknow," Tennyson.

From June 9th to August 5th, the Battalion did two spells in the line at Courtenay's Post and one at Quinn's. Between whiles it was in local reserve in Monash Valley, working, waiting, and "hanging on."

Courtenay's Post was taken over on the night of June 25th/26th. After Quinn's, it was a haven of rest. Two nights later, the Turks made their final attack at Anzac. Enver Pasha had arrived with fresh battalions and much ammunition. He was dissatisfied with the results of the campaign. The mere holding of position did not satisfy him. The challenge that was menacing the safety of the Turkish Empire had not only to be countered, but smashed. Liman von Sanders had learned his lesson, but the fierce young Turk would not listen to stories of previous defeat. At midnight on the night of June 29th every Turkish gun that could be brought to bear deluged the Anzac lines with shrapnel and high explosive in a sustained burst of fire, that continued for over half an hour. The massed Turkish columns of assault came forward steadily and bravely, only to be caught in the searchlights of the destroyers. They came on in vain against the steady lines of cool and determined riflemen. This attack was not pressed home in the vicinity of Courtenay's, and the preliminary shell fire had practically no effect on the deep, well-constructed trenches.

The trench line here, continuing on from Quinn's, ran along the crest of the ridge which fell away somewhat steeply below. Terraces had been cut on the steep slope for the accommodation of the supporting companies. "War is a frenzied burrowing competition, varied by tossing unpleasant missiles at one

June and July

another." The particular brand of unpleasant missile in favour with Johnny Turk who manned this sector was the catapult bomb. The catapult bomb, though an ingenious device, was not remarkable for its accuracy. The Turks, in trying for the trench line, not infrequently put on a little too much elevation, with the result that the bomb rolled nicely down the slope and created a nuisance amongst the terrace-dwellers. One overthrow landed fair in the midst of a party all congregated round a dixie, and caused terrible havoc. Lieut. King and nine others, including Mick Boyle, were wounded, and three or four killed. This proved a great incentive to the rapid completion of bombproofs in this locality.

Trench warfare here was quiet, mainly owing to the excellence of the trenches and the shortage on both sides of trench mortars—always excepting the catapult—and howitzers. The most offensive people were the snipers, of whom McCready and Fox were two of the most prominent. It was McCready who fought the duel with the mountain gun which the Turks had installed in their front line. This fired from a square black embrasure in the parapet. It fired and then swung out of sight to be reloaded. A quick shot could fire one round before and one after the discharge of this gun before it dropped out of sight, getting back into cover himself while the shell burst. The gun and McCready both did some very pretty shooting, and both lived to fight another day.

No-Man's Land being four hundred yards wide gave quite a restful sense of security. There was no longer the ever-present expectation of going to Heaven on top of a mine explosion; and even the most expert Turk could hardly throw hand grenades such a distance. Shrapnel and snipers were only a source of danger to people who exposed themselves above the parapet. In these happy circumstances Capt. Sinel and his 6th Company held a concert in their front-line trench, which proved a fine success. Here, perhaps, one may be pardoned a slight digression to mention Capt. Sinel for the continuous good work he had performed from the landing right on. He did well the first day, and supremely well during the

The Auckland Regiment

confusion and butchery at Krithia. Of the Battalion officers who had landed on the 25th, he and Capt. Algie were the only two still remaining.

On July 8th the Battalion was relieved and went into reserve in Monash, during which time Lieut. Simpson was killed by a sniper. Eight days later Otago were once more relieved in Courtenay's, which was held for a further period of eight days—a very quiet time.

The 21st July is a specially notable date. On this day gas helmets were issued to all ranks, with instructions as to their use. War was at any rate commencing to be more scientific. Fortunately, the Turks made no use of the deadly stuff. If they had done so, Anzac would have been quite untenable. The valleys and rest camps would have acted as natural sinks, where gas once accumulating would have hung about indefinitely. Moreover, with the enemy so short a distance away, holding higher ground, and having all the advantage of the wind, any effective retaliation would have been quite impossible.

The 31st July marks a very convenient break in the Battalion's history. During this period two great battles had been fought, the line held for several weeks, and two raids carried out. The losses had been extremely heavy. Of the original twenty-six officers who had landed the first day only three were still unhit—Captains Wallingford, Sinel and Algie. It is very difficult to determine exactly what number of casualties had occurred. The Battalion diaries are on this particular point certainly inaccurate. This is easily accounted for when the heavy losses, the constant changes in the *personnel* of the administrative staff, and the great difficulty in carrying out clerical work are considered.

Eleven hundred men actually embarked on the *Lutzow*. 1050 landed the first day. After the assault on Krithia 268 were left. 200 reinforcements brought this number to 468. Quinn's Post and incidental casualties reduced the strength to 326. The Fourth Reinforcement brought that total to 624. During June and July a very great number of men were evacu-

June and July

ated sick. The total fighting strength at the beginning of August was not very much more than 500.

A certain number of decorations and mentions in despatches had been awarded to various officers and men. Colonel Plugge received the C.M.G., and was also twice mentioned in despatches. Captain Wallingford won the M.C., while Sergt. Tilsley and Corporal W. J. Reid were awarded the D.C.M. Major T. H. Dawson was twice mentioned in despatches.

The following N.C.O.'s had been promoted on the field to commissioned rank:—R.S.M. Mooney, Sergt.-Major Fletcher, and Sergeants Ward and Graham Reid.

Toward the end of July Dr. Craig returned, and as he went up to Battalion Headquarters the men turned out and cheered him. This is an honour that was accorded to very few New Zealanders during the war.

X.

The August Fighting—Sari Bair

> "*So all day long the noise of battle rolled*
> *Among the mountains, by the . . sea.*
> *Until King Arthur's table, man by man,*
> *Had fallen in Lyonnesse about their Lord.*"
> —Morte d'Arthur.

> "*We have seen him flung in rank,*
> *Across the morning sky;*
> *And we've had some pretty shooting,*
> *And he knows the way to die.*
>
> *Yes, we've seen him dying there in front—*
> *Our own boys died there, too—*
> *With his poor dark eyes arolling,*
> *Staring at the hopeless blue.*
>
> *With his poor maimed arms astretching*
> *To the God we both can name.*
> *And it fairly tore our hearts out,*
> *But it's in the beastly game.*"

All attempts to break through in the Cape Helles sector had failed—Achi Baba was by this time a hill impregnable. So Sir Ian Hamilton turned to Anzac and prepared to strike the final blow of the campaign on the slopes of Sari Bair. His strategy was superb. A feint at Helles was to hold the enemy in force. A pretended landing on the Asian coast was to draw his reserves. On the right of the Anzac position the Australians were to make a holding attack against which the Turks would be compelled to concentrate. Bulair was threatened. The New Zealanders were to smash the "Anzac Ring" on the left, unmask the Sazli Beit and Chailak Deres, advance and clear Chunuk Bair, seize the dominating crests, and by so doing open the way to decisive victory. Two fresh divisions were to be flung ashore at Suvla Bay to fall on the exposed flank of the outmanœuvred enemy, and so complete his ruin.

The most careful preparations were made. Water was brought from great distances, put into petrol tins and stored away. Shells, and rifle ammunition, were quietly piled up. Fresh men were brought ashore and hidden in carefully prepared hiding places. The greatest precautions were taken to

The August Fighting—Sari Bair

conceal all signs of preparation from the Turkish airmen, who were continually flying across.

The country over which the advance was to take place was extremely rough. There were no good maps of it to be had anywhere. Aeroplane reconnaissance was only in its infancy. It was not easy or even possible for the greatest scouts to pass through the enemy's line at will. Nevertheless, there were some who did wonderful work in this direction. Warden was the finest scout the Auckland Regiment ever produced. A quiet, somewhat reserved man, he had not been at all conspicuous as a parade-ground soldier; but as soon as the fighting started, his exploits on the day of the Landing had brought him the immediate recognition of his superiors. At first with Colonel Plugge, and afterwards with Captain Wallingford, he was given great freedom of action. He always went about armed to the teeth. On one occasion, donning Turkish uniform, he penetrated great distances into the enemy territory. It is said that he once went over the hill and into Maidos itself. However that may be, he knew the whole of the Suvla Bay flat, and all the foothills of Sari Bair, on the left of the Anzac position. The information he brought in was quite invaluable.

The Turks, also, were preparing for a great battle. They had mustered all their available forces. There was a feeling of expectancy in the air. Both sides realised that the supreme hour was at hand.

In the last days of July the Aucklanders were busily employed carrying and digging. They relieved Otago in Quinn's Post August 2nd, remaining there until the night of the 5-6th, when they were relieved by Australian troops. The same night they marched across from Monash, beneath Walker's Ridge, along the great sap leading to No. 2 Outpost, and so to "Happy Valley." It was a long, hard tramp, and at that time very few were feeling in the mood for long marches. Practically every man was suffering from diarrhœa or dysentery. Many were on the verge of collapse. All were terribly weak. The physical condition of the New Zealand soldiers

The Auckland Regiment

who fought through the great struggle on the slopes of Sari Bair should never be forgotten by anyone who reads the story of their fight. It is one thing to go into battle as the Main Body went, on the day of the Landing, superbly trained, magnificently fit, and quite another matter to go in worn out by hard work, want of sleep, and weakened by disease.

Once in "Happy Valley," the Battalion stowed itself away in the scrub, with strict orders to show no sign of movement during the day. The sun blazed down with intense heat. The scrub was not high enough to give proper shade. It was abominably prickly, particularly as nearly everyone had bare knees. A plague of flies made sleep during the day almost impossible. The one redeeming feature of "Happy Valley" was the fact that a mail was served out. Mails always brought everyone to life again. Parcels, papers, and, above all, letters, were greatly prized. He was a happy man who had left behind him in New Zealand some good woman who remained steadfast and true, despite time and distance. Many a man went into battle with courage that was steeled by the letters of the day before.

During the day officers and N.C.O.'s went out along the great sap to Sazli Beit Dere and the Outpost, to view the heights of Chunuk, across which the advance was to sweep, while the men fastened on back and arm the white bands and patches which were to serve as distinguishing marks for our own artillery.

Lieut.-Colonel Young was in command of the Battalion, with Major S. Grant, of the Fourth Reinforcement, as his second in command. Lieut. Mooney was adjutant. Major Hume commanded the 3rd Company, Capt. Sinel the 6th, Capt. Algie the 15th, and Lieut. Gillet the 16th Company. Most of the 3rd Company were detached as escort to various Indian Mountain Battery Guns.

At four o'clock in the afternoon of the 6th, the 29th Division attacked at Cape Helles, and had soon joined battle in a desperately fought contest, which not only tied down thousands of Turks, but also, so vehement was the onslaught,

The August Fighting—Sari Bair

compelled them to draw upon their reserves. At half-past five the Australians went over the top to the storm of Lone Pine, one of the key positions of the Turkish left flank. The enemy trenches were of enormous strength and desperately defended. For five days the struggle for Lone Pine never slackened, until in the end the Australians were victorious.

So in two places the assault had swelled up in fury, and it may have appeared to the hard-pressed Turk that the battle was fully joined, and that, if he could but hold, all would be well. But it was his right flank at Chunuk Bair and Suvla against which the real menace was to develop, and so far everything was quiet in that quarter.

Amongst the rough tangle of hills, ridges and ravines in that locality were three long valleys, the Sazli Beit, the Chailak and Aghyll Deres, all winding up toward the heart of the mountain. These natural approaches were covered by the foothills of Sari Bair, No. 3 Outpost, Big Table Top, Sniper's Ridge and Bauchop's Hill, all of which were strongly held by the enemy. It was the task of the N.Z.M.R. to clear these hills, and by so doing open up the way to the infantry battalions, which were to pass on through them toward Rhododendron and the heights of 971.

The mounted troops attacked at nine o'clock in the evening, and immediately afterwards the leading battalions of the Infantry Brigade were on the move. Canterbury went by way of the Sazli Beit, while Otago, Wellington and Auckland proceeded up Chailak. At 10 p.m. Auckland wound out of Happy Valley, and with the 6th Company leading, followed by the 15th and 16th, connected up with the remainder of the column. The distance to be traversed was not so very great—a little over three miles—but a distance which, under the conditions of the night of August 6-7th, was very terrible. The ground was all new and strange. Once the long file had left the sap, passed over the little strip of level ground beneath No. 2 Outpost, and crossed the straight trench which led down to the Outpost Well, there came one long succession of blocks and halts. First of all, the covering troops were held up by the

The Auckland Regiment

wire entanglement which the Turks had built across the entrance to the valley. This meant delay. The scrub, the uncertain track, the darkness all hindered the advance. There would be a move forward of perhaps fifty yards, then a block in front, a crowding up behind, men standing wearily beneath their loads, expecting to move any second and not moving for five, ten or fifteen minutes. At last, tired of waiting, they would lie down, but no sooner had they done so than the file in front was moving, and they must race to join up again, and then, having done this, there was another halt. Nothing is harder than marching in this fashion at night, especially when men are loaded up with ammunition and weakened by privation and disease. The Otagos, leading, found the Dere still largely occupied by enemy troops. Rifle shots rang out from both flanks. Little groups of the enemy commenced firing. They were easy enough to overcome in detail, but each little affair cost a few men and, even worse, ate into the precious time. The passage of the Dere took nearly six hours. The Turks were commencing to realise what was happening, and long before dawn the rifle bullets were falling thickly. Prisoners were passed down. The Aucklanders even found a few more hiding in the scrub. All the way up there was a thin trail of dead and wounded of both sides lying beside the track. During the halts Dr. Craig was busy doing all that could be done for the men he was able to reach. The opposition at the head of Chailak grew fiercer. There was further delay. At dawn Otago were fighting hard for the lower slopes of Rhododendron, and it was not until 5.45 a.m. that the Brigade assembled on the ridge.

Auckland concentrated in a hollow, which was apparently dead ground, and commenced to make the best of a cold breakfast. After a few minutes, however, there came a burst of fire from snipers and machine-guns. Bunched together as the men were, casualties were numerous. Breakfast came to an abrupt conclusion, and there was a very hurried scatter.

All opportunity of surprise had now passed. Away to the left the Bay of Suvla was seen to be full of ships. Files of

The August Fighting—Sari Bair

men were moving over the Suvla Plain. It was now evident to all what the plan and scope of the battle actually was. The Turks were aware. They realised their danger. The first sudden surprise, the loss of so many points of tactical importance, had bewildered them, and for a while they had shown signs of demoralisation. But they could not afford to lose Chunuk. Hastily the thousand yards of crest-line were manned with what rifles and machine-guns they could muster. The volume of fire became greater every moment. Men were falling fast on Rhododendron and the Apex. At any cost an attempt had to be made to pass the hollow and obtain a footing on the slope beyond. The Auckland Battalion was detailed for the task. Orders came before the machine-guns of the Brigade had deployed out. Wallingford offered, if he were given but half-an-hour, twenty minutes, less even, to put up a barrage that would beat down the Turkish fire, so that the advance might stand a reasonable chance of success. He was told the advance could not stay.

The Battalion was drawn up, 6th Company in front, and informed roughly of the objective. Many of them were survivors of the Daisy Patch, most of them had seen something of the work of machine-guns in the open against advancing troops. They had a complete and clear realisation of what was being asked of them. The moment came. The word was given. For an instant there was an intaking of the breath, a tension, the hesitation as of one who nerves himself to leap into ice-cold water. What? were the leaders baulking? From behind came an indescribable growl and murmur. Then Major Grant rushed out in front with waved arm and a call to follow on. The mass moved, Lieut. Dittmer's platoon of the Hauraki's leading. Twenty yards of dead ground, and then a hail of fire—fire from a thousand yards of Chunuk; fire from Battleship Hill; rifle fire and machine-gun fire from front and flank. Two hundred and fifty yards to go, and every yard of it raked with fire. There was no faltering; every man went straight forward, running up the hill as fast as he could go. Killed and wounded, they went down in heaps, but the survi-

The Auckland Regiment

vors pressed on. The trench was reached, a small, narrow drain, and the foremost leaping in took what cover it afforded. It was soon too full to hold more, and the remainder lay down in rear. There was nothing to be done except wait and endure. The task was done, and at a great cost. All the way back to the Apex the ground was a tangle of dead, dying and wounded. For most of them nothing could be done, as the ground was so terribly swept with fire. The men in front scraped a little cover, but it would have been impossible to dig in, even if picks and shovels had been available. No movement was safe, and to stand up meant certain death. An order to get into the trench was passed round, and more were killed while endeavouring to do this. In the blazing sun the torment of thirst became very great. Heat, thirst, and flies—the wounded suffered hell tortures lying out on the slope. "God! Oh, God! When will it be night, and when will the stretcher-bearers come?"

The heroic Major Grant fell half-way. He lay out all that day and the next, and when at last picked up he made light of terrible wounds, saying it was only his leg, and that he would be back in six weeks. He died the same night.

If the Turks had counter-attacked immediately, they might have regained the lost ground; but in a short while their opportunity passed. As soon as the attack was ordered, Captain Wallingford had worked with all his energy to get the machine-guns placed. Now they were in position—too late to assist the advance, but in time to safeguard what had been won. After an hour's heavy fighting, the Turkish fire from the heights was beaten down, and superiority passed to the New Zealanders. If only the attack had been delayed until this time, how much slaughter would have been saved!

As yet the Suvla landing had not taken off the weight. All day our men lay flat in the tropical heat, waiting for the crash of firing from the left. It did not come. After dark the 6th Company held the trench while the 15th and 16th went back on working parties.

Very early in the morning Warden had guided a column

The August Fighting—Sari Bair

of British troops to their point of attack, taking them up in the darkness through a valley which no other British soldier save himself had ever trodden. His task finished, he had rejoined the Battalion on Rhododendron, and there fell fighting. He was buried that night by Father Dore. One thinks of the little cemetery at Coigneux in the pleasant fields of Picardy, the band playing the "Dead March," generals standing by the grave-side, the crash of the last three volleys, the sad wailing of the bugles as Sergeant Richard Travis, V.C., D.C.M., M.M., Croix de Guerre, the greatest scout of the New Zealand Division in France, was borne to his last resting place. When Private Richard Warden was buried, the stillness of the night was broken by the cries of the stricken in their agony. Carrying parties and stretcher-bearers toiled up and down with their heavy loads, the scrub breaking and crackling beneath their feet. The bursts from the Turkish machine-guns whizzed venomously overhead. Bullets fell everywhere, with the sound of heavy, slow drops before a thunderstorm. The night was full of noise, yet within a small space it was very still and quiet. Here in a shallow grave they placed the body of the great scout of Anzac. Two or three of those who loved him for his great valour stood round while the heroic priest recited the words of the Eternal Hope. The short service over, the mourners turned once more to the fighting front.

Succour from the left was slow in coming, but still the battle could not stay, the pace could not slacken. At dawn on the 8th, the Wellington Battalion, with some help from the Gloucesters, passed through and stormed Chunuk Bair. The key position was ours. If the force from Suvla would only press forward, the result was inevitable. But would help come? Wellington fought a most valiant fight. Their line was frightfully torn. Men scraped for themselves shallow pits and flung a little earth in front. The Turks crept up to bombing range, and along the whole line the fighting was hand to hand. Every moment our men grew fewer and fewer. Still they held on. Heat, thirst, wounds and death could not daunt them. "Hold on! Hold on!" If they could

The Auckland Regiment

but hold on for a few hours longer surely the English would come from Suvla, and all would go on over the crest to Maidos.

The English did not come.

So the manhood of New Zealand dwindled hour by hour through all the long day of August 8th, Wellington in front on the crest, Auckland in support in and about their captured trench. This day Captain Sinel was wounded.

The great flanking movement from Suvla had now been definitely held. Twenty-seven thousand fresh troops had been baffled by three thousand Turkish gendarmes. In the centre, although the casualties had been frightfully heavy, the attack had been successful. The door of opportunity was still open. One last effort might still clear the whole crest, and all would be well. The attempt was made at dawn on the 9th. All reserves were hurled into the fight. The crest was reached and passed along its whole length. Below lay the Straits of the Dardanelles and the town of Maidos. Victory seemed secure, when of a sudden a terrible thing happened. By some mistake the guns played for too long on the ridge, and the attacking columns were torn to pieces by their own artillery. The Turks saw their opportunity, came back and fell upon the shaken survivors. The supports were a few minutes late. The reeling line was pushed back, and the whole of Chunuk, with the exception of the south-western part held by the New Zealanders, was lost.

The fight had raged for three days, and the New Zealanders were utterly spent. They were withdrawn to the Apex and Rhododendron, with the exception of some of the 16th Company, who were holding a trench constructed a few yards behind the one captured in the Auckland charge.

As darkness fell on the 9th, the hope of victory had almost vanished. If the remnant of the crest of Chunuk could still be held, another attempt might be made after a rest and general reorganisation; but first it was necessary to obtain more men and more ammunition. It was now four days since the beginning of the struggle. The Turks had called up all their reserves. Thousands had crossed from Asia, and other thousands had come down from Bulair. All night they were massing behind Sari Bair, and on the morning of the 10th the whole mass was in motion, moving with the power of an avalanche

The August Fighting—Sari Bair

and the speed of a landslide. The English battalions in front broke and swept away the 16th. The Turks came on. The hillside was brown with their charging battalions. On toward the "Farm," and the Deres below, and the margin of the sea! It was a bold stroke, executed with determination and courage. For a moment it seemed that no power on earth could stop the moving mass, but the target they made was a good one. Aucklanders on Cheshire Ridge were firing—firing as fast as they could load and fire—and with them now were the Fifth Reinforcements. The Turks came on, three hundred men in a line, and twenty lines, following at a little space one behind the other. They stormed forward, crying on the name of God, calling aloud the proclamation of their faith; for them it was victory or the fields of Paradise. If fanatical valour, if contempt of death could win, then surely the host of the Turks would break through.

Wallingford had ten machine-guns in action, six of them well forward, two of the six, Auckland guns. They were trained across the line of the Turkish advance. The men behind, cool and resolute, set up a zone of death. The first line of Turks charged into it and went down to a man. The next line melted away on the same spot. But still they came on, line after line, and the leaden sweep reaped them in swathes. No hesitation; no faltering; the last line charged on with the same high courage. They also fall. Now the artillery have picked up the range, and the great heap of death and agony is torn and blasted by the bursting shells. The wounded Turks who were able to crawl back were unmolested, so full of admiration were the machine-gunners for the charge they had made. The Number Ones of the two Auckland guns who did so much to beat off this attack were Jack and (unknown).

Once more on the same day the danger became very pressing. On the Apex was Brigade Headquarters and also the Auckland Aid Post, which for seventy-two hours had followed the advance, working ceaselessly to succour the hundreds of wounded. Suddenly, twenty-five yards away, a party of the enemy showed up and commenced firing. They had crept up through the valley. More were climbing up every moment. It was a time of deadly peril. Most of the New Zealanders were on Cheshire Ridge, further back on Rhododendron, or in the

The Auckland Regiment

Deres below. On the Apex itself were only machine-gunners, some of the 3rd Company, and some men of the Fifth Reinforcement. Major Hume led on the men of his company. Lieutenant Ellis joined in with the new men. Lieutenant Jack and Captain Wallingford sprang in with some machine-gunners. In all, some fifty-five men, they raced for the threatened point, and went straight in with the bayonet. The Turks were caught in time, and after a moments fierce fight, they were pushed back and into the valley below. Major Hume and many others of that gallant band were killed.

The sufferings of the wounded during these days had been very dreadful. A man hit on the slopes had as often as not to lie all day in the blazing sun, tormented by thirst and tortured by the swarming flies. To attempt to move him would have meant certain death. At night he might well be missed, and so be doomed to another day of agony. Many were never found, and died amongst the thick scrub or in some tangle of rough and broken country, where no man passed once the first charge had gone forward. Even when the stretcher-bearers had found the sufferer and bound up his wounds, there was the three-mile carry to the sea-shore. The first stage was down a precipitous slope, where a man without a load was hard put to it to keep a footing. Imagine the difficulty of carrying a stretcher! The second stage was through the long and winding Dere. Here the foothold was better, but the path was jammed with traffic. Ammunition was going forward, also water, rations and all that was urgently necessary for consolidation. Line after line of mules plodded stolidly backward and forward towards the firing line. Shrapnel burst at all times and in all places. Bullets fell like rain. Imagine what a journey this was for a poor wretch with a fractured leg, to whom every jolt of the stretcher meant a spasm of intolerable agony! The New Zealand wounded were wonderful in their patience and self-restraint. Through all the terrible journey there would be no word of complaining, usually only expressions of regret "for causing the stretcher-bearers so much bother." One might have thought the wounded man was not in pain if it had not been for his drawn and twisted features. At last, after a journey of something like three

Brigadier General R. Young, C.B., C.M.G., D.S.O.

The August Fighting—Sari Bair

hours, the shore was reached. Close to the sea was one sap much travelled by all who passed No. 2 Outpost. This sap for nearly two hundred yards was crammed with badly-wounded men—all stretcher cases. For three nights they lay there without blankets; for three days they were scorched by the merciless sun. They had no food except scraps of hard biscuit, and no water save what was given them by passers-by. They were not even out of the fire zone, for many were hit a second time while they lay, waiting and waiting for the bearers who could not come. Some were killed, and to them death came as a merciful release. All wounded had to be evacuated by launch or lighter, and there had not been enough of these available. Remember, too, that it took four men three hours to carry from the slopes to the beach, and that stretcher-bearing is the hardest work, and taxes even the most powerful and courageous men to the uttermost. One trip was enough to tire anyone—the second brought a man to the limit of endurance, and after that the bearer staggered on, utterly spent physically and sustained only by that deeper spiritual side of human nature which gives victory over the flesh and its frailty. Remember, also, how many thousands of wounded men lay in the valleys and upon the mountain slopes. Was it any wonder that many a poor wretch died before succour reached him?

The great Turkish counter-attack was the last act in the terrible struggle for Sari Bair. Much had been gained in the territory of great tactical importance. The Turks were shattered and beaten to their knees. Another blow, even a weak one, would have broken them utterly; but the effort had been too great, and it was impossible to strike again. The high places remained with the Turk. Again he brought up fresh troops and fortified the blood-stained hill, until at last opportunity passed for ever.

The night of the 11th was a confused one. English troops were now holding the Apex, behind them were the New Zealand machine-gunners, and behind again the remnants of the New Zealand battalions. It was a sad wild night, and next morning Hamilton sent the New Zealanders back to the Apex and Rhododendron with orders to entrench and "hold on for ever."

XI.

Rhododendron Spur

"God," he said, "how painful is my life!"
—Song of Roland.

The fighting died away. After the high strain of the unnatural excitement came the inevitable reaction. The remnant of the Battalion was in a shocking condition. Diarrhœa and dysentery grew ever worse and worse. Scurvy made its appearance. Men broke out in septic sores that would not yield to treatment. The flies tormented the sufferers. Men of splendid physique were miserable, bent scare-crows, their faces haggard and drawn. As they walked they staggered with weakness. There was no energy, no vitality. Yet they hung on, and by slow degrees dug deeper trenches and communications, until all the hill was secure. All night they watched and worked, and then could not sleep during the day because of the heat and flies. Life was full of a most terrible monotony. Great-hearted men weakened, but refused to go away. "Very ill, but still sticking it," they write in their diaries. "We are in a most miserable state, yet we must hang on." In these terrible last weeks of August and the first two of September was established that steadfast character which is perhaps the best of all New Zealand's war traditions. Men grew so ill that some of them died in dug-outs or even in the open trenches. It was cruel work for the doctors, for they could do little, not even send the sick away in sufficient number. The Ridge had to be held, even if all the New Zealanders died in the holding of it. Hard as the doctors were compelled to be, the leakage was still very great. Men went down by dozens and by scores. Wallingford himself was evacuated a complete wreck. A price had been placed on his head by the Turks. His value to the Anzac Army was above all price. Day by day the little company grew fewer, and the limit of endurance for the remainder came nearer every day. There

Rhododendron Spur

were continual rumours of a rest, but so long was it delayed that the men at last despaired of its ever coming. Working, watching, sickening, dying—surely they would all soon die, and there would be an end to this intolerable agony.

During these days Padre Taylor was a great source of inspiration. He was as sick as anyone, but was quite tireless in his unselfish devotion. He did not belong to Canterbury, he belonged to all of us. Here was religion! No white collar, broadcloth and silk hat, no exclusive theology, no overpowering sense of aloof respectability, but a man of like passions to ours, of like fears and hopes, a man of a most human and brotherly type, fired with Christ's passion of love for all struggling and suffering humanity. He buried the dead, comforted the sick, passed the ready jest along the trenches. Tireless shepherd of the sheep, he knew every yard of trench-line, every gully and sap where men lived.

On September the 2nd, Auckland were relieved from Rhododendron, which they had entrenched, and went into reserve behind Brigade Headquarters in the Chailak Dere. September 8th saw them once more in the line, holding the Apex. Two days later this position was heavily bombarded.

At last, on the 14th, came orders to concentrate in the Chailak Dere. "Hallelujah!" The spell had come at last. The Battalion staggered down the Dere, past the Outpost, along the weary way to Anzac Cove, and then took lighter to the *Osmanieh*. A small boat, not very much if any larger than the *Manaia*, she was easily able to take off the remnants of the New Zealand Infantry Brigade. In Mudros Harbour an antiquated paddle-steamer, which must have been in its prime about the time of the Crimean War, wheezed alongside and took men and stores toward the "wharf." As the old craft did not capsize on the way, everyone landed safely after scrambling over the allegedly ingenious obstruction the R.E.'s had erected for the purpose. The march to camp was three miles —they seemed like thirty. The Battalion went by fits and starts. There were many halts and many stragglers. Some finished the journey in two hours, others in ten, and not a

The Auckland Regiment

few strayed in next day. A marquee had been put up, and everyone crowded inside, too weary, done-up and miserable to think of anything else than resting. The floor was rough and stony, but that was a detail. The weather was threatening, but no one could summon the energy to dig ditches. Next day came a thunderstorm. Rain fell in torrents. In a few minutes the water was pouring down the hillside in streams. It flowed in under the tent curtains and turned the floor-space into a running stream. Everyone stood up, holding his most treasured possessions in his arms, and so remained for an hour, until the rain ceased, when all turned out and dug the drains which, completed earlier, would have saved the situation.

XII.

Lemnos

"The winter winds of Lemnos,
They blow exceeding fast.
There's nothing quite so stiff on earth
As that persistent blast."
—H.B.K. in "Anzac Book."

That afternoon was a most joyful time. New bread, fresh eggs and fresh meat were served out, also a bottle of stout between every two men. Cooking fires were lighted between stones, so arranged as to keep off the wind. Steak and eggs were frizzling merrily, and the smell was good. For a whole fortnight the men did nothing except eat and rest. The food continued good, and there was a very large issue of milk. Apparently all the milk sent from New Zealand had been concentrated on Lemnos. The issue worked out to about a dozen tins per man, which was very acceptable, but much more than could be used at one time. If it had been sent across to Anzac during June, July, August and September, a large wastage of men would have been avoided. During all that time a tin of milk was worth a dozen tins of bully-beef. Yet bully-beef was landed by the ton and wasted by the ton, while the milk that would have saved thousands of evacuations for intestinal diseases was withheld.

The first Sunday was noteworthy, on account of the church parade, held on the open level flat before the camp. Everyone was of opinion that the New Zealanders had done enough fighting to last them for the whole war. Egypt was talked of. Garrison duty was thought of. Some cheerful optimists even discussed the possibility of a trip back to New Zealand. Then Padre Taylor preached a sermon, saying that no man had done his bit while he had a leg left to stand on and life in him. General Godley made the startling pronouncement that the war had only just commenced, and that there was much fighting still to be done.

The Auckland Regiment

"Oh, Hell!"

It was a hard note, but a necessary one.

On September 30th, the Sixth Reinforcement, under the command of Major S. S. Allen, arrived, and absorbed the Battalion. In the eyes of the old hands the new men were "lead-swingers." They looked down upon them with infinite scorn, and were at great pains to remind them that men who had fought at the Landing, at Helles, at Quinn's and Chunuk Bair were in a very different position to that of the men who had been forced out of New Zealand by sheer pressure of public opinion. It is all very laughable when one comes to think of the 42nd Reinforcements and the late arrivals of 1918, but in those days the Main Body took themselves very seriously, and, after all, who can blame them? The 6th Reinforcement, on their part, were torn between two emotions. On the one hand they were impressed by the fame these early men had won; for in those days the name of "Anzac" stood very high.

> "I'd count it the greatest reward
> That ever a man could attain.
> I'd sooner be Anzac than—Lord
> I'd rather be Anzac than—Thane."

On the other hand, it was very difficult to connect honour and fame with the handful of decrepit, homesick, thoroughly verminous and blasphemously "fed-up" scarecrows who represented the Auckland Battalion.

By this time a daily routine had been established. "Right turn! Left turn! Slope arms! Form Fours!" and so on, with the whole paraphernalia of barrack-square drill. There is no doubt that the Anzacs badly needed a straightening up; but, nevertheless, it went against the grain to do recruit drill with reinforcements.

On the whole, life was good and interesting. Leisure time was plentiful. A few miles away, over some rough and barren hills, was the tiny hamlet of Therma, where hot springs provided the luxury of a hot bath. Further on again was the considerable town of Castro, with a wonderfully strong old castle crowning the hill above the town. In all directions were small

Lemnos

villages inhabited by rather dirty, greasy-looking Greeks. The inhabitants of these, anywhere near the camp, immediately commenced to make their fortunes. They opened cafés and shops, endeavouring to do trade at exorbitant rates in anything they could sell. The children stayed away from school and sold grapes, chocolate, figs, raisins, etc., round the camp, varying this occupation by raking over the incinerators and begging for "backsheesh."

Water was scarce, and as the transport had all been sent back to Egypt, it had to be carried from the pumping station, in the heavy cooking dixies, over a distance of nearly half a mile. Water fatigue was hard work. The queue at the pumps was often a very long one, and it was here that the ancient and honourable game of "Crown and Anchor" flourished exceedingly. All sorts of hard-looking individuals, with raucous voices and a splendid control of the *Australian language,* here plied their calling assiduously, despite the Manual of Military Law and Brass Hats of all sorts.

Some camp-fire concerts were a great success. None who were there will forget one man with a magnificent voice singing "The Last Rally."

So the time passed pleasantly enough. The news of Loos made the Sixth Reinforcement fear the war would be over in a few weeks. They were very eager to prove themselves. All sorts of rumours were going round as to the next front the New Zealanders would be fighting on. Salonica, Mesopotamia, Alexandretta, Egypt, France, all had their supporters.

Time was up. The Battalion was something over half strength by reason of the reinforcements and a number of convalescent sick and wounded who had rejoined. Camp was struck early in the morning of November 8th. The men fell in, carrying enormous packs. Word had gone round that the destination would after all be Anzac; so everyone laid in what store of provisions he was able to procure. The Brigade moved out from Sarpi, embarked once more from the rough pier, and sailed out once more on the Anzac track.

XIII.

The Last Six Weeks

" Now snowflakes thickly falling in the winter breeze
Have cloaked alike the hard unbending ilex
And the grey drooping branches of the olive trees,
Transmuting into silver all the lead ;
And, in between the winding lines in No-man's Land,
Have softly covered with a glittering shroud
The unburied dead."
—M.R., N.Z.H.Q., in the " Anzac Book.

It was a misty, showery day. By nightfall the transport was nearing the shore. Soon the dark mass of Sari Bair was dimly outlined in the gloom. An occasional rifle shot rang out clear and distinct, "pit-pot, pit-pot." Bursts of machine-gun fire proclaimed that the Battalion was once more back again at the war, and that the old game was still being played. The men went ashore during the night, landing at the little pier below Walker's Ridge, and from there marched round to a bivouac between the Chailak and Aghyll Deres, from whence Auckland went up to the Rhododendron Spur, where they remained until the evacuation.

The weather had changed completely. The fearful enervating heat of the summer months was gone. There was a touch of keenness in the air. Most of the flies were dead, and those who by reason of strength still survived were looking very ill, and were suffering from general debility and cold feet. The lice, however, were stouter hearted and thicker skinned. They hung on with indomitable tenacity. Nothing could shake them off. They flourished in the summer heat, and multiplied in the cold of winter. If one died, however prematurely, ten more seemed to spring into being. They were as the sand on the sea-shore, or the stars in heaven for multitude.

In the Balkans, Mackensen with a mass of men and guns smashed down the Serbian defence, and by so doing opened a clear road from Berlin to Bagdad. The Turkish munition troubles were at an end. Down the Danube came the great

The Last Six Weeks

howitzers from the Skoda works. The heavy shells were very nerve-racking. There was a muffled report, then for several seconds the huge shell climbed up and up, high above Sari Bair, and having attained its highest elevation, turned, hung for a moment, and finally from the tremendous height dropped perpendicularly with a roar which gradually changed to a diabolic, blood-curdling scream. The projectile landed on the hard ground as if it had struck a stone road, and exploded immediately with a smashing, tearing explosion, practically unmuffled by soft earth. The second day after the return from Lemnos the Turks planted one hundred and thirty big high explosives in Chailak Dere. The menace of these guns, and still more the menace of the imaginary monsters which were to come, caused a great epidemic of "funk-hole digging." The hard clay hills, with their steep faces, were ideal places in which to drive tunnels. There was a keen nip in the air, and a bit of pick and shovel work kept the blood running.

Rhododendron Spur was turned into a splendid home. Seven hundred feet up above sea-level on the rough slopes of Sari Bair was formed a miniature Auckland Town. Every turning, sap and communication trench bore one of the old familiar names:—Queen Street, Quay Street, Customs Street, Fort Street, Shortland Street, Swanson Street, Wyndham Street, Wellesley Street, Manukau Road, and Seafield View.

The view was a glorious one. Every morning Imbros and Samothrace emerged from the morning mists, and every evening the sun set in splendour behind them. On the left, and far below, the plain of Suvla stretched from the Outpost to the Chocolate Hills and Kuchuk Anafarta. To the front and the right ran the ragged spurs of Hill 971. On the shining level of the sea, cruiser and destroyer were ceaselessly on the move. There is a great fascination in watching a destroyer on patrol duty. There is no beauty about her, no colour: she is drab, long and lean from one point of view—broad, low and squat from another. On a moonlight night she is a dark line, barely visible. Night and day she never ceases to move. Always there is the ceaseless, tireless moving, the keen look-

The Auckland Regiment

out, the instant readiness to strike. She has the range of every trench and landmark to the yard. A Turkish machine-gun has been pestering Chailak Dere. It is thought the Turk and his gun are concealed behind yonder screen of bushes. Rifles and machine-guns cannot shift him. The shore batteries do not command the spot. Word goes to the grey, weather-stained watcher on the laughing blue sea. She drifts backward and forward, so easily, so slowly, so lazily, as though every iron muscle was relaxed, as though nothing mattered, as though the day were too fine and the sea too smooth to do anything but drift. But of a sudden there is a flash, a wisp of brown and white smoke, the ear-splitting bang of the 4.7, a burst somewhere upon the hillside, and one more Turkish machine-gun has become scrap-iron, and some more of the faithful have passed from war to the Garden of Paradise and the dark-eyed houris. Kismet! The destroyer drifts up and down, so quietly, so easily, with such a lazy grace. She may not speak again all day, but always she is ready. The eyes of the watch are fixed on the dark hillsides, and the men in the long narrow trenches know that the vigil never tires and will never fail.

There are other craft to be seen. Sometimes a monitor creeps out from Imbros Harbour. She has a great 14-inch gun in her bow, and when she comes out there is something to justify the thunder-tones in which she speaks. Perhaps the enemy are dragging a gun into position. As the ox-team toils patiently along the rough road from Bulair there is a rumbling in the air, gradually growing nearer, a thud as the projectile buries itself in the earth, a rending explosion, and then men, machinery, bushes, rocks and débris rise slowly in the air, hang for a moment, while a pall of smoke rises, covering all from sight. The smoke clears. The watcher from Rhododendron can perceive no change; but the Skoda gun, brought with such toil down the Danube will never fire a shot.

A few days after the return to Anzac a working party from the Battalion were down by the little pier below Walkers Ridge. A group of Staff Officers came ashore. The central figure was Earl Kitchener. He was speedily recognised. The

The Last Six Weeks

Tommies and Indians fell in with appropriate clothes on. Australians and New Zealanders came just as they were. Some had hats on, others had none. Those who were smoking went on smoking, those with their hands in their pockets kept them there. The crowd pressed in to see the famous soldier. A number had cameras, with which they proceeded to take photos of the Field-Marshal under his very nose. The scene was not at all unlike a cattle show, with a group of farmers discussing the points of a prize beast. There was no disrespect. A Man met Men. The Man recognised the qualities of the Men, and the Men recognised in him the leadership, the steadfastness of purpose; and the inspiration which called the New Armies into being and mobilised Britain for war.

The air had had a nip in it for some time, and then one morning men woke to find the ground covered with snow. It was for many their first experience. The hillsides were very beautiful. Every little bush was outlined in gleaming white. The ground was frozen hard. It was cold, until the blood was running, and after that quite splendid. The air was cold, the water was cold, the dishes were cold, and, strange to say, many men never felt dirty for three whole days, and then only when the sun shone at mid-day. An Aucklander required more resolution to face cold water than to walk up to a machine-gun. During the days when the snow lay on the ground, delicacies such as fat bacon and bully-beef were devoured ravenously. The days of diminutive trousers were gone. Men no longer wandered round in identity discs, indecent apparel and wide smiles. Fortunate was he who had much clothing. Fortunate was he whose mother, sisters and sweethearts sent many balaclavas, scarves and socks, and still more fortunate was he who could salvage all these things from the careless. "Blessed is he that hath, for if he hath enterprise he shall have much more."

On the high slopes the snow disappeared slowly. Amongst the New Zealanders there were practically no cases of frostbite. Lower down, however, on the Suvla flat, the trenches were flooded out by the melting snow. Trench-foot and frost-

The Auckland Regiment

bite claimed as many victims as a big battle. For three whole days there was one long procession of poor Tommies and Ghurkas being carried out.

On November 20th Colonel Plugge returned, and took over the Battalion from Colonel Young. Life was very tranquil. A few casualties occurred from stray bullets and shells, but the trenches were so good, and afforded such splendid cover that the infantry in the line really ran very little danger. Rhododendron, in particular, was very safe.

The bombers were in possession of a Japanese mortar, which was regarded with a certain amount of suspicion and fear by those who were in the neighbourhood. Whether it was so regarded by the Turks it is difficult to say.

Very great attention was paid to the cleanliness of trenches, which were swept out every day. The prevalent disease was no longer dysentery, but jaundice. It was during this epidemic that men first commenced to get some idea of Major Allen's quality. He was a tall man, rather finely built, very deliberate in his movements and speech. Somewhat reserved, puritanical perhaps, he was never observed to be under the influence of liquor, and his language was most carefully moderated. His lisp when he commanded the "Houwakis to clean their wusty wifles," had become a standing joke. Who was this man? How would he turn out? There were not a few who were of the opinion that he would find war a very dirty, disagreeable, bloody business, and then retire gracefully from the scene to a more congenial sphere. Others suspended judgment, while odd men thought they detected some resemblance to Stonewall Jackson. In the meanwhile, as the Major commanding a company, the eyes of all were upon him. Apparently he had not yet realised that there was any danger in the air; if so, he gave no sign. Though suffering very badly with jaundice, he stayed on, performing all his duties. As a senior officer, he would have had not the slightest difficulty in being sent off. Also he was particular about the comfort of his men.

XIV.

The Evacuation

" Not unto us, O Lord, to tell
Thy purpose in the blast,
When those who towered beyond us fell,
And we were overpast
We cannot guess how goodness springs
From the black tempest's breath ;
Nor scan the birth of gentler things,
In these Red Bursts of Death."
—Capt. C. E. W. Bean,
"Anzac Book."

The decision to evacuate the Gallipoli Peninsula was reached soon after Earl Kitchener's visit. It was necessary to mystify and mislead not only the Turks, but also our own troops.

For two days, November 25th and 26th, the men were ordered to refrain from firing. During the night of November 30th much wire was placed in front of the fire-trench. A great deal of work was done "to prepare for the winter campaign." Deep dug outs were constructed.

Rhododendron Spur itself was made very comfortable. On the lower part of the slope was Captain Graham's store tent. A little further up lived the Battalion's two donkeys. These donkeys are noteworthy, because their driver was reputed to have the most forcible and fluent command of the *Australian language* in the Brigade. To hear the two little "donks" being "praised up" and called by their "Christian" names was to receive a lesson in the artistic use of language not readily to be forgotten. Dr. Addison had a most palatial residence, presided over by Davies and McDonald, the chief of the stretcher-bearers. The one drawback in connection with it being the fact that the roof consisted of one thickness of corrugated iron, and was therefore not to be relied on when the big shells were dropping round. In terraces on the slope lived the stretcher-bearers, signallers, ration-men, water-fatigue and the reserve company. Battalion Headquarters rejoiced in two *very* deep dug-outs, quite capable of keeping out even the heaviest shells.

The Auckland Regiment

Rumours of all sorts were about. Dunlop was an adept in the gentle art of rumour-mongering. He served out rumours and rations indiscriminately; his masterpiece probably being the yarn of the fifty ships of Japanese troops, with twenty-five shiploads of rice, all lying off, ready to be landed as soon as the cargoes of curry should arrive.

Rhododendron was shelled on the 4th, 5th, 7th, and 8th of December, but comparatively little damage was done. Heavy, high-explosive bombardments were a new type of frightfulness, not at all appreciated. Many a man who had stood everything else was not ashamed to admit that big shells were not to his liking.

At this time the men had not the remotest idea that the attempt to force the Dardanelles had been abandoned. Some thought we would hold on through the winter, and attack again in the spring. Others expected heavy reinforcements and another great effort before the bad weather set in. It became obvious that a move of some kind was on foot. Working parties were continually being sent down to move guns. Batmen and others on foraging expeditions to the beach found stores of all sorts thrown open. Several battalions of the New Army went away for a rest. Sections of the Field Ambulance moved away, none knew whither. More guns were moved. Fresh stores were thrown open. Rifles and ammunition were destroyed. The secret was becoming more open, but still men refused to believe the inevitable. The ground had been so hardly won, surely it would not be abandoned?

December 16th a small advance party left for Mudros. So it had come. The feeling amongst both officers and men was bitter in the extreme. "I am no lion-heart, but I would sooner go over the ridge in frontal assault, with all its chances of death with honour, than do this thing."

In these last few days R.S.M. Moncrieff was carried out, suffering from an attack of appendicitis. To the surprise of everyone he walked back next day from the Field Ambulance, very ill, but resolved not to spoil his record.

The most elaborate arrangements were made for the evac-

The Evacuation

uation. The success of the whole movement depended on accurate timing and on everyone knowing just exactly when and where he was to move. The evacuation, as far as Auckland were concerned, was to stretch over two nights—Saturday the 18th, and Monday the 20th of December. The first night two parties were to leave, one at six, and the other at nine o'clock. On the second night the remainder of the Battalion were to leave in three parties—one leaving at six, the second at nine, and the last—a small covering party of four officers and thirty-nine men—at two o'clock in the morning. It was generally thought that the movements set down for the first night would work out according to plan, and that the first two parties on the last night would, perhaps, reach the boats after very hard fighting. As for the small covering party, they were looked upon as the men who were to die for the sake of their comrades. Scores of men begged for a place in this little band. The Main Body and those who had seen much fighting were the keenest of all. They begged for a place as a privilege. They demanded it as a right. They entreated and cajoled—everything that could be done they did to secure a place in this fellowship of sacrifice. None expected them to come through alive—they, least of all, had any hope of life. It was a supreme act, made without fuss or show of emotion, in a fashion typically New Zealand. The names of the officers and men of this last party were:—Major Alderman, Lieutenant "Jock" McKenzie, Lieutenant Holland, Dr. Addison, Lieutenant Page, Sergeant Gasparich, Sergeant Francis, Sergeant Thompson, Sergeant Wilson, Sergeant Seddon, Sergeant Brook, Q.M.S. Stunnell, Sergeant Todd, Corporal Richardson, Corporal Cowan, Corporal Smith, Lance-Corporal Smith, Lance-Corporal McCready, Private Harding, Private Lauder, Private Lynn, Private Raymond, Private French, Private Rogers. (Other names unobtainable).

Main Body men who were refused for one reason or another were bitterly disappointed.

The first half of the Battalion moved away in two sections. From the heights the remainder looking down could see

The Auckland Regiment

the dark shapes of the transports lying in close to the shore. Next morning the sea was clear, the transports gone, and only the destroyers in sight. It was a day of tension. At 9 a.m. Monday the Turks commenced to bombard the Rhododendron trenches. Their ranging was very accurate, and but for the fact that there were so few men about very considerable casualties must have been inflicted.

The day passed. At six o'clock another big party moved off, and now the trenches were very thinly held. It was the most dangerous time of all. The next three hours were perfectly quiet. Nine o'clock came. The files assembled in Manukau Road. Rolls were carefully checked. There were quiet farewells. The rearguard stood to arms in silent, deserted trenches and waited for the sudden shout, the rush of Turks, the last bitter struggle and then Quiet Death, to whom they had given themselves that their friends might go free. The larger party filed down the steep slope to Chailak Dere, and there at the precise moment met the files of Wellington and Canterbury passing downward from the Apex and Cheshire Ridge. Chailak Dere had never seemed so quiet before. Scarcely a bullet fell anywhere. In the brilliant moonlight every familiar feature showed clearly out, the angles, the bends, the bracken, the scrub, and the graves of men. There were so many of them, the poor little graves, marked with the rough crosses of boxwood. So many sleep on the bloody, bitter slopes of Sari Bair, so many beneath the frowning Outpost Hill, so many by the margin of the Blue Ægean. These men elevated the Cross. They blazed a great trail. What valour was theirs, what steadfastness of purpose, what uttermost sacrifice of self!

The long file of men passed by the graves of their dead with no spoken word, but with a reverence that needed no words. In the hour of defeat men reconsecrated themselves to victory.

The lighters were ready. In half an hour all were on board. At two o'clock the rearguard withdrew. Just before their time was up a shout ran along the Turkish line. Surely the

Brigadier General C. H. J. Brown, D.S.O.

The Evacuation

enemy were coming now? They must have seen the transports in the moonlight and the boats moving to and fro between the ships and the shore. The rearguard "stood-to," ready to die like men. The slow minutes ticked past. They had offered themselves, but the offering was not taken. Nevertheless, their heroism is not lessened. In quietness they, too, reach the water's edge, where Colonel Plugge was waiting. All embarked.

The dark mass of Sari Bair stood out clear against the sky. The outline slowly vanished.

It was the last of Anzac.

> *"We only know from good and great*
> *Nothing but good can flow;*
> *That where the cedar crashed so straight*
> *No crooked tree shall grow.*
>
> *That from their ruin a taller pride,*
> *Not for these eyes to see,*
> *May clothe one day the valley side*
> *Non nobis, Domine."*

XV.

Egypt

After the Evacuation the various parties of the Battalion assembled outside Mudros Village in a camp of tents. The "Die-hards" of the Battalion were welcomed with much joy, but the greatest demonstration was reserved for the two Australian battalions which had been the last to leave Anzac. The road by which they marched was lined with cheering men; for the brotherhood of Anzac had been a very real thing. It was there that Australian and New Zealander got to know and appreciate each other as never before or after. Lemnos was not a wildly exciting place to be back in again. The camp was very ordinary, and the admixture of pebbles with turf did not improve matters when it came to turning in for the night. Mudros itself was a filthy little place. The only building of any beauty was the Church, which was really quite fine. Colonel Plugge took over the Brigade for a few days, and Major Alderman assumed command of the Battalion. Drill and discipline became the order of the day. This served to fill in time, at any rate. A shower of rain swamped out the officers' marquee, and made things unpleasant for all. The only real excitement, however, was a raid carried out by certain bold spirits of all units upon a certain guard of "Jocks," who had in their keeping sundry barrels of beer. The "Jocks" were surprised by overwhelming numbers and led away in one direction, while the barrels rolled off in another. When the barrels were "dry"—and what were they amongst so great a multitude?—both they and the guard were shamefully abandoned. Four days of comparative quietness passed, during which everyone yearned for the flesh-pots of Egypt, and were not a little disappointed when it became evident that Christmas in Cairo would be an impossibility.

Egypt

Orders for the move came Christmas morning. Very early indeed the Battalion fell in. The Colonel said he was sorry there was not very much for breakfast, but that if all hands would get to work and strike camp quickly they would be aboard the transport by mid-day and would find a first-rate Christmas dinner already waiting. Everyone set to work in high spirits and the best possible frame of mind. The work was done. The Battalion, headed by the band, moved down to the pier. Embarkation was a quick business. Shaking down on board was a somewhat more confused matter, but was finally accomplished successfully.

What about this Christmas dinner? Apparently it was to be on during the evening, instead of mid-day. That dinner never came, and to this day its loss is a bitter matter with every survivor. The officers fared sumptuously—no fault of theirs, for they would have shared if it had been possible—and the men had hard white biscuits, without even the familiar bully-beef. To wash down this repast a small quantity of cold water was available. This was the climax, and the Auckland Regiment was never, in all its history, in quite such a bad temper.

Next day things looked more cheerful. The *Marsova* was ploughing her way steadily toward Alexandria, and if Christmas had been rather a failure the New Year was still to come, and there were worse places than Cairo to spend it in. Memories of the first stay there were revived, and men made arrangements with one another as to what they would do and where they would go when all were safe back in Zeitoun Camp.

At last the quay at Alexandria! and there, right on the quay, a slip of an English girl in her Red Cross uniform at a little buffet. So fair and sweet and clean she looked—a vision of beauty and grace to men who for nine long months had not seen a woman, except some of the withered old Greeks at Lemnos. The very sight of her was a benediction.

There was to be no leave in Alexandria. Trains were already waiting, and in two hours the Aucklanders were once

The Auckland Regiment

more rattling down through the Nile Delta. Very homely and pleasant it looked, after the barren hills. There was a good time coming, and spirits were mounting high. Old Egypt seemed just the same, anyway, war or no war. One or two people fell off the train and damaged themselves rather badly, but otherwise nothing happened to mar the proceedings until it became evident that Cairo was not to be the destination after all. The train went down through a wide desert, past Zag-a-zig, past Tel-el-Kebir, to Moascar, close to Ismailia. This place had been chosen for several reasons. First there was a Turkish menace to cut the Canal, and sufficient troops had to be kept on the spot. Secondly, Moascar was an ideal training ground, with its great expanse of desert and the beautiful Lake Timsah, a bathing pool large enough for thousands of men. And, thirdly, it was *not* near to Cairo or any other large centre.

Arriving a little before dusk, it was found that the advance party had prepared tea, but had no camp ready, as tents had not arrived from Cairo. A bivouac was formed and, despite a shower of rain, the night passed comfortably enough. Next day a camp was made. The process was quite simple. A large square was formed, and then subdivided into four smaller ones, with roads running between. The four companies each occupied one square. In front of the main square were the officers' lines, and in rear of the camp the cookhouses, the Quartermaster's Stores, and the machine-gunners. Boundaries were marked off by heaping up little banks of sand. At first only a few tents were available, and the majority of men constructed rough bivvies, usually of oil-sheets. As the days passed, however, more tents arrived, and within a few days everyone was under canvas.

After nine months fighting the Aucklanders were once more back on the desert sands. They had left Egypt 1100 strong. During the campaign they had received another 1100 men as reinforcements, and now on landing back the strength was about 600. The total battle casualties were 19 officers and 344 other ranks killed, 35 officers and 901 other ranks

Egypt

wounded, and two other ranks prisoners of war, a grand total of 1301. Some hundreds of men were evacuated for sickness, thus causing the discrepancy between casualties and the final strength.

The following decorations were awarded during the course of the campaign:—

    C.M.G.—Lieutenant-Colonel A. Plugge, Lieutenant-Colonel R. Young, and Major W. Alderman.

    M.C.—Captain J. A. Wallingford, Lieutenant G. H. Holland.

    D.C.M.—Sergeants R. Tilsley, J. H. Francis, Corporals H. Spencer, W. J. Reid, F. W. Watson, and Private G. A. Tempany.

The above were all mentioned in despatches, Lieutenant-Colonel Plugge twice.

Other mentions were.—

    Major T. H. Dawson (twice).
    Major S. A. Grant.
    Private D. Davidson
    Private C. J. Maroni.
    Private E. L. Noakes.
    Bugler D. B. Treacher.

It will be seen from the above list that eleven decorations were given to the Battalion, and that another six names were included in the list of mentions. Compared with the number of decorations granted later in France, this seems a very scanty list. The recipients, however, have the right to feel additional pride in the fact that their valour was conspicuous at a time when the best and bravest men were in the field, and when recognition was very difficult to get. Those who were passed over have the satisfaction of knowing that they, too, fought at Anzac, and it is an honour for any man to be able to say that.

The following were promoted to commissioned rank during the fighting. Promotion of this sort was in itself a very great honour:—

    Lieutenant.—Fletcher.

The Auckland Regiment

Lieutenant.—Dittmer.
Lieutenant.—Graham Reid.
Lieutenant.—Holland.
Lieutenant.—John McKenzie.
Lieutenant.—Page.
Lieutenant.—Jack.

January, February and March were very important months in the history of the N.Z.E.F. In Moascar the Infantry Brigade swelled to three brigades, and with Divisional troops and Artillery became the New Zealand Division. This was made possible by the arrival of the Rifle Brigade, the Seventh, Eighth and Ninth Reinforcements, and the return of a great number of sick and wounded from hospital. The Auckland, Wellington, Canterbury and Otago Regiments formed two battalions, out of which, on March 1, 1916, the 2nd N.Z. Infantry Brigade was constituted.

2/Auckland were formed at Albury Hill—a point some four miles to the east of the Canal. The nucleus consisted of a small group, some thirty-five all told, who broke away from the old battalion and went out with nothing, execpt their personal belongings. Major, now Lieutenant-Colonel, Alderman was in command. Major S. S. Allen, Lieutenant Page, Lieutenant McKenzie, Lieutenant Seddon (recently promoted), Dr. Addison, Sergeant-Majors Hewitt, Goodwin, Cameron, Tuck, Sergeant Gordon and Corporal Carter were the best-known members of this nucleus party. Major Wyman, one of the most distinguished officers of the Auckland Mounted Rifles, was drafted in. Lieutenant McClurg, coming from the Rifle Brigade, was made Quartermaster. Gradually at first, and then very rapidly, the new battalion grew in numbers and acquired much property—not always by constitutional methods. Many sick and wounded swelled the numbers. The Eighth and Ninth Reinforcements joined up. Like the earth in the early stages of creation the new battalion was "without form and void." Colonel Alderman, however, had a genius for organisation and training. He brought the whole formless mass together into one place, and then in half an hour had

Egypt

formed a battalion, complete in every part from battalion headquarters to transport details. Immediately they marched off and commenced training. As a training officer, Colonel Alderman was unmatched in the N.Z.E.F., and until the Division sailed for France, 2/Auckland were never allowed to slacken. It was hard—just as hard as the men could possibly stand—but the purpose was achieved. A few broke under the strain, but the majority were in splendid condition. Keen as Colonel Alderman was on parade-ground work, he never overlooked the fact that he was training men for war, and the practical side was always stressed. Day by day the Battalion realised itself as an independent unit, and gained that sense of solidarity that is so essential for good fighting. The Company Commanders were:—

3rd Company: Captain Kirker.
6th Company: Captain Davis.
15th Company: Major Wyman.
16th Company: Captain Grainger.

The feeling with regard to promotions from the ranks became very acute. There were in all the battalions a number of exceedingly capable N.C.O.'s who had been very much to the fore throughout the Gallipoli Campaign. These men thought, and with reason, that as so many new officers were required it was only bare justice that they should receive the promotion they had so thoroughly well earned. To their dismay it was found that each reinforcement was bringing a quota of officers more than sufficient to meet all requirements. None of these men had anything to recommend them especially, except that in some cases they had had a certain amount of Territorial experience. If the system were to be continued it would mean that promotion from the ranks would be practically impossible, and that men inexperienced and unproven would continually be taking commands, ranging from a platoon to a company. Strong protests were made. The Commanding Officers were generally favourable, and three of them waited on Generals Russell and Godley. General Godley stated that the matter had received his attention. He was quite in

The Auckland Regiment

sympathy with the views expressed, but was powerless to act, as the authorities in New Zealand, despite his protests, insisted on sending men away with commissions. Here the matter rested, but there was much soreness. Amongst men who arrived with commissions were some, who, after experience of war, turned out most brilliant soldiers; the majority were men of average type and "filled" the positions in a "not unsatisfactory manner," while a minority broke under the strain and proved themselves utterly incapable or cowardly. The system provided for a succession of mediocrity, which, from beginning to end, was the curse of the N.Z.E.F. Fighting men of the calibre of the New Zealanders should have been officered only by first-class men of proven capacity and courage. In any future war, promotion should be made on the ground of ability and experience from the ranks of the fighting units. Talent should be given every opportunity and encouragement. The scheme, moreover, should be sufficiently elastic to provide for the reduction of the incapable, cowardly, or careless, in the most drastic fashion.

Training went on without interruption, very much on the same lines as in the days of the Main Body, with the exception that there was no Cairo in which to spend leisure time. After the work of the day, which usually finished up at 2 p.m., the main diversion consisted in bathing. Lake Timsah was quite ideal for that purpose. Thousands of men were bathing every day. It was a wonderful sight to see the blue waters of the lake, with the circle of sun-kissed sandhills just broken here and there by clumps of palms, and the splendidly developed bodies of the bathers.

Ismailia itself, though a pretty little place, had comparatively few attractions; yet, as there was nowhere else to go, except the wide desert, the town was thronged during all leave hours. It was at Moascar that the N.Z.Y.M.C.A. made its first appearance with the fighting troops of the Dominion. Two huts were erected, and much good work was done.

Life once more became monotonous, and the next move was eagerly waited for. No definite statements were made,

Egypt

consquently rumour had a clear field. Salonika, Mesopotamia and France were all frequently mentioned. Deep down there was no doubt whatsoever that France was the country most desired. Now that the Gallipoli venture had definitely failed, it was evident that France and Belgium were to be the decisive battlefields. It was there that the heaviest fighting would take place. Every little arrangement with regard to clothing, equipment or training which gave any indication of probable climatic conditions was most eagerly discussed. Training continued without respite all through March. On April 3rd Sir Archibald Murray inspected the troops.

The New Zealand Division, under Major-General Sir A. H. Russell, K.C.M.G., was to proceed to France.

On the night of April 5/6th, 1/Auckland entrained for Port Said, and there embarked on the *Franconia*. Next day 2/Auckland embarked on the *Ascania* from Alexandria. The voyage across the Mediterranean was quite uneventful, although the presence of German submarines created a certain amount of interest. The Huns were, however, distinctly unfortunate. A well-placed torpedo would have sent either of the Auckland Battalions to the bottom, and thus saved a very great subsequent waste of ammunition, not to mention the lives of many patriotic but unfortunate German citizens.

XVI.

France

Green hills rising from the sea! The Château d'If, the island prison of Monte Cristo! Churches and buildings of ancient grey stone! The City of Marseilles and the Land of France!

There was no delay. The transports ran alongside great wharves, and within a few hours disembarkation commenced. The men marched to the waiting trains, a distance of a few hundred yards only, and rapidly entrained. The famous trucks of "40 hommes et 8 chevaux en long" were for a later time. For this journey the rank and file had third-class compartment carriages. For three days the trains were passing through the pleasant land of France. Blooming orchards, green fields, white-walled and red-roofed villages, stately châteaux, beautiful towns, all were looking their best in the spring sunshine. Speed was apparently no object. Men, whose limbs were cramped with sitting so long in the confined space, would get out and walk alongside whenever a hill had to be climbed. Groups of French girls and French children stood by the side of the line, calling out a shrill welcome in classical Australian. Every here and there fatigue parties had dixies boiling beside the line, and tea heavily reinforced with rum, was served out. Incidentally, it may be mentioned, now the war is over, that not a few emergency rations of tea were opened without "an order from an officer" and brewed with water from the engine. Town after town was passed—Avignon, Orange, Lyons, Dijon. The Statue of Vercingetorix, the first hero of a struggle for the liberties of France, stood proudly on the hillside at Arles. At Versailles, Paris was side-tracked, and the trains went on through Rouen, Abbeville, Etaples, past Calais, through St.

France

Omer, and so to Steenbecque station, where the troops detrained.

1/Auckland arrived on April 16th, and marched away to look for billets somewhere between the village of Morbecque and the town of Hazebrouck. The interpreter was missing. It was popularly supposed that he had provided himself with a sweetheart in Hazebrouck, so as to avoid wasting time between the trains. While a search was being made for the missing functionary, who by the way ultimately turned out to be the village priest, the Battalion shivered on the cobble-stones of the street. Billets were finally discovered to be certain farmhouses between Hazebrouck and Morbecque. The most hazy ideas had been entertained on the subject of billets. Not a few had expected to be quartered by twos and threes on French families, to sleep in the best bedrooms, and generally to be entertained with considerable state. It was a rude shock to visionaries of this sort to be thrust into a lean-to off the pig-sty. The weather was not nearly so good as it had been in the south of France. There was a great deal of cold, misty rain. Everything was sloppy and muddy. It was not easy to keep warm, and, in consequence, the first impression of billets was not as favourable as it might have been. The French folk were soon well liked, and the language question was settled by the use of a few words often repeated, broad smiles and frequent gestures. "Mademoiselle" here came into vogue, but of her more later. The quaint French customs, their different outlook on many things, were all of interest, but in the cold weather the ones who possessed fires and sold coffee to the troops were the most popular. It was a terrible tragedy to find beer selling at a penny a glass and to have no money. Everyone was bankrupt, and so for a fortnight the French folk marvelled at the wonderful sobriety of the New Zealanders. They probably thought that it was one of the national characteristics of their guests to refrain from intoxicating liquors—evidently an idosyncrasy similar to the strange craze some of these Colonials had for bathing themselves. One day certain officers, who shall be nameless, desired of their

The Auckland Regiment

"madame" a tub and much hot water. "Mais oui, monsieur, certainement," and the hospitable old lady bustled round to fulfil this order. The family were warned off, and the bath commenced. As it was Good Friday, the family evidently concluded that this was some solemn religious rite in honour of the season. They gathered reverently round, monsieur, madame, the mademoiselles and the "piccanins," and gazed with awe on this wonderful ceremony of purification. Surely these men took their religion seriously and sadly! "Mon Dieu! Fancy exposing one's body to such cold for so unnecessary a reason!"

It is a very regrettable fact that madame's cows showed a deplorable lack of restraint, and were evidently quite prepared to be milked in any language.

2/Auckland arrived at Steenbecque station on April 19th, and immediately marched some kilometres to Rebecque, where the billets were found to be not very good. Here, again, there was a great thirst caused by lack of funds. At last, however, came the long-desired day—and the disillusionment of the villagers. Next day the Battalion marched to fresh billets at Bleu. It was a very long and hard march, and after the celebrations of the evening before, the tramp, tramp, tramp along the cobbled roads came none the easier. Many fell out, and the memory of that march still lingers.

Morbecque and Bleu were no very great distance from the firing line. In the still evening air the rumble of the guns could be distinctly heard, and from any eminence the flares could be seen, tiny points of fire, rising in the distance.

XVII.

Armentières

> "*There's a township torn and shattered,*
> *There are streets of broken brick,*
> *Where the shells have crumped and battered*
> *Where the mule-teams rear and kick,*
> *And the sweating driver curses,*
> *As the pellets zip and tear;*
> '*Oh, confound this German shrapnel;*
> *Up, you blighters! C'est la guerre.*'
> *There's a winsome little maiden*
> *Always greets me with a laugh,*
> *And her eyes with mirth are laden—*
> *Eyes that question, dance and chaff.*
> *There's a crash that shakes the pave,*
> *Splinters zutting through the air—*
> '*Ah, my God; one's caught the girlie!*
> *Pauvre petite: mais c'est la guerre.*'"

The New Zealanders took over the sector of Armentières. The place had a reputation for quietness, and for many months had been looked upon as one of the best "rest-camps" on the line. "Doan'e ye fire at him, choom, and he woan't fire at you," seems to have been the principle on which the war was conducted in these parts.

On May 13th, 1916, 1/Auckland went into the line at "La Chapelle d'Armentières," and on the following day 2/Auckland took over the "l'Epinette" sector. For the next three months trench warfare went on without interruption, and gradually increased in intensity and fury.

The trenches were old, and in many places not in the best condition. A very great deal of work was required, draining, revetting, clearing, sand-bagging, before they could be passed as satisfactory. Lieutenant-Colonel Alderman made particularly strenuous efforts in this direction. "Dig, men, dig! Do you want to live, then dig!" 2/Auckland perforce dug. Two-thirds of war is just sheer hard manual toil, digging and carrying.

Much interest was naturally centred in "No-Man's-Land" and the German territory adjacent thereto. A certain amount of mutual recrimination was always being carried on. "In retaliation for our strafe on Pont Ballot, the enemy vigorously shelled our supports at Vancouver and the Orchard with H.E. and shrapnel, and our front trenches with minenwerfers. Damage done was insignificant." Note these "minnies." They occur and re-occur from this time forward. They are the sirens who sing the song of "Where's your bivvy? Where's your bivvy? Where's your bivvy?" And then, having obtained local directions, burst with a large, wide noise, making a hole in the ground of similar dimensions. For moral effect their radius is seven and a half miles! Much objection is taken to the enemy's display of periscopes. One day "our snipers smashed five of them;" another day they smash three. "Two pigeons passed over trench 74 and settled in the enemy's line." It is evident spies are at work in the town. A certain "Red house" comes in for much attention. "Washing is hung-out" therefrom. Evidently the blood-stained Hun has his clean moments. "A woman was observed in the red brick house— the first woman seen on this part of the front." Who was she, this woman, traitress or slave? "A man was seen working in a sap. He disappeared when fired upon," evidently a man of understanding, this one, by no means void of worldly wisdom. "A man was observed on the parapet wearing a blue cap with a blue band." A rather ornate-looking person, using field glasses, was seen "to drop his field glasses and fall back into the trench, obviously a case for the "field-lazaret," if not for a burial party.

As time went on, gentlemen with blue and red round their field-grey caps made themselves less conspicuous, although the signs of their activities were still to be seen. "A maul was observed over the parapet driving stakes"; deduction would point to the fact of a certain motive power, probably a Hun, at the other end of it. "A dummy gun and a dummy man were perceived on the opposing parapet."

Our L.T.M.B.'s were very active continually bombarding sections of the enemy line. A few "ærial torpedoes" come over, and "our Lewis guns fire 4500 rounds in retaliation."

This mutual retaliation business catches the imagination of

Armentières

both sides. Whirlwind artillery strafes, trench-mortar duels, and continuous raiding become the order of the day. Fritz, who was by no means down-hearted at this stage of the game, made great play with minenwerfer, whizz-bang and "five-nine." The pace grew hotter and hotter, until all pretence of quietness passed, and Armentières was generally recognised to have grown "hot."

On June 2nd the Germans put up sign-boards giving notice of the sea-fight at Jutland. Mutual recrimination once more followed, with the result that 2/Auckland suffered a number of casualties. On the 22nd the same unit had the misfortune to lose Major Wyman, wounded. He had served with the Mounted Rifles at Anzac, winning the D.S.O. and a very great reputation. In the reorganisation he had been sent to the Infantry, and had been placed in command of the 15th Company. A man of the type of Donald Hankey's "Beloved Captain," he was at once greatly beloved and very highly respected. He naturally knew little of infantry drill, and so made mistakes, which drew upon him the stinging censure of the commanding officer. Such a gentleman, and such a soldier as Major Wyman, could afford a few technical slips in parade-ground orders, for the 15th, to whom he was father, brother, leader and commander, would have followed him anywhere and done anything for him. He was hit through the chest by a chance machine-gun bullet while supervising some work in the vicinity of Tissage Dump, and although he lived, he was never again fit for service. His loss was a very great one.

A few days later, Lieutenant-Colonel W. Alderman was evacuated through the Field Ambulance, suffering from a nervous breakdown. Major S. S. Allen took command of the Second Battalion until the new Commanding Officer, Lieutenant-Colonel C. H. J. Brown, D.S.O., should arrive from England. This officer had already been associated with the Regiment in the affair of Quinn's Post, where he had been very badly wounded. Already he was looked upon as one of the best soldiers in the N.Z.E.F. 2/Auckland were fortunate in securing so fine a man to command them.

The Auckland Regiment

1/Auckland went into the l'Epinette sector on June 21st, occupying trenches 73, 74, 75 and 76, the strong points SPX and SPY, Willow Walk and Buterne Farm. Willow Walk, Plank Avenue and Japan Avenue led to the front line, which was held by the 15th and 16th Companies. Everything went well until the afternoon of July 3rd, when the Germans commenced to range with a big naval gun. This was an ominous sign. At 9 p.m. a coloured flare went up from the enemy rear line. There was a feeling of impending danger. At 10.30 p.m. hell suddenly broke loose. Every kind of missile rained down upon the front line. The parapet was blown in, dug-outs smashed, men killed, wounded and buried alive. For an hour the noise continued, the detonations filling the night with sound, the flashes lighting up the darkness. The Huns were about to raid. It was impossible to move about, but every man grasped his rifle, crouched down beneath what shelter was left, ready to leap up and fire as soon as the barrage lifted and the raiders should endeavour to push in. The air was heavy with smoke and fumes and the smell of phosphorus. In a little trench ahead of the front line, Corporal Best and five men of the 16th Company were stationed on outpost duty. It was impossible for them to get back, as the enemy barrage was falling between them and their own front line. They determined to fight, and as soon as the enemy barrage lifted fighting commenced. The little party, well supplied with bombs, made a most gallant resistance, and were not taken until their supply of bombs was exhausted and nearly every man wounded. Their stubborn and unexpected fight undoubtedly disorganised the raiders' plans. The telephone wires were all cut, but before communication quite ceased Battalion Headquarters got in touch with the front line, and Major R. C. Allen was ordered to take up a platoon of the Hauraki Company and reinforce. As Plank Avenue and Japan Avenue were both blocked and under very heavy fire, the party went overland, straight through the barrage of high explosive that was falling between the front and support lines. There was comparative quietness for the space of an hour, during which

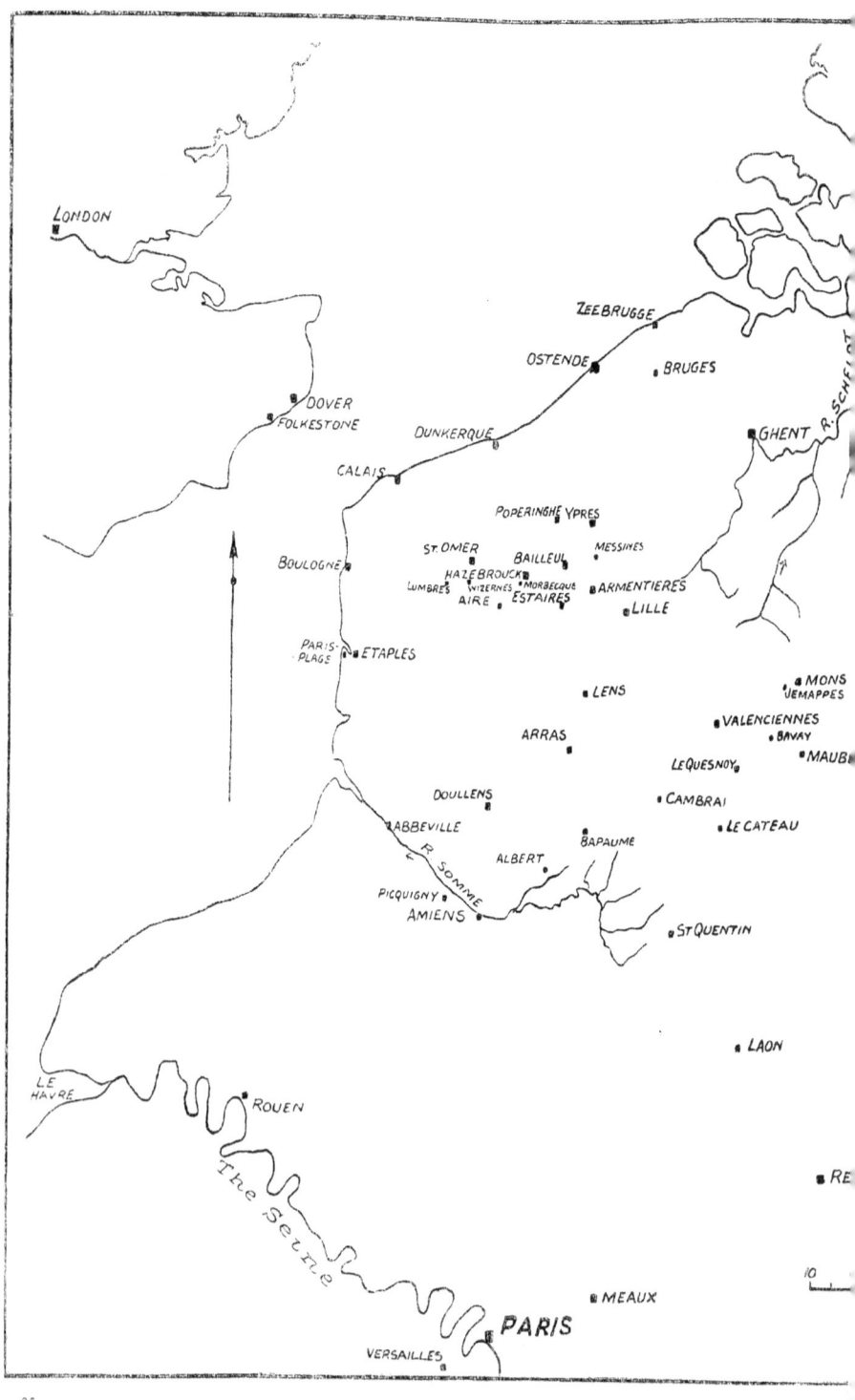

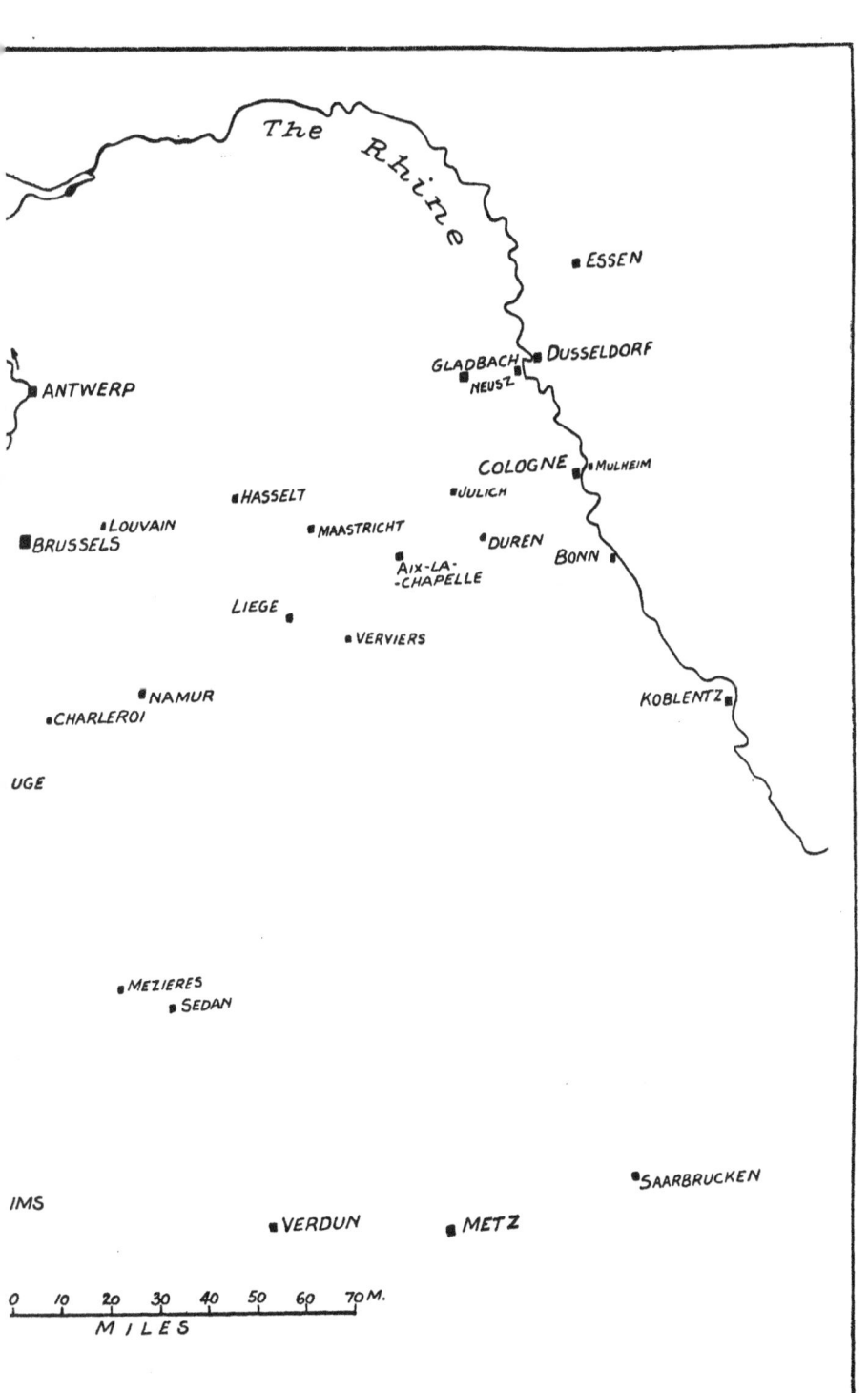

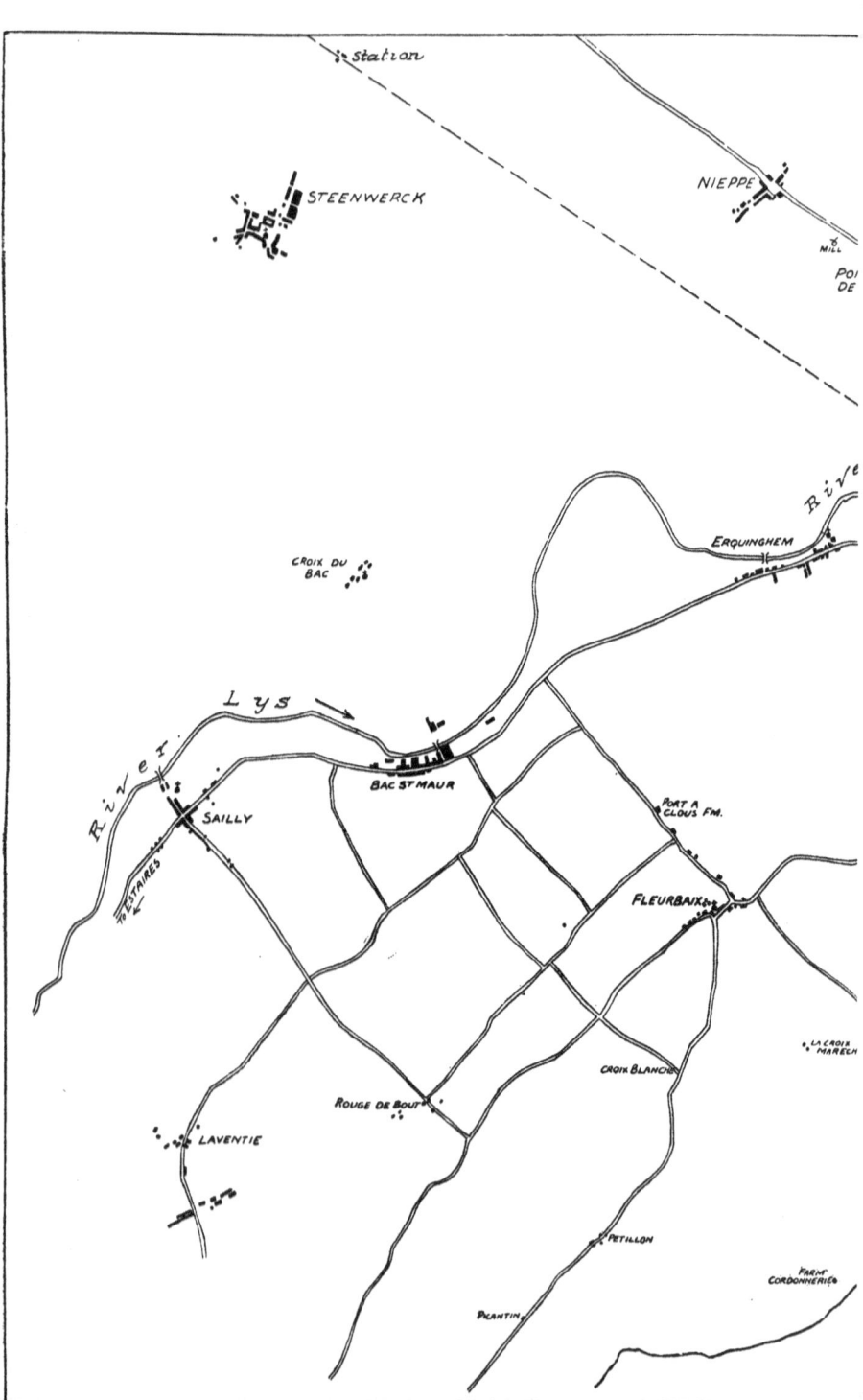

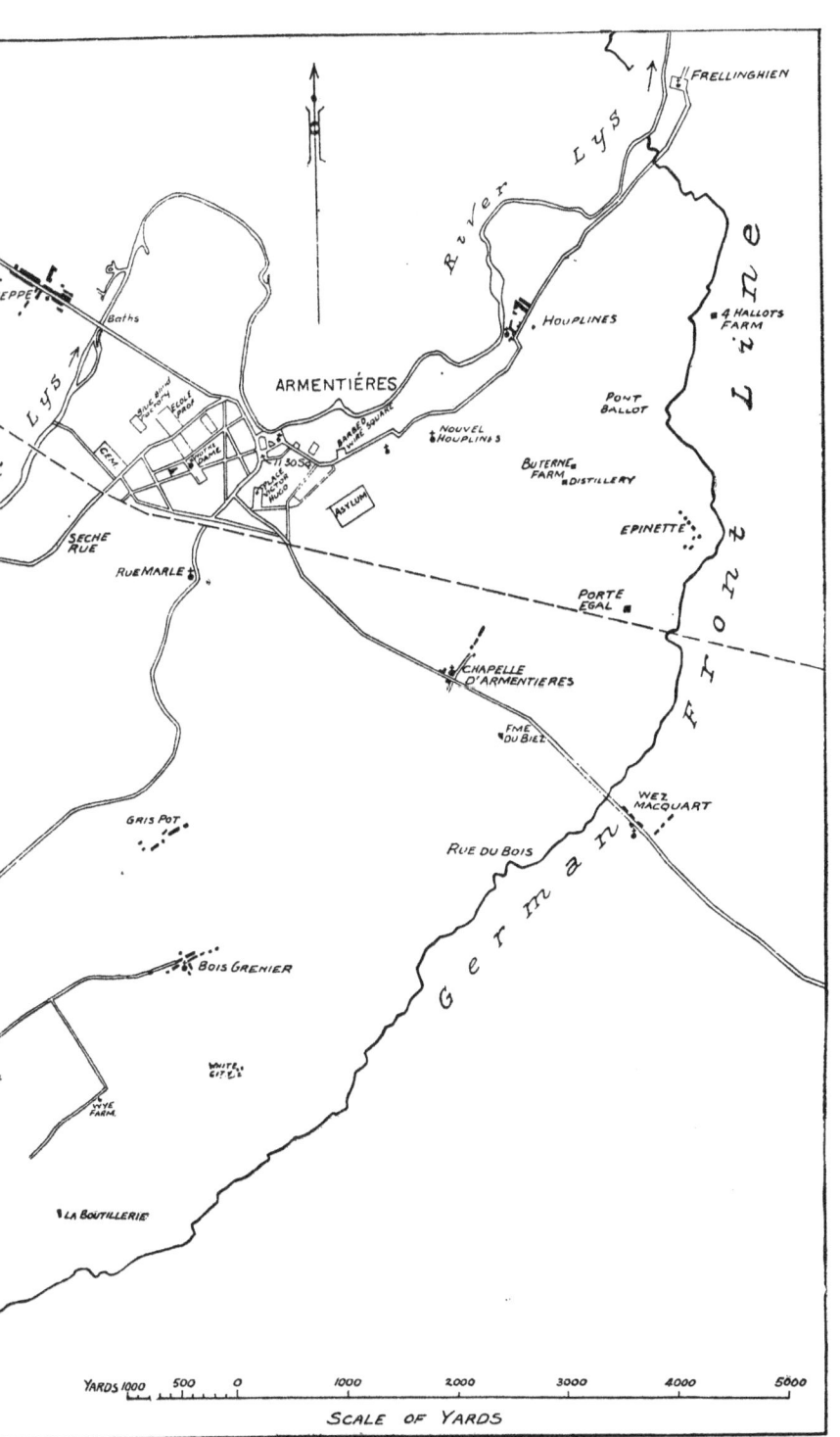

Armentières

the wounded were cleared and everything possible done to restore the line. Major Allen returned, and the survivors were congratulating themselves on their good fortune, when of a sudden the German barrage fell once more. This time it was largely a "minenwerfer" strafe. Another hour of terror, more men killed, wounded and buried alive, and then the raiders, reorganised after their first check, tried once more to rush the front line. They tried obstinately, but with no success. The Aucklanders "stuck it" steadfastly, every man fighting just where he stood, shooting and bombing straight ahead at the indistinct figures moving in the wire. After half an hour of constant effort the raiders withdrew, baffled, leaving behind them a large canister of powder which they had brought as far as the parapet (and with which they intended to destroy our mining system), a few hand-bombs, and one dazed man who was found next morning wandering about the line. Major R. C. Allen once more came up through the barrage, bringing with him R.S.M. Thompson and some 1/Otagos from the subsidiary trenches. They helped to put the line to rights and clear the wounded.

Altogether it had been a very bloody and expensive business, 33 O.R.'s being killed, 1 officer and 63 O.R.'s wounded, and 5 O.R.'s missing. The officer, Captain Morpeth, was a very brave and excellent soldier. He was singularly unfortunate, having been badly wounded the day of the Landing, and now, after a few weeks only of trench warfare, he was so badly hurt as to be incapacitated for further service. Sergeant-Major Todd, of the 16th, especially distinguished himself in holding the company together. His coolness, resolution and cheerfulness were most marked. When the artillery fire first opened, R.S.M. Thompson was in Houplines, chatting with friends in the 2/Auckland R.A.P. As soon as the uproar was heard, he stopped suddenly, drew himself up, listened for a moment, and then said that he must go to his battalion at once. He was trembling; everyone knew that he feared to go into the bursting hell of noise ahead; but he did go, and went not only to his Battalion Headquarters, but right up to the

The Auckland Regiment

smashed front line, and there worked like any private soldier to straighten out the smash. Few men with the Regiment ever commanded such genuine respect as R.S.M. "Andy" Thompson. Major Allen's extreme coolness was remarked on by all.

On the 19th July 1/Auckland were to carry out a raid from the Port Egal sector. This was not a success, owing to a certain confusion in the arrangements. Sergeant Fox and three men were the only ones to enter the enemy trenches. All through the Armentières period Sergeant Fox continued to uphold the very high reputation he had won at Anzac, doing very much fine patrol work. During the preliminary movements before the raid, Lieutenant Gasparich, a hero of the Daisy Patch, and one of the most popular members of the Main Body, was wounded for the third time, and permanently incapacitated.

2/Auckland during this period were holding the line in front of Houplines, and continuing to have quite an uneventful time. On the night of 12/13th August, Captain Armstrong carried out a highly successful little raid. The party had been carefully trained. Captain Armstrong had with him Lieutenant Cooper, one of the best and ablest of the Gallipoli men. The ground had been most carefully reconnoitred, and everything went exactly according to plan. The party assembled in No-Man's-Land under a covering barrage, moved up toward the gaps in the enemy wire, dashed in the instant the barrage lifted, bayonetted a few Huns, captured a machine-gun, the first taken by the New Zealanders in France, and two prisoners, and then, having achieved their purpose, withdrew without loss.

The only other incident of any importance during the time in the line was the discovery by Dr. Nelson of 1/Auckland of a large store of red wine in one of the abandoned buildings at La Chapelle d' Armentières.

After the barren life at Anzac and the isolation of the desert, Armentières was a good place. It was a quaint old-world town, built almost entirely of red brick. The churches, the religious foundations and the schools were the most prom-

Armentières

inent buildings. The streets were the famous "pavé" roads of France, a barbarous survival of mediævalism. Five-sixths of the population had fled long before the arrival of the Division. Those who remained were for the most part the most courageous of the poor folk, who were prepared to risk much rather than leave the humble homes which meant so much to them. Most were women and children, for the men were under arms.

Armentières, except for certain parts, was a city of silence. Grass was growing between the cobble-stones. Street after street was empty and silent. The glass in the windows was smashed by the detonations of the bursting shells. Every here and there a house was torn by a shell-hole in roof or wall. Some had been burst open, and all the pitiful relics of the once happy homes were lying in confusion amidst the tangle of rubbish on the floor. The life of a happy and industrious town was gone. More tragic than the loss of prosperity and the shattering of bricks and mortar was the death and wounding of women and children. Every day some of them were hit. The sight of a woman horribly dead, lying in the shattered smash of her home was terrible; to hear the groans and cries of a girl who half an hour before had been the life and soul of a crowded estaminet—a superb example of bright and splendid womanhood—and to realise that she was dying in agony was very terrible; and to find a little maid of six, golden-haired and blue-eyed, the very picture of hundreds of the little sisters of our own homes—dying on the stones of the street from shock, was most terrible. War is horrible. Imagine the tragedy of this French town, with its shattered and desecrated homes, its silent streets, its long roll of women and children killed and wounded. But tragedy was never allowed to obtrude itself. The French folk were far too brave for that. Armentières was for the New Zealanders a most cheerful place.

In between trench spells the Battalions were billeted in the town, 1/Auckland in the basement of the large blind factory at the rear of the town, and 2/Auckland in the Breuvert Fac-

The Auckland Regiment

tory, off "Barbed-wire-square." Both of these billets were exceedingly popular and very comfortable. 1/Auckland were roused in the morning by a troop of "gamins" and "mademoiselles" entering their dormitory in the "Blue Blind Factory" to sell the morning paper, eggs and chocolate. Mademoiselle was an adept at rough wit, and the jokes flew round fast and furiously. People arising to wash found another "troop of damsels glad" arriving for the day's work in the factory. As often as not the day was free, for the working parties on which the Battalions in rest were employed were for the most part required at night. Quite close to the factory was the "Ecole Professionale," a very fine structure, though now of a somewhat dilapidated appearance, resulting from an intensive application of Hun "Kultur." This institution was the centre of the Divisional social life. The Y.M.C.A., the Church Institutes, the Canteen, the Picture Theatre, were all established in various parts of the great building. In close proximity were numbers of estaminets and cafés. To the Anzac men, in particular, this seemed a very fine kind of war. Nevertheless, it was war. Even at the best of times there was some reminder. One day the Hun left his visiting card at the door of the picture show, in the shape of a huge shell-crater. For the next two or three sessions the patrons were not as enthusiastic as heretofore, and sat somewhat lightly on their seats, ready to beat a hasty retreat in case of need. The aeroplanes, either a "Fritz" or one of ours, were always passing overhead and drawing to themselves the attentions of the anti-aircraft guns. The unconquerable optimism of human nature was never better displayed than when men, after three months in the town, still watched for the result of each shot, in the hope that something interesting might happen to the "flieger" up aloft. The planes themselves were a never-ending source of interest. As a rule they flew backwards and forwards without any tangible result, as far as the infantrymen could observe; but just now and again something did happen. One day a British plane dashed over Houplines and flew straight for the line of German captive balloons. He was over the first, and a second

Armentières

or two later it burst into flames, the next and the next came down burning furiously. It was a great sight, and the cheering that went up was most exasperating to the Hun, who replied after the objectionable manner of his kind by turning on the "Minnie-guns."

The "estaminets" and "chip-shops," whether in the vicinity of the Blue Blind Factory or Barbed-wire-square, were centres of great revellings, where many a tall story was told in a dialect which consisted of distorted French mixed with English of an elementary and often sulphurous sort, accompanied with much gesture and more laughter. Chips, eggs, coffee and beer were all good in their way; but brave, cheerful, generous, good-natured mademoiselle was much better than them all. What a wonderful creature she was—jamais fachée, jamais vexée; how willing she was to "promenade avec monsieur apres la guerre," or to go back with him to New Zealand "after de nex war per-r-raps." "Mademoiselle from Armentières," you were a good friend to the New Zealanders. You and they went through some hard times together, and you are not forgotten. Men in the bush camps and on the sheep runs, in the mine and factory, busy town and quiet countryside still talk of and think of you. They have married their old fiancées now, or are looking round for better ones—and you, your heroic men have come back, those who are left, and you, too, will be marrying and settling down. Fate and chance sent you the New Zealand men for a little while. For a brief space you were their womenfolk. You opened your hearts and your homes. You said that the "soldats de la Nouvelle Zelande étaient beaucoup bien aimés." They thank you, and do not forget.

The trenches were only twenty minutes walk from the town. At three o'clock in the morning a man might be wiring in No-Man's-Land, every now and again dodging the bursts from "Parapet Joe," whose favourite melody, "Where is my wandering boy to-night?" went to all hearts. At dawn, or a little before, he would file down through the saps and the silent town, have breakfast, sleep for a few hours, and then

The Auckland Regiment

go down to Pont Nieppe for a bath. These baths at Pont Nieppe were the most famous in France. Never were such baths. Great round vats, capable of holding a dozen and more, were filled with water five feet deep, steam-heated. Into these vats the bathers piled themselves, and commenced a jolly scramble. Then emerging like giants refreshed, they clothed themselves in clean underclothing and received back coats and trousers, minus sundry boarders, who had succumbed to the "pressing" attentions of the mademoiselles armed with hot irons, whose presence behind certain screens of sacking was betokened by frequent outbursts of song. That afternoon, clean and well "swanked up," the soldier would be cracking jokes with plump and jolly Marie in the coffee and pastry shop near "Half-past-eleven-square," or buying luxuries for tea from Marie, Madeleine and Bertha Vandamme.

Until "eight o'clock finèèsh" there were the estaminets of innumerable madames and mademoiselles, Simonne, Louisa, Darkie, Ginger, and many another, at that time known to fame. Of course, all this sociability and real good fun gave opportunities for espionage, which otherwise would not have existed. Nevertheless, the "moral effect" of the civilian population was more than worth any harm that ensued. Armentières, without its shops, estaminets and cafés, would have been as bad as Anzac.

Armentières was only a trench spell, yet the casualties were by no means light. 1/Auckland lost a total of 265 officers and men, of whom 62 were killed, while 2/Auckland lost a total of 149, 22 being killed. The majority of the dead were carried back and buried in the cemetery behind the town. This cemetery will always be a sacred place for New Zealanders, as more than 300 of our dead are buried there—more than in any other one place in France.

July 1, 1916, the storm burst on the Somme. At that stage of the war there was no opening for brilliant strategy, no hope of large movements. The German was almost at the climax of his strength. He had guns, he had able commanders, he had brave men. The only thing that could be done was

Armentières

to stand and fight face to face; to join battle; to feed the furnace with the fuel of fresh divisions; to co-ordinate into one mighty machine the full force of Britain and France and to strike with it a weightier blow, and, if possible, a faster blow, than the German machine could strike.

All through June a mighty prelude was played on the whole line from Nieuport to Verdun. Every week the artillery fire grew more intense. Every week raids were more frequent. There was a tense feeling in the air—the expectation of battle. In the darkness of the night men looked southward to see if the sky was red with flame; in the quietness of the long night watches they listened for the rumble of the massed guns beating on the German lines. The battlefield of the Somme, like some huge magnet, drew to itself the imagination of all the Armies.

For six weeks the struggle waxed greater and greater, and then toward the middle of August the 51st Division marched into Armentières with German pickelhaubes on their heads and the souvenirs of famous Prussian regiments in their haversacks. There was a wild time in the old town that night, with New Zealanders and Jocks holding high revel, greeting and parting in the same night. A wild night! and Fritz, to make it wilder, threw five-nine's about and therewith slew certain Scotchmen.

Next morning the Battalions fell in and marched to Steenwerck railway station. "Good-bye, madame! Good-bye, mademoiselle! Good-bye piccanins! Nous allon kill beaucoup Bosches, come back promenade avec vous! Au revoir! Bon santé!" It was a straggling march. No one had done any marching for over three months, and everyone was soft. Moreover, it was the morning after the night before, and loads were heavy. Not a few dixies and other essential parts of the impedimenta were shamefully abandoned by the wayside.

XVIII.

The Battle of the Somme

*" The New Zealand Division was a tower
of strength on the right hand and on the left."*
—Report of Battle of Somme.

At Steenwerck the Battalions entrained on the famous trucks of "40 hommes et 8 chevaux en long," and so arrived at the little village of Ebblingham, from whence 1/Auckland marched to Campagne and 2/Auckland to Le Carnois. A night and a day in cramped billets, and then a night march to Arques, and from there by train through Abbeville to Pont Remy, from whence, on August 20, 1/Auckland marched to Neuville-Forceville and 2/Auckland to Allery. The next twelve days were spent in re-equipping, organisation and battle training. These days were amongst the happiest in France. The sun shone, trees and fields were green. Everyone ate well, drank well and slept well. Training was not too hard. Above all, madame and madamoiselle were kind, and loved their new guests well. Friendships are formed wonderfully quickly when there are only a few days for the business. Months and years afterwards many of these friendships were still kept up, and there were several men who had "beaucoup correspondence" with the village maidens. Field days, route marching and good living made the Battalions very fit. While in this area Sergeant-Majors F. E. McKenzie, F. R. Wilson, H. R. Brumby and H. Hogg of 1/Auckland, and Sergeant-Majors Goodwin, Hewitt, Tuck and Dagg were promoted to commissioned rank. Of these men, two in particular, F. E. McKenzie and Tuck, had both seen a very great deal of fighting, and were men of splendid reputation. All of them had seen considerable service, and without exception they were fine soldiers.

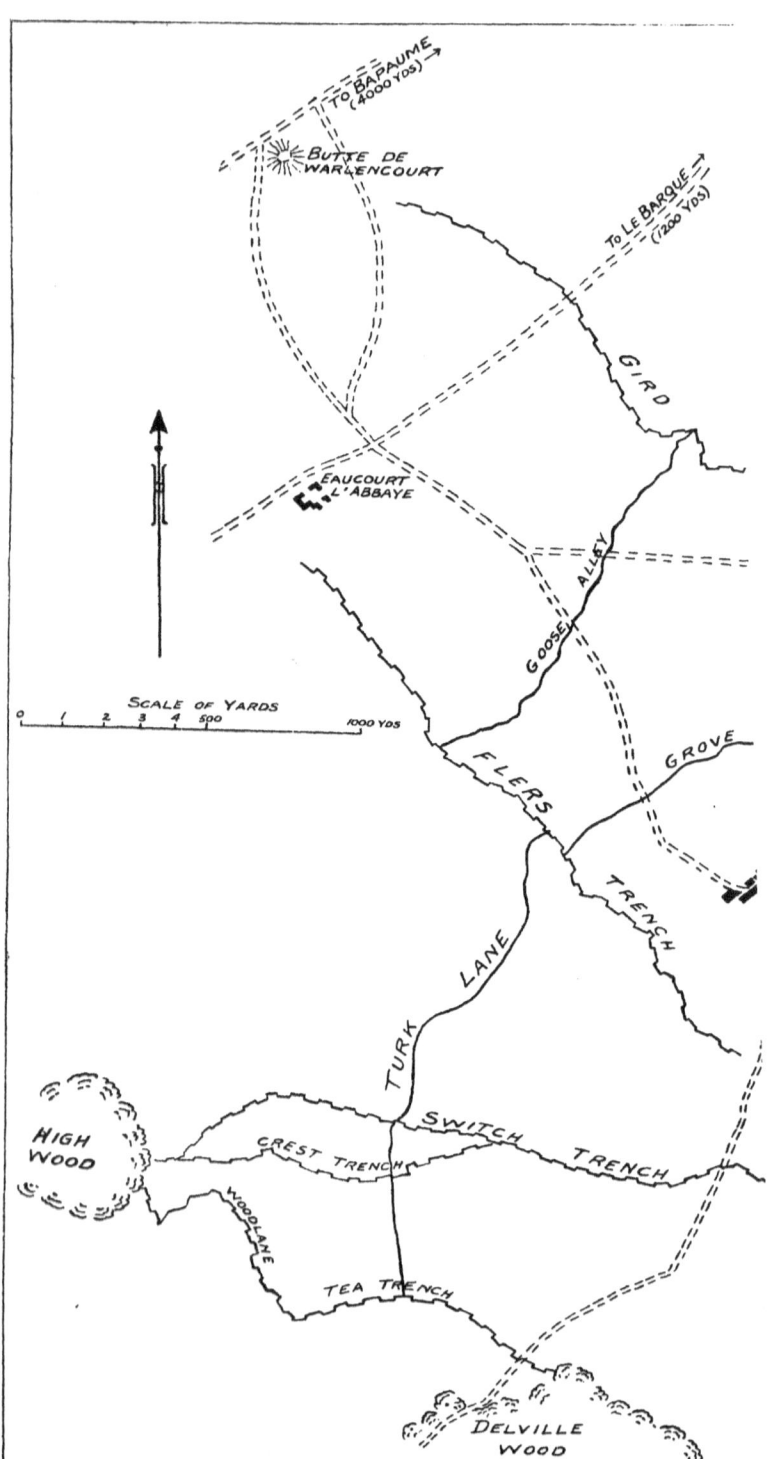

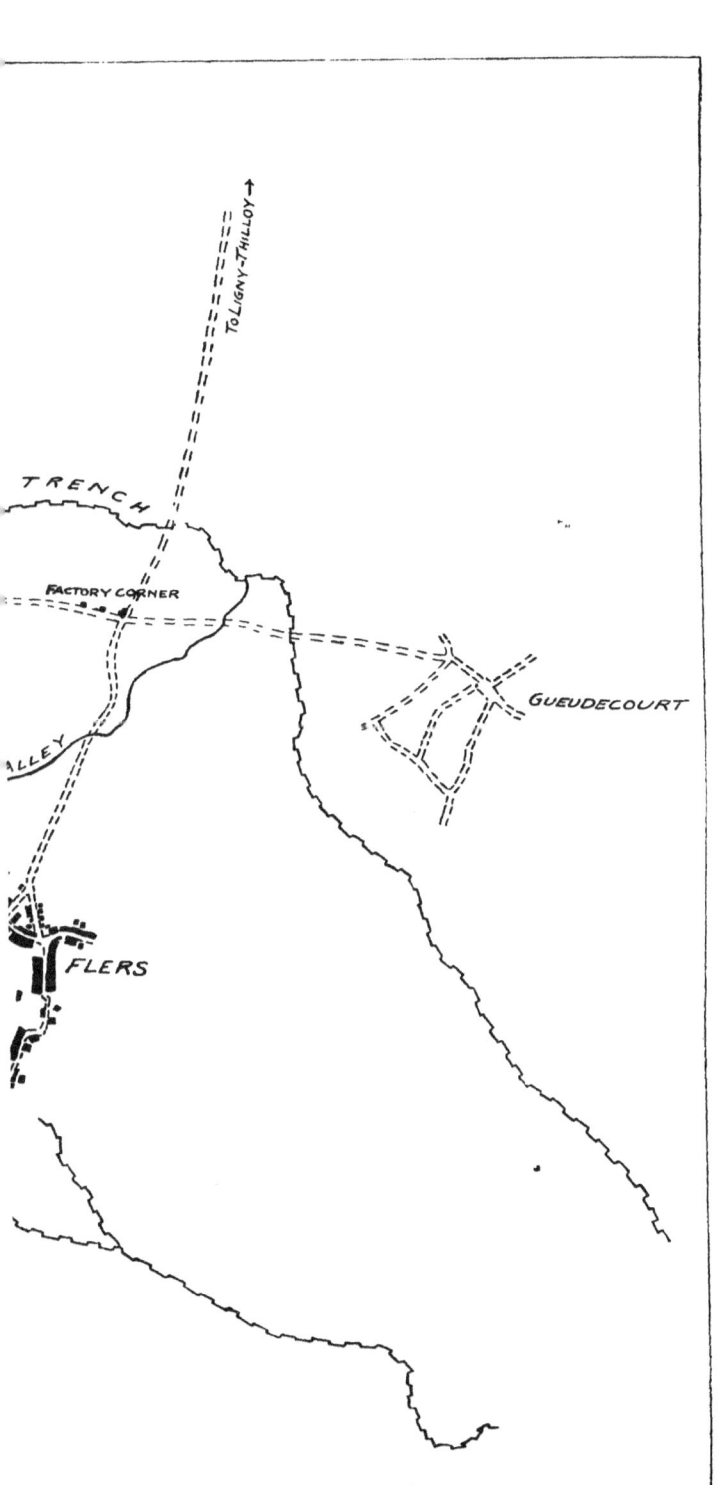

The Battle of the Somme

September 2nd saw the Division once more on the move, 1/Auckland marching to Airaines and 2/Auckland to Riencourt. During the afternoon, just as everyone was thinking it high time to stop for the day, when packs were growing heavy and feet sore, several motor lorries passed crammed full of German prisoners, at which sight there was considerable murmuring.

The general opinion was that positions should be reversed, Auckland on the lorries and Huns trudging wearily along the "pavé" roads. Another march through green fields and country lanes brought the First Battalion to Yseux and the Second to Picquigny, a typical little French town, and a place of considerable historical interest. A peace between England and France was once signed here, probably in the old mouldering castle which crowns the hilltop and looks down upon the gently-flowing Somme. Now every night the flares could be seen rising along the fighting line, and the thunder of the guns was like the sea-surf rolling in on the long ocean beaches. A four days halt, with shooting and training, and then once more the march went on past Amiens, through Poulainville and Cardonnette, until, on September 8th, the Battalions bivouacked in the fields not far behind the 12-inch naval guns and the edge of the battlefield. The Albert-Amiens road was dense with traffic guns, motor lorries of provisions, waggon loads of ammunition all moving in; Red Cross cars, broken and empty limbers moving out. It was a greatly travelled way, and during the next two days men would sit by the roadside for hours at a time gazing at the traffic passing to and fro. Many walked into Albert and saw the famous figure of the Virgin hanging from the front of the Cathedral. Everyone was splendidly fit. The New Zealand Division was marching down to its first great battle in the land of France. All were determined to demonstrate to friend and foe alike that they could fight as well in Picardy as on the slopes of Sari Bair.

The whole effort of the British Army was for the time being centred on the tactical objective of Bapaume, as that of the French on Peronne. It was thought that the taking of

The Auckland Regiment

these two towns would open up great strategic possibilities. In any case, the fury of the fighting had relieved the pressure on Verdun, and the terrific nature of the struggle was telling heavily on the German reserves of men, munitions and morale. At first the attacks had gone well. Not quite so much had been gained as was at first hoped for, but the wedge was strongly pushed in. For the last six weeks, however, the enemy had maintained their hold on High Wood, Delville Wood, and the spur which connected the two. On and behind this ridge they had constructed a very strong position. It was backed by a great power of artillery. Some of their élite regiments were holding the line. Wave after wave of assault had broken on this rock of defence. The unburied dead lay thick all about—English, Scottish, German. The ground was a maze of shell-holes. Switch Line—the name given to the enemy position between the woods—and the villages of Flers were the first objectives assigned to the New Zealanders. The 2/Brigade, under Brigadier-General Braithwaite, were given the task of storming the Switch Line. 2/Auckland and 2/Otago were to lead the assault, and in so doing lead the whole New Zealand Division into action.

On September 10th 2/Auckland left the Albert area and moved up through Fricourt, Bazentin and Contalmaison to Mametz Wood. Once the old front line was passed, evidence of tremendous fighting became ever plainer. Fricourt was a heap of ruins. Cemeteries were frequent. Débris of all sorts was lying everywhere. The guns became more numerous. Men realised the magnitude of the conflict raging so short a distance in front. Mametz Wood itself, where the Battalion bivouacked, had been blasted with fire. Two days were spent in the wood, and then on September 12th the Battalion took over the line in front of Green Dump.

The fighting strength was 600. Lieutenant-Colonel Brown was in command, with Lieutenant McClurg as his adjutant. Captain Armstrong was in command of the 3rd Company, Captain Hunter of the 6th, Major McKenzie of the 15th, and Captain Grainger of the 16th. Dr. Addison was in charge of

The Battle of the Somme

the Regimental Aid Post and the Battalion stretcher-bearers. Major S. S. Allen was attached for liason duties to the Brigade on the right flank.

Throughout the 13th and 14th the Aucklanders made a steady creep forward in preparation for the battle. The Hun artillery was very active, and a number of men were killed and wounded. The Battalion was to attack in line of companies in company column, with the 3rd, 15th, 6th and 16th in order from right to left. Companies were drawn up in four waves, with an interval of fifty yards between each wave on a total frontage of six hundred yards. The night was bitterly cold. A light misty rain fell intermittently, and the hours passed miserably.

All night the guns were active, and toward morning the firing grew more intense. At six o'clock there was a considerable rattle of machine-gun fire. The stationary barrage was falling in rear of the enemy line, and there was a constant sighing and droning in the air as the big howitzer shells went over. At 6.20 a.m., in a wide circle of flame and a great crash of sound the "creeping barrage" fell on the German trenches. It was the signal, and the whole attack moved forward with a thrust and weight that was irresistible. The Aucklanders and Otagos went straight forward in lines of assault, and behind them, as far as the eye could see, were the battalions of the Rifle Brigade moving in sections in artillery formation. To the right and left were the files of Guardsmen, South Africans, English Territorials and Irishmen. Here and there, not quite keeping pace with the infantry, were the "tanks," the mysterious new weapons of war, whose advent had been heralded by a confused rumour, but no certainty. Now they were a real presence, an inspiration of victory to our men, a great fear and terror to the enemy. There was a steady surge forward of the whole vast mass. It was a wonderful, an inspiring, a stupendous sight.

Scarcely, however, had the first line left the shell-holes in which they had assembled than the rockets went soaring up from the German posts, calling urgently for the protective

The Auckland Regiment

barrage of their guns. The response was immediate, accurate and very deadly. It took a terrible toll, but did not shake the steadfast courage of the moving mass. Men dropped quietly by twos and threes; sometimes a whole section was blown out. What had been No-Man's-Land was full of dead.

Very eagerly the Aucklanders press forward close to the heels of their barrage. They are too eager. They press too closely, and many fall from the bursts of their own shells. "Crest Trench," the Hun observation post, is reached—a few shots and bayonet thrusts and it is passed. Now there is a quickening of the pulse. Below in the rain of shells is the Switch Line. They close down upon it. Forty yards away the leading waves merge. They wait for the barrage to lift. There is shooting and bombing at short range. The line of gleaming bayonets, of staring eyes and of set, drawn faces, is waiting for the signal to dash in on this trench, packed with Huns. In places the enemy stand shoulder to shoulder. Now the stick-grenades are coming over in showers, for there are brave men amongst them, who see that if they can but stay this attacking line, hold it at bombing range for a few moments, then the time of grace will have passed, the machine-guns will come into play, and the "verdamnt Englanders" will be mown down, as they have been time and time again during the last few weeks. But now the third wave has come up. Lieutenants Tuck, Cooper, Senior and Stewart, the platoon commanders, Sergeant Hill, Sergeant Gordon, the section leaders, men here and there all along the line, take the initiative. The wave breaks and floods over the Hun line. Many of the enemy died fighting very bravely, many were shot down endeavouring to retreat down the hill, some were bayoneted screaming for mercy, but none except the wounded escaped. Few prisoners were taken by 2/Auckland.

The fourth wave, under the company commanders, came in, and at once a start was made with the consolidation of the position. Generally speaking, the new line was taken up about fifty yards in front of Switch Trench.

The Rifle Brigade passed through and went on to the more

The Battle of the Somme

distant objectives, a few of the Aucklanders going with them. Indeed, Lieutenant Tuck and some of his men had made no stop at all, but pushed on through the barrage, until they saw before them the ruins of Flers.

2/Auckland dug for dear life. It was well they did so, for the German fire was extremely heavy all day long. During the period of consolidation the Battalion lost some of its best officers. Captain Armstrong started off, his walking stick in one hand, his overcoat thrown over his arm, walking coolly through the bursting shells. He reached his company objective, and, with magnificent coolness and an utter contempt for danger, was directing his men where to dig in, when he was hit through the arm and chest, and fell mortally wounded. He was a man who, if he had lived, would have risen high.

Captain Keith Hunter, one of the most able and popular officers the Battalion ever had, was sitting in the same shell-hole as Captain Grainger, of the 16th, who, though very ill, insisted in coming into the battle. Word was brought of the death of Sergeant-Major Wallace Hunter. "Well, he died like a soldier, anyway," remarked his cousin. The words were hardly out of his mouth when there was a shrieking in the air, a burst, and he, too, lay dying, while Captain Grainger was wounded.

Carter, the signal corporal, followed the whole advance. He it was who took the telephone wire across Switch Line and then right into Flers village, from where, at 9 a.m., he transmitted the first message through to Brigade Headquarters. Then all day long, under extremely heavy shell fire, he passed backward and forward, mending breaks and keeping the line of communication clear.

Brown, the stretcher-bearer, commenced the wonderful work that, continued through the next three weeks, was to earn him a reputation for bravery and devotion to duty second to no man in the whole Battalion.

The Regimental Aid Post earned great praise for its work. The doctor and his assistants worked all day in one of the most heavily shelled areas of the whole battlefield. All around

The Auckland Regiment

the ground was torn to pieces. Battalion Headquarters, only a hundred and fifty yards away, but fairly well sheltered, was certain the post had been wiped out. Three times Colonel Brown sent down special messengers to see if any were left alive. Dr. Addison and Corporal Taylor deserve the very highest credit for the bravery, efficiency and speed with which all day long they worked to clear the great numbers of wounded, who were continually passing through.

Colonel Brown won for himself the confidence, esteem and devotion of his whole command. He set a fine example of personal courage. His practical common sense removed difficulties, and ensured smooth working, while his sympathy and thoughtfulness gained for him the affection of all.

2/Auckland held Switch Trench through the night, and next morning were relieved, going back to Check Line and Thistle Dump. The losses had been considerable. Six officers, Captains Hunter and Armstrong, Lieutenants Dagg, Sheridan, McLean and Bremner were killed, while Lieutenant Page, one of the original Main Body sergeant-majors, a very brave and able soldier, died of wounds. Fifty-two O.R.'s were killed. Seven officers, Captain Grainger, Lieutenants Cooper, Hewitt, Tuck, Hudson, Raine and McClurg, were wounded, also 231 O.R.'s. Twelve men were missing, making a total of 309 casualties.

1/Auckland, on the morning of the 15th September, moved from Fricourt Wood to Mametz Wood, where they beguiled the time by raiding the Guards' canteen. Next day they marched to the battlefield and took over from a battalion of the Rifle Brigade. Orders were issued for an attack on Goose Alley, but after the preparations had been made these orders were cancelled, and the Battalion dug the left defensive flank for the New Zealand Division. At 6 p.m. the following evening a party of bombers successfully bombed up a section of the Flers Trench. On the 18th the Battalion was relieved and went back to Check, Savoy and Carlton trenches, and there remained for several days, doing carrying and working parties.

The Battle of the Somme

The night of the 18/19th, 2/Auckland took over part of Flers Trench, adjoining Goose Alley, which, together with sections of Flers Trench and Flers Support, was still held by the enemy.

A night relief over a torn battlefield, where men have a long way to go to a goal that even the guides are not certain of, tries the temper of the most good-natured. Progress is very slow. Often the saps are blocked by men coming out. There is a stop every fifty yards, while a file of dirty, tired, cursing men jam past. The men going in are loaded up, not only with arms and equipment, but with sand-bags of rations, machine-gun panniers, and all the numberless essential things that may be required. They stumble on for three or four hours, floundering through mud, falling into shell-holes, tripping over the broken strands of barbed wire, losing touch and direction. German shells fall at random, and as the files come nearer to the long line of brilliant green flares which mark the far side of No-Man's-Land, there is the "rat-tat-tat" of the machine-gun and the wheen and whizz of bullets passing overhead. At last the parados of the fire-trench looms up, and there are whispered welcomes from the worn-out watchers, who immediately hand over and vanish back in the darkness. The relief is complete. Some huddle up in little scrapings in the wall of the trench and so endeavour to snatch a little sleep. Others stand silently on the fire-step peering out into the uncertain gloom. A few stamp up and down to bring back circulation to numbed feet. Patrol parties creep out to search No-Man's-Land and to guard against surprise.

These terrible night reliefs were a feature of the Somme Battle. Being relieved was a somewhat more cheerful business, inasmuch as there was usually less to carry, daylight was at hand, and there was prospect of a hot meal at the end of the march. 2/Auckland, holding about a thousand yards of front line, found themselves in a somewhat curious position.

The Germans were holding a considerable portion of Goose Alley, in particular the crossings of Flers Trench and Flers Support. For all practical purposes the enemy were not on

The Auckland Regiment

the Battalion front, but on the left flank. Between the Aucklanders in the Flers Trench and the enemy were a party of English troops in a most pitiable condition. Their faith in the "Anzacs" was most touching. Every assistance possible was given them—bombs, bombers and stretcher-bearers. Later in the afternoon, by special arrangement, the section of the trench they were holding was taken over by the 15th Company.

The trenches had been dug, but never finished, and, in consequence, the continuous rain soon turned them into quagmires. The greater part of the Battalion simply stood and shivered for three days and nights, feet gradually getting colder and colder, while the German artillery shelled intermittently. On the exposed flank there was more excitement without any lessening of the discomfort. Lieutenant Seddon, who had been too shaken to take part in the battle of the 15th, was now back, and led a bombing party along Flers Trench, gaining something like fifty yards of line.

2/Canterbury were ordered up to take Goose Alley during the night of the 20/21st. They passed through 2/Auckland, and drew up at 8.30 p.m. in the sunken road. After some very stiff fighting, in which the issue was for a considerable time in doubt, the objectives were taken, very largely as a result of the help and encouragement given by the Aucklanders. Sergeant Gordon, "old Tom Gordon," of the 15th Company, was particularly prominent, and at one critical moment rallied the attacking force when they were giving way, and led on to victory. The enemy counter-attacked at dawn, but were driven off. They came again in the afternoon, but had no better fortune. During this attack the Auckland Battalion Headquarters did some excellent sharp-shooting, and the Trench Mortar Battery, under Lieutenant "Jock" McKenzie, also did some very fine work. While in this portion of the line the Battalion ration parties, under Major S. S. Allen, had an extremely difficult task. It was not possible to come up during the day, and, in consequence, the carrying had to be done at night. The nights were extremely dark, the path obscure and frightfully rough, the loads heavy, and the shell fire frequently very

Colonel A. Plugge, C.M.G.

The Battle of the Somme

intense. Major Allen and his men deserve the very greatest credit for their work—especially Roberts, who quickly established a moral superiority over the other men and was an inspiration to all.

During the night of the 23/24th, after another day of misery in the wet and cold, 2/Auckland were relieved, and after a weary march back arrived in the Black Watch Area, and there settled down to recuperate.

Up to this date 1/Auckland had played a very small share in the battle. They had been in the line once for a short while only, and for the remainder of the time had been doing working parties or waiting in the reserve areas. Now the army was ready to exploit the success of the previous ten days fighting. The guns had gone forward, the position had been consolidated. Masses of cavalry were concentrated in rear, and their scouts were continually riding forward. To the infantry it seemed that at last the great hour had come for the break through. Rumour grew. The 1st New Zealand Infantry Brigade, the veterans of Anzac, were to smash the last line of German defence, and then through the breach they made would pour an avalanche of mobile troops. So it seemed to the glowing imagination of men somewhat intoxicated with the success of the first few days.

Colonel Plugge was in command, with Captain N. A. Duthie as his adjutant. Captain Herman commanded the 3rd Company, Captain Mahan the 6th, Captain Alexander the 15th, and Captain Dineen the 16th. Dr. Nelson was in charge of the R.A.P., while Major R. C. Allen, the Second-in-Command, was detached for liason duty with the Brigade on the flank. The Rev. Gavin was the Battalion's chaplain.

1/Auckland took over 750 yards of line running from Factory Corner, with Canterbury on one flank and Otago on the other. The objectives were Gird Trench and Gird Support. The distance between the Gird and Flers system left a very wide No-Man's-Land, and hence it was necessary to make a preliminary advance to secure a suitable jumping-off position for the main attack. This was done on the 25th, and the opera-

The Auckland Regiment

tion was carried out with little opposition and light casualties. The new line was dug and then everything was ready. In the meanwhile the howitzers had been firing on the enemy wire, endeavouring to prepare the way for the assault. Patrols sent out during the night and observation from the line itself established the fact that the wire was almost intact. This was disquieting, but few knew of it, and hopes were high. Zero hour was fixed for 2.15 p.m. on the 27th September. All was ready. The steady line moved forward across No-Man's-Land. Down came a counter-barrage. Men were falling, but there was not the least weakening. The Hun trench was near. Canterbury had no difficulty—the wire in front of them was cut—and they passed right in. Otago were shot to pieces. Auckland came fair up against uncut wire. Held up by the unexpected obstacle they were delayed, while the barrage passed on and left them. The Huns in the line manned their parapet shooting, bombing and machine-gunning. They had the Aucklanders at their mercy. Desperate efforts were made to rush in through the gaps which had been torn every here and there. The Hun machine-guns were trained on these gaps, and the attackers were mown down in heaps. All, with the exception of the desperately brave, were down in the shell-holes sniping where a chance offered, bombing where they were close enough in. One or two Lewis guns got into action, but for a moment it seemed that no impression could be made. Then Sergeant Clarke, bombing a machine-gun into silence, rushed through the gap and obtained a lodgment in the line. Captain Alexander, Lieutenant Hogg, Lieutenant Ellisdon, Francis, Tribe, Lauder, Mitchell, Whitehouse, Prendergast, Bright, Torrens and others won in, and now the tide commenced to turn. The Huns lost their nerve. Instead of instantly concentrating on the gallant few who had entered the line, they wavered. Some drew back, some commenced to run. More of the Aucklanders came in. A Hun officer tried to rally his men, but was shot dead by a lipless man lying out in one of the shell-holes. Now the enemy were running all along the line. Quickly the Lewis guns were placed on the new parapet, and the fleeing enemy

The Battle of the Somme

mown down. Another rush forward of fifty yards or so, and the support line was carried—this with little opposition. The objective was taken—but at what a cost! Eight hundred men went over against the Gird System. When the line was taken two hundred were left. Three times 1/Auckland had charged as a battalion—once at Helles, once at Chunuk, and again over the shell-torn field of the Somme—and on every occasion they had been slaughtered by a cruel concentration of machine-gun fire. The 16th Waikato Company had been especially unfortunate in this last charge, Lieutenant Hogg and six men being all that remained. Many brave men had fallen. Captain Dineen went over, leading the first wave of the 15th Company, to fall mortally wounded half-way across. The Regiment never lost a finer officer. Enlisting at the outbreak of war, he had trained for the Royal Flying Corps, and at the last moment, when his training had been completed, was rejected for some trifling defect in vision. He at once joined the N.Z.E.F., offering to throw in his commission and serve as a private in the ranks. He was not allowed to do this, and was attached to 1/Auckland as a captain. The trench warfare at Armentières had shown him to be the very finest type of soldier, a man endowed with a splendid physical self, of great mental ability, with a will like steel and a nerve that nothing could shake; absolutely conscientious, strict, but just and very thoughtful, a man who "reverenced his conscience as his king." He was the bravest man in his company, because he was the best. Terribly wounded as he was, he continued to direct his men as the successive waves passed him. The stretcher-bearers, Porter, Forrest and other gallant men, made great efforts to save him, but after three of them had fallen in the attempt they were compelled to wait. He died on the way to the Base. Padre Gavin, a man of very quiet and gentle manner, but strong in faith, a man who loved much, and so had the mastery over fear, brought up the rations when the Quartermaster was incapacitated, buried the dead under heavy fire, and showed himself most worthy of his calling.

Next day, the 28th September, the remnants of 1/Auck-

The Auckland Regiment

land were relieved and went back in reserve, a battalion of the 2/Brigade taking over the newly-won line. 2/Auckland held from near the junction of Goose Alley and the Gird System to L'Eaucourt-Abbaye road. Communication to the front was difficult until the Maoris completed Turk Lane right through. The hottest part of the Battalion sector was on the road itself, round Battalion Headquarters and the Regiment Aid Post, which were so placed that the German artillery were able to fire right across the salient into the entrances of the dug-outs. Here Canterbury, with support from 2/Auckland, carried out a second attack on Goose Alley, in which they were completely successful. A feature of the attack was the use of flame projectors to assist the advance. Many scorched Huns testified to the success of the new weapon. Very early in the morning of October 3rd, 2/Auckland were relieved by a battalion of the Rifle Brigade, and went right back, moving in comfort through the great communication sap, Turk Lane, which had been pushed forward with wonderful speed by the Maori Pioneers. The Battalion concentrated below Mametz Wood, where the cooks were waiting with stew and hot tea, and then after the hot meal marched back from the battle area to King George's Hill, Fricourt. Next day 1st Auckland were relieved from Worcester, Dorset and Seaforth trenches, in the support area, and also marched out.

Men were tired and overwrought. Those who came out were but a few compared with the numbers who had gone in. The Aucklanders went into battle a little under 1500 strong. More than three hundred were left dead on the battlefield, while close on seven hundred were on their way to hospital. Heavy as the losses had been, they were counterbalanced by the greatness of the victory.

There was a great glow of feeling—a mood of exaltation. The New Zealanders had won a great reputation at Gallipoli, but yet there were critics who under-rated the fierceness of the struggle at Anzac. Now their doubts could no longer stand. On the battlefield of the Somme the New Zealand Division had been a tower of strength on the right hand and on the

The Battle of the Somme

left. They had not only done all that was asked of them, but more. From the time of the Somme the New Zealand soldier took undisputed place as one of the finest fighting men of the war. It had been a great shock battle. Massed guns were countered by massed guns, infantry division was flung against infantry division. The enemy was strong, well organised, well led, and determined to maintain an unbroken line. Progress could only be made by hard fighting, and even then progress was slow and very costly. Good soldier as the New Zealander is in open warfare, he is nowhere better than in the shock of battle. His ability to take punishment, his steadfastness, endurance and cool, desperate daring have never shown out more splendidly than on this great occasion.

XIX.

The Winter of 1916-1917

" When the snow lay round about,
Deep and crisp and even.
Brightly shone the moon that night,
Though the frost was cruel;
When a poor man came in sight,
Gathering winter fuel."
—Good King Winceslas.

The Division took three days to concentrate round about Albert, and then, when all had been withdrawn from the trenches, moved back by rail to the training area, 1/Auckland going through Longprè to Airaines, while 2/Auckland moved from Longprè to Liercourt. As the men marched by moonlight from the detraining stations through the beautiful countryside of the Somme Valley, they burst once more into song. For a time, at any rate, the horrors of the battlefield were left behind, and there would be estaminets, no doubt, and mademoiselles, and quite certainly hot meals and sleep.

"So pack all your troubles in your old kit-bag
And smile, boys, smile.
What's the use of worrying?
It never was worth while.
So as long as you've a lucifer to light your fag
Smile, boys, that's the style!"

As soon as the news got round that the New Zealanders were out of the battle the French folks walked miles to renew old acquaintances and very sincerely to mourn for friends who had not come back. The stay in the pleasant villages was all too short. The trains of "40 hommes et 8 chevaux" were soon running north, and the Division, detraining at Bailleul, proceeded almost at once into the line, the 1st and 3rd Brigades occupying the Fleurbaix-Sailly sector, which based itself on the little town of Estaires, some eight kilometres south of Amentières, while the 2/Brigade went back as part of "Frank's" force to its old sector in front of Houplines. The

The Winter of 1916–17

Division had left the Somme battlefield on October 7th, and on the 14th were once more in the line. It had, therefore been "out" for just a week.

2/Auckland returning to Armentières were welcomed back with joy. The line was very quiet, and the sector seemed to have relapsed right back to its old peaceful state. There was very little to complain of, except the rather flooded condition of some of the trenches. In the first few days after the return from the Somme, the Battalion had the misfortune to lose Lieutenant Ancell, a very promising young officer, who was hit by a stray bullet while on patrol. A few other casualties occurred, and there were also a certain number of evacuations for sickness, brought on by the wet and cold.

The only incident of the six weeks spent on this sector was a raid carried out by Lieutenant Hally and thirty men. The party went straight across, found the gap in the wire by means of an electric torch, and entered the German line. They bombed the dug-outs and took three prisoners, one of whom came to a bad end on the return journey, owing to his insubordinate behaviour. The other two, very mild and inoffensive people, were brought back safe and sound. No one was hurt, and the only ones to suffer any inconvenience were three Canterbury men, whose bay was blown in on top of them during a little retaliation by the Hun artillery. They were only half buried, and, having their heads free, lit cigarettes to pass the time until some friendly soul should arrive to dig them out. Unfortunately for them, the first to come by were the raiders, very elate at their success. Unlike the man in the parable, they did not pass by on the other side, but marched straight on over the top of the prostrate Canterburians, whose cheerful resignation at once gave way to a very peevish exhibition of ill-temper.

The remainder of the time passed quietly enough, and on December 3rd the Battalion moved from Armentières and rejoined the remainder of the Division in the Sailly-Fleurbaix sector, going into billets at La Gorgue, close to Laventie.

1/Auckland had been going in and out of the right sub-

The Auckland Regiment

sector at V.C. House, and had also been having a very quiet time. The weather became increasingly miserable, wet, raw and cold, windy, showery, sleety, and then toward the end of November came the frost and snow. Early in December the winter had set in properly—the hardest, coldest, most terrible winter known in Europe for half a century. For many it was the first winter after four successive summers. Gallipoli had been the extreme torment of blazing heat, with thirst, flies, lice and smells. The French winter of 1916-1917 was the extreme of cold, with frozen hands and feet and shivering nights in trench and billet. Frozen snow has a most unfortunate habit of sopping through boots, and cold feet are almost the limit of torture. The scenery was magnificent. Branches of trees were all delicately lined with white, the roofs were white, the wide expanse of level field was all white and gleaming, broken here and there by the dark line of a road or hedge. Very beautiful, no doubt! But the shivering infantry would gladly have exchanged all the beauty for a New Zealand fireside and a warm bed.

In front of the V.C. House sector the enemy had withdrawn from their front line, going back to the higher levels of the Aubers Ridge. The position, therefore, was not well defined, and on December 1st three strong patrols went out and indulged in a very interesting wander round, which established the fact that the enemy were certainly not holding portions of their trenches, owing to the bad condition of the ground. The same night a German patrol bombed Cellar Farm. Then came three weeks of an almost depressing quietness. Sometimes it seemed that the war had stopped. It became possible not merely to look over the parapet for a continued period, but to sit on it, and even to walk about in No-Man's-Land during the daytime. The Medium Trench Mortars commenced to demolish the abandoned German trench, and the infantry crowded up on the parapet and watched the "plum-duffs" bursting with very much the same sense of security as a football crowd watching a match.

Quiet as the sector was at this time, there were ghastly

The Winter of 1916-17

reminders of previous activity. No-Man's-Land was full of dead Australians. It was here the great disaster had occurred when the 5th Australian Division failed completely in their attempt to take the Aubers Ridge six months before.

On this sector the Aucklanders first met that peculiar type of atrocity, the deep dug-out, built for the accommodation not of a few officers or a company headquarters, but as a home for three hundred men. The particular one in question was deep down in the bowels of the earth. It was wet, steaming, dimly lighted and badly ventilated, and the air was an unspeakable pollution.

Lieutenant Oxenham, on the night of December 21st, while out with a patrol party, endeavoured to pass the enemy wire and enter the trench. Unfortunately this particular section was held strongly, and heavy fire was at once directed on the party, with the result that two men were wounded and left in the enemy wire, while another fell in No-Man's-Land before he could reach safety. Next morning Major R. C. Allen and Lieutenant Tilsley, passing along the line, were looking over to see if there were any signs of the missing men. They perceived the man lying in front, and Tilsley, although it was now broad daylight, went out to him. It was an extraordinarily brave thing to do, for he was clearly visible to the watchers in the German line and offered a certain target to any Hun sniper who cared to shoot. Would they do so? He approached the wounded man, while the men in the line held their breath, waiting for the crack of a rifle from the enemy line. It did not come. Instead, a German stood up on his fire-step and waved across. In less than a moment there was an impromptu armistice. A stretcher was hurried out and the wounded man brought in. Germans were busy binding up the two men in their wire. Some Aucklanders crossed, hoping that these two also might be brought in, but the enemy waved them back, one of them calling out, "It is good for us to take them in—we will take care of them for you."

For nearly three weeks 2/Auckland had been billeted in La Gorgue, mostly in French farms, places which have been

The Auckland Regiment

aptly described as "a number of buildings with a rectangular smell in the middle." During this period the Battalion, with others, paraded for inspection by Sir Douglas Haig, who highly commended 2/Auckland for their creditable turn out.

The New Zealand soldier was not a very religious person, but yet, being of a charitable nature, he was generally prepared to respect and even admire religion in others. The Army was vastly tolerant on all matters of individual character and conduct. One man's little peculiarity was to get drunk too often, another's idiosyncrasy was "two-up," the sport of kings, still another showed an alarming fondness for patrolling No-Man's Land, while one here and there was religious and held prayer meetings. "Well! what would you wish?" They were all good fellows, and small failings and eccentricities of this sort were really not worth noticing. At this time there were two men with the Battalion, Corporal Taylor of the attached N.Z.M.C. and Corporal Madill of the 3rd Company, a Presbyterian minister serving in the ranks, who felt called to publicly proclaim the Word of God. The service was held in the 3rd Company's billet, and will not readily be forgotten by any man who was there. A huge barn littered about with farm implements, the roof high up and in darkness, was the meeting place. Glowing braziers scattered here and there showed groups of men, playing cards, letter writing, reading, sleeping, gossiping. Outside the night was wet and cold. The report of a distant gun, the flash of the explosion were continual reminders of the fact of war. From the darkness outside a little group of men entered the circle of firelight, passed round hymn books, and then commenced to sing the old familiar hymns. Gradually the groups round the braziers joined in, until the old barn was full of the music of the English hymns. Corporal Taylor, standing on an old waggon, preached a sermon of wonderful power. For a space there was quietness, and then the service closed. The murmur of conversation swelled up again, the cards came out, the letters were finished, and all went on as before, save that many a man felt better for the flood of home memories the hour of devotion had called to mind.

The Winter of 1916–17

During the winter the N.Z.Y.M.C.A. grew very rapidly. The main hut in Sailly will be remembered by all who were with the Division on the sector. Smaller out-stations became increasingly numerous. One "buckshee show" was installed in the support line on the right sub-sector. These Y.M. centres were very much appreciated and were always crowded.

On December 23rd 1/Auckland were relieved in the line by 2/Auckland, and so managed to have Christmas Day in billets. It was a much merrier day than that of the year previous on board the *Marsova* in Lemnos Harbour, with nothing but hard biscuits and cold water on which to make merry.

The New Year saw a complete reorganisation of the 1st and 2nd Brigades. The North Island Battalions now formed the 1st Brigade, and the South Island ones the 2nd Brigade. This change brought the 1st and 2nd Battalions of all the infantry regiments into very much closer touch with each other. From this time until the end of the war the 1st Brigade consisted of 1/Auckland and 2/Auckland, 1/Wellington and 2/Wellington.

Certain important promotions were also made at this time. Colonel Brown, D.S.O., was promoted to the command of the 1st Brigade, with the temporary rank of Brigadier-General. Major S. S. Allen was sent to the Senior Officers' School of Instruction in England prior to taking over the command of the Battalion, which in his absence was commanded by Major McKenzie, D.S.O., of the 15th Company. Captain West, promoted to Major, acted as Second-in-Command, while Lieutenant Seddon took over the duties of adjutant. From the 1st Battalion Colonel Plugge, C.M.G., was detached for special work in connection with physical and recreational training, his place being taken by Major R. C. Allen, who was succeeded as Second-in-Command by Major Orr, Lieutenant W. P. Gray becoming Adjutant.

Immediately after the reorganisation the 1st Brigade took over the Fleurbaix sector, and for the next month 1st and 2/Auckland relieved each other in the Tin Barn Avenue and J-Post trenches. The cold was intense, and the enemy only

The Auckland Regiment

moderately quiet. The main occupation was shooting hares, a sport which was enthsuiastically pursued at considerable risk, not only to the hares, but also to anyone that happened to be within a few hundred yards. Rifle bullets richocheted off the frozen ground in all directions. Hun frightfulness at this time consisted mainly in the discharge of minenwerfers into certain areas of the front and support lines. Fleurbaix itself had for a very long while been immune from the attentions of the enemy artillery, although early on in the war considerable damage had been done. Toward the end of January it once more commenced to draw its allowance of iron rations, and there was more than a suspicion that the Huns were about to lay on the gas. Lying in bed at night with only a few tiles overhead, it gave one a queer feeling to hear the "five-nines" dropping all round, bringing down slates, smashing glass, and generally making the night hideous. During this period the Y.M.C.A. held a competitions carnival at Sailly. 2/Auckland won the debating championship after a very keen contest, in which a number of teams from all over the Division took part. Corporal Taylor and another man walked six miles down through the snow from the front line to take part in this contest.

February 10th, when 1/Auckland were in the line, an enterprising party of Germans, clothed in white, waited in the snow outside the wire for the patrol. The corporal in charge going first was seized—to use his own words "the snow flew up and hit him"—and rushed over No-Man's Land to the enemy line. Two days later a party of the enemy were discovered in the gap between Auckland and Wellington. They retired after an interchange of bombs.

December had been very quiet. January saw the armies still frost-bound. In February was heard the first sound of the gathering storm which was to burst in fury with the coming of spring. All along the line there was continual raiding, as each side strove to test the enemy defence, and raids, not of twenty or thirty men, but raids of companies, and finally of battalions. 2/Auckland had the honour to be chosen from

The Winter of 1916-17

the New Zealand Division to carry out a battalion raid. On February 28th they were withdrawn to the little village of Bac St. Maur for training, which was of the most thorough sort. Major West was responsible for practically all the arrangements, except for the fixing of the actual zero time. The most minute details were carefully gone into. A plan of the enemy trenches was laid out by the engineers, and over this the men practised the assault. Patrols searched every yard of the ground ahead. Every creek and drain was explored. The Sunday before the raid aeroplane photographs of the Hun trenches to be raided were thrown on the screen at the divisional picture show. Great precautions were taken to ensure silence before zero hour. The duckwalks, both in the communication saps and the front line were covered with straw and canvas. Pine lozenges were served out to prevent coughing.

Sixteen officers and 500 men formed the raiding party. The 16th, under Captain Hubbard, and the 6th, under Lieutenant "Jock" McKenzie, were to form the first wave, while the 15th and 3rd Companies, under Captains King and Mewett respectively, were to form the second. At two o'clock in the morning the men were awakened, and after a hot meal marched off toward the line. Lightly equipped, they carried rifle, bayonet, bandolier and bombs only. Pioneer parties had gone on before and cut gaps in the wire. The parties filed up past Wye Farm, through Gunners' Walk and Bay Avenue to the front line, every one being in place half an hour before zero. They waited quietly, bayonets fixed, looking backward for the flash of the signal gun. It came, and immediately after a circle of flame shot up around the horizon as the barrage opened. The first wave were away at once. They were in the wire before the roar of the first discharge was heard from the guns behind —they were half-way across No-Man's Land when the enemy trench burst with a roar into a line of light, as the barrage fell. The frost had just broken, and the first thaw had weakened the ice over pools and shell-holes, melted most of the surface snow and softened the frozen ground. Everywhere was sloppy and muddy. Floundering across, the leaders were close on the

The Auckland Regiment

broken German wire, when almost from beneath their feet the S.O.S. rockets went soaring up. The Hun listening post had done his duty like a brave man. He was shot by Corporal McGuinness, one of the bravest men in the Battalion. So prompt was the German counter-barrage that it seemed as though the gunners had been waiting, pieces trained, and fingers on the triggers, for the signal. The second wave had hardly cleared our own wire when the shells were bursting over the trench they had just quitted. A mass of shell-holes, full of mud and water, marked the position of the enemy front line. In the darkness and the pall of battle-smoke it was barely recognisable. Here the waves merged and passed on to the support line. It was a wild, confused fight. In places the Huns fought heroically, and elsewhere they surrendered tamely. Some were bombed in dug-outs, some were shot, some bayoneted. Many fell endeavouring to escape back through the box-barrage. Lieutenant Taylor, going right on past the trench, found two light field pieces blown out. He and the small group with him would have wandered right on but for a party of prisoners who very politely guided them back. Captain Mewett, though his arm was broken, shot three of the enemy, and refused to go back until time was up. Sergeants Brady, Cuthbertson, Corporals Yorke and Ashwin were all leading well and doing splendid work. Time was up, the whistles blew, and the survivors commenced to make their way back, some guarding prisoners, some helping wounded companions. It was still dark, and, in consequence, not only were many of the enemy missed, but a very considerable number of our own wounded were left behind. The German shelling was very heavy, and many casualties occurred on the return journey. Not a few were hit recrossing the parapet, and some after they had actually reached the shelter of the trench. It was thus Captain King was killed.

The stretcher-bearers were busy from the first. Brown was wounded in the back by a flying splinter very early, but carried on until every man was clear. The Huns very quickly reoccupied their front line, and then occurred a very remark-

The Winter of 1916–17

able thing. As day broke, dead and wounded men were seen to be lying in No-Man's Land. Hun snipers were active. It seemed certain death to venture to their aid. Yet one or two made the venture, gambling on the chance that the Germans might be chivalrous and permit the wounded to be brought in. They crossed the parapet with nerves tightened, knowing that 150 yards away the Mauser rifles were levelled at heart or brain, and knowing that if a trigger was pressed the shot could hardly miss. A German stood up and waved his hands, others got up beside him. New Zealanders came up on the other side. Firing ceased, except for one enemy machine-gun some distance back in the supports. One of the enemy, standing right up on his parapet, signalled back to the crew, and this gun ceased also. Stretchers came out on both sides, and in ten minutes every wounded man in No-Man's Land was taken in, and the dead also. When all was clear a shot was fired in the air. Both sides took cover, and the war went on. 2/Auckland streamed back into their billets, leaving 2/Wellington to hold the line and build up the broken parapets.

The great raid was over, and there remained but to balance the results. On the one hand, 198 of the enemy were counted dead in the line, and 45 prisoners had been taken; on the other side, Captain King and 17 men had been killed, 6 officers and 75 men wounded, while 56 men were missing; a total of 159.

Next morning in the Clearing Station at Estaires died Lieutenant John McKenzie, one of the most famous and certainly the most beloved of all the Main Body men. From the onfall at Anzac to the chill dawn of February 21st, when he fell mortally wounded, he had never missed a day of the fighting. A very gallant soldier, the equal of Holland, Tilsley, Tuck and Gordon in personal courage, he was loved beyond any of them. No man in the Regiment approached more closely the knightly ideal. He lies in the cemetery of Estaires, "Fighting Jock" of the old 1/Auckland, of the Trench Mortars, of 2/Auckland, a very perfect gentleman, "without fear and without reproach."

The Battalion marched to Estaires the day following the

The Auckland Regiment

raid, and from there followed the remainder of the Brigade to the new sector in front of Le Bizet, going into billets at Nieppe, where on the 25th they were reviewed by General Plumer. On the same day 1/Auckland went into the front line at Despierre Farm.

Lieutenant-Colonel W. W. Alderman, C.M.G., D.S.O.

XX.

Le Bizet—Ploegsteert—Hill 63

" Day by day we dig new trenches,
Bury war-created stenches,
Build up castles in the mud, and drain the floor.
Night by night the big guns thunder,
Trench and castle rend asunder ;
And at dawn we start to dig and build once more."
—K. L. Trent in " N.Z. at Front."

The sector, Le Bizet—Ploegsteert, was adjacent to the old Houplines one, and lay just across the canalised River Lys. Le Bizet itself was a suburb of Armentières, and was connected by means of a bridge with the town itself. "Mademoiselle of Armentières" was therefore quite handy, and so many old friendships were renewed. Would-be visitors, however, were very much restricted by reason of passes being demanded by the bridge guards. As there were only two bridges this was something more than a formality, especially when the guards were composed of conscientious Tommies.

1/Auckland took over the Despierre Farm sub-sector, which consisted of "two gaps and three localities." The trenches had been shockingly neglected, and were simply tumbling to pieces. Apparently no maintenance work had been done for months. The Germans in the line opposite had gained a decided ascendancy. Rumour even ran that they were in the habit of coming over at meal times and taking the steaming dixies back with them. They were certainly active, both with snipers and minenwerfer guns. Despite their hostility, they were a courteous people, and the day after the Aucklanders took over the line the following notice was displayed over their parapet:—

"Engl. Ober leutnant
Gefallen.
Er Ruht in Friedhof
von Quesnoy."

This news of the death and burial of an English officer,

The Auckland Regiment

missing after a raid, was one of those touches of human kindness which occasionally flash out amidst all the bitterness and hatred of war.

On the night of February 28th the Germans, following a heavy barrage of minenwerfers, raided the 16th Waikatos. Despite very determined attempts, most of them penetrated no further than the wire. The Waikatos were on the alert, and for a quarter of an hour there was a very lively exchange of bombs. A German officer was the only one to reach the trench. Badly wounded though he was, he stood on the parapet bombing, and then leaped in, to be bayoneted by the defenders. Sergeant-Major Todd and "Jimmy" Greenwood, a recent transfer from the N.Z.M.C., both distinguished themselves greatly. Before dawn the enemy removed their wounded, but left thirteen dead men "standing up" in the wire. The Auckland casualties were ten killed and fifteen wounded. During the day a party was told off to go out after dark and bring in the German dead for the purpose of identification and burial. They were a little late in starting, however, and on arriving at the spot found that the enemy had stolen a march on them, and had removed all traces of their previous visit.

March 1st, 1/Auckland were relieved by 2/Auckland, going into support at Le Bizet. 2/Auckland's stay in was entirely uneventful, although rather uncomfortable for the men in the dilapidated front line. They, in turn, were relieved by the 1st Battalion, and after another period of eight days the two battalions went back to Nieppe, from where 1/Auckland proceeded to Aldershot Camp and 2/Auckland to De Seule. On the 31st March 1/Auckland went into support at Ploegsteert, and on the following day 2/Auckland relieved the 3rd Battalion of the Rifle Brigade in front of Hill 63.

The weather at this time was very variable. The dry cold had gone. Snow, rain, hail and sleet alternated. In between whiles there was a miserable drizzle. Although warm, the slush and wet made things even more uncomfortable than during the three months of intense cold. Occasionally, however, a fine, warm sunny day brought a promise of spring

Le Bizet—Ploegsteert—Hill 63

weather and a reminder that the time of great battles was rapidly coming.

Hill 63 faced the famous Hill of Messines, and the British line ran along the Valley of the Douve, in front of Ploegsteert Wood and between the two hills. The village of Messines itself, crowning the heights, showed plainly out. It seemed very little damaged, its church towering over the lesser buildings, a most conspicuous landmark. The slope from the hilltop to the valley below was green and not greatly torn. The outlines of the German trenches were clearly visible. The fact of the hill impressed itself on the consciousness of the Division. It rose up before them as a perpetual challenge. It flaunted itself in mockery. Gradually the hill became a lure. Was it always to be a German hill, or were New Zealand bayonets to go up and over it?

Major S. S. Allen, now promoted to the rank of Lieutenant-Colonel rejoined the 2/Auckland Battalion, and took over the command from Major McKenzie, who in his turn proceeded to England.

Hill 63 was the buttress of the British line in these parts. It covered the railhead at Steenwerck, the town of Bailleul and the main road running between Bailleul and Armentières. Behind it, as far as the eye could see, stretched level country, which would offer little natural difficulty to an advancing enemy. Branching off from the highway at Canteen Corner, the road ran through the small village of Romarin to the foot of Hill 63 at Red Lodge, now a somewhat dilapidated but picturesque ruin. From here it skirted the foot of the hill as far as Hyde Park Corner and Ploegsteert Wood. Here, close to Charing Cross Dressing Station, it junctioned with the Le Bizet-Ploegsteert road, which ran on between the trench lines to Messines. The rear slope of Hill 63 was heavily wooded, and in consequence of the excellent natural cover thus afforded it was nearly always densely populated. Huts were scattered amongst the trees, and deep dug-outs driven into the side of the hill. Social welfare was catered for by two well-known philanthropic institutions—the Y.M.C.A. and the Honourable

The Auckland Regiment

Society of Two-Up Kings. The Y.M.C.A. built a hut, which was later on destroyed by shell fire, and the Two-Up Kings organised large "schools"—not, however, for educational purposes. This popular diversion was a source of much perturbation to the Higher Command. Periodical edicts were issued for the suppression of gambling. Why such a fuss should have been made about gambling it is hard to see, for the results at the time were altogether good from the point of view of morale. Gambling occupied men's minds under circumstances where otherwise an opportunity would have been given to that terrible foe of all good discipline—mental depression—to do its deadly work, sapping away at those foundations of faith, hope and courage, without which an army cannot exist. The money used for the purpose was the two shillings a day of the field pay, and the worst result was that the man who lost everything went without chips, eggs, beer and cigarettes for the fortnight at most until the next pay day. Immediately after the Hun raid on the l'Epinette, in which the 16th Company suffered so heavily, Sergeant-Major Todd started a "two-up ring" in the wrecked front line. In no other way could he so easily and effectively have restored the breaking nerve of the survivors of that terrible night. Of course, from the disciplinary point of view, he should have been "crimed." From the point of view of military efficiency a much stronger case could be made against smoking than against gambling, for the heavy smoking that was frequently indulged in had a very harmful effect on the nerves. Yet what man in his sane senses would have issued an order for the abolition of smoking? Both of these "vices" had immense psychological effects which were wholly beneficial from the "win-the-war" point of view. Army methods of inculcating morality were not without a certain humour. They strained at gnats, but with the most cheerful good humour swallowed immense camels.

Saluting was another matter that required a periodical offensive. It was looked upon either as an imposition or as a big joke, and very seldom in the best light. From the time of General Godley's Gallipoli Manifesto to the effect "That there

Le Bizet—Ploegsteert—Hill 63

was too much swearing and that saluting was conspicuous by its absence" until after the cessation of hostilities the same old trouble was continually coming up. New Zealanders are, taking them as a whole, an eminently commonsense folk, and, in consequence, discipline of the real sort was usually excellent. The mass had a perfectly good understanding of the necessities of the position, and, in consequence, practically all orders were cheerfully and properly carried out. But, generally speaking, the New Zealander is not a demonstrative person. He does not cheer, or even sing, as readily as other troops. When in agony he does not scream or forget that a man should endure with fortitude in silence. Revival preachers say that he was the hardest man in all the Armies to touch, harder far even than the Australians. Individual freedom, self-respect and keen perception make a man very quick to perceive "humbug," and the Army doctrine of saluting was widely regarded as such. The saluting of the "King's Commission" was an excellent thing in theory, and if all officers had been in practice what they were in theory—officers because of their courage, ability and capacity for leadership—there would have been little difficulty. Observation of English troops made it clear that saluting was one of the main buttresses of military autocracy, and the Prussian behaviour of numbers of English officers toward the Tommies under their command did not go unnoticed. A small section of New Zealand officers would have been only too pleased to introduce a similar spirit and the same methods. It was the fear of this, partly unconscious of course, which kept alive the opposition to the practice. Men fighting for the principles of democracy were not over anxious, even under the exceptional circumstances, to practice the observances of class distinction.

To return to Hill 63 and the amusements thereof, it was found that not only the Higher Command of the British Army, but that of the German also, was opposed to the means of sociability. In fact the Huns went further, not only did they break up the "two-up rings" with H.E.'s, which were much more effective than M.P.'s, but they also destroyed the

The Auckland Regiment

Y.M.C.A. Hut, quite a dastardly thing to do, considering that there, and there only, was the supply of hot coffee.

2/Auckland's stay in the line was quite uneventful, and on the 6th April they were relieved by 1/Auckland, who took over the sector to the north of Ash Lane, 2/Auckland going back in support. It was during this spell that Plum-duff Dump, close to Battalion Headquarters, was blown up. The explosion was a tremendous one, and everybody in the vicinity was well shaken up. Fortunately very few casualties occurred, and as the cook's fire was not put out things were "not so bad." On April 15th, 2/Auckland relieved the 1/Battalion at Plus Douve Farm, and eight days later were themselves relieved. April 27th saw the 1st Battalion back on Hill 63 and the 2nd in the hutment camp at De Seule. Three days later 1/Auckland moved to Aldershot Camp and the 2nd Battalion to Neuve Eglise.

During the whole of this period the time not actually spent in the line was employed in preparing for the coming battle. There was little attempt at secrecy. The enemy were to be overwhelmed by a tremendous concentration of guns, aeroplanes, tanks and infantry. A battle of this description called for no subtle strategy, but for the most careful preparation and exact co-ordination of all branches of the service. An enormous amount of work was necessary digging new communication trenches, assembly trenches, gun-pits and burying cables. 1/Auckland were for the greater part of their working time employed on the latter job. With the success or failure of the battle depending so much on the work of the artillery it was supremely important that telephonic communication with all parts of the battlefield should be rendered as secure as possible. To ensure this, cable was buried six to eight feet deep right up to the front line. The greater part of this work had to be done at night. Working parties would fall in at any hour of the night deemed most suitable by the authorities, and march through the darkness to the allotted place, which in the case of 1/Auckland was usually Ploegsteert Wood. Engineer sappers were ready to mark out the task for the night. As a

Le Bizet—Ploegsteert—Hill 63

rule, each man was given a distance of two yards to dig down to the required depth of six or eight feet. In daylight on clear ground such a task took from one-and-a-half to two hours; at night in difficult country it might take twice as long. Ploegsteert Wood, for instance, was often very difficult, owing to the number of roots which had to be removed before any progress could be made. Close up to the front line the enemy frequently heard suspicious sounds and intervened actively with machine-guns and whizz-bangs. The extremely variable weather was also a very great hindrance. Occasional days which seemed to give a promise of spring were followed by snow storms, hail, rain and sleet. There was little frost, and, in consequence, there was much mud. 2/Auckland were at first employed on the digging and wiring of the assembly trench, afterwards known as "Hanbury Support." Falling in soon after dark, they marched all the way from De Seule, a distance of about six kilometres, to the rear of Hill 63, where, picking up shovels, they went on over the crest and filed on down to the work, and then having done the allotted portion filed back in silence, dumped the shovels, and commenced the long tramp back to billets.

On April 30th, 2/Auckland moved to Neuve Eglise and the 1st Battalion to Aldershot Camp, from where, on May 4th, they went into the line near Wulverghem. By this time the weather had definitely taken a turn for the better. Spring was coming, fields were green, and all the trees were bourgeoning. Activity on both sides increased. On May 5th and 6th the Huns brought up heavy guns and shelled the back areas, especially Neuve Eglise. It was a wild night. Some of the working parties had just come in and were settling down to a well-earned rest after a hard job cable laying; others were preparing to go out, when of a sudden the big shells came flying over. A huge convent, however tranquil and secure a place it may have seemed to the Good Sisters and their flock of little maids in the quiet days of peace, gives small sense of sanctuary when the big guns are firing and the projectiles crashing down amongst the buildings. Most of the Battalion

The Auckland Regiment

scattered over the countryside, returning in all sorts of moods to carry on once more the interrupted slumbers—keeping one ear open to catch the whine and whizz of the first salvo that might herald another bit of German frightfulness. The same night, after a bombardment of "minnies" and H.E.'s, the Huns attempted to raid 1/Auckland, meeting, however, with no success. It may be remarked here that 1/Auckland made a habit of repelling enemy raids. Somehow or other, they seemed to attract the errant Hun of nocturnal habit in a way that the 2nd Battalion never could. Next day there was intermittent shell fire, sometimes swelling up to quite a burst of fury. During the afternoon the 2/Battalion had the misfortune to lose Major West, who was for the second time very badly wounded. Captain Champion was also wounded. Throughout the night of the 6/7th the "Hun Travelling Circus of Heavies" gave another demonstration, but the night was made hideous mainly by the British retaliation for the proceedings of the night before.

At Neuve Eglise there was a fine field that lent itself admirably to the playing of cricket. The game was making progress, but unfortunately a Hun O.P. amongst the spectators very unfairly took sides at the wrong moment, considerably marring the perfect wicket by a well-placed H.E. Sundry bursts of shrapnel overhead could not deter such enthusiasts from carrying on, and it finally took a Brigade Order to stop play. At the time this was rather resented as a piece of unnecessary molly-coddling on the part of the "Heads," but, after the fall of Messines, men walking about in the ruins realised what an excellent view old Fritz must have had of the play. Perhaps, after all, the much-abused Higher Command could see a little further than ordinary individuals!

On May 8th, 1/Auckland were relieved, and two days later the whole Brigade moved back to the Strazeele-Cæstre area to commence the preparatory training for the coming battle. The 1st Battalion went into excellent billets at Pradelles, while the 2nd Battalion occupied a number of farmhouses on the outskirts of Strazeele itself. While in this area a Brigade Horse

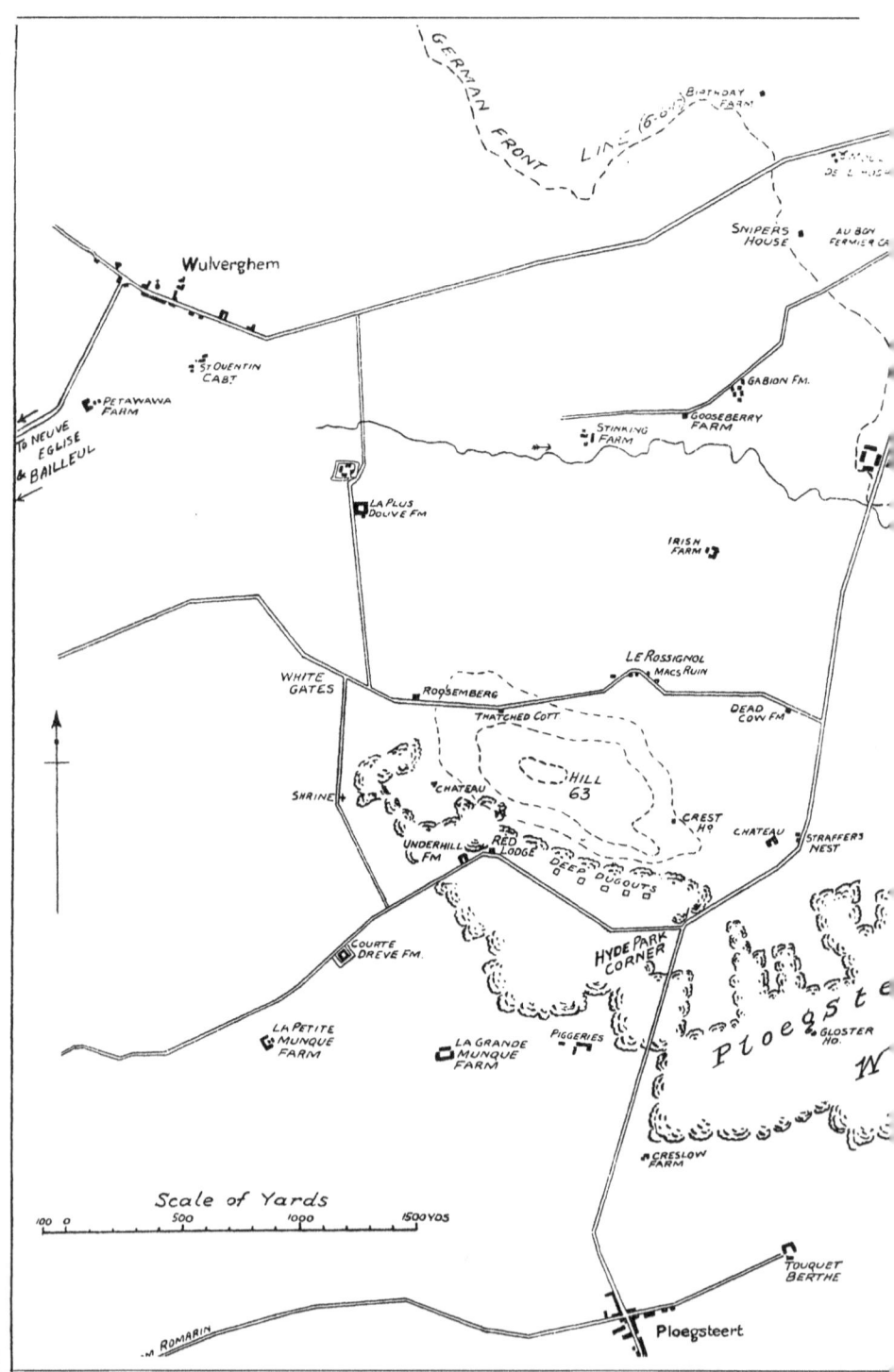

Le Bizet—Ploegsteert—Hill 63

Show was held, at which the two Auckland Battalions divided most of the prizes between them. Transport was always a matter of the very greatest importance, and in any future "war of movement" would be of even greater importance. It was perfectly true, in the strict military sense, that the life of a horse or a mule was of more importance than that of a mere man. Men could always be replaced, but horses and mules only with difficulty. No means that would tend to secure efficiency in this all-important side of a battalion's organisation was ever neglected by a wise commander. For the next few days training went on with little out of the ordinary to mark the course of events. Pleasant spring weather, green fields, reasonable billets and a sufficiency of estaminets made a welcome change after the hard trench life and the discomfort of the long winter. It was here that the rank and file of 2/Auckland commenced to get a real knowledge of their new commander. Colonel Allen took the first opportunity of making a speech to the assembled Battalion, in which he traced its history from the first beginnings in Moascar up to the commencement of the training period. The life of an individual with a combatant unit was usually so short that lectures of this sort were of the utmost value in the development of that esprit-de-corps so essential to the development of the best fighting spirit. Colonel Allen's own intense pride in the Battalion was infectious, and from that time men became increasingly proud of the Red Diamond badge. It was a well-known fact that the New Zealand Division was looked upon as one of the finest in France, and to realise that one's own battalion was perhaps the best in this élite Division was a very proud thing.

For the coming battle it was necessary that every man should not only be physically fit and expert in the use of his weapons, but also that he should have an accurate knowledge of his own particular task. In the Army training area a few kilometres outside St. Omer a full-size model of the Messines fortifications had been laid out, so that the attacking troops could rehearse as nearly as possible under actual conditions the operation they would have to perform when the day of

The Auckland Regiment

battle should at last arrive. By this means everyone, from the Divisional Commander himself to the humblest private, gained a complete understanding of his own particular share in the tremendous undertaking that lay ahead. On May 18th the 1/Brigade entrained from Bailleul and proceeded to St. Omer, from where 1/ Auckland marched to Setques and 2/Auckland to Esquerdes, two pleasant little villages some eight kilometres outside of the town itself. Accommodation was good, and there was really nothing left to be desired. Every morning the Battalions marched away to the training ground, and by platoon, company, battalion, and finally brigade practised their particular part of the scheme of attack. After a hard day's work they marched back again, hot and dusty, to plunge into the river that so conveniently flowed through the middle of the village. It was a somewhat novel sight to see hundreds of men without the superfluity of bathing costumes swimming in the midst of a civilian population, which could hardly fail to see the whole proceedings. Under abnormal conditions even the most civilised drop back, almost without noticing, to the primitive; and conventions, under the pressure of necessity, just drop off for the time being. Tired, dusty men and a smooth-flowing river. "Que voulez-vous," says madame, "c'est la guerre, monsieur." And so bathing goes on without any protest from the village father in the person of "Monsieur le Maire," who, by the way, is not backward if a few francs can be made out of the benevolent British Government. A trip to St. Omer for bathing parade was full of interest. Fortunately the interior economy of the baths had been somewhat disarranged, and in consequence there was an excellent excuse to let all hands have a look round the historic old town. St. Omer was well outside the danger zone, and was therefore very much more normal than Armentières, Estaires, Ballieul or even Hazebrouck. The main evidence of war in these parts was the great number of officers in St. Omer, due to the town being an extremely important centre of Army organisation; the huge aerodrome just outside; and the spare Huns kindly lent by the Kaiser's Army. There were hundreds of

Le Bizet—Ploegsteert—Hill 63

them employed on various kinds of work in the vicinity. Generally speaking, they seemed a well-fed, happy-looking people, by no means ill-contented with their lot. Many newspapers during the war made much of the miserable appearance and physique that was supposed to be the mark of the degenerate Hun. This was so much nonsense, as the average German soldier was a good type of man. Journalism of this character has given rise to the feeling that the German Army was after all a very miserable organisation, needing but a breath to overthrow it. As a matter of fact the German Army and the German soldier compared very favourably with the average of any of the armies. This foolish talk, although useful as propaganda to hearten the war-weary civilians, was only another way of belittling the work of our own men. Huns were hard people to beat, and it took heavy fighting to win victories. If the German Army had been as contemptible as it was made to appear on paper, the Allies would have won the war in a few weeks at a small cost. But it was far otherwise. The twelve days training in the pleasant villages passed only too quickly, and the battalions made ready for the long tramp back to the battle sector and the great event toward which everything had for so long been moving. All through the winter the Australians had been busy on the Somme. They had taken Bapaume, and their patrols had pushed on to the Hindenburg Line. At Arras the storm had burst, and the Canadians, taking Vimy Ridge, had won much praise. Australians busy, Canadians fighting, it was time for New Zealand to pass "Onward" once again. Hardened up by the marching and training, all were fit and eager.

XXI

Messines

> "From out the smoky pall of battle strife
> The Ridge looms grey, but with uncertain line;
> And all it's stricken fields are brown. No green remains.
> Our dead lie thickly in the broken town,
> All strangely still and quiet, unheeding now
> The thunder of the conflict they have won."
> —M.R. in "New Zealand at the Front."

The first day's march of about fifteen miles brought the Battalions through Wizernes and Arques to the Wallon-Cappel area, the next, another hard day, saw them passing through Hazbrouck and the Fôret de Nieppe to the La Motte area, leaving a comparatively short march through to the Bailleul road and so along the pavé, under the avenue of trees to De Seule and Canteen Corner. Tents were pitched in a little wood beyond, and the Battalions settled down for a brief spell, which many employed for the purpose of visiting the newly-arrived 4th Brigade, who were under canvas half-way between De Seule and Bailleul. The quiet period during the winter, when casualties had been reduced to a minimum, had led to the building up of a considerable surplus of men in the English Base Camps. Many of the Gallipoli and Somme men were now fully recovered, and once more ready for active service. With so many men on hand, and with a continual stream of reinforcements arriving, the authorities determined to organise another brigade of infantry. Experienced officers and N.C.O.'s were sent over from France to season the new recruits. The Brigade consisted of the newly-formed 3rd Battalions of the Auckland, Wellington, Canterbury and Otago Regiments. Formed at Codford March 15th, 1917, the new brigade had two months training, and then, after being reviewed by the King, was sent to France—joining up with the Division only a few days before the battle.

The 3/Auckland Battalion was commanded by Lieutenant-Colonel D. B. Blair, M.C., an officer who had seen much

Messines

service with the Mounted Rifles on Gallipoli and with the Canterbury Regiment in France. His Second-in-Command was Major Sinel, whose Gallipoli record was a very fine one. Captain Baker—a new officer—commanded the 3rd Company. Captain Dittmer, who had fought from the Landing without a break, came over from France to the 6th Company. Captain Evans, another very experienced officer, had the 15th, while Captain Closey, a man of great determination, courage and intellectual ability, came over to command the 16th Company. Lieutenant Thompson, of 1/Auckland, was of immense service, particularly in the work of training and organisation, Captain Gillett, Lieutenants McLean, Nicholls (the adjutant), McClurg, McAdam, McIntyre, Aitken, Gordon, Richardson, had all seen previous service. A great number of the N.C.O.'s were experienced and reliable men, sent over from France to stiffen the new men. Many of the men in the ranks also had seen much fighting.

On June 3rd, 1/Auckland moved from Canteen Corner and went into support on Hill 63, while 2/Auckland took over the whole of the Divisional front. During the move forward it became increasingly evident that the time for the assault was close at hand. Everything was ready. Heavy railway tracks had been laid down as far forward as possible, and from these the light lines diverged in all directions, running up to the guns and ammunition dumps, which were everywhere. The massed guns were ranged in rows, clustered into little valleys, sheltered behind crest-lines, and in many cases standing boldly out in the open, protected from observation by camouflage netting only. W, X, Y, and Z overland routes from the concentration areas to the assembly trenches had been cleared and pegged out for the use of infantry moving up. Other routes were marked out for the walking wounded and prisoners of war. Red Lodge itself, heavily protected by means of reinforced concrete and sand-bag walls, had been fitted up as an advanced dressing station, the same thing had been done at Kandahar Farm, while at Hyde Park Corner a strong concrete dug-out had been built at the Charing Cross

The Auckland Regiment

Junction. Wire cages were provided here and there for the accommodation of the German prisoners.

Day by day the firing increased in intensity. The trench mortar, the flying pig, the eighteen-pounder, the six-inch howitzer, the nine-point-two, the twelve-inch, the fifteen-inch, the long-range naval gun, all pounded, hammered and searched the enemy lines. Every day the creeping barrage moved up Messines Hill. The green slope was gone; the clean outline of the trenches effaced; the village itself a heap of ruins. From the middle of No-Man's-Land to the reverse slope was a brown waste.

The Germans, knowing of a certainty that an attempt would be made upon the Ridge, had strengthened their defences, brought up fresh troops and more artillery. From the 1st June their guns were extremely active. They blew in the front line and practised a counter-barrage across the valley of the Douve. Barrage and counter-barrage, the whole dreadful machinery of attack and defence was tested in every part.

2/Auckland in the line had an extremely trying time. Every little while the enemy shelled heavily with whizz-bangs and five-nines. Dug-outs were blown in, and the line rapidly commenced to crumble away. Men crouched up against sandbags, squeezed into the safe corners or lay down beneath the fire-step to obtain a little overhead cover from the flying splinters that came zutting down upon the duck-walks. "Bang! Crash! Bang! Crash! Whizz-bang! Zirr-Zut"—for half an hour the air is full of splinters, flying débris, dust, smoke and infernal noise. Men sit quietly, nerves and muscles tensed up, braced for a shock, or ready to roll away if the parapet shall give way above them. They think of many things. The minds of some are clouded with fear. As each shell shrieks toward them they feel the agony of wounds, and suffer many times all the bitterness of death. Others, with a certain scientific detachment, speculate on the probable point of impact of an approaching shell, and then from its explosion the calibre of the enemy gun. A few force the sensations of the present moment back into the fringe of consciousness and focus their

Messines

attention on past pleasures or future hopes. Some cheerful souls make a jest of the whole business. The nobler minds feel a lifting up of spirit. Death is near and there is a certain solemnity. They are lifted from the plane of the commonplace. Such men think of God, and to them in the broken trench the Presence is near and real. The hour of terror is an hour of vision. During the enemy bombardment, when ruin is all around, when nothing can be done save watch and wait, then is seen the finest valour. Men move amongst their fellows with a word, a gesture, a smile, bringing good cheer to the over-wrought, the trembling, and the much afraid. In some indefinable fashion virtue goes forth from them, and the weak looking to them are made strong. The same men may afterwards do great deeds, winning the Victoria Cross or a great name, yet the men around them know full well that the supreme hour of their valour was an hour when nothing could be written of deeds done only when some could say, "He gave us the courage." And as the shells crashed in amongst the entanglements or thudded against the parapet men thought to themselves to-morrow, or the next day, or perhaps the next, I must leave the shelter of the trench and go out into the storm of flying steel. What will the chances be?

The German guns ceased for a while, and those of the British opened up on the Hill in front. Messines vanished in smoke and drifting columns of dust. The fiery hail rained down on trench and dug-out. Nothing on the surface was safe, and twenty feet below ground the flying pig rooted and tore. German diaries show what a hell it must have been for them. "This everlasting murder. They send over shot after shot. The casualties increase terribly. All the trenches are clodded up. The English demolish our dug-out also. Casualty after casualty. No shelter left. They blow up the earth all round us. To look on such things is utter misery."

> "O'er all the sand fell slowly wafting down
> Dilated flakes of fire."

As dug-out and trench collapse in heaps of smoking débris little groups of men run across country seeking a fresh shelter,

The Auckland Regiment

if such may be found. But the Lewis-gunners in the Auckland trench are on the look-out for just such an opportunity. "Br-r-r-r-rt-t-tt," and they run no more.

Back on Hill 63, 1/Auckland were in huts and tents beneath the trees. Guns of all calibres were firing round them, and, in consequence, drawing retaliatory fire. At night the Germans sent over gas shells. Alarms were frequent, and rest was much disturbed. Respirators were in use a great part of the time. On the afternoon of June 5th, the 1st Battalion were relieved and went back to Canteen Corner to get a night's rest and to be served out with its final issue of gear and ammunition. 2/Auckland remained in the front line until the afternoon of the following day, and then, being relieved by a Battalion of the Rifle Brigade, went back to Midland Support—their battle-station.

The amount of extra equipment issued was very great. Perhaps in no other battle of the war did the private soldier carry quite so much. Steel helmet, rifle, bayonet, Webb equipment, full pouches of S.A.A., and an extra hundred rounds carried in bandoliers, entrenching tool, haversack and water-bottle, with the small box respirator slung on the chest, were quite sufficient to make a good load. In addition to these, every man carried two Mill's bombs in his breast-pockets and extra rations in his haversack, also a pick or shovel. Then distributed amongst the members of a platoon were wire-cutters of all sizes, shapes and descriptions, buckets of bombs, carriers full of rifle-grenades, spare Lewis-gun panniers and ground-flares with which to signal position to contact aeroplanes. All officers and section commanders were supplied with small scale maps, showing in detail the enemy trench system in the area to be assailed by the New Zealand Division.

At dusk on the 6th, 1/Auckland fell in and commenced the march from Canteen Corner to their battle-station in Hanbury Support. Lieutenant-Colonel R. C. Allen was in command, and had with him on Battalion Headquarters Lieutenants W. P. Gray, the Adjutant, and W. P. Fitchett, the Intelligence Officer. The O.C.'s Companies were:—

Lieutenant-Colonel S. S. Allen, C.M.G., D.S.O.

Messines

3rd Auckland: Captain C. L. Knight.
6th Hauraki: Captain G. H. Holland, M.C.
15th North Auckland: Captain A. E. Alexander.
16th Waikato: Captain R. Tilsley, D.C.M.
Dr. Nelson was in charge of the R.A.P., and the Rev. Gavin was Chaplain. The Battalion never went into action with a finer fighting staff.

The march across open country was very slow, and owing to numerous delays and halts it was after midnight when the Battalion reached Hill 63. From there on progress was still more difficult. Strict orders had been issued that all troops moving forward must keep to the saps. The main sap leading from the crest of the hill forward to the assembly point was crowded, and stoppages were frequent. All night long the German gas shells were bursting on the slope. Every now and again helmets had to be worn, and progress ceased for the time being. Casualties occurred. At last Colonel Allen ordered the men out of the communication trench and led them directly overland to the allotted position, which was reached half an hour before zero. The British Artillery was silent. A few machine guns were firing, and an aeroplane flew low down over the trenches to drown the noise of the tanks moving forward.

2/Auckland, concentrated in and about Midland Support, had a fighting strength of 20 officers and 660 men. Lieutenant-Colonel S. S. Allen was in command, with Lieutenant Seddon, M.C., acting as Adjutant. The Company Commanders were:—
3rd Auckland. Captain F. E. Beamish.
6th Hauraki: Captain W. Watson.
15th North Auckland: Captain F. R. Foster.
16th Waikato: Captain C. H. McClelland.
Dr. Addison was still in charge of the R.A.P., while the Rev. C. T. H. Dobson was the Battalion's Chaplain.

During the early part of the night the extra equipment and supplies had been served out, and then all ranks endeavoured to get what rest was possible. Gas shells were coming over continuously, and, in consequence, men had a choice of

The Auckland Regiment

two evils—to sit up with a gas-mask on all night or take the risk, go to sleep and hope for the best. A short while before zero the men were roused and given a hot meal. Everything was now ready.

General Plumer's objective was the Messines-Wytschaete Ridge, which was the buttress of the German line in the north. The New Zealand Division were given the task of storming Messines itself and of passing through some five hundred yards to the reverse side of the hill. On the right flank the 3rd Australian Division were attacking, and on the left the 25th Division of English troops. If the first part of the attack was successfully carried out, then troops of the 4th Australian Division would pass through the New Zealanders and go on to the final objective. The area to be occupied was divided by imaginary lines, the Blue, Brown, Yellow, Black, Black Dotted and Green, into six successive areas. The taking of the first three of these, which included the 1st and 2nd German trench systems on the forward slope and Messines Village itself, was entrusted to the N.Z.R.B. and the 2nd N.Z. Infantry Brigade. As soon as the village was taken the 1st Brigade (Brigadier-General C. H. J. Brown, D.S.O.) were to go forward to the Black Line, and from there push posts out to the Black Dotted Line.

At 3.10 a.m. there was a shaking of the earth, a column of leaping flame quickly obscured by smoke and débris, and then a muffled roar. The mines had gone up. A brief pause, the sudden rattle of thousands of machine-guns, a flash round the horizon, and then with a thunderblast of sound the great barrage fell on the German line. The long roll of the heavy guns and the quick, stabbing, bang-snap-bang of the eighteen-pounder blended into one tremendous volume of sound. Up from the enemy posts went the signals of distress and warning, but their urgent appeal met with small response, for the Hun artillery had been overwhelmed by the weight of the British counter-battery work. For hours their field guns were out of action, and the only reply they could make was with long-range guns of heavy calibre.

Messines

Behind the moving wall of steel and flame the infantry flung themselves on the demoralised enemy. With little opposition and light casualties the N.Z.R.B. and the 2/ Brigade took the Blue, Brown and Yellow lines. A few scattered groups of Germans made a show of resistance, but little more than a show; by far the greater number were too dazed and shaken to think of anything but immediate surrender.

The Auckland Battalions remained in the assembly trenches until 3.55 a.m., by which time dawn had broken, and then moved forward by half-platoons in file across the Douve and the old front line. Heavy black H.E. shrapnel burst overhead, but did little damage. Gas was met with in the valley, and respirators had to be worn during part of the ascent. Fortunately there was no lachrymatory mixed in with the phosgene-chlorine preparation which was at that time generally used by the enemy and so it was only found necessary to adjust mouthpiece and nose clip to ensure perfect safety. Prisoners passed on their way to the cages—well set up men, who, from their spruce appearance, had evidently been but a short while in the line. Some of our wounded going back and a few dead lying here and there on the slope showed that the success so quickly attained had not been won except at a price. 2/Auckland concentrated round the Moulin de l'Hospice, and there took shelter in shell-holes and hastily dug trenches, waiting orders, while the 1/Battalion, passing to the right of Messines, drew up on the Wytschaete-Messines road in readiness for the attack on Ungodly Trench. At 4.55 a.m. the barrage moved forward. Nothing could face it, scarcely anything live under it, and so the 6th and 16th Companies had no difficulty in occupying the trench. With the same ease the 3rd and 15th Companies attacked and captured Unbearable Trench, finally digging in on the Black Line at 5.20 a.m. A strong point was established on the Black Dotted Line, and the Battalion's work was done. Battalion Headquarters and the 3rd and 6th Companies of 2/Auckland moved forward at 6.40 a.m. to a position in rear of the Black Line, from where they established four posts in the Black Dotted Line. Here a 77mm. gun was

The Auckland Regiment

captured, which, with the two that were taken at the same time by the 1st Battalion, were the first guns to be taken by the New Zealand Division. At 9.40 the barrage ceased, and patrols sent out to the Green Line reported that the wire in front had been cut.

The blow staggered the enemy army in the salient, and for two or three hours the Huns were utterly demoralised. A bold and daring sweep forward while the Battalions were flushed with victory, still comparatively fresh, and very little reduced in numbers, might have led to very great results. Instead, a policy of safety was adopted, and the consolidation of the newly-gained ground became the prime business of everyone. The Germans recovered quickly. What guns were still in position and undamaged opened a furious fire on the lost ground. Fresh batteries were rushed up, and the fire became more intense, and every moment made a strategic exploitation of the tactical victory a more difficult matter.

15th Company, 2/Auckland, were ordered to proceed to the front and dig communication between Ungodly and Unbearable Trenches. Moving round to the right of the village they came under direct observation, and were heavily shelled, only by extreme good fortune escaping with light casualties. On the completion of their task, the Divisional Front was fully established and held in its entirety by the Aucklanders.

From this time forward there was nothing to be done except watch, wait and endure. The day was hot, and the exertion, with the battle-smoke and the acrid fumes from the explosives, caused intense thirst. In some parts of the line the digging uncovered numbers of tiny springs, the water from which, muddy and dirty though it was, served to supply the urgent need. Up in the front posts men ran greater risks from the short bursts of our own artillery than from the German fire. One battery of four big guns was continually firing short, and inflicted many casualties. For some reason or another, despite our complete control of the air and the large number of observation 'planes continually flying overhead, no message was got through to this battery. Its continued activity

Messines

caused considerable loss and the slight withdrawal of two posts. The Hun barrage fell heavily on the Yellow Line, in the vicinity of which the two battalion headquarters had been established, with the result that runners, signallers, and stretcher-bearers had a particularly dangerous and difficult time. All through the morning the heavy guns continued active, while the field batteries were rushed forward. At 1.17 p.m. the 3rd Company, 2/Auckland, reported a counter-attack forming on their front. Concentrated artillery fire was at once directed on the spot, and the attacking formations dispersed. A local counter-attack developing against one of the posts was dispersed by the Lewis guns.

At 3.10 p.m. the Australians moved through to take Owl Trench and Owl Support. For various reasons their attempt was far from a success, and they became entirely disorganised. Some stayed in No-Man's Land, others joined the garrisons of the posts, while others fell right back on the Black Line, and then could only with difficulty be restrained from going back further still.

During the afternoon Colonel Robert Allen was very badly wounded by a shrapnel burst. His loss was a very great one. It is perfectly true that a good officer is of more value than many men. No one in a battalion has anything like the same influence for good or for evil as the Commanding Officer. There are many things he should be, for he has many parts to play—wise in administration, careful over business, watchful for detail, just, purposeful, sympathetic, of clear brain and good understanding. To achieve success, moreover, he must be a good combining medium for men of widely different temperament and ability. Above and beyond everything else, however, he must have about him a subtle power of touching the hearts of men, of capturing their imagination; for he is the source of inspiration and the beginning of all true discipline. Such an one was Colonel Allen. It was one of 1/Auckland's greatest misfortunes to lose him at a time when so much heavy fighting lay ahead. He was never replaced. The same shell which wounded him killed Captain Foster, the brave

The Auckland Regiment

commander of the 2/15th Company, who had been doing excellent work throughout the day.

German machine-guns and snipers came into action again during the evening, and before nightfall were active. There was constant expectation of a counter-attack developing, and to make the position doubly secure numbers of machine-guns were rushed up to the forward side of the slope. Night fell. Under cover of darkness, organisation which had been impossible during the latter part of the afternoon, was rapidly carried out. Rumours got round that the advanced posts had been driven in and that the enemy were coming over in force. Men nerved themselves to resist to the uttermost, and took courage from the bursts of fire which rattled overhead from the machine-guns massed in rear. Nothing came, and when the sun rose on the morning of "A" Day it was generally felt that the position was secure. Throughout the battle Captains Holland and Tilsley, Lieutenant Fitchett, of 1/Auckland, and Lieutenants Tuck, Frank McKenzie, Stewart and Lorie, of 2/Auckland were a great source of inspiration to their men. That very brave and able soldier, Lieutenant Cooper, was killed. Sergeant Calame, of 1/Auckland, and Sergeant-Major Gordon, of 2/Auckland, especially distinguished themselves.

Early in the morning Brigadier-General C. H. J. Brown, D.S.O., was killed. He was universally looked upon as one of the best soldiers in the N.Z.E.F. At the Landing, Helles and Quinn's Post he had demonstrated his courage and ability to command. His handling of 2/Auckland through the Somme fighting had been masterly, and at the first opportunity he had been promoted to the command of the 1st Brigade, passing over many who were senior to him in rank and service. Two distinct types of commander achieve the greatest success. There is the dominant character, severe, masterful, efficient, compelling, feared rather than loved, but absolutely trusted—such a commander was Earl Kitchener; and then there is the other type, the loved leader of men, who is served with a passionate devotion by men who count a smile from him or a word of thanks to be the best reward they know—such a leader

Messines

was Earl Roberts. Of the latter type was General Brown. From batman to Major-General, we all loved him, and would have done any thing for him.

Colonel S. S. Allen took over the command of the 1st Brigade, and proceeded with the reliefs that had already been agreed upon. The 15th and 16th Companies of 2/ Auckland moved back to Moulin de l'Hospice in readiness to relieve in the Yellow Line after dark. All day shelling was exceptionally heavy, and very little movement was possible. At 10 p.m. the 15th and 16th relieved the 1st Battalion N.Z.R.B. in the Yellow Line, while 2/Wellington relieved the 3rd and 6th Companies from the Black Dotted Line. The 3rd Company relieved part of the 4th Battalion N.Z.R.B. about midnight, and early in the morning the 6th Company completed the relief. 1/Auckland remained, as they were holding the ground they had won. There was no slackening of the German fire. During the whole of this trying time Dr. Nelson did splendid work. He pushed his R.A.P. up almost into the front line, and always under heavy fire successfully cleared numbers of wounded. Padre Gavin also did excellent work.

The continuous strain of the last three days was commencing to tell on all ranks, and the order received that night to go back to Bulford and Kortypyp Camps was very welcome. The journey back was slow and tedious. Once across the old front line and passing along the saps to the crest of Hill 63, every man was carefully checked at Brigade Station. This at any rate was a rest, and tired men dozed off, leaning up against the trench wall or lying flat on the duck-boards. Up again, and moving down the slope, they passed through the mass of heavy guns. Brilliant green and yellow flames stabbed through the darkness, to be followed by a bellowing crash of sound. "Cr-r-r-a-a-sh." Twenty yards away a monstrous weapon explodes with a hideous clamour. A moment of intense blackness and then once more the flame of fire and the shock of the discharge. For half a mile, on both sides of the track, batteries are in action. The ordeal is terrible. A battery just ahead has the muzzles of its guns almost touching the road.

The Auckland Regiment

It fires a salvo, and the file of infantry see what is ahead. Can they pass before the next discharge? Tired as they are they quicken pace. No. 1 is being screwed up to its right elevation. No. 2 is ready, but still silent. Perhaps they will just clear! But no! The battery commander megaphones his warning order. "Hurry up there in front, before the b—— b—— goes off!" Too late! "Fire" comes the muffled voice through the megaphone. "Crash" from No. 1. "C-r-r-a-sh" from No. 2 just in rear, and then the solid earth shakes as 3 and 4 bellow out. "Oh, Hell! Get on! Get on!" At last the guns are passed, and on the good road faster progress is made, until at last all stumble wearily into the camp, and as soon as possible fling themselves down and sleep luxuriously after the week of strain and stress.

Casualties for the Auckland Regiment, although the heaviest in the Division, were very much lighter than in the Somme Battle. They were:—

1/Auckland: Killed, 3 Officers, 39 O.R.'s; wounded, 4 Officers, 228 O.R.'s; missing, 16. Total, 290.

2/Auckland: Killed, 3 Officers, 57 O.R.'s; wounded, 8 Officers, 290 O.R.'s; missing, 23. Total, 381.

XXII

The Aftermath of Battle

From the 11th until the 18th the Aucklanders were resting, re-equipping and re-organising. Not the least interesting part of the business were the attempts on the part of numerous section commanders to prove that sundry bomb-carriers and wire-clippers had been "destroyed by shell fire." It is quite possible that the articles in question had been so destroyed—after their tired owners had abandoned them in some convenient shell-hole. "Destroyed by shell fire" was a convenient formula which covered a multitude of sins. On the 12th, 1/Auckland moved to Regina Camp, a short distance from Romarin. Next day Sir Alexander Godley reviewed the 1st Brigade, and complimented them on their work during the battle.

As the war progressed, there were constant improvements in the art of killing. When the New Zealanders first went into the trenches at Armentières there were many alarms and much sounding of Strombos' horns, but no gas. After sweltering a few times in slimy, evil-smelling "P.H. helmets" the alarm of "gas" came to be looked upon as rather a bad joke. On the Somme the infantry had encountered lachrymatory gas, but this, although sometimes a nuisance, had no result, except a temporary irritation of the eyes. Goggles were served out to combat the effect of this gas, and were quite effective, though somewhat clumsy. Nothing occurred during the winter, and nearly everyone grew careless. "Cloud gas" had not been a great success. The cylinders from which it was released were difficult to carry, and were most dangerous things to have about in the line. Even when a cloud had

The Auckland Regiment

been successfully discharged there was no certainty that a sudden change in the wind might not blow it aside, or even back from whence it came. The evolution of the gas shell changed everything. From being a rather expensive and ineffective novelty, gas immediately became one of the most terrible and deadly weapons of modern war. It could be used safely at all times, concentrated on a particular spot, or spread over a wide area.

At Messines, gas casualties were numerous, and there was a general realisation of the seriousness of the thing. Much greater attention was paid both to the care of helmets and training men in the quickest and best methods of using them. The "small box respirator," issued shortly after the Somme, was an absolutely safe protection against any gas then used. A rubberised mask with eye-pieces, nose clip and expiratory valve fitted over the face. A rubber tube led from the mouthpiece to the tin canister containing chemical preparations which neutralised any harmful gas in the atmosphere. Only pure air passed through. In action the brown canvas haversack containing the apparatus was carried slung on the breast, and at other times slung at the side. At first the S.B.R. was looked upon as rather a mixed blessing. It certainly gave an extra sense of security, but then it made more to carry. Still there were compensations. With a scarf on top it made a most excellent pillow, and the mask compartment of the satchel was useful for the carrying of anything from socks to loveletters. This casual treatment of the soldier's best friend had anything but good results. Valves became choked with dust and dirt. Eye-pieces were neglected, and a man moving through a gas belt found himself blind and in danger of losing touch. Some, through lack of practice, were very slow in adjusting the mask. Gas experts now came into their own, and from this time forward the rank and file suffered many things at their hands. Adjustment of masks by numbers, route marches with the things on, lectures, demonstrations, tests of various sorts, became an utter abomination, especially after the fiftieth repetition of the same old thing. Still it was all necessary, for

The Aftermath of Battle

on the least slackening of the pressure careless human nature reasserted itself, and sooner or later trouble occurred.

The weather was exceedingly fine, and the few days spent out of the line in Regina and Kortypyp were very pleasant ones. After a big battle it is always a satisfactory thing to realise that one is still alive and in possession of the correct number of limbs. "If that big H.E. had not been a dud —— —— ——!!!" Such a lot might have happened, such a lot did happen—to others. A "buckshee" was all very well, a neat little hole through the arm or leg, with a trip to "Blighty" at the end of it; but some frightful smash from a jagged chunk of poisonous shell-case was quite another thing. Many a man feared the shattering bone smash, with its inevitable months or years under the surgeon's knife and its prospect of lifelong crippling, more than death itself. In a short while the men who had come out almost in the last stages of collapse were strong and fit once more, and ready for the next move.

On the morning of June 7th the 3/Auckland Battalion had marched from De Seule to Hill 63. For the next three days they were employed making and repairing roads, and then received orders to take over the sector to the right of Le Bizet. The enemy here had the River Lys behind them and Messines almost directly on their right flank. Their position was quite untenable. Accordingly they withdrew the greater part of their garrison to the other side of the Lys, leaving a few posts to cover the retirement and to hold the trenches until such time as the British should make a serious attempt to occupy them. 3/Auckland received orders to establish posts in the enemy front line, and on the night of the 12/13th parties of the 6th and 16th Companies went over and occupied the trench with little opposition beyond some sniping. Captain Ruddock was mortally wounded, but otherwise casualties were slight. At 2.30 a.m. the enemy shelled his old line, and the 6th, after losing several men, were finally compelled to withdraw. An enemy bombing attack on the Waikatos was driven off. Heavy shelling continued all day. Hauraki patrols made further progress, entering the support line, and then at 8 p.m. the three

The Auckland Regiment

lines of German trenches were seized. On the 15th the Battalion was withdrawn and went back to bivouac at Pont Nieppe. During this spell in the line the enemy artillery fire from the direction of Frelinghien was frequently heavy, and caused a number of casualties.

The New Zealand Division, withdrawn from the sector of Messines, took over the La Basse-Ville-Warneton one, which stretched away from Hyde Park Corner and Ploegsteert Wood over an almost level expanse of torn field to the outskirts of the two villages which were both occupied by enemy troops. On the 18th, 1/Auckland went into the Prowse Point sector, holding the front line from Douve to La Truie Farm, while the 2/Battalion in support occupied the Catacombs. Forward of Prowse Point the newly-won ground was ill-defined and only very roughly organised. Vigorous patrolling was at once commenced and enemy posts discovered at an average distance of four hundred yards. The second night in, strong patrols went out under cover of a barrage, but were only partially successful. Running diagonally across the New Zealand front was an old railway line. Between this track, the Douve and our posts the enemy were holding strongly. It was decided to raid the whole area, destroy their posts and kill or capture the garrisons. Zero hour was 1 a.m. the morning of the 23rd, and the whole of the 16th Company, with two platoons of the 3rd, were detailed for the task. On the right no opposition was met with, but elsewhere the Huns fought well. In the centre they were holding wired shell-holes, and on the left, in the angle by the creek, a cleverly-concealed pill-box caused a lot of trouble. One German, standing in front and alone, coolly shot down man after man. Such a man might well have turned the tide but for "Jimmy" Greenwood, one of the most desperately brave men in the N.Z.E.F., coming at that moment on the spot. For a second the two faced each other, and then with a shout the New Zealander leaped in, the bayonets crossed, and the brave German fell. Single combats were rare in the war of great guns and magazine rifles, and rarer still was a meeting between two men of so splendid a type. Nine

The Aftermath of Battle

prisoners were taken, and very many of the Huns were killed, while Auckland lost 4 killed, 20 missing, and 1 officer and 52 O.R.'s wounded.

The whole area in the vicinity of Hyde Park Corner was heavily shelled at all times, and 2/Auckland, doing working parties from the Catacombs, had continually to run the gauntlet. For two hundred yards all round there was an excellent prospect of being blown out any moment by eleven-inch high explosives. Gas shells rained over, falling on the hillside, in the wood and round the entrances to the dug-out. The atmosphere in the long, stuffy galleries reeked with the pungent odour. Working parties picked up their engineer taskmasters at Hyde Park, and then got away from the danger zone with all speed, going along the Messines road to the Douve, or through Ploegsteert Wood to the forward area. The organisation of the newly-gained ground entailed immense labour, digging trenches, putting down duck-boards and "A-frames," revetting, burying cable, making roads. Frequently the Huns picked up the location of the working parties and shelled heavily, sending everybody helter-skelter to the nearest cover. A bombardment was not a bad excuse sometimes to clear away home, and so escape two or three hours digging in the mud, but it was an intolerable nuisance when it stopped traffic during the return journey, with breakfast and bunk only fifteen minutes away.

On the 23rd, 2/Auckland relieved the 1/Battalion. The newly-dug line ahead of the Potteries was the main line of defence. In front of this was a line of posts connected by a shallow trench, and a couple of hundred yards in front of this again was a recently occupied position, from which the garrison, with the exception of a few observers, was withdrawn during the day. A few hundred yards away were the buildings of Warneton, and close up a tangle of hedges and clumps of trees, behind which were the enemy posts. Their observation was fairly good, and in consequence their artillery was very active, firing on any movement. Lieutenant Stewart, with a platoon of the 15th Company, occupied and consolidated

The Auckland Regiment

"Stewart's Post," as it was afterwards called, and patrolled out toward the railway.

The 1/Battalion went back to De Seule on the 28th, and next day were followed by 2/Auckland, both units going under canvas near De Seule.

Once the battle was actually over the British Higher Command commenced to withdraw great numbers of guns and many squadrons of aeroplanes from this part of the front, leaving the Germans with a gradually increasing predominance both in gun-power and in the air. Night bombing was becoming more and more a regular feature of war. Every night now the Hun airmen were over trying for the billets, stables, dumps and rail-heads. The Aucklanders while under canvas had reason to take a particularly keen interest in the new departure. Back from the Y.M.C.A., from the Pierrot show, from the estaminet or from a walk to Bailleul, miles behind the line, and feeling quite unusually secure, men went to sleep in comfort, taking off boots and clothes. It was a most luxurious feeling to realise that the whole night long was for uninterrupted slumber. Lights out, and the only sounds to be heard were a few whispers, coughs, the snores of the musically-minded, and the muffled report of a distant gun. There is a drumming in the upper air—gradually coming nearer, and then the unmistakable beat of a Hun engine. A sleeper awakes, "Hallo, boys, there's a blanky Fritz overhead!"

"Shut up, and go to sleep, you windy beggar!"

"Cr-r-r-r-ash-sh," somewhere a mile off. The whole tent is awake now, and speculating.

"The blankety-blank something has dropped an egg!"

"Cr-r-r-r-ash-sh," this time only half a mile away, and in a direct line. "The b—— b——'s coming nearer; where are my boots?" and a nervy individual makes a bolt outside. Nothing is to be gained by so doing, for he is as likely to run into the danger he is seeking to avoid as to escape it. Now the searchlights are flashing across the sky, and the anti-aircraft guns barking furiously. The converging beams fail to pick the raider up, and the crashes grow nearer. Many find the

The Aftermath of Battle

strain of lying still too much for their nerves, and get out and on the move. Others lie quiet, cursing a little, or just by a concentration of will waiting for whatever the issue may be. No one sleeps, and however successfully anyone may pretend "to care for none of these things," it is only pretence.

"C-r-ash. C-r-r-ash. C-r-r-r-ash-sh," behind, level, and then a big sigh of relief, for the last explosion is clear of the camp and the danger has passed. Perhaps no great material harm has been done, but, nevertheless, it is just this kind of thing that in the long run breaks men's nerves and renders them entirely useless for the moral strain of modern war. The Germans placed much faith in the "loud noise theory," and, undoubtedly, they were very largely right. Frightful, crashing detonations have a most demoralising effect on all except troops of the highest order.

On 30th June the 1st Brigade moved back to the training area, 1/Auckland to Bleu and 2/Auckland to Steentge, for a fortnight's rest and training. The weather was delightful, the billets good, and training easy. As a general rule the afternoons were given up to recreation. Division held athletic and swimming sports and a gymkhana, while a good deal of cricket was played between company teams. One team from 2/Auckland had the immense satisfaction of beating the redoubtable 3/Field Ambulance Eleven. To commence with, the Red Cross people regarded the Infantry in the same light that a crack town team regards an eleven from the backblocks. They were speedily undeceived, and as their wickets crashed one after the other they realised that their opponents could throw other things besides bombs.

Bailleul was quite close, and scores of men walked in during the long evenings to visit the shops, estaminets and restaurants of the quaint old town, and to inspect the trophies of battle which had been collected in the square. Many had pilgrimages to make to the graves of comrades, who, dying of wounds received in the fight, had been buried in the military cemetery on the outskirts of the town. Here General Brown was buried and many another good comrade.

The Auckland Regiment

On July 19th the Brigade went back into the line, 1/Auckland going in to the Prowse Point sub-sector, while 2/Auckland moved first to Kortypyp Camp and then to the Catacombs. Shelling was heavy and continuous, and the Huns were making a most liberal use of poison gas. Ploegsteert Wood was literally drenched with the stuff. Hyde Park Corner was commencing to look as brown and torn as parts of the battlefield. On the 30th, 2/Auckland relieved the 1/Battalion, who went back to Hill 63, with Headquarters at Red Lodge.

The Third Battle of Ypres—the bloodiest, most terrible fight of the war—commenced on the 31st July, when the British and French attacked from Dixmude to La Basse Ville. The New Zealand Division, on the extreme flank, had the task of storming the latter village and of advancing its line in conformity with the forward thrust of the Army. 2/Wellington and 1st and 2/Auckland were detailed for the purpose. Wellington had La Basse Ville itself as their objective, while the Aucklanders on their left were to push forward and establish a new outpost line.

For three weeks Captain Coates had been training the 1/15th Company in readiness for an offensive operation against the enemy position in the Warneton sector. They arrived in the line during the night of the 29/30th, and were in readiness to carry out their raid, when, with little warning, the German barrage came down. It was heavy and destructive. The men lying round in the shell-holes and shallow trenches suffered severely. After some hours of heavy shelling, the German infantry came on the heels of their barrage, and, penetrating the gap between two of the outposts, got right in amongst the 15th. There was a confused and very bloody fight in the darkness. The North Aucklanders, maddened by their losses, and glad of the opportunity to get amongst the enemy, fought savagely. There was little opportunity for direction or co-operation. Every man fought as best he could. Revolver, bayonet and bomb were busy. Very few of the Germans returned to their own line. Almost the whole of their party were

Lieutenant-Colonel R. C. Allen, D.S.O.

The Aftermath of Battle

killed. The 15th lost heavily, but there were still enough of them left to go over on the morning of the 31st. Some ninety strong they raided in the triangle between the railway, the Douve and our own front line. They swept through the enemy shell-hole system, killing many and taking prisoners. The line was pushed well forward. Parties of the 2/6th Company moved up immediately and established three posts to the left and in line with Stewart's Post, which until this time had been dangerously isolated, only fifty yards from the Huns, but two hundred and fifty from our own front line. When these posts had been established, the 15th Company were withdrawn. They had done excellent work, and had had a very rough time. Throughout the operations Captain Coates had displayed great powers of leadership, and had set a fine example. Lieutenant Lang had been conspicuous for his coolness and bravery, and also Sergeant Rogers.

At daybreak Sergeant Cusack, in charge of one party of the 6th Company, discovered that somehow or another a party of twenty-two Huns had been missed by the assaulting troops and were still holding their position a few yards only from his own post. Sergeant Cusack, although he had only ten men with him, attacked and killed the whole of the enemy party, with the exception of one man taken prisoner, captured a machine-gun, and then transferred the enemy wire to the front of his own post. The whole operation had been quite successful. Wellington had taken La Basse Ville, and the new line was everywhere established.

Conditions for the forward troops were miserable in the extreme. Heavy shell fire caused numerous casualties. Rain turned the whole battlefield into a quagmire. The posts filled with water and mud. Men were wet, chilled to the bone, and unable to rest or sleep. Even when parties carried hot food up through smashed trenches where the duck-boards were swimming on top of three feet of water or sunk out of sight under a like depth of mud, the food was wasted because "dixies" were lost in the slime or so coated with filth as to render them utterly useless. A man stood in a narrow ditch facing the front, his feet buried deep in the slush, at first numbed, then hot and burning as the first symptoms of "trench foot" made their appearance; his clothes were wet through and stiff with clay; his fingers frozen and useless; his rifle, breech and barrel choked with mud, had slipped from the nerveless grasp. So he stood and waited, in imminent deadly danger, without food, without sleep, while the Hun artillery shelled heavily. "Whizz-bang! Zutt!" and a man rolled slowly over badly wounded. If the wound were merciful he relapsed at once into a blessed unconsciousness of all his misery, but if not, he suffered the tortures of the damned. Under cover of darkness the stretcher-bearers came, and after hours of heartbreaking effort got him out to the light tram line, and so on a jolting journey to Hyde Park and the motor ambulance. Even in the naked, sordid horror of such an experience as this there is a touch of glory. Flashes of chivalry and self-sacrifice run like a thread of gold through the dark welter of agony, weariness and misery, and in some measure redeem the wickedness of it all. Victor French gave his overcoat to a wounded German, and for three days endured without complaint the terrible rigour of the cold and wet.

2/Auckland were relieved, and with the 1/Battalion, went back to Canteen Corner, where they remained until August 17th, re-equipping and doing working parties. Enemy aeroplanes were extremely active, and bombed stables and billets with great regularity. About this time the Germans brought into action a long-range, high-velocity naval gun, firing heavy armour-piercing shells. They used this weapon for the purpose of shelling back areas. Prospective victims were certainly not held long in suspense as the first report of the discharge and the arrival of the shell seemed almost simultaneous. On the other hand, there was little opportunity of carrying out that manœuvre so popular with all ranks of "ducking for cover."

On August 17th the two battalions moved from Canteen Corner, 1/Auckland to the hutment camp at Romarin and 2/Auckland to the line in front of La Basse Ville. The new

The Aftermath of Battle

trenches were in fair condition, and a continuous front line had been established on the near side of the Lys. Shell-holes full of mud, water and mosquitoes, and covered over with camouflage netting formed the outpost line. The mosquitoes were of an enormous size, and of a most voracious appetite. Hun aeroplanes hovered just overhead, taking photographs and dropping bombs. Control of the air seemed to have passed entirely to them. At dawn heavy barrages went down on the front and support lines, and men stood-to in expectation of a raid or an attack. On the 22nd, 2/Auckland were relieved, going back to Regina Camp, while the 1/Battalion took over the Prowse Point sector. A few miles to the north the battle for the ridges was proceeding with increasing fury and varying success. The Germans were apprehensive of a further blow in the very delicate sector before Messines, and so strengthened themselves with more guns. They made a prodigal use of gas. All the woods, the hollows, the roads, tracks and camps in the forward areas were systematically deluged with phosgene and chlorine. Men returning from a working party would be caught in the middle of Ploegsteert Wood. Gas helmets were immediately adjusted, and the file sat down on the duck-boards to wait for better times. Shrapnel commenced to burst freely. There was no shelter, and so the only thing to do was to stumble on, perspiring and half-suffocated. The road was reached, and after various halts behind sheltering banks the party straggled into camp, and tired out lay down at once on the wire bunks. But the rest was a short one. A poisoned breeze was blowing through the camp. A few tried to sleep with the masks on, but without much success, and after a little while nearly everyone streamed out of the camp away down the road to Romarin. So the night passed in alarm and discomfort.

From July 1st to 7th, 3/Auckland were at Brune Gaye, supplying working parties for the front line, and then took over the Le Toquet sector, facing Frelinghien. Much work was put in on Long Avenue, despite heavy enemy artillery fire. Patrol work was carried out, and on one occasion a sharp

The Auckland Regiment

brush occurred with an enemy party in the midst of No-Man's-Land. Heavy artillery exchanges took place daily. After eight days in, the Battalion was relieved, and went back on working parties until the last day of the month, when the Warnave sector was taken over from 3/Canterbury. Here there was no definite touch with the enemy, and, in consequence, a great deal of patrolling was undertaken. Lieutenant "Andy" Thompson was killed on July 4th. He was a great loss to the whole Regiment. Four days later the Battalion went back to Brune Gaye, where they remained for a week training, until on the 16th they once more took over the Warnave sector. Much work still remained to be done, digging and wiring the new front line. Shell fire was again heavy, and many patrols were out on both sides. One party of Germans strayed right on to an Auckland outpost, which immediately fired on them, wounding one, at least. The next relief saw the Battalion go back first to Brune Gaye and then to Bulford Camp.

By this time the Division was heartily sick of the whole area from De Seule and Canteen Corner to Messines, Warneton, La Basse Ville and Ploegsteert. There had been one tremendous day of moving excitement, and then months of hard work and miserable conditions, heavy shelling, gassing, bombing, and a continual heavy drain of killed and wounded. Orders for the Divisional relief were eagerly looked forward to, and when at last they actually came there was much joy expressed by all. On the 25th the 1st and 2/Auckland Battalions proceeded by motor-lorry to the Cæstre area, from whence they entrained four days later for Wizernes. 3/Auckland entrained at Steenwerck on September 2nd, and proceeded by train and motor-lorry to Le Waast.

XXIII

Ypres

" There's a little hill in Flanders
Heaped with a thousand slain;
Where the shells fall night and noonday,
And the ghosts that died in vain.
A little hill,
A hard hill,
To the souls that died in pain."

—"Three Hills," by Everard Owen.

At Wizernes the Battalions detrained and found the Y.M.C.A. in readiness with a cup of cocoa and a packet of biscuits for each man. Thus refreshed, the men clambered on the waiting motor-lorries and rattled off through the moonlight past Setques and Esquerades, along the St. Omer-Boulogne highroad to the villages of the Lumbres area. 1/Auckland billeted in Quesques, a charming little village nestling at the foot of high hills. 2/Auckland occupied the two small hamlets of Fromentelles and Harlettes, which, although somewhat deficient in estaminets for those of a bibulous habit, were yet pleasant places enough. 3/Auckland, some kilometres along the road toward Boulogne, were perhaps the most fortunate of all. Their village of Le Waast was not only of considerable size, but was sufficiently close to Boulogne to make an occasional trip to that interesting town quite a possible thing.

Training was commenced at once, and was of a most practical nature. Great stress was laid upon platoon and section tactics, and on the "taking of pill-boxes." Wood-fighting and the counter-attack also received a considerable amount of attention.

For some time there had been a strong rumour to the effect that the Main Body and the first three reinforcements were to be given an extended furlough, for the purpose of visiting New Zealand. At last it seemed that the rumour was about to materialise. Applications were invited, and many of the

The Auckland Regiment

Main Body began to take quite a fresh interest in life. Most of them, naturally enough, rushed the opportunity, being very tired of war, and very eager to get home again. A few, however, refused point blank to consider the proposition until such time as the war was won. However, nothing more was done at that time, and it was many months before the first man got away. On the other hand, leave both to "Blighty" and to Paris was fairly liberal.

The Y.M.C.A. had gradually become one of the main features of the Division. In Armentières it was represented by one man—J. L. Hay, an enthusiast, a tireless worker, and a man of vision. During the Battle of the Somme it flourished in the rest camp near King George's Hill. Throughout the winter of 1916-1917 it extended its activities. How many men of that period have forgotten the hut at Sailly? On the Messines sector the work grew. The N.Z.Y.M.C.A. had a genius for rapid improvisation, for quick moves, and was the most expert agency in France for "souveniring" anything likely to be of use to itself and therefore to the "Diggers." Round the Y.M.C.A. centred the social, intellectual and religious life of the Division. Large marquees were erected at Quesques, Fromentelles and Le Waast, and within a few hours of the arrival of the Battalions activities were in full swing. 2/Auckland were particularly fortunate in having with them Victor French, a member of the Battalion who was "on loan" to the Y.M. He had enlisted, despite a leg injury that many conscripts would have given large sums to possess. From the Fleurbaix raid until after Messines he fought as an infantryman, and then, being no longer able to march or carry equipment, applied for permission to join the Y.M. This was granted, and Vic. rapidly became one of the celebrities of the Division. He was not clothed in fine raiment, nor did he fare sumptuously. His buttons were never known to dazzle the eyes of anyone, and it is very doubtful whether the Grenadier Guards would have regarded him as a desirable acquisition. But Vic. had a heart of gold. Unselfish to a fault, devoted entirely to the business of serving, always cheerful, always on his job, there was no

Ypres

one quite so enthusiastically whole-hearted as he, no one with the same infectious quality of brotherhood.

During the period of training in the Lumbres area the New Zealand Division had the honour of being reviewed by Field-Marshal Sir Douglas Haig. The review took place in a large field outside Fromentelles, and was a most brilliant spectacle. Steel and brass glittered in the sunshine. Platoon by platoon, the Battalions of the 1st, 2nd and 4th Brigades marched past the saluting point. They looked well, and Sir Andrew Russell must have been a proud man as he watched his men go by.

Training finished, and on September 25th the 1st Brigade marched from Lumbres to Renuscure, and then by Wallon-Capel and Wardrecques to the Watou area, where the Battalions billetted for two days.

On October 1st the three Auckland Battalions marched along the crowded highroad from Poperinghe to Vlamertinghe, and so into and through the town of Ypres. Once again there was the thrill of expectation. The broken tower of the ruined Cloth Hall had its appeal, even to the most unimaginative. In its glory of desolation and ruin it typified the splendid valour and steadfastness that had saved Europe. It stood foursquare, battered, but still standing—the wall against which the Old Army had set its back and fought to the death. Now it pointed to the skies and spoke of victory. Ypres was no longer the gate bolted and barred against the invader; it was a wide open way through which poured the rising tide of triumph.

Ypres! The very name is a trumpet call to the man of British race. What heroism was there; what steadfast enduring; what faithfulness unto death; what a terror, and horror, and tragedy of defeat, and yet what a glory, and splendour of victory rising crowned from the ashes of despair. Ypres! What a link this name will be between nation and nation in the great Federation of British peoples. Here died the Old Army, and in dying saved the Allied Cause. Here lie the dead of Canada, Australia, South Africa, New Zealand, and interningled with them everywhere the men of the New Armies. For ever this will be sacred soil.

The Auckland Regiment

Ridge after ridge the wilderness stretched back from St. Julien and Pilkem to Polderhoek and Passchendaele, and from Messines on the one side to the Forest of Houlthurst on the other.

All the beautiful woods were dead, horribly dead. There was no green grass or pleasant herb. The villages were heaps of rubble. The streams that once made glad the smiling valleys were horrible bogs. Over all the wide area no bird sang. For mile after mile shell-hole touched shell-hole, with here and there a great, gaping crater torn by a mine explosion. As far as the eye could see was a wide expanse of dull and dreary brown.

One could hardly follow the line of the old German trenches, so ploughed and torn was all the earth. Line after line their pill-boxes crowned every height, swept every slope, enfiladed every approach. Solidly and with much labour were they built, but frightful was the storm which had burst upon them, rending and smashing the stoutest walls of iron and concrete. Most of them were charnel-houses, from which the garrisons, bombed, or crushed by the falling ruins, had never emerged.

The débris of the battlefield was everywhere; tangled heaps of rusty wire, broken rifles, smashed field guns, rotting pieces of equipment, filthy and torn clothing, empty shell-cases, old tins, riven helmets and all the ruined litter that makes still more hideous the ugly desolation of an old battlefield.

Here and there along some corduroy track leading through the morass is the Via Dolorosa of the horse and the mule. One sees an upturned waggon, then one wheelless, and after that the poor brown carcases, sometimes singly, sometimes in twos and threes, covered with a little earth, quicklime, or altogether uncovered. The tanks look in a pitiful fashion like some huge, terrible uncouth monsters of a prehistoric age, that have had the life blown out of them, or that have been choked in a frightful struggle to flounder through the quaking slough.

Everywhere there is desolation, destruction, and the visible signs of death and decay. On one side of the wilderness are

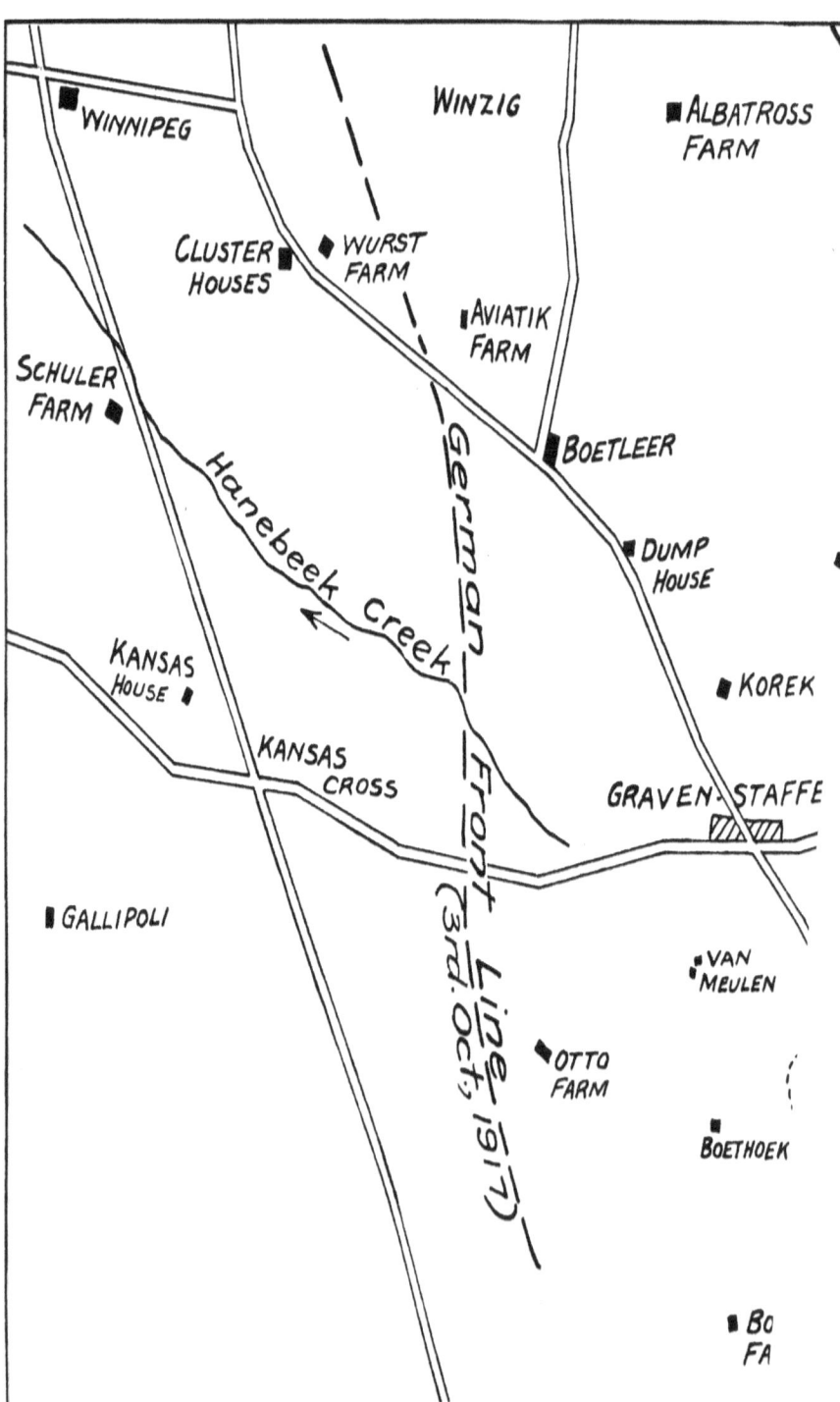

Map

- KRONPRINZ FARM
- YETTA HOUSES
- WOLF FARM
- CALGARRY GRANGE
- PETER PAN
- WATERLOO
- BERLIN
- To PASSCHENDAELE
- BELLEVUE
- BERLIN WOOD
- ABRAHAM HEIGHTS
- BORDEAUX FARM

New Zealand Line (4th Oct. 1917)

Scale of Yards
500 YDS. — 0 — 500 — 1000

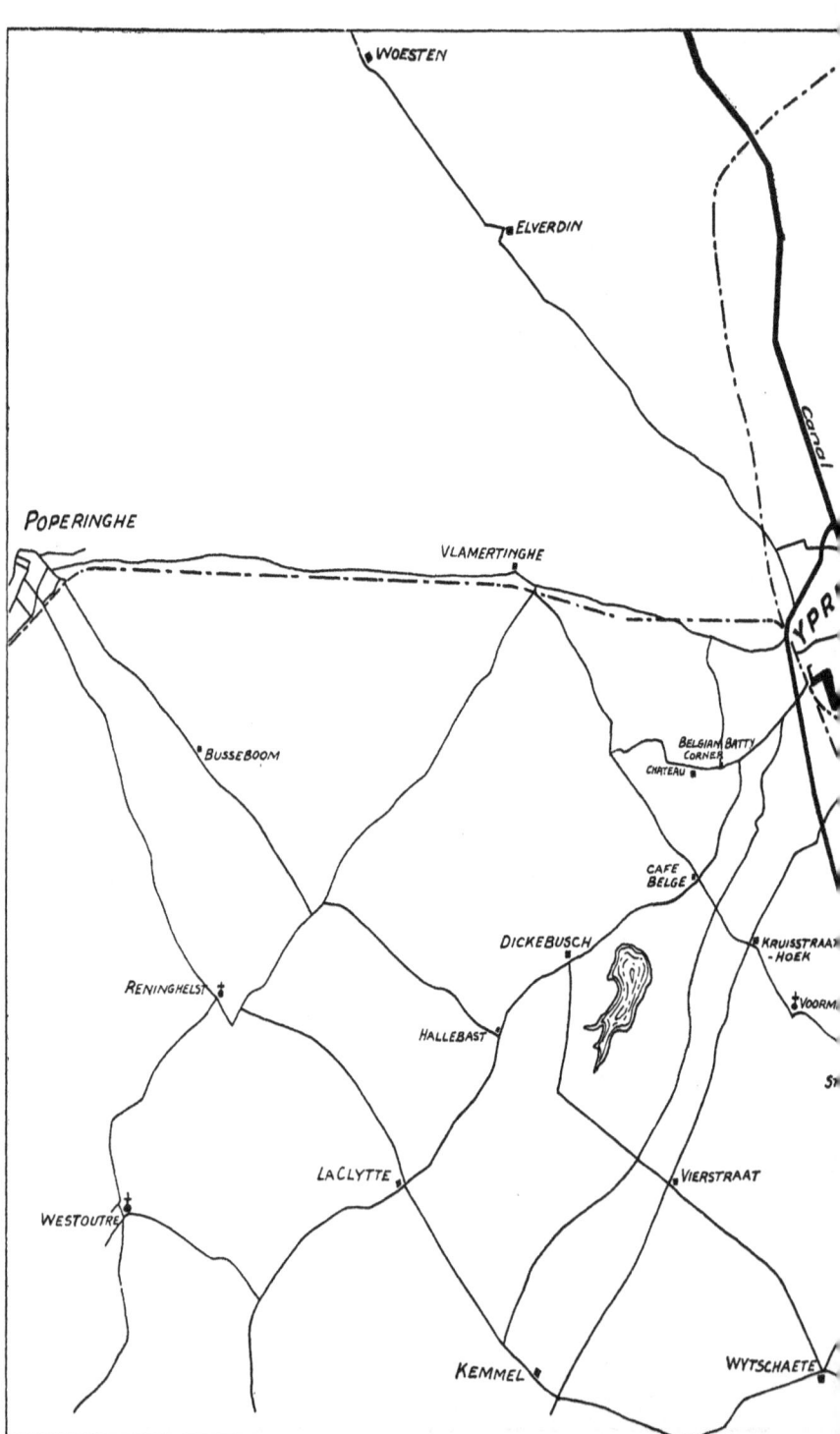

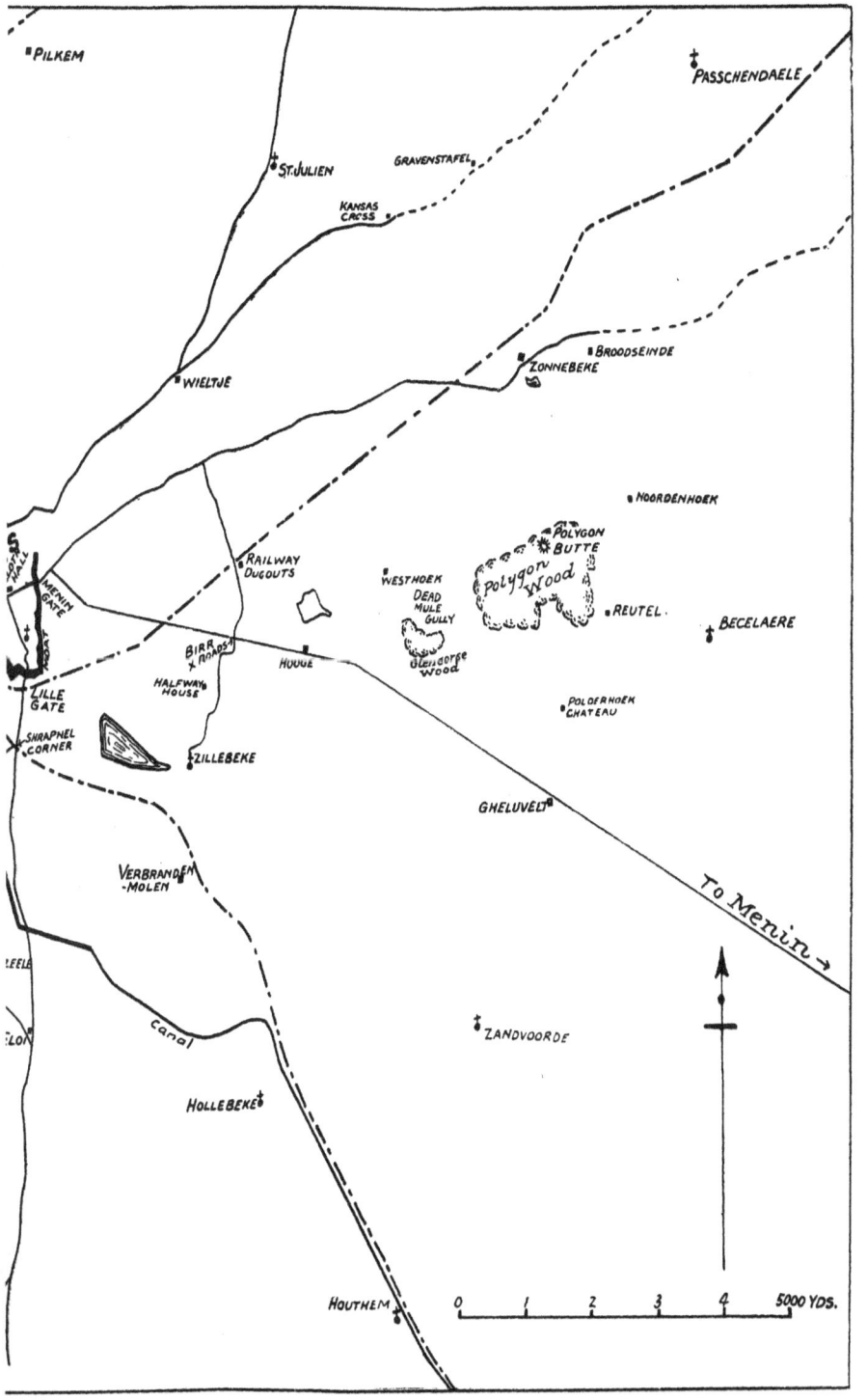

Ypres

the cemeteries of the British; on the other from the Butte of Polygon and beyond those of Germany. On the one side is "Rest in Peace," on the other "Hier Ruht in Gott," but above all is the Common Cross. In the central wilderness itself lie a tangle of the dead of all nations in graves which for the most part no man has marked. Here and there a few have been gathered together, and there is a cross rudely shaped and pencil-marked, or perhaps an upturned rifle or broken helmet to mark the spot. Here lies "Ein unbekant Englander," there "An unknown German soldier."

The battlefield of Ypres! It is a dreadful place, hideously bare of all comfort, with no beautiful, or decent, or pleasant thing anywhere to be seen. It is a field of agony and death. No place on earth has been so desecrated by slaughter, no place, save Calvary, so consecrated by sacrifice.

The succession of low hills stretching back from the town to Passchendaele formed the buttress of the German line in the north. If these were taken the flank of the enemy would be turned, and he would assuredly be driven from the Flanders coast, thus losing the submarine bases of Ostend and Zeebrugge. The matter was urgent. Submarine sinkings were rapidly on the increase. Unless the loss of tonnage was reduced it became increasingly obvious that Germany would win the war. Time was fighting for the enemy. Russia was beaten to the ground, and in a few weeks or months hundreds of thousands of Germans would be transferred to the Western Front. At any price a decision must be quickly reached. So the British Army attacked with all the force it could muster. Once more, as at the Somme, it was a shock battle. During August and September blow after blow had been struck, and ever the final objective was brought nearer. Two things saved the German Army—first the bad weather, and second the 'Pill-box System." There were literally thousands of these concrete forts, which as long as any considerable number of them remained intact, rendered a position impregnable to infantry attack. Before every advance these forts had practially to be blasted to pieces. For this an enormous concentra-

The Auckland Regiment

tion of artillery was necessary. The guns used were mainly heavy howitzers. Roads had to be made to get them into position; light railways constructed to run the heavy shells up to the gun teams. Scores of kite-balloons were flown to observe the movements of the enemy. Aeroplane squadrons buzzed and circled overhead, each one doing its own particular bit. Some bombed the German lines, some observed and sent back wireless messages to the artillery, some guarded the line of balloons, some cruised backward and forward to keep watch that no hostile machine flew over the British lines. Here and there, alone, soaring high, flew a champion of the air ready to swoop down upon his prey or sweep headlong into fight if any valiant man of Germany should fly out to attempt some deed of arms. The organisation of the battlefield was a masterpiece of administrative skill, of ingenuity, of adaptation and of sheer hard work.

Another great battle was at hand, and for the first time since the fight for Sari Bair practically the whole of the Australians and New Zealanders were fighting together. Much had happened since the Peninsula days. In the intervening time New Zealand had become once and for all a nation. No longer was the New Zealander English, Irish, or Scotch. No longer was he even an Australasian. He was a New Zealander, proud of his nationality and passionately proud of the deeds which had given his people a place amongst the free nations of the world. So Australia and New Zealand took their places in the line. The two nations were equally proud of their record; both were resolute, both high-hearted. They claimed, and with reason, that no troops, allied or enemy, could be found to match them. Both were resolved not to be outdone by the other. Rivals in fame, they trusted each other implicitly and trusted fully no other race on earth.

On October 1st, 1/Auckland billeted in the Ypres north area. Lieutenant-Colonel Alderman, C.M.G., who had rejoined after Messines, was in command, with Captain W. P. Gray as adjutant.

The Company Commanders were:—

Ypres

3rd Auckland: Captain Coates, M.C.
6th Hauraki: Captain Holland, M.C.
15th North Auckland: Major Mahan.
16th Waikato: Captain Parry.
Dr. Nelson and Padre Gavin were still with the Battalion. The fighting strength was 20 officers and 660 O.R.'s
2/Auckland bivouacked in the old British line. Lieutenant Porrit was temporarily acting as adjutant. The Company Commanders were:—
3rd Auckland: Captain Taylor.
6th Hauraki: Captain Thomas.
15th North Auckland: Major McClelland.
16th Waikato: Captain Hubbard.
Dr. Addison had been transferred to the Field Ambulance, and his place was taken by Dr. Lee. The Rev. Dobson was chaplain. It is worth mentioning that Lieutenant Tuck acted through the battle as transport officer, the only occasion on which this officer served as a non-combatant. Both he and Lieutenant Stewart were extremely desirous of commanding their respective platoons in the forthcoming action, but after repeated applications were forbidden to do so. Under the circumstances, the best that could be done was for the one to take the Battalion transport, while the other solaced himself with a Brigade carrying party. The strength was 20 officers and 660 O.R.'s.

3/Auckland, also in the old front line area, had a strength of 20 officers and 660 O.R.'s. They were commanded by Lieutenant-Colonel Blair, D.S.O., M.C., with Lieutenant C. Nicholls as adjutant. The companies were commanded by:—
3rd Auckland: Lieutenant H. A. E. Milnes.
6th Hauraki: Captain Dittmer.
15th North Auckland: Captain Evans.
16th Waikato: Captain Gillett.
The chaplain was the Rev. Steele Craik.

Throughout the night and the following day there was desultory shelling, which caused a few casualties, and then on

The Auckland Regiment

the night of the 2nd/3rd, 1st and 3/Auckland moved up and took over the front line.

Two attacks were planned for the New Zealand Division. The first, which was to be undertaken by the 1st and 4th Brigades had the Gravenstafel-Abraham Heights section of the Broodseinde Ridge as its objective. Success in this operation would clear the way for the final assault on the Belle Vue Spur and Passchendaele, which was to be undertaken in part by the 2nd and 3rd Brigades. For the Gravenstafel action the Division was attacking on a four battalion front, and had orders to penetrate the enemy defence for a distance of about 1700 yards. Crossing the Hannebeek Stream, 1/Auckland, 1/Wellington, 3/Otago and 3/Auckland were to take the enemy system of trenches, pill-boxes and strong points as far as the "Red Line," which ran approximately along the crest of the ridge. 2/Wellington, 2/Auckland, 3/Otago and 3/Canterbury were then to "leapfrog" the leading battalions and go forward to the "Blue Line" at the foot of the Belle Vue Spur. On the right flank of the New Zealanders were the Australian Divisions, and on the left British troops.

Throughout the whole of August the German losses had been very serious, and they were now threatened right at the heart. For several days they had been counter-attacking, but had met with little success. Heavy reinforcements arriving, they had prepared a very great attack for the morning of October 4th. Intelligence of this had reached the British Higher Command some time before, giving them the opportunity to anticipate the enemy move.

On the night of October 3rd/4th the battalions of the second wave moved up to their battle-stations, 2/Auckland occupying the shell-hole area of the Canvas-Capricorn system. During the night the weather broke, and a fine drizzling rain commenced to fall. Men huddled together in the shell-holes, without overcoats, shivering under their oilsheets. The enemy artillery fire became very intense, and remained so during the early hours of the morning. Before daybreak all were standing-to in readiness for the barrage to open. At this hour

Ypres

vitality is always at its lowest. Scarcely anyone has slept, all are chilled to the bone. Breakfast has been a few mouthfuls of bully beef, dry bread and water. Officers and N.C.O.'s move round, giving final instructions; the men stand quietly about, waiting with nerves somewhat on edge after the ordeal of the night. Within a few minutes they will be passing through the deepest and most soul-searching experience that men can undergo. Physically they are quite unfit, but when the body would fail the stronger spiritual forces assert themselves, and the spirit triumphs over the frailty of the flesh.

1/Auckland, occupying the ground round Cluster-Houses, were lying very close to the enemy strong points at Winzig and Aviatik Farm, from whence came a considerable volume of machine-gun fire, which caused many casualties throughout the night.

Zero hour was at 6 a.m.—ten minutes before the time fixed by the enemy for their counter-attack, and about a quarter of an hour before dawn. Suddenly the sky was red with leaping flame, and the air was full of the rushing of innumerable shells. The long roll of the drumfire beat out into the morning air, while the sharp rattle of the thousands of machine-guns pierced the duller roar of the cannon.

Between the jumping-off point and the first objectives was the bed of the little brook of Hannebeek. The constant heavy shell fire had turned the running stream into a wide bog, which could be traversed only in certain places by winding paths, along which men could pass very slowly and in single file. Crossing this swamp was a terrible strain, as progress was so very slow. The German shell fire was playing with remarkable accuracy on the narrow tracks. Only the softness of the ground, in which the shells failed to explode or were smothered, saved the attacking troops from very severe losses. Immediately on the other side of the swamp resistance was met with, and then all up the hillside groups of the enemy were found. Some were demoralised and surrendered at once. Others fought desperately. The leading companies of 1/Auckland, the 15th and 16th, had a bitter fight for Winzig. The garrison of this

The Auckland Regiment

strong point were very brave men, and fought with desperate courage. It had been impossible to hide from them the preparations for attack. All night their machine-guns had been active, and as the Aucklanders closed in upon them they rattled in burst after burst of destructive fire. Men went down fast. "Come on, you fellows, follow me!" cried Lieutenant White, as he rushed straight on to the enemy guns. He fell, riddled with bullets. Major Mahan and Captain Parry were killed. But now the flanks, meeting with little opposition, had got round to the side and rear of the German post. Corporal Speakman brought his Lewis gun into play. Lieutenant Lang and his platoon were within bombing range. Captain Coates sent forward men of the 3rd Company to reinforce. The Germans commenced to lose heavily, and their numbers were thinned. From all sides the Aucklanders closed in. Hinchco, Brewer, and many another did gallantly. They rushed in, and Winzig fell. The advance was at once continued under the direction of Captain Coates. On the left flank the British troops had to a certain extent lost direction and touch, thus leaving the Auckland flank exposed to the fire from the entrenched position known as Albatross Farm. Captain Coates swung the 3rd Company into the gap, and then the Red Line having been reached, pressed on along the crest, and finally dug in on the further side of our own barrage. Except for the fight at Winzig, the task had been an easy one, and the casualties were comparatively slight. Battalion Headquarters settled down correctly, but receiving no reports, and seeing no sign of the men sent word back to Brigade that the objectives had been taken, but that only thirty-five men remained— a somewhat disquieting report. The Brigade-Major, Major N. W. B. B. Thoms, D.S.O., M.C., coming up in hot haste to find out if 1/Auckland were actually so much reduced, by carrying out a personal reconnaissance, had little difficulty in finding Captain Coates and the Battalion safely dug in.

Immediately in front of 3/Auckland was the large pill-box known as Otto Farm. This was rushed without difficulty. Fifteen prisoners and four machine-guns were captured. Here

Ypres

fell Lieutenant H. A. E. Milnes, Principal of the Auckland Training College—a man who has left his mark on New Zealand. Crossing the swamp the Battalion very nearly missed the barrage, owing to the hard going across the mud. Boethoek and Bordeaux, on the further slope, were stubbornly defended, but were finally taken, with three more machine-guns. Sergeant Lloyd here distinguished himself. The Van Meulan pillbox, on the crest of the ridge, showed fight. The British barrage was falling all round it. Its left flank was guarded by a machine-gun firing from an open position. Lieutenant Aitken, together with Private Johnson, went out by themselves into the barrage and captured the machine-gun. They then fired into the door of Van Meulan, which a few moments afterwards surrendered. Fifty minutes after zero the Battalion was digging in on the Red Line, where Lieutenant McAdam did excellent work in organising the position.

On the summit of the Gravenstafel Ridge was the strong redoubt of Korek, which was resolutely defended. The machine-gunners, in their concrete shelters, manned their guns, riflemen in shell-holes stood to their weapons. The swing over of 1/Auckland caused a corresponding swing in the direction of 1/Wellington, with the result that certain of these enemy groups, once the barrage had passed over them, were left unmolested until the leading sections of 2/Auckland advanced to go through to the final objective. As the Aucklanders neared Korek they found the conflict still raging fiercely, and were themselves soon fighting.

A section moving forward in file suddenly commenced to lose men from rifle fire. One man lurches forward into a shell-hole, another falls with a cry, clutching at the breast of his tunic, another stumbles to one side and gazes stupidly at a spreading red stain. The remainder take cover. Fifty yards ahead are a file of Huns—their helmets scarcely discernible against the brown background. Rifle fire is opened at once, but it is amazing how many shots miss the mark, even at such an absurdly short range. The morning mist, the battle-smoke, the excitement all have a part in this. One or two of

The Auckland Regiment

the more venturesome walk, crawl or run forward, and by good fortune reach the flank or rear of the enemy. Under fire from two sides the small centre of resistance commences to crumble. The attackers rush in from front and flank, and the Huns, realising the hopelessness of their position, put up their hands and cry for mercy. Sometimes quarter is given; at other times there is only the shriek of agony as the bayonet goes home. There is even some sort of an attempt at justice. The man whose bayonet is red with the blood of men whom he considers to have forfeited their lives by fighting until the last moment is quite solicitous for the safety of others who have obviously taken no active part in the defence of the position.

When fear enters into a man, body, mind and soul, the result is a condition of abject terror distressing to behold. Many of the Germans had been demoralised by the barrage. In the faint dawn light they had seen the waves of assault sweeping forward, overwhelming machine-gun post and strong point. Isolated and almost alone they felt helpless, hopeless and lost. The wave was surging up toward them. They fired a few shots with fingers that trembled on the triggers and hands that shook. Perhaps a couple of hundred yards away a man dropped here and there, but there was no slackening in the steady push forward of the attacking host. Nothing seemed able to stem the resistless tide. No supports were coming from behind. There was still time to run, but in the path to safety thundered the British barrage. Knees weaken and they cannot run, fear becomes terror, and terror panic, and the panic a madness. Men wrap oilsheets round their heads and cower down dumbly expectant of death—they are no longer men but driven cattle. Some are shot, some are bayoneted, some dragged out and half-kindly, half-contemptuously sent back to the rear without escort.

All night the attackers had lain miserably in the drizzling rain, heavily shelled, cold and sleepless. Vitality went low. As the barrage opened they moved forward. At once there was a transformation, a glow of feeling as the immensity of

Lieutenant Colonel D. B. Blair, D.S.O., M.C.

Ypres

the whole thing entered into and lifted up a man's whole being. They pass the swamp and the German barrage—with loss. They encounter the first opposition, and see comrades killed and wounded. Rage enters in—a cold, silent, terrible rage. Men stalk on up the torn hillside, conscious of danger, but disdainful of it. They feel their strength is that of ten, and that their advance is inevitable and resistless—and it is so. There is a great exaltation of soul and a wonderful consciousness of power. So Hector must have felt when the Trojans stormed the Grecian Wall and carried fire and storm through the camp and to the ships. In some the elemental blood-lust comes to the surface, and they kill the enemy who bravely resist, they kill the prisoners whose surrender they have accepted, they kill the wounded lying helplessly in the shell-holes. One man boasted after the battle that he had killed no less than twenty of the enemy, most of them wounded and prisoners. Others coldly and terribly do their duty, killing if necessary, but showing mercy if it be possible. Others again fight with cheerful good humour, shooting Huns as if they were taking wickets. Some fight for glory, some that a woman back in New Zealand may perchance feel a thrill of pride for some deed done this day, but most because the task is there and it is their duty to do it. In the hour of advance and victory the spirit of the brave is always the infectious spirit. Cowards and weaklings are swept away by the bravery that is in the very air.

2/Auckland and 2/Wellington went over the crest and advanced to the Blue Line. Calgary Grange, at the foot of the hill, was taken by a Wellington sergeant and an Auckland corporal, who went through the barrage and bombed the pillbox from the rear, taking a machine-gun and a number of prisoners. One of the stiffest fights of the day was that of the 15th Company for a strongly-held trench at the foot of the hill, and right on the Blue Line. They had nearly five hundred yards of shell-hole country to cross under rifle fire. Many men had become scattered in the small combats here and there, and when a hundred yards from the Hun line the

The Auckland Regiment

attack had to be pushed home there were only some forty still left. The barrage had passed on. They were in the open— the Huns in a good trench. Nevertheless the 15th pressed doggedly on, outnumbered four to one, losing heavily, but still going forward, led by Lieutenant Ellis, Sergeant Balle and Corporals Maynard and Faithful. It was an impossible task, and if the Germans had kept their nerve, every one of the attacking party would have been shot down, and with the bare hillside before them the enemy could have developed a local counter-attack, which might well have crumpled up the New Zealand forward line. As it was their nerve failed at the critical moment, and they surrendered.

Colonel Allen—"Old Steve" nowadays—was not much given to waiting at headquarters for reports to come in. Like a wise commander, he knew perfectly well that nothing can replace personal observation and direction. So with a single runner he went forward to the most advanced part of the line. Here he was blown up by the burst of one of our own shells. "Got him at last, have they?" was the general remark, as his stretcher was carried back. Fortunately for the Battalion, he was not hit until the success of the operation had been assured.

The battle was won. It had been a clean sweeping success, and the enemy were for the time being utterly broken, so much so that if fresh troops had been immediately pushed to the front they would probably have had little difficulty in taking Belle Vue Spur. As it was, consolidation was commenced and the position made secure. The enemy artillery were active, but they were unable to concentrate men for an effective counter-attack. Next day there was more heavy shelling, and the men suffered considerable discomfort in the newly dug and muddy trenches. During the night of the 5/6th the Battalions were relieved and went back, 1/Auckland to Salvation Corner and the 2nd and 3rd Battalions to Gold-fish Chateau.

Considering the magnitude of the success, the losses had not been heavy. They were:—

1/Auckland: Killed, 7 officers, 52 O.R.'s; wounded, 4 officers, 185 O.R.'s; missing, 29 O.R.'s. Total, 273.

Ypres

2/Auckland: Killed, 2 officers, 39 O.R.'s; wounded, 14 officers, 165 O.R.'s; missing, 40 O.R.'s. Total, 260

3/Auckland: Killed, 4 officers, 33 O.R.'s; wounded, 5 officers, 124 O.R.'s; missing, 6 O.R.'s. Total 178.

Padre Gavin once more earned great praise for his devoted work. The purity and earnestness of this quiet, selfless man had won for him a high place in the hearts of all. He buried the dead, British and German, in the same grave, often dug with his own hands. No matter how heavy the shelling he stood by the graveside with bared head and repeated his service, omitting nothing and hastening nothing, but reciting the words of hope with a reverence and feeling that touched even the roughest men. They stood beside him, their heads also bared, while the shrapnel burst near by and the splinters whizzed through the air. If one asks those men to-day about Padre Gavin they will probably first declare with oaths that they themselves are not religious, but—this with a certain enthusiasm—that religion of the type of the padre's they reverence. The battlefield is a hard, cruel and terrible place, and on it the finest traits of character are often crushed and soiled, but the battlefield, no less than the cloister, has its saints, and the perfect flowers of faith grow sometimes in their utmost beauty on the fields red with blood.

The next few days passed quietly enough for the 1st and 4th Brigades in the reserve area. The Battalions rested, reorganised, and did a certain amount of work, while the 2nd and 3rd Brigades held the line in readiness for the final assault on Passchendaele. Preparations were hurried on for the attack. The weather broke, rain fell, and in a few hours the battlefield was a morass. It was almost impossible to get guns forward. By almost superhuman effort field pieces were got sufficiently close, but it was out of the question to move forward the heavies. The artillery had not cut the wire and had not smashed the pill-box system of Belle Vue Spur. They could not promise a barrage. Nevertheless, the Higher Command insisted that the attack should go forward on October 2th. It was a pure gamble on whether the Germans would

The Auckland Regiment

keep their nerve and fight or whether their nerve would break and they would surrender. The Staff had every reason to believe that the enemy were demoralised. It was a problem in psychology.

Once more in the cold dawn the guns opened, but this time the thunder roll was absent. At the first discharge many of them slipped from the small patch of firm ground on which they had been placed and stuck fast in the mud. Few batteries had half their guns working at any one time. Poor as the barrage was the infantry could not keep with it. They had six hundred yards of bog to cross before they reached the slope and their first objective. This bog was a mass of shell-holes, with craters six, eight and twelve feet deep. These craters were full of water. The advancing men floundered along the edges knee-deep, sometimes waist-deep, in mud. German machine-gunners, secure in their undamaged works, looked out, and seeing the opportunity, took heart of grace. They swung their guns with terrible effect on to the struggling men in the black slough. Men slipped, fell and were drowned in the brimming craters, dragged down by the weight of their equipment. Machine-gun bullets claimed their victims by scores and hundreds, yet the stubborn battalions pressed on over the swamp until the survivors were held up by the uncut wire. This could not be passed, and all the while the death hail rained upon them from the pill-boxes. With desperate valour men worked forward into the wire, and tried to cut a way through for their comrades. They were shot down. The Huns kept their nerve, and the result was the inevitable massacre. For the first time New Zealand Brigades had completely failed, and their defeat had cost them as tragic a price as the barren victory on the blood-stained slopes of Sari Bair.

As soon as possible the shattered battalions were relieved. On October 16th, 1/Auckland relieved 2/Otago in the support position, and 2/ Auckland moved up in reserve. 3/Auckland had already, on the night of the 14/15th, relieved the two forward battalions of the Rifle Brigade. Three days later the 1/Battalion took over the left sector with Battalion Headquar-

Ypres

ters at Krönprinz Farm, the 2/Battalion came up in support, while the 3/Battalion were relieved and went back to the old British front line, from where, on the 22nd, they entrained. Canadian Divisions were on their way to take over from the Australians and New Zealanders. The relief took place the night of the 23rd-24th, and the Battalions moved back to bivouacs in the St. Jean area, where they were heavily bombed by German aeroplanes. The next day, entraining at Ypres and Dickebusch, they proceeded to Wizernes, and from there to the villages of the Lumbres training area—1/Auckland to Coulomby and 2/Auckland to Senningham. 3/Auckland had already settled down at Alquines.

Training, reorganisation and re-equipping were immediately proceeded with. The weather was damp, drizzling, and not at all pleasant. Winter was definitely setting in, and the season for great battles closed down.

XXIV

The Winter in the Salient

On 11th November 3/Auckland marched to Esquerdes, and from there to Wizernes, from where they went by train to Poperinghe. After staying a night in Forrester Camp, and another in the Railway Dug-outs, Zillebeeke, they went into the line in the Nordenhoek sector beyond Polygon Wood on the 14th. The 1/Brigade detrained at Hopoutre on the 15th and proceeded to Mic-mac Camp. The Divisional area stretched back over miles of the dreadful battlefield, from the Polderhoek Chateau to the ruined town of Ypres and the village of Dickebusch. An ugly dreariness was the prevailing feature. The outlook was sordid and revolting. Skies were grey, and the damp mists hung low. Everywhere was a sea of mud. The whole atmosphere was dispiriting and distressing. Men lived in comfortless iron huts, in old gun-pits rotting with age, grimed with smoke and swarming with rats, and, further up toward the line, in the captured German pill-boxes. Few of these had escaped altogether. Even where the walls and roof were secure the foundations had been cracked, and the water was rising. Often beneath the floorboards were horrors unmentionable, and the stench rising was sickening. Yet these fearful dungeons where the German machine-gunners had fought, died, and after that been buried were the only shelters in the wide muck of desolation. Men lived in them, and so utter was their need that these horrible places were looked upon as homes.

There is a limit to human endurance, and during the winter of 1917-1918 this limit was very nearly reached. At no other time was the morale of the British Army so low. At

The Winter in the Salient

no time was the war so nearly lost. It is impossible to fight once the will to victory has gone, and during this winter hope and faith in the final triumph almost died away. The terrible disaster before Passchendaele, and the fearful price which had finally to be paid for it, had disheartened so many. Then, too, it was obvious that, despite the tactical success, the strategic objective had not been reached. The German submarine campaign was being only too successful. Russia was disorganised and helpless. She was compelled to conclude a humiliating peace, which set free hundreds of thousands of German troops for the Western Front. The Italians met with frightful disaster. The Battle of Cambrai, so brilliantly successful in its earlier stages, closed badly after a heavy sacrifice of life. After three years of war men everywhere were sick of the slaughter, home-sick, weary, worn out with the labour, disgusted with the sordidness and the naked, dirty horror of the bloody business. Victory seemed as far off as ever. Mentally, morally, physically, the ordinary man was done. Many talked of a drawn fight, some even despaired of that. Nevertheless, even in the Ypres salient there were men whose resolution no hardship or danger could shake. These men were the prophets and apostles of victory. Mud, filth, ugliness and the comfortless desolation of the wilderness could not sour them; they smiled and kept their poise; defeat could not discourage them, they looked forward only to victory; opposing numbers, swelling daily, did not daunt them. High of hope, strong in faith, death had no terrors for men like these. It was nothing to these men if they died, if all the men of their race and time died, if by that sacrifice there might be a dawn of hope. In the blackness of despair they kept the flame burning, a flame which in the months to come was to blaze up into a great light, chasing far the shadows and the darkness. These men won a victory which no historian will relate, but a victory the hardest won of all, and which alone made possible the final triumph. Some were generals, some officers, some N.C.O.'s, some privates in the ranks. Many are dead, and many more maimed. Some have come home. All honour to the great-hearted few who

The Auckland Regiment

endured so stoutly and valiantly when all around was despondency and despair.

3/Auckland, in the line, found that a very great deal of work was required to make it secure and comfortable. They proceeded with this task. On the 21st one of their patrols was broken up by machine-gun fire at close range. Private Campbell earned distinction by carrying a wounded man three hundred yards to safety, although he himself had been hurt. The following evening the Battalion was relieved and went back to Railway Dug-outs and Half-way House, where they remained until December 1st, doing working parties. Proceeding to Howe and then to Walker Camp, they continued to supply working parties until the 14th, when they again went into the line in the Nordenhoek sub-sector. Two days later came the first fall of snow, and with it the frost. For the next two months the battlefield was frost-bound. The shell-holes had six inches of ice on top, and the landscape was white as the flakes came drifting down. The British artillery fire was still intense, and the enemy suffered considerably. One day two of them surrendered themselves, and the following day one more came in. On the 22nd the Battalion was relieved, and went into support at Half-way House and Railway Dugouts, doing working parties.

From here Lieutenant-Colonel Blair, D.S.O., M.C., left for England, and his place was taken by Lieutenant-Colonel A. G. McKenzie, D.S.O., and the Battalion, after a week in support, once more moved up to the front line. Here Lieutenant Lorie, a very able, energetic and brave officer, was killed. On January 2nd the Battalion once more moved back to the support area and then to Dickebusch, from where they entrained each morning and went up by the light railway to tasks at various points in the Corps Area.

The greater part of the sector consisted of land won during the heavy fighting of the previous months. As there was a practical certainty that, with the coming of spring, the heavily-reinforced German armies would take the offensive, very great labour was expended on the organisation of the battlefield and

The Winter in the Salient

the strengthening of the defences. Light and heavy railways were pushed forward, roads were built, both corduroy and metal, miles of duck-boards laid down, trenches strengthened and reserve lines dug, blasted woods and hidden valleys tangled with masses of wire, while the broken pill-boxes were, wherever possible, cleaned out, repaired and made defensible. Beside the work of construction, much salvaging was done. Long before this time the shortage of raw materials had become very acute, and the greatest economy was practised. Even horseshoe nails and scraps of rubber were picked up from the road, while great dumps of spoil were accumulated from the battlefield itself.

A few days after their arrival in the area 1st and 2/Auckland detached 600 men each for working parties. These men took up their quarters near Belgian Chateau in old gun-pits, tents, huts and dug-outs, while the remainder went back with the Battalion Headquarters to Hoograaf, where schools were established for the purpose of giving refresher courses in all specialist departments of infantry work. "Working parties" and "schools" were the main features of the winter.

An hour before dawn the Company Sergeant-Major would be up and stirring the working party for the day out of bunk. No easy job this, for the old gun-pits were snug and warm, and outside was very cold and bleak. Human nature always has a tendency to turn over on the other side, despite sergeant-majors. At length, by threats, persuasion and cajolery, but mainly through the smell of bacon and beans, the toilers were mustered in time. Clothed in leather coats, with hands muffled up in big gloves, they stamped up and down on the duck-boards until the light railway train came puffing and rattling along. "All aboard," and so away past Ypres, Birr Cross Roads, and right out on to the battlefield itself. A tramp of two or three kilometres along a corduroy road and duckboard brought the party to the task which might perhaps be the wiring of a little wood. No one is ever in the least enthusiastic over a working party, unless sometimes a very new and conscientious officer. The rank and file looked upon working

The Auckland Regiment

parties as an unmitigated evil, to be avoided on all possible occasions, by every means. On the job it was not considered good form to make a display of surplus energy. Wire is abominable stuff to handle at any time, especially in the bitter cold, in mud, and amongst tangled débris. It tears clothes, flies up into one's face, cuts and scratches. Gloves save the hands, but make the handling of the wire four times as difficult. Old soldiers make a particular point of not putting out the wire. New hands are inveigled on to this part of the business, while the others do the carrying from the dump, a very much pleasanter business. The "go-slow" policy is frequently in evidence, but the work proceeds—if not apace. Occasional black "coal-boxes" burst overhead, causing much disturbance, but doing little damage, and sometimes a Fritz battery becomes active and causes a temporary scatter. On a working party very brave men suddenly discover the dangers of shell fire, and urge a retreat for the day, particularly if a new officer shows signs of caution. Most companies endeavour to keep enough rum in store to provide an issue when men are actually on their tasks. At about half-time the rum jar, accompanied by an officer and the senior N.C.O., goes the rounds and instils fresh energy into the workers, who, thus refreshed, carry on until about mid-day, when work finishes and the party moves off in the direction of home. A few of the most energetic set out to walk all the way back to the camp. Some fortunate ones catch an early train, the majority, in groups of half a dozen or so, make along the duckboards to "Hellfire" and the Y.M.C.A. "buckshee" show at that point. Great care is taken to salvage any wood lying about for the brazier fires. The train rattles in, and there is a hurried rush from the "buckshee" show, a bundling on board of the spoil, and somewhere about two o'clock Belgian Château is reached. There is a clatter on the duckboards as the workers push into the huts and gun-pits. Gear is thrown off, and everyone is free for the remainder of the afternoon. Many go off to the "Y.M." Hut at Howe Camp for afternoon tea, a talk, and a smoke. Before dark and dinner time all are back. The braz-

The Winter in the Salient

iers are glowing redly in the bivvies, and hungry men are rattling dixies, waiting for the mess orderlies' call. "Come on, there, tumble out!" and at once there is a joyous scramble to be first in the line. "What is she, to-night? How's it holding? Any chance of coming the double? What about some spuds? Go on, push on, there—you've got your issue." And so the jostling, good-natured crowd are quickly served. After dinner men settle down for the evening. One, a black and white artist of some parts, works busily by the light of a guttering candle, touching up a sketch of the "Crucifix of Polygon," near where he has been working for the last few days. It is a drawing, somewhat crude in execution, but full of power because of its utter realism and its accurate, detailed portrayal of the ugliness, the horror, the sadness and the underlying hope of better things that in dim and obscure fashion lies underneath the terror of the present. Others lie round reading all sorts of literature. The Continental Edition of the *Daily Mail* has come up with the rations. It is read eagerly and believed—with reservations. One or two are not ashamed to be seen reading the little pocket Testament—the last gift of some proud, sorrowful, loving mother. One man is openly reading the *Labour Leader* or George Lansbury's *Herald*. In the Ypres salient it is refreshing to know that ideals have not utterly perished from the earth—the *Daily Mail* notwithstanding. Novels are in great demand, and it is a poor author who cannot get a reading. A couple are wrestling with a pocket set of chess, many are playing cards, some are writing letters, while the remainder sit around the brazier and talk of many things. Some time during the evening an N.C.O. comes in with "orders" for the next day—and the rum issue. The "orders" are listened to with attention, containing as they do the names of the working parties for the next day, while the rum is received with joy and drunk with eagerness. There is nothing now to wait up for. The brazier is smoking abominably, and everyone's eyes are full of smoke. Outside it is freezing hard, and if for more than a moment or two the crazy doors are opened the cold night air rushes in, and

The Auckland Regiment

the pleasant heat vanishes as if by magic. One by one everyone curls up on the wire bunks, or on the floor, wrapped up in all available garments, for before morning and the Sergeant-Major's call the cold will be very intense. By nine o'clock all are fast asleep. Gradually the red flames from the brazier die down. The black shadows fall everywhere, and one more day of the war has passed.

All not employed on working parties were despatched to schools, either the Battalion schools at Hoograaf or the Brigade N.C.O. school at Berthen, close to the Mont des Cats. The 1/Brigade school was commanded by Lieutenant-Colonel Alderman, C.M.G., and was conducted with great efficiency. It provided a refresher course in all departments of infantry work, bombing, musketry, Lewis gun, bayonet fighting, wiring, gas, map reading, platoon and section tactics, drill and recreational training. Expert officers and N.C.O.'s were in charge of all branches of the work. R.S.M. "Bill" Bates, of 1/Auckland, the chief drill instructor, soon became one of the celebrities of the school. Without doubt, he was the most amazing drill instructor the Regiment ever had. He could abuse you horribly and profanely without causing the least feeling of bitterness. His sense of humour was exceptionally keen, but those who were the most frequent targets for his satire often liked him the most. Sergeant-Major Taylor, of the Imperial Forces, was attached for physical training and bayonet fighting. "Round-me-nip" was a rather brilliant graduate of London University, and a geologist of some standing, who, owing to the loss of one eye, was refused as unfit for actual fighting service. Having always taken a keen interest in physical culture, he had been drafted into this department, and attached to the 1/N.Z.I.B. He was an exceptionally efficient instructor, and rapidly became very popular. The snow lay thickly on the hard ground, and the man who kept his men moving was held in the highest esteem. Six hours a day, with an occasional lecture in the evening by the C.O., and Saturday half-holiday was the routine of work. There are all sorts of soldiers. Some of the best fighting men are also exception-

The Winter in the Salient

ally keen on the parade ground. One has only to think of men like Sergeant Faithful; while others, Prendergast, for instance, an unmatched fighter, abhorred all endeavours to make soldiers of them. Many a man, who in a hot corner would not hesitate to assume command of a platoon or company over the heads of all sorts of superior officers, showed a strange diffidence in calling a section of eight men to attention. Another man, who in the line was scrupulously careful about the care of bombs, S.A.A., and the posting of sentries, came on to parade with his puttees falling off, two buttons undone, and made a really foolish showing when it came to mounting a main guard with full pomp and circumstance. Some men loathe schools, others like them; some grow homesick for their battalions, others would be content to stay at school for the duration of the war. The trench failure is always ready for a school, because for one thing it is safe, and for another he has the opportunity to reassert himself. On the other hand, the best type of fighting man, however much he may appreciate a good refresher course, is never desirous of a long stay away from his unit.

Christmas Day passed happily enough. A general holiday was declared for all those on working parties and at schools. There was plenty to eat and drink, Christmas mail, and any quantity of "buckshee" parcels sent by the Women's Patriotic Society were eagerly and gratefully received.

On January 18th, 1st and 2/Auckland concentrated as full battalions at Dickebusch Huts and Hussar Camp, preparatory to going into the line. The 4/Brigade, relieved by the 1st, went out into Corps Reserve and carried out a similar programme of work and instruction to that just completed by the 1/Brigade, Captain Dittmer taking command of the school which was formed at Ottawa Camp.

On the night of January 20th/21st, 2/Auckland went by train to Birr Cross Roads, and from there along the duckboard track to the Cameron Covert-Polygon Veld sector, immediately in front of the famous Polderhoek Château, against which many assaults had broken down, including one carried

The Auckland Regiment

out by troops of the 2/Brigade. Many dead were lying about —English, Scotch, New Zealand and German. The sector was quiet enough usually, but was extremely uncomfortable, as the melting of the ice and snow had caused the ground to become very wet and muddy. Everyone suffered a great deal, either through standing about in the mud or living in the foul pillboxes, which served as Company or Battalion Headquarters. A certain amount of patrolling was carried out, but otherwise there was little to note. 2/Auckland were relieved on the 26/27th by the 1/Battalion, and went back in support near the Crucifix. The weather was steadily growing warmer, and the ground firmer. Again nothing of consequence took place, and six days later the battalions once more changed over. On the 7th February, 2/Auckland were relieved from the Reutel sector and Dead Mule Gully, and marched back to the infantry barracks at Ypres. The 1st Battalion went in on the Broodseinde sector, where they found the ground high and dry. There was a temporary break in the weather, which for some days was wet and stormy. Four Germans came in one day and gave themselves up to a post of the 15th Company. They had had enough of the British shell fire. Enemy artillery also was active, and maintained a harassing fire on the posts. After a cold night's vigil, or a couple of hours on patrol spent in slithering from one wet shell-hole to another, a nip of rum sets the blood running, and enables a man to get off to sleep. It cheers men immensely, having much the same effect as "two-up," cigarettes, love-letters, mademoiselles and "buckshee" cocoa. Nearly all men drink to some extent, and the little taste of liquor gave great pleasure. Properly controlled, the rum issue was, from the military point of view, wholly beneficial. The trouble came just on that point of "proper control." Relatively large quantities of rum had to pass through the hands of a few men, with the result that the temptation was often too strong, and a Company Headquarters or a few senior N.C.O.'s took out as much as they required for their own purposes before issuing to the men. This meant a certain amount of drunkenness, and in the Army, as in civil-

The Winter in the Salient

ian life, more trouble was caused through drunkenness than through anything else. On this matter, as in many other things, there was far too much tolerance. In war time, when troops are actually in the face of the enemy, the most drastic measures should be adopted to deal with cowardice, inefficiency and drunkenness. For the first two, offenders should be reduced immediately to the ranks. A coward may do excellent service in some administrative capacity away from the front, but there is no place for him even as a lance-corporal in a fighting unit. Only the efficient ones amongst the brave should be promoted to any rank of responsibility, and for men of this sort promotion should be as rapid as possible. The crime of drunkenness when troops are actually in the line should never be considered apart from the rank of the culprit. A drunken private is a nuisance and deserves to be checked, a drunken N.C.O. is a prolific source of trouble and should be reduced, while a drunken officer, being a public danger, should be tried by court-martial, and, if found guilty, shot, no matter what his rank or attainments might be. If a drastic policy of this sort had been adopted from the beginning it is unlikely that more than half-a-dozen shootings would have been required amongst commissioned ranks, and as a direct result of clearer thinking at critical moments many hundreds of valuable lives would have been saved.

February 14th, 1/Auckland were relieved, and came back to Walker Camp, from where on the 23rd they moved to Halifax Camp. 2/Auckland had for some days been billeted in West Farm Camp, near Birr Cross Roads, and both battalions now supplied large working parties for tasks on and about the Corps Line. While here, Colonel "Steve" Allen returned from England, and once more took over command of his battalion. He was very lame as a result of the wound received at Gravenstafel, but by dint of much persistent effort had secured the reluctant consent of the authorities to return to France. The Battalion was as glad to see him back as he was to be once more with them, particularly as heavy fighting was expected to break out almost any day.

The Auckland Regiment

That the enemy would take the offensive was a foregone conclusion; the only question was as to just when and where he would attack in real force. There was a distinct threat against the Ypres salient, and the British artillery was continually active. On at least two occasions the full barrage was thrown out, and once a considerable enemy attack was actually launched on the Reutel sector.

Some time before this, on February 8th, the 4/Brigade was formally disbanded. Many of the officers and men were immediately drafted into other units, while from the remainder the Auckland, Wellington, Canterbury and Otago Working Battalions were formed. Later on these working battalions became the 1st, 2nd and 3rd Entrenching Battalions, under the command of Lieutenant-Colonel Mitchell, D.S.O. They served as reinforcement depôts for the Division, and at the same time were able to do a very great deal of work on reserve positions some distance behind the line.

On March 10th the New Zealand Division moved by train and motor-lorry to the villages round about Cassel, for what was intended to be a month's training. 1/Auckland billeted at Staple, while the 2nd were in the village of Zuytpeene. Billets were good. The spring weather was splendidly fine, and the blue skies, the sunshine and the green fields were such a contrast to the hideous desolation of the Ypres battlefield that men could not but help feeling joy at the change. The French folk were very kind, and after the months in Belgium it was a pleasure to be amongst them again. Training was carried out during the mornings, and the afternoons were devoted to games. Great efforts were made to smarten the men up. Equipment was scrubbed, brass polished, bayonets rubbed with emery paper until they shone and sparkled in the sun, while barrack-square and guard-mounting drill formed a not inconsiderable part of the training programme. By the time General Russell inspected the battalions a wonderful transformation had been wrought. This was important, but not so important as the marked improvement in morale that accompanied it. The Brigade football competition held at this time

Lieutenant Colonel A. G. McKenzie, D.S.O.

The Winter in the Salient

was very keenly contested, 1/Auckland and 1/Wellington winning the preliminary rounds, while the latter battalion won the final.

On the 21st March, 1st and 2/Auckland marched from their billets to Moule, some distance the other side of St. Omer, for the purpose of carrying out musketry practice on the range which had been constructed there. The day was hot and dusty, and the pavé roads very hard on the feet. Two very tired and footsore battalions arrived late in the afternoon at the new billets. Orders were at once issued for the shooting to take place the following morning. There had been rumours during the day of a great enemy attack opening on the Somme. Rumour ran that it had been repulsed with heavy loss to the attackers, who had been mown down by the machine-gun fire. Late in the evening came news of disaster. The 5/Army had broken before the tremendous onrush of the massed German armies, backed as they were by an immense power of artillery. The British line on the Somme was broken and the grey tide, sweeping on over the old battlefield, was surging on toward Amiens to cut the railway communications, isolate the Channel ports and destroy the British Army. The orders already issued were cancelled, and the men warned to be ready for an early start back to the Cassel area—there to join the remainder of the Division, ready for the next move.

XXV

Mailly-Maillet

"Ils ne passeront pas!"
—The French at Verdun.

During the next two days, news of the real magnitude of the disaster commenced to come through. Orders for the Division to entrain for the Somme were received.

1/Auckland, who were at full strength, were commanded by Lieutenant-Colonel W. W. Alderman, C.M.G., with Lieutenant W. P. Gray, M.C., as adjutant. The Company Commanders were:—

3rd Company: Captain Coates, M.C.
6th Company: Captain Alexander.
15th Company: Captain Holland, M.C.
16th Company: Captain H. R. Vercoe.

Dr. Ardagh was still with the Battalion, while the Rev. Grigg had taken the place of Padre Gavin.

2/Auckland, who were also at full strength, were commanded by Lieutenant-Colonel S. S. Allen, D.S.O., with Captain Tuck, M.C., as adjutant. Company Commanders were:—

3rd Company: Captain Paterson.
6th Company. Captain Moncrief.
15th Company: Captain McArthur.
16th Company: Captain McFarland.

The Rev. C. J. Dobson had been with the Battalion ever since the Hill 63 days, and was very well known to all. Dr. Harpur, the R.M.O., on the other hand, had only recently joined up.

On the evening of Sunday, March 24th, the Battalions entrained at Cassel station. The villagers turned out to see the last of their guests, who were in a distinctly hilarious mood, as the result of Saturday having been pay-day.

"Bon soir, mademoiselle, you promenade with me?"

"After de prochaine guerre, per-r-r-aps!"

"Hello, Marie! How's the beer standing?"

Mailly-Maillet

"Allons gourmand! You have drink all de biere—no more left for nex soldat."

"Ah! Madeleine! You embrassez-moi for bonne chance?"

"Brigand! You kiss beaucoup mademoiselles—me write your fiancée—tell her you no good!"

"You plenty zig-zag—too much vin-blanc!"

And under all the merry badinage ran a deeper tone, for after all this was a supreme hour in the agony of France. Who knew what might befall if these men failed to stay the onward rush to Amiens? They were not Frenchmen, but they were the friends of France, and in a few hours they would step into the breach and hold for the sake of France.

"Dieu vous aide, messieurs! Dieu vous garde! Vous combattez pour nous! St. Jeanne d'Arc vous aide."

All night the trains were running down toward the Somme, St. Omer, Etaples and Abbeville, until midway through the morning they reached Hangest-sur-Somme, where the battalions detrained at the little station familiar enough to the men of 1916. A battalion as it arrived dumped its heavier stores and set out at once on foot, or by motor-lorry, for the divisional concentration point, which was somewhere in the general direction of Pont Noyelles. 1/Auckland were fortunate, and caught the motor-lorries, which conveyed them to some distance the other side of Amiens. 2/Auckland set out to march. The day was clear and fine, with a cool breeze blowing, and rapid progress was made. For the first few kilometres the road was unfamiliar, but then, at the foot of a slope, was an estaminet known to not a few, and in half-an-hour's time the companies were taking a brief spell in the market square of Picquigny. Once through the town and marching along the high road toward Amiens, refugees were met with in increasing numbers. Some of them had waggons piled high with their household stuff, some only the clothes they stood up in. All were weary and worn, and many of them very hopeless. Behind them were the little homes they loved so much, and they were moving, where they knew not, hoping only that they might escape the Bosche. The sight of

The Auckland Regiment

these poor folk hardened the resolution of the marching men. The Hun should not pass.

The Battalions bivouacked, 1/Auckland at Dernancourt and 2/Auckland in an orchard close to Breilly. Here final preparations were made. Packs and greatcoats were stored away, and, with fighting gear only, the men were prepared for immediate action. At midnight 2/Auckland were roused from their chilly bivouac and proceeded by motor-lorry through Amiens to Pont Noyelles. From here the last stage of the journey was commenced. Early in the morning the Battalions were moving in the chill dark hours before dawn to Hedauville, near where the Division was being assembled. There was no stay. Dawn came, and then hour after hour the steady tramp, tramp, tramp along the high road ate into the tale of kilometres. There was a short spell for a cold breakfast, and then once more the steady move forward through a countryside that was curiously deserted. One thing only was certain, and that was that where the march stopped there the fighting would begin. Men were desperately tired and footsore, yet scarcely anyone dropped out. Albert was passed some distance on the right hand side. The stronger took a heavier burden upon themselves, carried extra panniers, bags of rations, or took a comrade's rifle, and so the steady march went on. Once the road was blocked by a six-inch howitzer battery that had been retreating for some days. Two or three wandering Scotchmen and Tommies were met with, but no sign of an army or of resistance was seen, until just outside Hedauville, where several tanks of the new "whippet" type were manœuvring. A long-range naval gun outside of the village was firing at intervals. By mid-day two-thirds of the Division had assembled in a large field between Hedauville and Mailly-Maillet, a village some twenty kilometres from Amiens, and about the same distance from Doullens. For an hour there was a welcome spell, during which time final arrangements were made and orders issued. One thing was clear. The New Zealanders had marched straight into the gap that had developed between the 4th and 5th Corps. Somewhere ahead of them were the

Mailly-Maillet

enemy, who had found the weak spot, and were racing desperately to pass through before it should be closed. If they succeeded the fall of Amiens and of Doullens would be almost a certainty. At all costs this gap had to be closed, and closed without an hour's delay. Everyone was in the highest spirits, and fit for anything. No one was in the least daunted by the events of the last few days. The Tommies had broken, but what of that? This was the New Zealand Division going in to save the day. What the Turks had failed to do on Chunuk Bair and Rhododendron, the Huns should not do here on the Somme.

As the Wellington Battalions had not yet arrived, the 1/Brigade was reorganised, and for the time being consisted of the two Auckland Battalions and the 2/N.Z.R.B. The plan of battle was for the 1/Brigade to advance astride of the Mailly-Maillet-Pusieux Road in the direction of Serre, while the 2/Brigade on the right were to go through Auchonvillers, and if possible reach Beaumont-Hamel. Soon after two o'clock the leading battalions were moving off with intervals between the platoons.

The Germans, flushed with victory, had crossed the old battlefield. Their leading troops had been assigned so many kilometres for that day, on the completion of which they were to be withdrawn and rested. Eagerly they pressed on to complete their task. They passed the old German front line, they passed the British line of 1916, and in high spirits set foot on what for four years had been inviolate soil. Amiens was before them—Amiens, which meant victory for the German arms; Amiens, which would give the supremacy of the world and "Deutschland! Deutschland uber alles!" They were not far from the city of their desire. At any moment, as they topped one of the rolling chalk ridges, they might catch a distant glimpse of the spires and belfries of the famous town. For four days their advance had never ceased, and they had met with no serious opposition. Their patrols, advancing boldly, and with no great amount of caution, suddenly encountered the leading sections of the 1/N.Z.R.B. There was

The Auckland Regiment

a shout of alarm, shots, and then a moment's fusilade. The Hun advance guards were driven in, and the riflemen occupied an outpost line in front of Mailly-Maillet, to cover the advance of the 1st and 2/Brigades.

1/Auckland advanced along the Serre road, in threes, with intervals between the platoons. In an orchard just outside the village they passed two English eighteen-pounder guns, which for the last four days had been retiring and fighting all the way. Three hundred yards further on, near the "Windmill," two Hun machine-guns opened fire on the column. The Aucklanders immediately swung half-right and deployed, with the 15th and 16th Companies leading and the left flank just touching on the Serre road. They advanced in artillery formation toward the "apple-trees" and a long hedge, which ran across the front. Here the enemy fire became intense, and at this point casualties commenced to occur. Henry Beery, one of the oldest soldiers with the Battalion, a very brave man, was killed. From the hedge the ground fell away for some little distance, and then, after a small level space, rose again to the Serre Ridge. At the foot of the ridge, and just to the right of the sugar refinery the 16th were checked. Many men had fallen. Lieutenant Swayne, one of the company's most gallant soldiers, was wounded. The machine-gun barrage was too heavy to pass, and so a halt was made in a sunken road, while the men recovered their breath, and ways and means were found to continue the advance. In the meanwhile, the 15th Company, under Captain Holland, had gone well forward. Getting into a tangle of old saps, and led by their Company Commander, Sergeant-Major Rogers, Prendergast and other brave men, they bombed forward, past the chalk pits, through the Bowery and into the enemy positions beyond. Three machine-guns were taken and a number of the enemy, who were fleeing in all directions, were killed. This brought the 15th Company well ahead of the 16th, took off much of the pressure, and opened up the way for a further move. In the meanwhile, Captain Vercoe had worked with great energy to reorganise his men, Captain Coates had pushed up reinforcements from the

Mailly-Maillet

3rd Company, and shortly before dusk everything was ready. The Lewis gunners, coming practically out into the open, engaged the enemy guns and drew nearly all the fire upon themselves. They suffered heavily. Few of them were left, but their purpose was achieved.

From the sunken road to the enemy guns there was only some hundred and twenty yards of open, gentle slope. As darkness commenced to fall, Captain Vercoe gave the signal. "Come on, boys; rush them, rush them!" The Waikatos, and the 3rd Auckland with them, went up the hill in the teeth of the German fire. Lieutenant John Allen led the charge with magnificent courage. Looker, Moffitt and Brewer were amongst the first to break into the German line. The Aucklanders closed in with the cold steel, and in a few moments the Huns were a crowd of panic-stricken fugitives. It was in vain that their officers endeavoured to rally them—a few were taken prisoner, many were killed, and the remainder ran. Night fell as victory was secure. The sugar refinery, on the left of the Serre road, taken by the Rifle Brigade, and set on fire by the German artillery, was burning luridly. It was a wild night. Numbers of the enemy were on the front, and several times they came up against the Auckland posts. Once a number of them were observed to be deploying out on the road ready to counter-attack. Lance-Corporal Bray and another man, going out by themselves, reached the flank of this party and dispersed them with Lewis gun fire.

The Huns made no further attempts to retake this portion of the line, but all next day they bombarded it heavily with minenwerfer and artillery fire. Many casualties occurred, including Lieutenant Allen, who was killed, and Lieutenant Quartley wounded. Throughout the whole of these operations Captain Vercoe's conduct had been most distinguished. He had led his company with great determination and ability, and now he performed one of the coolest and most valiant deeds done by any member of the Regiment throughout the war. Two of his posts were isolated. They had been heavily shelled, and from the main position it was obvious that casualties must

The Auckland Regiment

have occurred. Captain Vercoe left the trench and commenced to walk overland to the post. For a few seconds nothing happened. Then he was observed from the enemy line. They turned a machine-gun upon him. He continued his walk. Two light minenwerfers tore up the ground all round, but he never faltered or even quickened his pace. He reached the post, entered it and found two wounded men. He carried one of them back to safety, and then returned and brought the other in also. The enemy never slackened their fire. The minenwerfer shells repeatedly burst within yards of him, and the smoke and dust of the explosions drifted across his path. Several bullets pierced his clothes, while his puttees were in ribands. It was a magnificent exhibition of coolness and valour.

Captain Coates once more distinguished himself greatly.

2/Auckland, in reserve during the attack, settled down on the outskirts of the village, expecting to stay there the night. They saw the wounded and prisoners go through, and then salvaged the deserted houses for anything that would make the cold of the night more tolerable. Blankets, scraps of canvas, odds and ends of female raiment, were requisitioned, and everyone lay down to sleep in fair comfort. Hardly, however, were all settled than orders came for the Battalion to move up as far as the "apple-trees," preparatory to relieving the 2/N.Z.R.B. On completion of the move, there was a long wait in the bitter cold. Groups here and there huddled up under their oil-sheets, and endeavoured to get a little sleep. Tired as they were it was too cold, and before long nearly all were stamping about in a vain endeavour to keep warm. At last, in the early hours of the morning, the relief took place, the 15th and 16th Companies taking over the front posts, which had been established in the old communication trenches which ran from the Hébuterne road to the old front line, now held by the enemy. On the right of the Serre road, 1/Auckland had reached the rim of the saucer-shaped valley which stretched from Beaumont-Hamel to Hébuterne, Rossignol Wood and Puisieux. Their observation was good, and as the ground commenced to fall away almost immediately in front

Mailly-Maillet

of them their position was a strong one. From one post on the extreme right of 2/Auckland it was possible to observe for a considerable distance along the Serre road and across the valley to the long slope on the other side. Further over, however, the ground rose slightly, and the enemy line was everywhere slightly higher. The long hedge running in front of La Signy Farm effectually screened all movements on the part of the enemy, and enabled them to muster unobserved for their attacks on the posts.

Dawn came, and in the first faint light the Huns were seen streaming across the Serre road into their front trench without apparently the least attempt at concealment. They were evidently an assault battalion that had been used to easy victories, light casualties and every consideration from their opponents.

"Look at the b—— b——s coming up the road!" In a trice men were up on the fire-step, and it was not long before the road was clear. To reach their position a number of the Huns were compelled to cross the road in full view of the Auckland snipers. When they could no longer walk over with their hands in their pockets they tried running and crawling, with not much greater success. For two or three hours the shooting was good, and the Aucklanders enjoyed themselves immensely. So great was their ascendancy that although the Hun line was packed with men, scarcely a shot came from them all the morning, while the Aucklanders, right up on their parapet, showed themselves freely, and shot at anything, adding insult to injury by shooting the enemy with captured Mauser rifles.

By the middle of the morning the Huns had completed their preparations for attack. Their machine-guns and trench mortars opened up a heavy and continuous fire, to which it was not possible to make any effective reply, while the artillery that they had rapidly pushed forward barraged behind Battalion Headquarters and made things particularly lively round about the sugar refinery and Euston Dump. Down the old communication saps, that led from one line to another, the

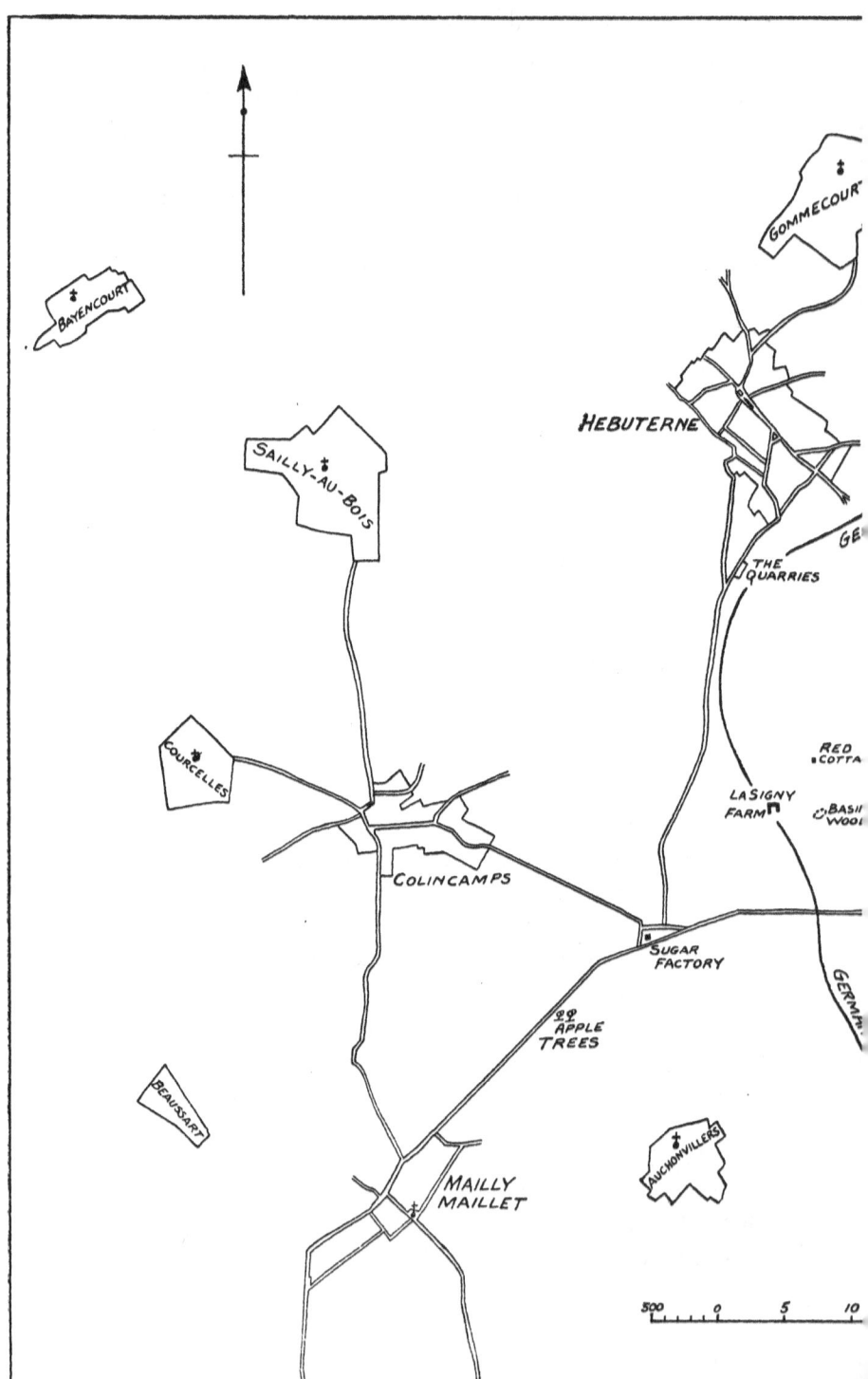

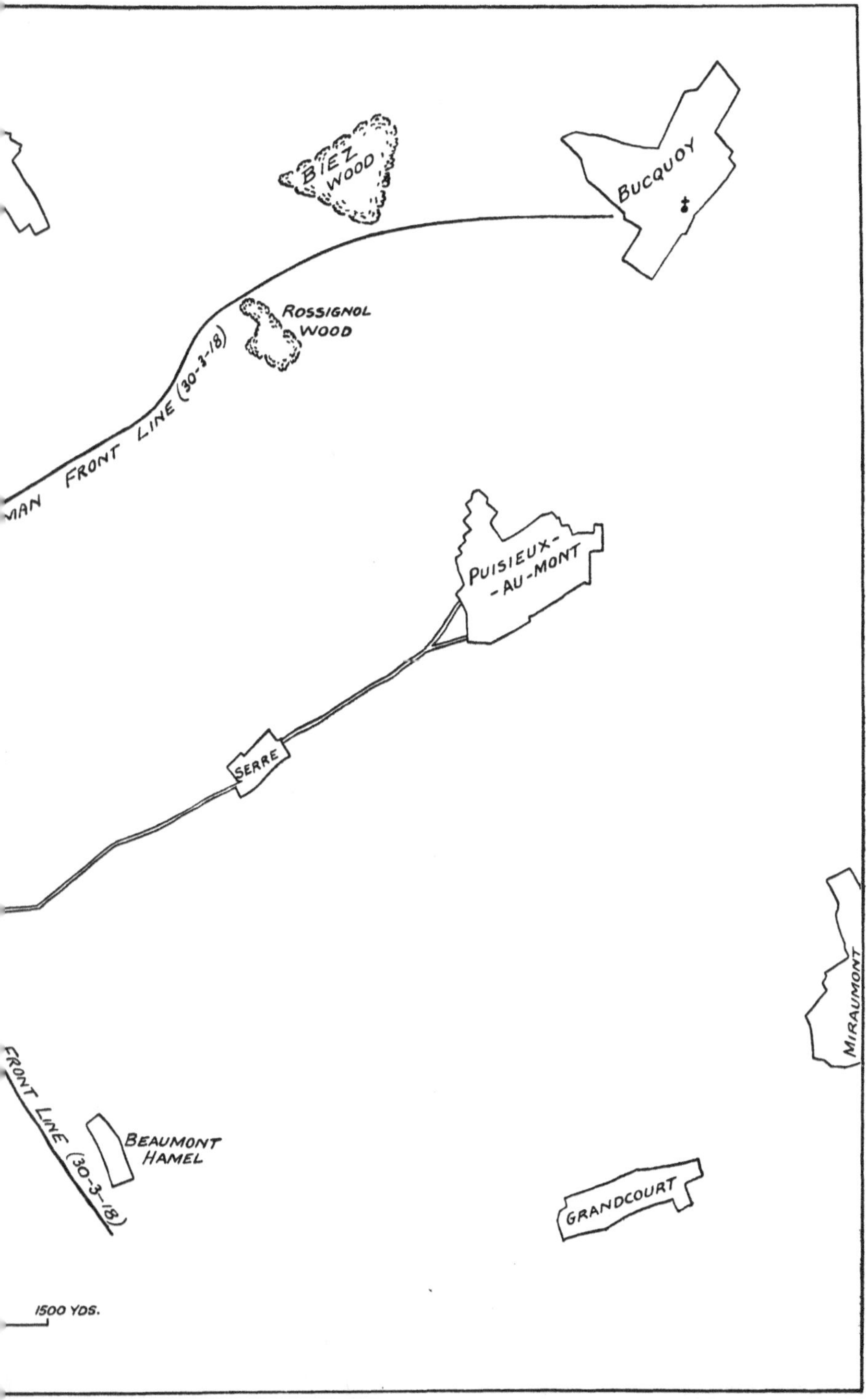

BIEZ WOOD

BUCQUOY

GERMAN FRONT LINE (30-3-18)

ROSSIGNOL WOOD

PUISIEUX-AU-MONT

SERRE

MIRAUMONT

FRONT LINE (30-3-18)

BEAUMONT HAMEL

GRANDCOURT

1500 YDS.

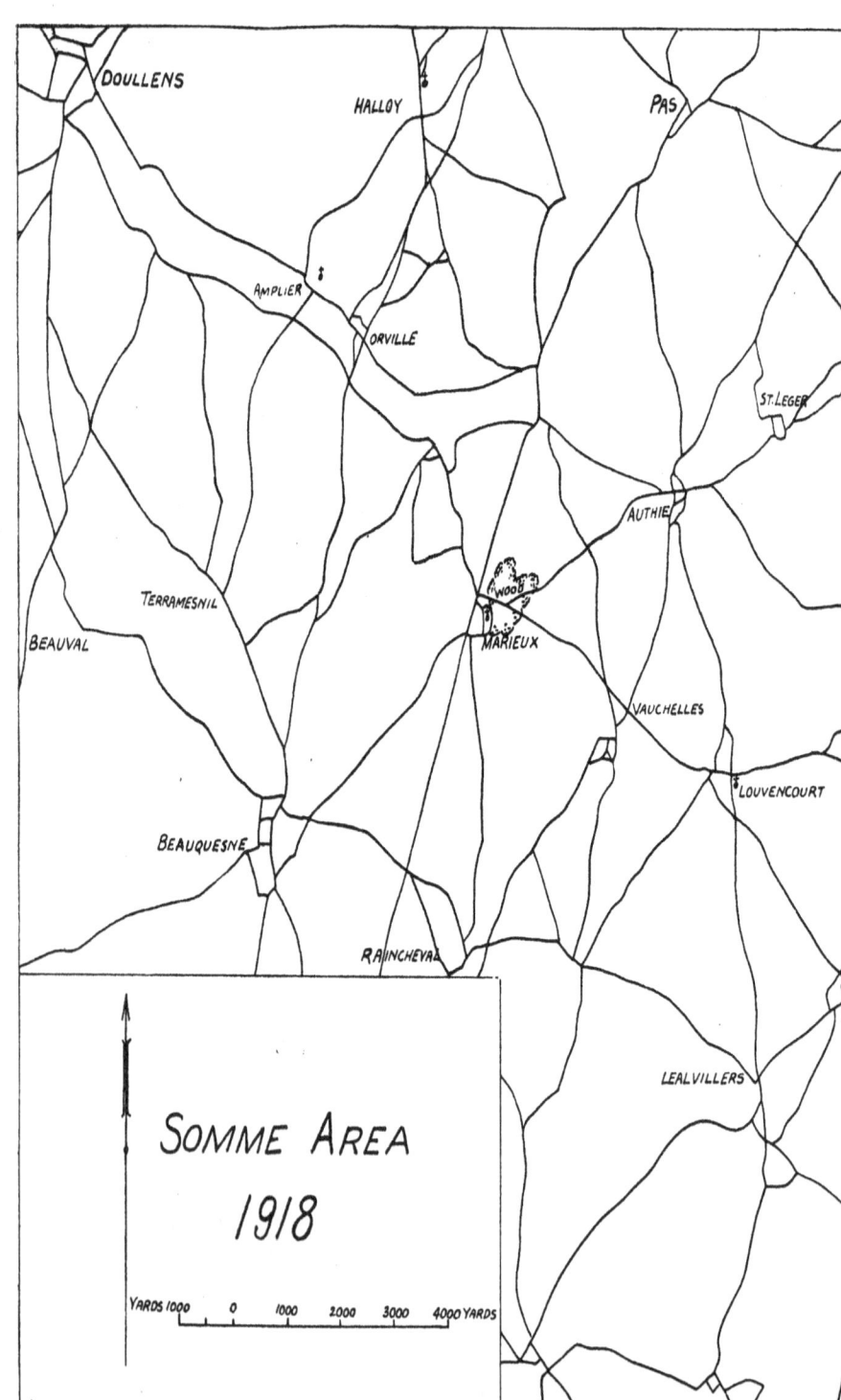

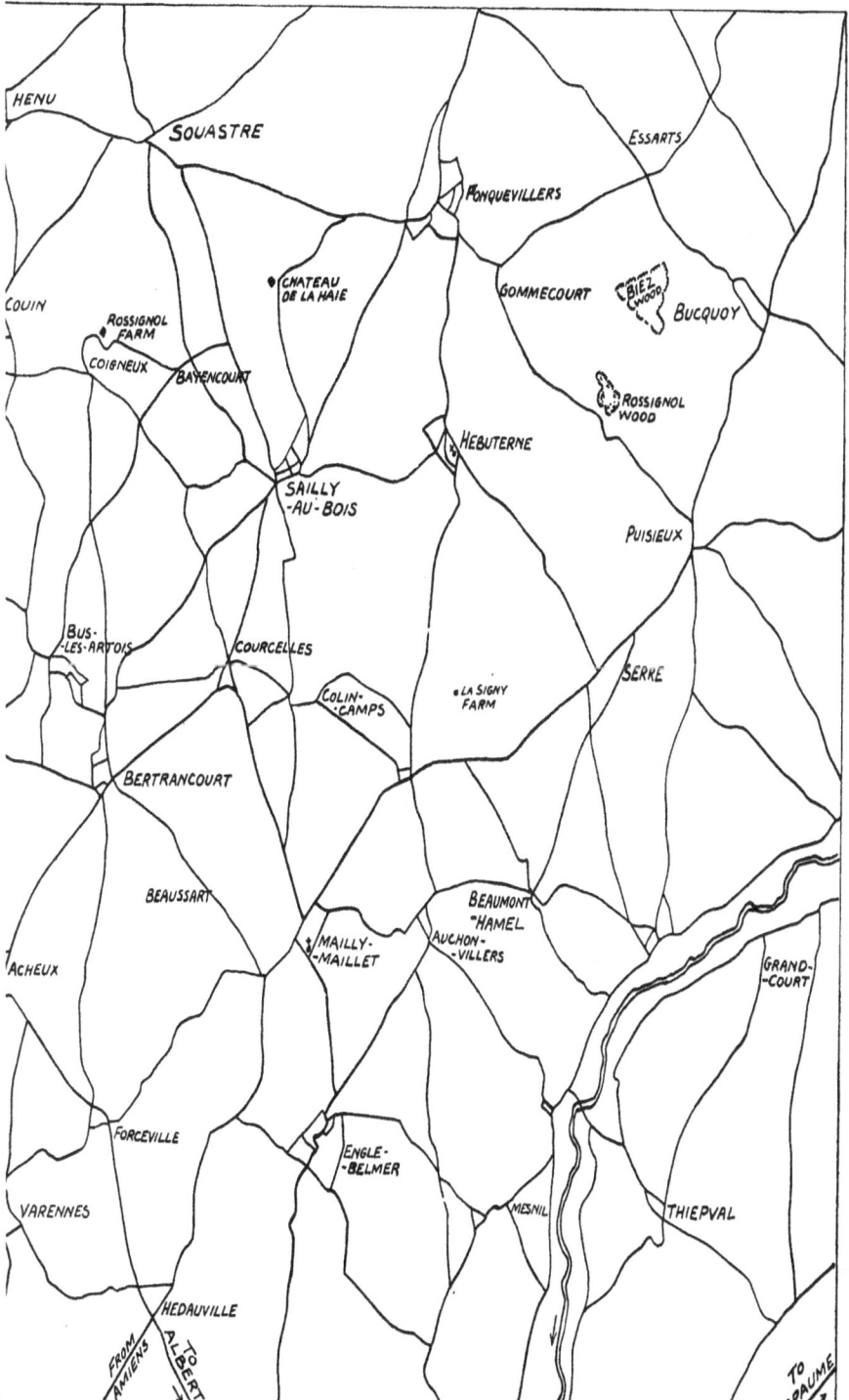

The Auckland Regiment

Huns developed their attack by the "infiltration" method mainly. They did not rush large bodies of men across the open, but coolly, scientifically and with determination they worked forward, taking every scrap of cover, bombing down saps and seeking for weak spots which they could overwhelm, or empty and unguarded places through which they could enter, and by flanking movements gain what they could not get by direct frontal assault. 2/Auckland were at a tremendous disadvantage in having no bombs. The Huns were plentifully supplied. They crept up to within a few yards of the posts, and from there bombed in perfect security, while the men in the posts were helpless to retaliate. They were too few to sally out and counter-attack. All they could do was to endure and hang on, and with rifle and bayonet stop the rushes which every now and again were made against them.

A Hun scout peers round the traverse. It is a moment before he can focus his gaze, and in that moment a rifle has been aimed and fired. He drops forward, dead, but so suddenly smitten that the half-smile is still upon his face. His comrades are close behind, and in a moment the air is full of the stick-bombs. Some are caught and hurled back before they explode, others burst and scatter splinters all round. A wounded man staggers out and is dragged away by the stretcher-bearers, while the remainder of the little post, huddled up against the bank, so as to obtain all the shelter available, await the sudden rush. It comes, but the rifles are ready, and the foremost Huns fall dead. The remainder draw back, and once more commence to bomb. All through the afternoon they were alternately rushing and bombing, while their machine-gun and trench mortar fire never slackened. Captain McArthur, who had been a great inspiration to his men, fighting in the front line with them, fell mortally wounded. Other officers and many men were down, but on the right, Sergeant Faithful dominated the situation, and not a Hun got in, nor was an inch of ground lost.

On the left of the 15th Company the bombs came raining into the trench, and, despite the fact that no casualties had

Mailly-Maillet

occurred, a new officer commenced to withdraw his platoon. It was a critical moment. The whole army was depending on the New Zealand Division to hold its ground. 2/Auckland were holding the most delicate portion of the divisional front, and the left post of the 15th Company was the key to the whole position. Captain Tuck, from Battalion Headquarters, saw the retirement, and dashing out intercepted the retreating men and ordered them back. He was obeyed, and with Sergeant Yorke at the head, they rushed back and retook the trench, into which the enemy had already penetrated. Shortly afterwards Lieutenant Harrison took charge of this part of the line, and under his direction the post was defended with the greatest determination against constant attacks. The night was quiet, except for a little bombing, but next day the attacks from La Signy were renewed, and, though they were held off, the 15th Company's losses were heavy, and that evening they were relieved. Massing under cover of the hedge, the enemy now launched a determined attack overland against the 16th Company and the battalion on their left. Half an hour's heavy artillery and machine-gun fire preceded the attack, which broke down completely under the flanking fire poured in by the Waikatos' Lewis guns.

Throughout the long hard days of the 27th and 28th, the line opposite La Signy Farm had been held by 2/Auckland against an enemy superior in numbers and well supplied with bombs, who, despite their advantages of position and their superiority in machine-gun, trench mortar and artillery fire, had failed completely in their attempt to break through. The Brigades of the New Zealand Field Artillery had been racing south from Ypres, and late in the afternoon of the 27th the leading batteries were coming up the Doullens road. All next day they continued to arrive, and by the morning of the 29th were in position and firing. The new line was secure.

Lying in front of the New Zealand line, and in some parts dominating it, was the ridge and farmhouse of La Signy. Possession of this would very greatly improve the strength of the line, and would drive the enemy everywhere into the valley,

The Auckland Regiment

leaving him in such a position that a general assault on his part would be very much hampered by the lack of a suitable jumping-off point. It was resolved to take La Signy and to entrust 2/Auckland with the task. The attack was planned as a pure surprise, and was to take place at 2 p.m. on the afternoon of March 30th. There was no preliminary artillery bombardment, but at zero hour a shrapnel barrage went down on the Hun line, and at the same moment the infantry leaped from the trenches, deployed out and went straight forward. The Hun sentries were evidently extremely careless, and fearing nothing, stood down and kept their heads below the parapet when the shelling commenced. It was the most impossible and most improbable time for an attack to take place. The greater part of the trench garrison were asleep in their dugouts. Some were writing home on British Y.M.C.A. paper. They were in great numbers—the trench was packed with them. Machine-guns were mounted every few yards. So sure, so confident were the Huns, in their own strength, in their feeling of certainty that their opponents would remain entirely on the defensive, that the idea of a surprise attack over that two hundred yards of level grass field never entered their heads. The Aucklanders were half way across before they were seen. They were on the parapet of the German trench before the machine-gun crews could reach their weapons. The 3rd Company, on the right, and the Waikatos on the left, went straight in with rifle, bayonet and bomb. Many of the enemy were killed actually in the trench. Many more were shot down as they endeavoured to escape. Numbers of them surrendered. In two places only was there strong opposition. Right in the centre of the position, at the end of Southern Avenue, an enemy strong point held out. A platoon of the Waikatos, advancing up the sap, found the enemy on the alert. For a moment the whole line of them were exposed to the direct fire of an enemy gunner. Fourteen fell—every man shot through the head. Two or three more were wounded, including Captain McFarland. The attack here was held up until Colonel Allen, in response to an urgent message, came up to the spot,

Mailly-Maillet

and with him the trench mortar officer, Captain Morgan, who with all speed brought one of his guns into play. This played havoc with the Huns, who speedily surrendered. On the extreme right, by the Serre road, another post still held out, but a bombing party of the 3rd Company under Sergeant Buckthought quickly reduced it, while the Colonel and the Padre looked on. This established touch with 1/Wellington on the right. During the night Captain Napier, who had come up to take charge of the Waikatos in the left sector, completed the whole operation by co-operating with the 4/N.Z.R.B. in squeezing the enemy out of the only portion of high ground they still retained. Everywhere now the New Zealanders held the high ground, and the enemy were forced down into the valley. There was every reason to fear a counter-attack, but it did not come, and the night passed quietly enough, the outstanding event being the capture of the "Hun Major" by a patrol party. This rather ornate-looking individual was found wandering about No-Man's-Land, and being evidently of a "kamaradely" disposition was "souvenired" and conducted to a Company Headquarters, where someone with the reputation of being a German scholar pronounced him to be of "field rank." Captured majors are scarce, and the captive was conducted with considerable state to Battalion, who in perfect good faith forwarded him to Brigade. Here he was received with great cordiality and generally made to feel at home. By this time the Hun, who had received several "nips" of rum, had become very good company, and all would have gone well if some more accurate German linguist had not made the discovery that the alleged "major" was only a quarter-master-sergeant. He was promptly relegated to the nearest prisoner cage, but, if he has a sense of humour, he must often laugh to himself at the way in which he was received by the British General and his staff. One of the prisoners had done remarkably well for himself during the advance. He had evidently made a practice of searching all prisoners, and as a result was in possession of sixty treasury notes and also some hundreds of francs. He was a valuable prize, and was very much appre-

The Auckland Regiment

ciated by those who searched him. In the attack a most valuable position had been gained. One hundred and forty of the enemy dead were counted on the sector, and there were many more who had been shot during their flight lying further down the slope. One hundred and fifty prisoners were taken and also forty-two machine-guns, two light minenwerfers and one Lewis gun. 2/Auckland lost 130 in killed and wounded. This operation was surely one of the most successful surprise attacks of the war. When it is considered that the attackers were greatly fatigued and were part of an army that had been heavily defeated, and that the Huns were flushed with victory, the full merit of the achievement becomes obvious. Small as the operation was, compared with the mighty happenings of those critical days, it was yet the first successful attack made by Allied troops since the opening of the German offensive.

Easter Sunday, March 31st, 2/Auckland were relieved by 2/Wellington, and went back in reserve to Courcelles-au-Bois. It was time, for everyone was tired out. Since leaving Zuytpeene men had not had their boots off for a week, and there had been very little sleep for anyone. Fighting had been severe and continuous. During the last two or three days, rain had fallen, there was much mud, and many were suffering from the first stages of "trench foot." It was a weary trudge back, but at last all were back to the hot meal awaiting them, and the delights of an uninterrupted sleep.

XXVI

Holding the Line

> "*The magpies in Picardy*
> *Are more than I can tell.*
> *They flicker down the dusty roads,*
> *And cast a magic spell*
> *On the men who march through Picardy—*
> *Through Picardy to Hell.*"
> —T. P. Cameron Wilson.

Throughout the months of April, May, June and July the New Zealand Division was employed holding the line. During this time extremely heavy fighting took place round Armentières in the north and Rheims in the south. In both these localities the enemy launched very heavy attacks and penetrated to a great depth, but in both cases they were stopped before irretrievable disaster occurred. The New Zealanders would probably have been withdrawn and flung into one or the other of these areas but for the fact that a renewed German thrust toward Amiens was continually being threatened. On more than one occasion such an attack was expected almost daily, and all troops were warned to be in constant readiness.

1/Auckland had been withdrawn from the line on March 28th, and then on April 2nd came in once more, relieving 1/Wellington. They were themselves relieved forty-eight hours later by the 3/N.Z.R.B. Next day, April 5th, the enemy attacked with great violence on a wide front. Their artillery fire was very heavy, not only on the front lines, but also on the back areas. The Aucklanders of both battalions had rather a lively morning, but, fortunately, few casualties were sustained. Determined infantry assaults on the New Zealand position broke down before the steady resistance of the Rifle Brigade. This was the last effort made by the enemy to break through in the area of the Somme battlefield.

The position was now reasonably secure, and the next business was to consolidate it in such a fashion that no future attack, however heavy or sustained, would be likely to succeed.

The Auckland Regiment

Within the divisional area three distinct trench systems were constructed. The front system, known as the Green Line, was largely made up of the old 1916 trenches renovated. Three thousand yards or thereabouts to the rear was the Purple Line, a very strong defensive position, which had at all costs to be held. Further back still was the Red Line, and still further to the rear were other lines constructed by Corps and Army troops. Switch lines connected up the various systems. An enormous amount of work was necessary before the defensive works in the divisional area were complete, and battalions not in the line were always sure of employment.

2/Auckland stayed in the Purple Line round about Courcelles until April 9th, when they relieved 2/N.Z.R.B. in the sector stretching from Waterloo Bridge to a point half way to Hébuterne. The sector was a long one, but quiet, except for a certain amount of desultory shelling. Here the 15th Company had the misfortune to lose Company-Sergeant-Major Brown, a very old, tried and trusty soldier, who from the days of the Main Body had been engaged in all the fighting. He particularly distinguished himself in the Battle of Messines. At this time there were very few Main Body men with good fighting records still remaining with the Regiment, and the loss of any of them was a very serious matter. "Old soldiers never die, they only fade away," is not quite correct. Certainly the less steadfast element did drift back to base camps and "soft jobs," but the finer sort were killed sooner or later. It was just a question of time. Some survived for a year, and were lucky to do so. Some came through a second year. Not many lived through a third. A very few, and one could name them on the fingers of one hand, went right through the war and fought in the last six months with the same dash and daring that had marked them out in the first weeks at Anzac; but even with these it was just a question of time, and if the war had lasted a little longer they, too, would have gone. Death came to all—to the brave man and to the coward. Sometimes he reaped a wide swathe, and other times as a gleaner does, he gathered his harvest one by one, but

Holding the Line

always it was the best and the bravest who were most likely to meet the dread reaper. To a very large extent men were able to make their own choice. Some, despite physical infirmity and the breaking of all their material prospects, enlisted at once, and then, volunteers always, exposed themselves to every danger and hardship of war. They lost their lives, but in the memory of those who knew them they still live. Others there were who chose to live. They sheltered behind legal technicalities; in the first and second year of the war took unto themselves wives, and from behind a petticoat gave expression to a fine patriotism; they became indispensable to the community and could not be spared; they discovered physical defects that, while in no sense debarring them from the hardest manual work or keen participation in all games, could yet be made much of when it came to a medical inspection. They walk our streets to-day, and they think that all is forgotten. They saved their lives, but we who knew those others, though we say nothing, find it not easy to forget.

2/Auckland were relieved on the 14th by 2/Wellington, and went back to Colincamps, while, on the same day, 1/Auckland went into the line, taking over from the Serre road to Waterloo Bridge. Though fairly quiet on the whole, the crossroads by the Sugar Factory were heavily shelled. Captain Alexander was badly wounded by a sniper early in the morning of the 15th, and on the same day three bombing attacks were carried out on a Hun post in one of the saps. There was some lively bombing, but nothing definite was achieved. On the 17th, the Battalion was relieved, going back to posts in the Purple Line. At the same time 2/Auckland moved back to a tarpaulin camp near Bertrancourt. The weather was not good, and the men were not very comfortable, but the spell out enabled them to have a clean up and get new underclothing. A week later the 1/Battalion took over the trenches in front of Hébuterne, while the 2/Battalion were in support in and behind the village. The sector was taken over partly from English and partly from Australian troops. Much work was necessary to put the trenches into good order. New Zealanders

The Auckland Regiment

had plenty of this kind of thing to do, as it was always their custom to leave a sector in better condition than that in which they found it. Simply as a working division the New Zealanders had a very good name. So many of them had been used since boyhood to an outdoor life, to digging, road-making and the simple engineering on a farm, that this aptitude for doing "war work" is not to be wondered at.

On the 30th, 1/Auckland was relieved by 1/Wellington, and went back in support, while the 2/Battalion took over the right half of the Brigade's sector—a very strong portion of the front, which completely overlooked the enemy position in the valley below. The enemy, so inconveniently placed, very sensibly kept quiet.

Another move back took place on May 6th, when 1/Auckland went back to the locality known as J 22 Central, not far from the Château de la Haye, while 2/Auckland went into the Purple Line near the windmill of Bertrancourt. It was now well into the middle of spring, and the weather was becoming much finer, and the conditions in every way more pleasant. After a week in reserve the 1/Brigade took over the right sub-sector of the divisional front, 2/Auckland remaining in brigade reserve at Colincamps, while the 1st Battalion once more took over the Serre road sector. All through the next day there was considerable movement behind the enemy lines, but no resulting activity. At 6 p.m. Sergeant-Major Rogers, with five O.R.'s, left the trench by Mountjoy Sap, and raided an enemy strong point, for the purpose of obtaining identification. They found the trenches fully occupied and were unable to bring back any prisoners, although in the lively fight that took place they were successful in killing a considerable number of the enemy and managed to get back to their own line without loss. The following night the enemy endeavoured to retaliate by raiding an advanced Lewis gun post. A patrol fortunately located the raiding party while they were assembling in No-Man's-Land, and so enabled a destructive fire to be poured into the party, which was dispersed with loss. Although a big German attack was expected at any time, everyone was in the

Holding the Line

best of spirits. Morale was at its very best, and if the Hun did come no one had any very great fear of the result. The general opinion was that although in the first surprise he might rush some of the front posts, his penetration would proceed no further—a very comfortable theory for all except those who for the time being happened to be garrisoning the posts in question.

During the evening of the 15th a platoon of the North Auckland Company, commanded by Lieutenant Stunnell, one of the old Main Body men, now promoted to commissioned rank, carried out a raid on the enemy line. Under cover of an artillery and trench mortar barrage they filed out into No-Man's-Land, and immediately the barrage lifted rushed in. They quickly bombed five dug-outs, killing some twenty of the enemy, and then returned with two prisoners and a light machine-gun, suffering no loss themselves. The whole operation barely took five minutes, and was a splendid example of the perfectly successful raid. A retaliatory barrage put down by the enemy caused a few casualties—amongst them being Major Holland, M.C. His death was a heavy blow, not only to the Regiment but also to the Brigade and the Division. Enlisting as a private in the same section of the 6th Company as Tuck, Tilsley and Melville, he had earned a wonderful reputation during the Gallipoli days. For his services there he was granted a commission and awarded the Military Cross—an honour which he and Captain Wallingford were the only Aucklanders to receive throughout that campaign. A man very keen on winning the war, extremely conscientious, and though not loved as well as some, yet universally respected, and greatly admired for his thoroughness, devotion to duty, and his great valour. When one thinks of the best fighting men the Regiment produced—men like Wallingford, Holland, Tilsley, Warden, Tuck, Forrest, Jock McKenzie, the Allens, Vercoe, Todd, Brewer, Prendergast, Rogers, Roberts, Robertson, Brown the stretcher-bearer, Campion, Greenwood, Stewart, Tom Gordon, Dr. Craig, Faithful, and if it be permissible to include him, Forsyth, V.C., the engineer—it is barely pos-

The Auckland Regiment

sible to say this man or that was the bravest of them all. They differed in character, rank and attainments, but as far as courage was concerned they stand very much on a level. Major Holland's name will always be one of the most honoured of them all, equalled by some, but not surpassed by any. One more of the "Old Brigade" had gone. Continuous movement on the part of the enemy and much shell fire marked the remaining days spent in the line, and then on the 18th the Battalion was relieved by 1/Wellington.

2/Auckland came in, and occupied their old position before La Signy Farm. For the first few days there was quietness, undisturbed by anything more serious than a few rather badly aimed minenwerfers. Sergeant-Major Roberts was, as usual, very active on patrol work. It was during this spell in that the Battalion was raided for the only time in its history. Just before daylight the enemy guns played a heavy barrage on the front and support lines, which he followed up by a dash on the salient in Central Avenue. The raiders were observed and dispersed by Lewis gun fire, leaving behind them two dead and six rifles. On the evening of the 20th, the Battalion was relieved, and marched right back to billets in St. Leger Authie, a small village some miles behind the line. This march to billets was memorable, as owing to a late start the hour for the wearing of gas masks occurred actually during the march. For those who could raise no reasonable excuse for dropping behind, and then out of sight, the march was exceedingly unpleasant. St. Leger Authie was a typical little French village and though the billets were not of the best, at the same time they were a very pleasant change after two months in the trenches and open fields.

The countryside of Picardy and Artois was different altogether from that around Armentières and Ypres. Instead of level flats, stretching for mile after mile, there was here for a long distance alternating hill and valley. Both alike were well grassed, and much of the ground was down in crops Patches of woodland were frequent, and were much used for camping grounds. From Hébuterne, which may be taken as

Holding the Line

the central point of the New Zealand line, the road ran back to Sailly-au-Bois, an extensive village, considerably damaged by shell fire, but which before the war must have been an exceedingly pleasant place, nestling amongst its beautiful hedge-rows and trees. From here it continued down a long valley past Rossignol Farm, Couin and Coigneux, and so to Authie St. Leger. Authie itself, a considerable village, with a fine chateau in the middle of it, was a kilometre further on. Authie was in many ways the social centre of the Division when troops were out of the line. It possessed a large Y.M.C.A., a number of excellent estaminets, and also a first-class natural amphitheatre, which served excellently for concerts given by one or other of the divisional troupes. From here the road continued down the valley through Orville to Doullens, the only considerable town within reach. Without being of any great size, it yet had sufficient attractions to justify a visit when funds were available and a day's leave could be obtained. As one faced the front line, Marieux Wood, Lovencourt, Bertrancourt, Bus, Courcelles and Colincamps were all on the right hand side of the road from Doullens to Hébuterne, while on the left were Pas, Henu, Souastre, Fonquevillers, and finally, right on the line, Gommecourt. Marieux Wood was the divisional centre for the "B" teams, who were all concentrated here for the purpose of training. Ever since the fighting on the Somme in 1916 it had been the practice to leave a certain percentage of the personnel of a battalion in reserve whenever heavy fighting was anticipated. Experience had shown that in case of very heavy casualties it was often extremely difficult to carry on again, when things returned more or less to normal, owing to heavy losses in officers, N.C.O.'s and trained specialists. The object of the "B" team was to have a sufficient nucleus of experienced men always available from whom, in case of any disaster, the battalion could readily be built up again, still retaining that "continuity of command" and of "feeling" so necessary if a unit is to be a really good one. The practice had been extended by this time, and a battalion in the later stages of the

The Auckland Regiment

war sent back its "duds," as they were familiarly known, even when it was merely going in for an ordinary trench spell. It was usual for the Battalion Commander and his Second-in-Command to take turns in staying back. The same rule was followed by company commanders and their seconds-in-command. Three platoon officers went in with each company. The Regimental-Sergeant-Major and two Company-Sergeant-Majors, with a certain number of junior N.C.O.'s and men formed the remainder of the party to stay out. As far as 2/Auckland were concerned, Colonel Allen always made a rule of leaving Major Sinel with the "B" team. In consequence, the Major, who had left Anzac with a very fine reputation, had little chance of displaying his ability as a fighting soldier.

Louvencourt was for a considerable while the railhead for the New Zealand Division, and, in consequence, was the home of the various battalion transport details, those of the 1/Brigade camping close to the windmill of Lovencourt. This village was for a long time crowded with the men of a very fine French Division, which was there lying in reserve in case of a renewed effort by the enemy to break through.

The Entrenching Battalions had established themselves in the large and beautiful wood above the village of Pas. As all reinforcements passed through here, including men returned from hospital, the camp under the trees was frequently visited by all those who had got word of old friends coming up to the Division. Rossignol Farm, renamed "Diggerville," a frequent home of 1/Auckland, was a very large Y.M.C.A. centre.

1/Auckland in the Bois de Warnimont, and 2/Auckland in St. Leger, settled down to a week's concentrated training. There was much to be done. After two months in the line a considerable deal of smartening up was necessary, much attention was paid to gas training, and a considerable deal of time was also spent in carrying out battalion battle manœuvres. The difficulty with which these operations were sometimes carried out showed how necessary training of this sort really was. Certain hilarious people from the Entrenching Group

Holding the Line

celebrated a pay-day in Authie, and, being considerably elevated, became entangled with certain members of 1st and 2/Auckland, 2/Wellington and the Military Police. As the "M.P.'s" failed to carry off the honours of the day—or night rather—they raised a storm at Brigade Headquarters, which resulted in the three battalions aforementioned doing an hour's extra gas drill. Colonel Allen's contention that 2/Auckland were not concerned is probably correct, although this abstention on their part was due, not to the fact that they were too proud to fight, but that their estaminets lay further up the road. The average infantryman, no matter how law-abiding a person he may happen to be, had a tremendous averison to military police. It is safe to say that the only body of police who were ever really popular were the regimental police of 2/Auckland—and they never made an arrest.

A brigade horse show and transport competition was held at Vauchelles, whither the battalions marched one bright summer's day. The show ground was a very pleasant meadow with patches of woodland scattered about. Some New Zealand nursing sisters and some ladies from the district gave a touch of colour to the mass of khaki-clad men. Everything went off splendidly. 2/Auckland were successful in carrying off practically all the prizes, including General Melvill's Cup. Incidents like this made men forget the war for brief hours, though not for long.

Every night there was a droning in the air, and the heavy-laden Hun bombing 'planes flew down the line of the valley to Doullens—often not so far. It is never a pleasant feeling waiting for the last 'plane to get safely past, especially when there are only a few tiles overhead.

On June 1st, 2/Auckland went into Brigade reserve in and behind Sailly, while the 1/Battalion went into the line in front of Hébuterne. With the exception of a little shelling, the sector was quiet. A patrol party, endeavouring to locate a Hun strong point, were unlucky enough to be observed and to have a heavy machine-gun fire directed upon them, which wounded eight of the party. Nothing else happened, and then on the

The Auckland Regiment

6th the Battalion was relieved by Manchester troops, and went back to J 22 Central, near the windmill of Bertrancourt, and then after a week in that position moved back to the tented camp at Couin. 2/Auckland carried out a similar move, and then a few days later 1/Auckland moved to Louvencourt, and 2/Auckland to a very comfortable camp at Vauchelles. With the exception of three battalions which were garrisoning the Purple Line, the whole Division was now out of the line, and busily employed in training.

This period of training was noteworthy for the number of social events which took place. First and foremost, Colonel S. S. Allen went over to England and got married.

A divisional horse show and sports was a very great success. It was largely attended. Many generals and other distinguished people were present. Not the least interested was a Hun airman, who came over to see the boxing. Someone evidently disturbed his peace of mind by shooting upon him with an anti-aircraft gun, for he shortly after flew away. Not long after, probably on his instigation, a big gun commenced to fire shells round about the area of the show ground. The programme was almost over, and so the shelling was taken as a broad hint to go home.

The 1/Brigade's debating competition resulted in 2/Auckland scoring a victory in the first round over 1/Auckland, but losing the final to 2/Wellington. This final excited a great deal of interest. It was held out in the open before an audience of several hundred men, the subject being: "Is a League of Nations Desirable?" 2/Wellington's victory was well earned.

Mr. Massey and Sir Joseph Ward, otherwise "Bill and Joe," took this opportunity of visiting the Division. Their first appearance was at the pierrot show in the open-air theatre at Authie. It is very regrettable, but nevertheless a fact, that the politicians were not taken altogether seriously, and were regarded more or less as a "star turn" on the programme. Something of the same sort happened a few days later, when they appeared again, this time at a church parade. Unfortunately, they were not allowed to preach, and so enliven the

Holding the Line

proceedings a little; but at the conclusion of the ceremony their turn came—and also that of the congregation.

The mention of "church parades" brings up the question of religion. It is a subject that cannot be passed over as lightly as one might think. New Zealanders were generally supposed by army evangelists to be a very hard type to touch—harder even than the Australians—and very little religion was apparent amongst them. To start off with, very few men even in civilian life are at all deeply interested in the subject. A considerable number fall in with the ceremonial and social demands of the church simply from long-established habit. War came, and established habits went to the winds. Once overseas men did as they pleased in all the private relationships of life. It was very easy to run wild—it was rather difficult to keep straight. The influence of the chaplains, taken as a whole, was exceedingly small. Perhaps the real cause of this ineffectiveness was the disunion of the Church and her utter inability to give any clear leadership on any of the great issues of the time. This mental and moral cowardice was reflected in the Army. Chaplains always had a tendency to be obsessed with the fact that they were army officers, and to forget that first and foremost they were "men of God." One example will make things clear. A divisional order was issued to the effect that chaplains must not accompany their battalions into the line. Almost inconceivable to relate, this order was obeyed by the majority of the chaplains then with the Division. The Army was perfectly right in issuing the order, and the clergymen were quite correct in obeying it, but the whole underlying principle was wrong. As a rule chaplains were men whose moral conduct was unimpeachable, but who were not distinguished above ordinary men for courage and self-sacrifice. They were a good average—perhaps a little better than average—but from the followers of One Crucified, whose primary business, according to their creed, was "to lay down their lives for the sheep," it was perfectly justifiable to expect much more than mediocrity. One of the most saddening things of the war from the point of view of the Christian man was the

The Auckland Regiment

ease with which a padre could win for himself a reputation for bravery. Compulsory church parade did a tremendous lot of harm to real religion. It disgusted the average man. He was quite willing to give up his freedom and to submit to a rigorous discipline; he was prepared to give his life, but it seemed rather an unnecessary infliction compelling him to be religious "by numbers." From the point of view of the Higher Command church parade was an excellent institution. It was an admirable opportunity for some of that "ceremonial drill" which is so very essential to give the sense of battalion and brigade solidarity. However admirable as discipline, from the point of view of religion, church parade was a deplorable failure. From disunion, timidity, lack of vision and leadership the official representatives of religion failed even more deplorably than under civilian conditions to touch the hearts of men in the mass. Despite the failure of the padres, religion did not entirely die out. Before the first sailing from Egypt a group of men gathered frequently in the Y.M.C.A. tent of Mr. Oatts at Zeitoun. Sadly depleted, they maintained a precarious footing at Anzac, revived strongly at Lemnos, grew again during the reorganisation in Egypt, but almost disappeared in the early months of the French campaign. They came together again before Messines, forming groups in units, and linking these groups together in a divisional movement under the name of the "Brotherhood of Men of Goodwill." Many were killed and wounded at Messines, but during the spell for training the movement gathered impetus, and though nearly shot to pieces at Passchendaele, it went steadily forward, growing in numbers and influence. Denominationalism simply vanished —the very simplest essentials being found sufficient basis for unity of effort. Here on the Somme the movement made splendid progress, and the first great rally of the religious element in the Division took place. Representatives of every unit in the Division assembled in the large upper room of the biggest estaminet in Authie. It was a remarkable gathering or Catholic Christianity. From this time on the Brotherhood grew from more to more, until it reached its culminating point

Holding the Line

in the magnificent rally held after the Armistice, when General Russell addressed the gathering. Throughout the later stages of the war the Brotherhood notice was a familiar one in all the Y.M.C.A. centres. At this time, however, the prospect of an armistice or peace seemed a very long way off. Even as men knelt to receive the Sacrament the windows rattled and the house shook as great pieces of cannon rumbled through the main street.

Authie was the centre of reunions of all sorts. Freemasons, Grammar School Old Boys, Old "A"s of the Training College, all held most successful functions. Altogether the spell was an exceeding pleasant one, and when the time came for a move forward the morale of the men was excellent. The general health and fitness was also good, except for the influenza epidemic which now broke out. Commencing in the east and centre of Europe, amongst populations whose resisting power had been lowered by the food scarcity, the disease rapidly spread westward, through the German army and across No-Man's-Land. A number of New Zealanders went down with it, but there were very few really serious cases, and scarcely any deaths. All the "flu" patients were concentrated in a camp at Marieux Wood, as delightful a spot as could have been found anywhere.

XXVII

To Bapaume!—Rossignol Wood, Grevillers, Bapaume, Bancourt

"Onward!"

As the summer passed the power of the German Empire slowly waned. Furious assaults on the Western Front yielded great tactical victories, but, despite colossal losses, the Huns were at no place able to win through to their strategic objectives. The people of the Rhineland were demoralised by the bombing raids of the British Air Service. The flower of the German manhood was dead on the battlefields. Food was short. Many raw materials essential for the manufacture of munitions were terribly scarce. Material hardships and privations were at last commencing to wear down the morale of the German people. Russia, broken, conquered and humiliated, by preaching and propaganda stirred the revolutionary elements toward action. Not only did the Bolsheviks fling the secret treaties into the ash-barrel of history, but they denounced even more strongly the Imperialism of Prussia. Karl Liebknicht, the prisoner of the Kaiser, the Communist leader, who had from the beginning stood out uncompromisingly against the war, became more and more a power in Germany. From his prison cell his voice reached from one side of the Fatherland to the other. The whole country was honeycombed with the British propaganda directed by Lord Northcliffe. Every day the position of the War Lords was growing more desperate.

On the other hand, the power of the Allies waxed greater and greater. The mood of depression had passed with the coming of the enemy offensive. All through the summer there

To Bapaume!

was no thought of anything but victory. The British rushed over every man they could lay hands on. Base depôts were cleared out, and many veterans of the "Sling Front" found themselves once more with the Division. The brilliant exploit of the British Navy at Ostend and Zeebrugge was a big factor in raising the Allied morale. For three years the Americans had delayed before they came into the struggle, but now at last their succour was being brought to Europe. They did not play a very important part in the actual fighting, but they did enable Marshal Foch to do what otherwise he could not have done, and use the French and British Armies to the very uttermost without fear of a disaster in the event of a check at any point.

The German War Lords, faced by the spectre of defeat, were now desperate. They could not cease attacking, because once on the defensive their last hope of victory would be gone, and in that case they feared the people. So they thundered on, endeavouring to smash a way to Paris. Their blows were heavy, but there were not lacking signs of weakness and indecision. The Allies supremacy in the air was gradually blinding the German army. Then at last, when it seemed as though the Germans were endeavouring to deal a death-stroke, the blow was arrested in mid-air and the counter-blow was struck. Marshal Foch opened the counter-offensive which in three months of furious, breathless fighting broke the power of Germany and brought victory.

From the middle of June, old soldiers in the New Zealand Division began to notice the preliminary preparations for a big move. Heavy guns were brought up by ones and twos. Tanks came in quietly by night and were hidden away in the patches of wood. Gradually the sector grew hotter. Shell fire became more intense as the enemy commenced to lose confidence. Raids were more frequent. In front of Hébuterne and about Rossignol Wood a small affair of some sort or another happened every day.

On July 1st the 1/Brigade took over the sector from Rossignol Wood to Hébuterne, thus shifting the divisional front

The Auckland Regiment

one brigade sector further north. The battalions embussed and proceeded by motor to Souastre. It was real midsummer weather, and the white dust was flying in clouds. From Souastre there was a march of some kilometres along a straight tree-lined road, bordered by green fields, to the village of Fonquevillers—a place much battered in the fighting of 1916, and still a frequent target for the Hun gunners. 1/Auckland proceeded through and took over the support position in Gommecourt. Here men noted with admiration the care and thoroughness with which the enemy had fortified this place in the days when it was the most western point on their line, and one of the strongest positions they possessed. The width of the wire-belts, the depth of the main trench, and the immense caverns and dug-outs driven into the hill, made it a matter of small wonder that all attacks on this stronghold in 1916 had broken down.

2/Auckland, waiting for nightfall—sunset was not until eight o'clock—moved up and took over the Rossignol-Biez Wood sector. Rossignol Wood was of immense value to the enemy. It was the one place where they had a footing on the western rim of the basin. Not only did it afford much excellent observation, but it was also a fine jumping-off point for an attack. As long, moreover, as the enemy could hold the wood securely, offensive operations against weaker portions of their line in the valley below could be carried out only at a great disadvantage. The trenches were in rather bad repair, and a considerable amount of work was necessary to put them to rights. One fairly extensive bit of digging had to be done to connect Railway and Ash trenches. While in this position, Colonel Allen, Captain Tuck and the Padre should have been shot, but escaped, owing to the reprehensible carelessness of the Hun sentries. Nearly every morning these three officers approached the front line, exposing themselves in the most reckless manner. Strange to say, they were only fired on once, and then the Hun missed, although he could not have been more than a hundred yards away. At night the enemy in their posts along the edge of the wood were very nervy. They

To Bapaume!

bombed and machine-gunned their wire on the very slightest provocation, and a harmless and inoffensive patrol wandering round No-Man's-Land was made the occasion for a most liberal display of fireworks.

Patrol work is always fascinating, and in front of Rossignol Wood it was even more so than usual. The dark line of the wood across the hundred yards of grass field seemed very specially mysterious. At midnight four men cross the parapet and move quietly through the wire. They carry rifles only, with a few spare rounds, and perhaps a bomb in the tunic pockets. Once clear of the wire they adopt a diamond formation, and then, with the leader in front, go forward slowly and with the utmost caution. Every now and again they slide into a shell-hole and listen intently for any sound, and then, satisfied that all is safe, move forward once more. Half way over No-Man's-Land an old trench is found and cautiously searched. There is nothing in it. A wooden cross with a piece of tattered cloth fluttering from it is the next mark, and from there the slow, careful, doubled-up walk becomes a crawl. Now the wood itself, dark, silent and mysterious, is but a matter of yards away. There is a halt for three or four minutes, and dead silence. Fifty yards away on the left a flare goes up, making everywhere as bright as day. The patrol lies flat, faces to the earth, until the flare falls with a last dying hiss amongst them. Nothing more—they have not been detected, and so after a little longer pause the leader glides forward. Straight ahead, not twenty yards away is a mound of white chalk on the very edge of the wood. Black stumps and broken branches form the background. Dark objects just visible may be men or may be trees. Is it a Hun post? There is but one way to be sure, and the patrol work on their stomachs toward it, moving inch by inch, fingers on triggers, with the first pressure already taken. The rear man of the party has the pin in his first bomb loosened, and is ready in the fraction of a second to launch it over the heads of the others. Five yards away from the mound the leader half rises and creeps in. It is an empty shell-hole—fortunately un-

The Auckland Regiment

manned. Close beside it is a heap of rails, wire, iron standards and beams of wood—evidently the place had once been an engineers' dump. For ten minutes the patrol lie quiet and listen. They have reached the line of the wood, and from the flares which rise on the left it is obvious that they are level with and perhaps in between the enemy posts. Shall they proceed further? Once more the leader goes ahead straight into the dark and tangled mass of torn trees. There has been very violent shelling here, for in between the stumps are huge craters, six and eight feet deep. They penetrate almost to the other edge of the wood—not too quietly, for in the darkness it is impossible to avoid brittle sticks or to help sending a clod of earth rattling down. Finally they stop and turn back from a point some twenty feet from a Hun pill-box, that a few days later is to get for itself a sinister reputation. The dim and silent wood, mysterious and full of unknown danger, is left behind, and the little party moves in the open field, creeping from shell-hole to shell-hole. Thirty or forty yards away a cough or a muttered word betrays the presence of the enemy. Suddenly one man places a hand on a dry stick. It breaks. Up goes a flare and two machine-guns rattle out. Fortunately their elevation is eighteen inches too high, and the prostrate four slide safely into a friendly crater. Brother Fritz has evidently caught a glimpse of their movement, and immediately goes mad. All his machine-guns along half-a-mile of front open up on to nothing in particular. There is a great banging of bombs in his wire, and a brilliant display of flares. The four who have caused this extravagant demonstration of hate sit securely in their crater and laugh noiselessly. Nothing could have done their work better for them. Sentries in the line itself will be able to take direct and accurate bearings on to the enemy posts, and next morning the "Toc Emmas" will be busy. When the Hun has recovered his equilibrium, and all is quiet again, the patrol walks back to Railway Trench, is challenged, and then recrossing the parapet, is finished for the night, once the leader has handed in his report.

On 9th July the Brigade went into divisional reserve,

To Bapaume!

1/Auckland going back to Rossignol Farm, while the 2/Battalion occupied the hutted camp at Coigneux. Both camps were comfortable places, and training of all sorts was carried out. It was during this period that one of the minor satellites of the Divisional Headquarters—the museum officer to be exact—made a tour of the Division, for the purpose of instructing all and sundry in the best methods "of ratting the Hun." One of the educational staff, the recently organised department, which had for its ultimate purpose the fitting of men to go back once more to civilian life, also paid a visit to the battalions. During this period the weather was changeable, and there were several wet days.

Whilst the Auckland Battalions were out of the line the N.Z.R.B. made the first move, and in a very successful little operation occupied Fusilier Trench, the highest part of the Hun line between Hébuterne and Rossignol Wood. From this time the advance went forward practically without a stop.

The 1/Brigade relieved the N.Z.R.B. in front of Hébuterne on the 17th, 2/Auckland going into Brigade reserve at Sailly, while the 1/Battalion went into the left sub-sector of the Right Brigade, some little distance to the left front of Hébuterne. At this time 1/Auckland was commanded by Lieutenant-Colonel Alderman, C.M.G., with Major Orr, D.S.O., Second-in-Command, and Captain W. P. Gray as Adjutant.

Dr. Ardagh was in charge of the medical arrangements, while Chaplain Grigg was still with the Battalion.

The newly-occupied trenches which the Battalion was occupying were in very poor condition. German troops on this sector must have been in the line for extremely short periods, otherwise their working discipline must have been remarkably bad. Their communication saps were in particularly bad order. From the number of helmets and rifles lying about it was evident that losses from artillery fire must have been heavy. The very fact of so much useful material lying about unsalvaged was another proof of diminishing morale. The Aucklanders set to work to improve and make defensible

The Auckland Regiment

the new position, but the work was much hindered and delayed by heavy artillery and machine-gun fire. Next day there was considerable movement in the enemy lines, and the gun fire was again heavy. In the afternoon patrols went forward to test the strength of the enemy line, but were unable to make peaceful penetration at any point. Patrol activity continued by night and day. It was known that the enemy were considering a retirement to more securely fortified positions, and it was of great importance that once they commenced to move back they should be so harried and hustled that the retreat should become a rout. On the 19th, a daylight patrol worked down to the enemy block in Nameless Trench, and before retiring shot the Hun sentry. At mid-day came information that the enemy were vacating Rossignol Wood, where Sergeant Richard Travis with his picked scouts and Sergeant Forsyth, the Engineer, were doing wonderful work. It was here the great scout reached the height of his fame and received his death wound. Auckland patrols were immediately pushed forward, and stiff bombing fights occurred, which resulted in the occupation of Owl, Swan, Fish and Duck Trenches. Hawk Trench was too strongly held, and the best that could be done there was to put in a block at the junction with Nameless Support. Two machine-guns and three prisoners were captured as a result of this fighting. Consolidation went steadily forward, and during the night the trench from Owl to the Sixteen Poplars was completed. Next day further progress was made along Hawk Trench and Nameless Support. Very heavy rain fell during the night, and the trenches quickly became quagmires. At 3 p.m. on the 23rd, after an hour's bombardment, the enemy attacked with bombing parties down Dugout Lane, but were unable to penetrate. On the following day patrol activity was continuous. Small advances were made in Lob Street and Hair Alley. A strong fighting party fought its way along Hawk Trench, and in an hour and a half had taken three enemy posts, finally being held up by a strong point, which was protected by machine-guns on the flank. The garrison of this post counter-attacked, but were

To Bapaume!

repulsed with the loss of three killed and fifteen wounded. In conjunction with 2/Otago, Slug Street was occupied, and here another machine-gun was taken. During the afternoon of the 25th, while the Battalion was being relieved, the enemy artillery suddenly opened up, and a picked company of their storm troops attacked Slug Street and Dugout Lane. Their first rush penetrated the line on the Otago sector, and they were moving to the left to exploit their success. Sergeant Judson, who happened to be in the vicinity, went across by himself, and, re-organising a party of Lewis gunners, reoccupied part of the lost ground. Corporal Webster, with two men, drove twelve of the enemy before him, until they fell into the arms of a counter-attacking party of the Otagos, he himself capturing the machine-gun they had with them. From Huns captured in this affair the New Zealanders had the pleasure of hearing that amongst other things they had the reputation of being cannibals. Once the position was again secure the relief proceeded, and 1/Auckland went back into support between Hébuterne and Sailly-au-Bois. They had had a most exciting and adventurous week, and, as a result of almost ceaseless activity, had occupied much new ground and taken four machine-guns, with several prisoners. Ten men were killed and two officers and seventy-two men wounded.

2/Auckland meanwhile had been having a very pleasant time in reserve between Sailly and the Château de la Haye. Here they were joined by a company of the 317 U.S.A. Regiment, which was distributed a platoon with each company of the Battalion. These troops were Virginians—grandsons of the men who had fought with Lee and Jackson. They were not at all of the average Yankee type—they were anxious to learn, and were not obsessed with the idea of teaching veterans how things should be done. They were very likeable folk, and with their quaint sayings, strange manœuvres, their faculty for getting lost, and remarkable simplicity, provided much amusement for all. Perhaps one of the most humourous things of the war, as far as 2/Auckland were concerned, was to see Sergeant McMurdo leading his "gol-darned to a cinder

The Auckland Regiment

Yanks" round "by the hand." McMurdo was an Irishman, and a splendid mimic—it is needless to say more. The Battalion, with its attached Americans, took over the line from 2/Wellington. Owing to the Division on the right flank not moving forward in conformity with the New Zealanders, the forward positions held by 2/Auckland were dangerously exposed to flank attack. Chasseur Hedge was therefore abandoned, after all dug-outs had been blown up, and Jena Trench became the front line. It was at this time that Sergeant-Major Roberts took up his residence in a dug-out of immense depth in what was now No-Man's-Land. His theory was that if any wandering Huns should investigate and throw bombs into the cavern below the bombs would explode long before they reached him—so he would be quite safe. Much work was done, and the Americans were given plenty of experience of living in mud. On August 2nd, 1/Auckland moved back to the hutted camp at Coigneux, while the 2/Battalion went to the Château de la Haye Switch behind Sailly. Eight days later the 1/Brigade relieved the N.Z.R.B., 2/Auckland going into the support line in front of Gommecourt, while the 1/Battalion took over the front line with Battalion Headquarters at Salmon Point. This spell in was very similar to the last—newly-won ground had to be organised, and at the same time continuous patrol work was necessary to keep in close touch with the enemy, who were expected to make a further retirement at any hour. Conditions were exceedingly unpleasant, as the trenches were very narrow, wet and muddy, and there were frequent short, sharp bursts of shelling. On 14th August word was received from Brigade that the enemy were withdrawing. Patrols immediately moved out down Jigger and Kaka Trenches, and though little progress was made on the left, owing to the inertia of the battalion on that flank, the right pushed down Crayfish and Crayfish Support. Later, after nightfall, the trenches from Fork Wood southwards were occupied. Next day scout patrols were unable to make any progress, but on the following day, after artillery and trench mortar preparation, strong bombing parties, working along

To Bapaume!

Jigger, Crayfish and Crayfish Support, entered Fork Wood, which they cleared, and after some fighting established posts on the Bucquoy-Puisieux road. Two machine-guns and seventeen prisoners were taken.

The constant patrol activity of the last three weeks had resulted in the occupation of Rossignol Wood, Puisieux and Serre. Bapaume was the immediate objective on this part of the front, and the time had now come to strike directly for it. For weeks preparations had been quietly and secretly pushed forward—so secretly, indeed, that it was not until the 19th that even senior officers were aware of the magnitude of the operations that were to be carried out within the next few days. The New Zealand share in the first phase was to be a very small one—the Rifle Brigade being the only part of the Division to be employed. 2/Auckland, in close support to 1/Wellington, found their main business was to squeeze as tightly as possible into a very small space to make room for men of the 5th Division, who were to make the advance. This led to a certain amount of recrimination between the opposite members of various platoons and companies. When your platoon has successfully settled down in the only dug-out or trench in the neighbourhood you are apt to look coldly on anyone who pushes a rival claim, however plausible a case he may advance from a legal point of view. In the army possession is usually much more than the proverbial "nine points of the law."

The attack went forward on the morning of the 21st of August. Under cover of a heavy mist the attacking troops had little difficulty in penetrating deeply into the enemy's position. Prisoners came back in fair numbers. 2/Auckland, having nothing better to do, made a point of examining what "kamerads" chanced to come their way—not without an eye for wristlet watches and other articles of value. It may be here remarked in passing that Hun watches were often most excellent timekeepers, and some of them are going still. The "ratting" of prisoners was a very interesting process. Some men were too proud to plunder,

The Auckland Regiment

and stood aloof from the whole business; others, out of a thirst for knowledge, or a desire for souvenirs, displayed a deep interest in all that was Fritz's, from his jewellery to the photos of the "frauleins" he carried in his pocket-book. Fritz was usually quite amiable, and showed a very proper spirit of resignation. Usually the search was conducted in a perfectly friendly spirit, and the unfortunate was consoled for the loss of his girl's photo, or of his Iron Cross, with cigarettes or tobacco. Occasionally the thing was carried too far, as in the case of the Field Ambulance man whom some members of 2/Auckland will remember. This gentleman, with a few others, was in charge of a small post on the main road. Little groups of prisoners were frequently passing, and he was making in every case a most thorough and systematic search through their pockets. One Hun came up, very faint, and evidently almost swooning. His arm was almost off, and as the frightful wound was undressed and without a tourniquet, the man was rapidly bleeding to death. The ornament of the Red Cross went on plundering, and when the matter was pointed out to him by those standing about, refused with oaths to touch the b—— b——. Only direct threats from the infantrymen round about and the intervention of an officer made him come to his senses. Such an inhuman type as this, however, was rare. As a general rule, once prisoners were taken by our people, and had got back out of the actual fighting, they were sure of decent and kindly treatment.

For two days the Brigade waited for orders, expecting a move forward at very short notice. On the 22nd, officers went up to reconnoitre Logeast Wood, but this place, together with Achiet-le-Grand, fell during the night. Bapaume was now within reach. Of the series of ridges which run in a semi-circle to the south and west of the town, all except the last were now in the hands of the British. If the line Loupart Wood-Grevillers-Biefvillers could be taken, the way was open for a direct encirclement of the town itself. During the afternoon of the 23rd, when the 1/Brigade received their orders to move up in readiness for battle in the morning, the exact

To Bapaume!

position was somewhat obscure, and remained so through the greater part of the night. About 4 p.m. the Brigade was moving, 2/Auckland leading, followed by 1/Wellington, 2/Wellington and 1/Auckland. Everybody was in high spirits and quite ready for all that might befall. Once through Bucquoy, where was a dead mule—a significant sight in a smashed village where the barbed-wire barriers were still across the street—and up the short, steep rise that faced the village, the Battalions commenced to march across a wide field, which here and there bore evidence of fighting—helmets and rifles lying about, and here and there newly-dug graves. At the same time it was hard for the men who had fought on the Somme, at Messines and Ypres to realise that this was a battlefield. Very few shell-holes scarred the surface of the meadow-land. Half way to Achiet-le-Petit there was a halt, and the men settled down in old German trenches to wait for the next move. A little shelling caused a few casualties. The night was rather chilly. At 10 p.m. a Brigade conference was called. 2/Auckland and 1/Wellington were ordered to attack before dawn in the direction of Bapaume. Two alternatives were given. If the 5th Division had taken the Loupart Wood-Grevillers-Biefvillers line, as was rumoured, then the objective was to be the town itself. If this had not been done, then 2/Auckland were to take Grevillers and 1/Wellington Loupart Wood. Zero hour was to be at 4.15 a.m., and an artillery barrage was to cover the attack. At 2 a.m. the Battalions, while on the road, received word that, as the English troops were moving, they would have to carry out the second part of the programme. This information, however, was quite wrong, and on arriving at the cross-roads known as the "Starfish," 2/Auckland found that they were for all practical purposes in No-Man's-Land. The road running from the "Starfish" to Biefvillers faced directly on to Grevillers, and along this road the Battalion deployed out and then lay down in readiness for the move forward.

Lieutenant-Colonel S. S. Allen was in command, and had with him Lieutenant Nicholls acting as adjutant in the absence

The Auckland Regiment

of Captain Tuck, who had gone on leave. Dr. Harpur, the Battalion M.O., was also on leave, and his place was taken by Dr. Simcox. Padre Dobson was with Headquarters. Company Commanders were:—

    3rd Company: Captain Wood.
    6th Hauraki: Captain Moncrieff.
    15th North Auckland: Lieutenant Clapham.
    16th Waikato: Major McClelland.

A thousand—fifteen hundred yards away Loupart Wood and Grevillers showed up, dark masses of trees against the lighter background of the fields. These, with the road running from the "Star-fish" to Grevillers, were the only landmarks to give direction. 1/Wellington Battalion arrived, but were too late to establish proper contact. There was no one on the left, and that flank was exposed. Where the enemy might be no one knew, except that on the left he was sending up flares from a post some three hundred yards from the road. Along the rest of the front he gave no sign, and from the reports received he was at least a thousand yards away. The general plan of attack was for two platoons of the 15th Company to go to the right of the village and two to the left, while the 3rd Company were to pass over the ridge between Grevillers and Biefvillers and reach the valley beyond. Very few had a clear realisation of just what had to be done, or how it was to be done. By the time the deployment had taken place and the Company Commanders had received their orders it was time to move. In other battles the zero time was marked by the crash of the barrage opening, but on this occasion a quiet word of command put the Battalion in motion, and very quietly the men moved out into the darkness, knowing little save that they must go forward. The first obstacle was a belt of wire, through which everyone scrambled as best he could. Enemy machine-guns on the left opened up, and also one or two in the centre. So hot was the fire that Lieutenant Vickerman's platoon, on the extreme flank, was held up, and the remainder of the company considerably disorganised. In the centre, however, the resistance was less stubborn, and the

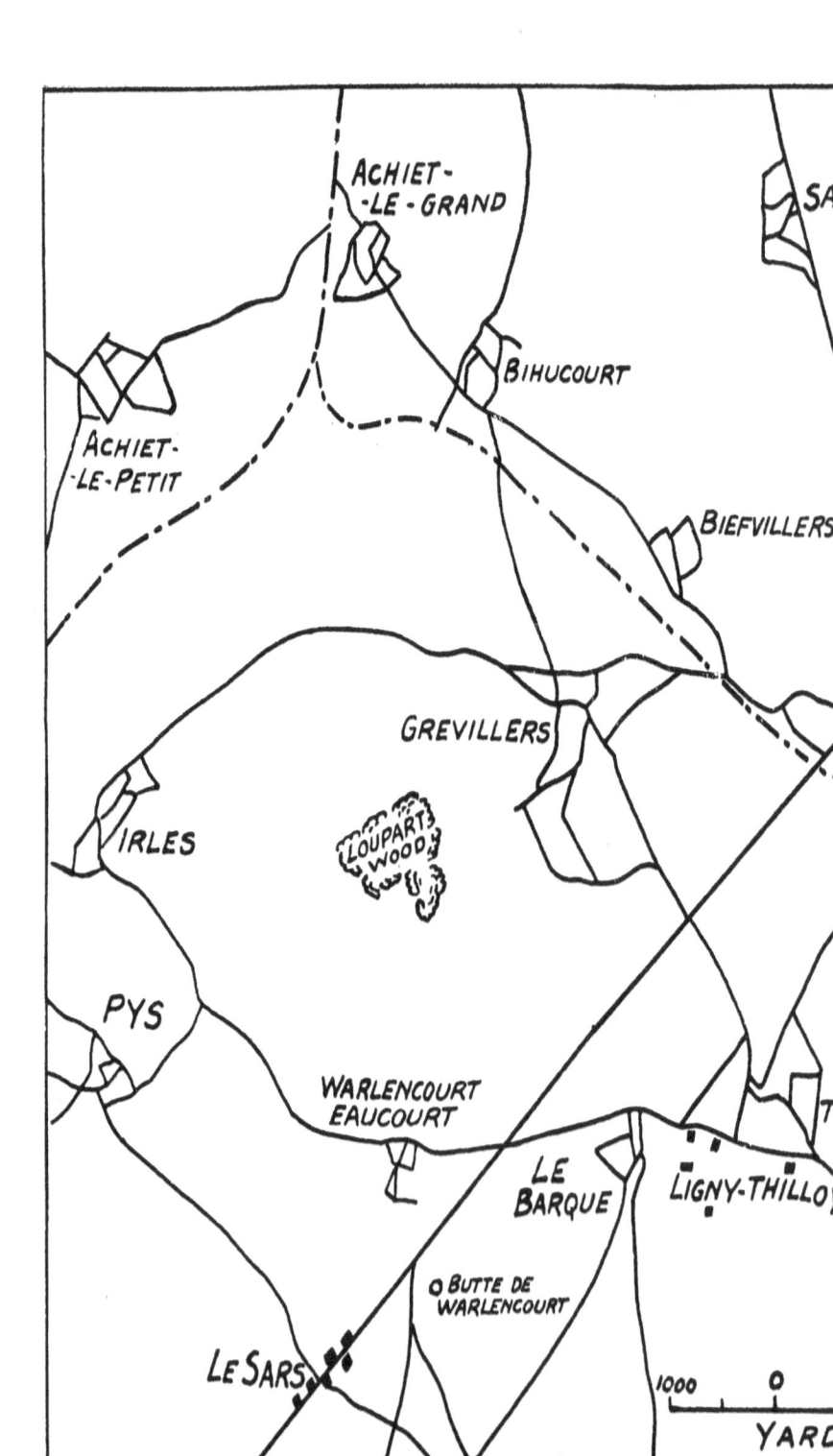

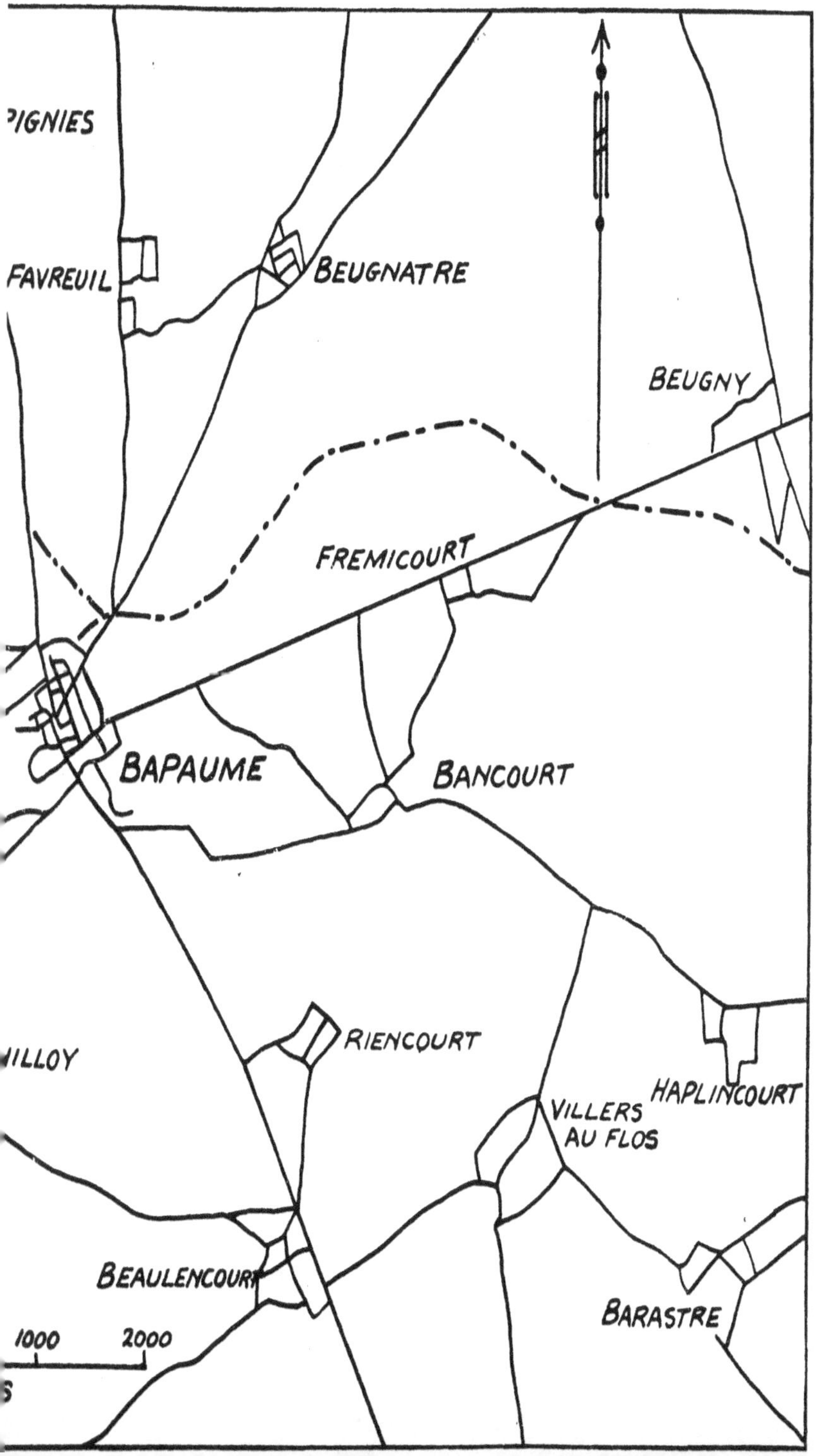

PIGNIES

FAVREUIL

BEUGNATRE

BEUGNY

FREMICOURT

BAPAUME

BANCOURT

ILLOY

RIENCOURT

HAPLINCOURT

VILLERS AU FLOS

BEAULENCOURT

BARASTRE

1000 2000

To Bapaume!

enemy outpost screen was rapidly broken through, many machine-guns and prisoners being taken. A small party, under Sergeant O'Brien of the 3rd Company, was now able to move round and take in the rear the machine-guns which were causing all the trouble. The crews surrendered, and the 16th were thus enabled to get well ahead, meeting with little opposition until they commenced to cross the ridge just in front of their final objective, when they once more came under very heavy fire. In the centre the 3rd Company met with little opposition, moving swiftly on the village along the line of the road. The main part of the 15th Company, on the extreme right flank, crossed below the wire belt, through a trench they were fortunate to discover, thus escaping a very well-directed stream of bullets that were knocking sparks out of the wire. Once through, dark figures were seen moving on the right. Who were they—Huns or men of the Wellington Battalion? They were where the Wellington men ought to be. A guttural challenge and a rifle shot, a short fierce little fight, and then it was obvious from the prostrate figures that there had been no mistake. Under two or three senior N.C.O.'s—amongst whom by far the most prominent was Sergeant McMurdo, a very brave, popular and efficient man—they extended out, and, maintaining touch both with the Wellington Battalion and the 3rd Company, moved on toward the village. The gap widened rapidly, and the thin line stretched out for some hundreds of yards. Just at dawn all were very close to the fringe of hedge and the tall trees that marked the village boundary. The 3rd Company plunged right in, meeting with no opposition. In the middle of the village, marked by the Red Cross, was a large dressing station, which had been hastily evacuated. On the outer edge, where a railway siding ran into the trees, they were just too late to capture a big railway gun, which was hastily towed away by its engine. Four eight-inch howitzers were not so fortunate. Their teams, or traction engines, were not on the spot, and so they could not be moved. These guns were the most important capture yet made by New Zealand troops.

The 15th Company, moving up to the edge of the village

The Auckland Regiment

and the high crest line between it and Loupart Wood, saw figures moving in front of them. Dawn broke very suddenly. From thirty yards in front came a cry of alarm. The long thin line of the 15th hesitated whether to dash right in or not—the Huns hesitated whether to run or stick to their guns. The initiative lay with any bold leader on either side who could impose his will on the waverers. A Hun gunner was the first to act, and the rattle of his gun restored the confidence of the others. Half-a-dozen more joined in, and the 15th went to cover, while the streams of bullets cut up the earth in all directions. It was impossible to raise a head while the Huns continued to rattle through belt after belt at such a furious pace. There was nothing to be done but lie still and wait for better times. Back across the valley three tanks were seen coming up. Helmets went up on bayonet points to attract their attention, and then Sergeant Forsyth, who had been scouting far in advance, went back to the nearest and explained the position. Under heavy fire he led it up the slope toward the sunken road.

Two small quick-firers open on the tank and the little shells burst all round as fast as the gunners can loose them off. The brave sergeant never flinches—hit in the arm by a flying splinter, he still leads on. The German machine-gunners see the danger. Their weapons avail nothing against this iron monster—their nerve fails, and they run. At the same moment the infantry rise up, keeping abreast of or following the tank. They take the sunken road with its row of machine-guns. Then "Bang"—clear and hard—a shell has caught the tank fairly in front. It gives a funny little lurch, slews half round, and then stops dead. But the infantry press on, and, though coming immediately under heavy fire, gain possession of the crest and work some little distance down the slope before flinging themselves down in the old grass-grown shell-holes of 1916.

Forsyth and McMurdo moved freely round on the bare and exposed slope, organising the new line. Enemy snipers not a hundred yards away were very busy, and one of them

To Bapaume!

shot Sergeant Forsyth dead. He had been in front from the moment the advance started, and had acted throughout with the most cool and desperate daring. It was quite certain that he would be killed. He had as fine a record of fighting service as any man with the Division. Enlisting with the Main Body Engineers, he was one of the few who went right through Gallipoli. In France he had been through every general engagement in which the New Zealand troops had fought, in addition to which he had been in two fights with Australian and one with British troops. His was a wonderful record, crowned by a day of glorious deeds. The Victoria Cross awarded to him was one of those which has never been disputed. All were agreed that he was worthy of it, and that there was no one who could be named in any way equal to him.

With the exception of a certain amount of open ground in front of the 15th Company, 2/Auckland had now obtained the whole of their objective, and at an astonishingly small cost. When it is considered that the Battalion took thirty-five machine-guns, all of which were well placed with a splendid field for fire, it is seen that the task set was no easy one. Success can be attributed to the surprise attack in the darkness, which had penetrated deeply before the enemy realised exactly what was happening, the exceedingly patchy defence of the Huns, who fought well in places, but very weakly in others, and the bold leadership displayed by various junior officers and N.C.O.'s in the resolute tackling of the various posts which gave trouble. The 16th Company, in particular, performed the whole of their task in a most satisfactory manner, great credit being due to the manner in which Lieutenant Vickerman pushed forward with his platoon after the initial check. Great results might have been obtained on the right if there had been better combination between the 3rd and 15th Companies, combined with strong, intelligent and resolute leadership. Unfortunately, Colonel Allen was wounded soon after dawn, before he could reconnoitre this part of the front, the command of the Battalion passing to Major McClelland. Casualties were only eighty all told, including seven offi-

The Auckland Regiment

cers, only one of whom—Lieutenant Webster, a very fine man—was killed. Beside the thirty-five machine guns, the three howitzers and the two 77mm. field guns, the Battalion captured five minenwerfers, three waggons, one "pineapple" gun, and nearly four hundred prisoners.

On the flanks, Loupart Wood had fallen to 1/Wellington, and Biefvillers to parties of 2/Wellington, which had been acting as support battalion. Later in the morning the 2/Brigade passed through on the left and kept up the pressure. The same evening 2/Auckland were relieved by the 1/Battalion, and went back in reserve.

After the fall of the Loupart Wood-Grevillers-Biefvillers line the resistance of the enemy in front of Bapaume was much stiffer than had been expected. He clung tenaciously to the Albert-Bapaume road, endeavouring to save time until his defences in rear should be more strongly organised. 1/Auckland for the third time running found themselves actively employed in patrol work, so as to maintain a constant pressure and to be prepared to exploit without loss of time any retirement of the enemy. They took over the position won by 2/Auckland, and held on during the 25th under heavy shelling from 5.9 and eight-inch howitzers. Rain fell through the night, and the next day was showery. At mid-day the 15th Company were ordered to support 2/Wellington in an operation to the right of Grevillers, which had for its object penetration to the south of Bapaume and the crossing of the Bapaume-Albert road. 2/Wellington made no progress, but a patrol of the North Aucklanders, Lieutenant O'Gorman, Sergeant Judson and four others, bombed for two hundred yards up a sap until they reached the road, taking three machine-guns and a couple of prisoners. It was here that Sergeant Judson, who had already distinguished himself in the patrol operations at Hébuterne and Puisieux, was awarded the Victoria Cross for "most conspicuous bravery and devotion to duty, when in an attack on enemy positions he led a small bombing party under heavy fire and captured an enemy machine-gun. He then proceeded up a sap alone, bombing three machine-gun crews before him.

To Bapaume!

Jumping out of the trench he ran ahead of the enemy. Then standing on the parapet he ordered the party, consisting of two officers and ten men to surrender. They instantly fired on him, but he threw a bomb and jumped down amongst them, killed two, put the rest to flight, and so captured two machine-guns. This prompt and gallant action not only saved many lives but enabled the advance to continue unopposed."

Sergeant Judson joined 2/Auckland with the Ninth Reinforcement, and served with them through the trench spell at Armentières until he was badly wounded in the storming of the Switch Line on September 15th, 1916. He rejoined the Regiment after the Hun offensive, and was sent to the 1/Battalion, then holding the line in and about Hébuterne. His feat of winning the D.C.M., the M.M. and the V.C., all in the space of six weeks, is a record probably unequalled by any other British soldier.

The ground gained by the gallant sergeant and his companions was, however, not held, as the Division on the right retired, and, in consequence, the New Zealanders had also to draw back to avoid exposing their flank to attack. Later in the afternoon 1/Auckland were ordered to be ready to follow up in case of an enemy retirement after a short bombardment by the trench mortars. The enemy, however, showed no signs of retiring, and became exceedingly hostile, whereupon the Battalion received orders to "stand fast." Later, orders came to relieve 2/Wellington, and this move was carried out before the dawn of the 27th. During the evening patrols of the 3rd, 6th and 16th, the front line companies, moved out behind a heavy barrage and occupied several hundred yards of ground, going forward until they were held up by enemy strong points. One patrol of the Waikatos crossed the sunken road, but, coming under heavy machine-gun fire, was compelled to withdraw, with the loss of two men killed. Rain set in, and this, with much shelling, combined to make the spell in, a miserable one. The Aucklanders had very little shelter, and an oil-sheet is a poor protection against continued rain. It is good only as far as it goes, and that is not quite to a man's waist. Men

The Auckland Regiment

and water soon make mud, and mud is always a misery in war time. Boots get wet through, and wet feet are never a comfort. Rifles are jammed with the mud, and the lot of the man in the line is altogether an unenviable one, particularly when hot food fails to arrive.

On the morning of the 29th, after a fairly quiet night, 6th Company patrols advised that the enemy showed signs of evacuating the position. Orders were immediately issued to push forward. This was done, and a rapid move at once took place. In an hour 3/Company patrols had pushed forward a thousand yards. The Rifle Brigade, on the left, at the same time commenced to push through Bapaume itself. 1/Auckland, keeping to the right of the town, pushed past it, and, crossing the Bapaume-Peronne road, took up a line beyond the reservoir on the embankment by the large railway siding, some thousand yards ahead of the town itself, and facing the village of Bancourt, which was strongly held by the enemy. 1/Auckland had been continually busy through the whole of the month of August. Without being actually involved in any considerable action, they had been fighting almost continuously and very successfully. The ground they had gained by peaceful penetration and otherwise, was all of extreme value. The casualties had been far from light—4 officers and 31 O.R.'s having been killed, and 5 officers and 123 O.R.'s wounded. Captain Knight, one of the officers wounded, belonged originally to the Fourth Reinforcement draft, and had seen a very considerable amount of service. Amongst the killed was Sergeant Fraser, M.M., a Gallipoli man, who had been badly wounded on two or three occasions. He was a quiet, strong character, a hard worker, and a brave man, who was very highly thought of in the Battalion.

It was decided without any delay to attack the enemy in their new position on the line Frémicourt-Bancourt-Riencourt, which they had organised on the high ground that ran in a northerly direction from Riencourt behind Bancourt to the Cambrai road. Over the whole area of the Ancre and the Somme the country was much the same. Villages scattered

To Bapaume!

here and there were embowered in groves of trees, while, beyond, wide open fields stretched without a vestige of cover for thousands of yards. A succession of chalk ridges, nowhere running to any great height, ran like so many waves across the whole battlefield, and in every case formed admirable defensive positions, giving excellent observation and a splendid field for fire on advancing troops. In accordance with their usual custom, the Huns were holding in depth and relying on their machine-gun nests to hold up attacks made against them. If they had had men behind the guns of the calibre of those who manned the New Zealand guns on Chunuk Bair there would have been little chance of an advance being successful. Fortunately, however, the morale of the German troops was breaking down rapidly, and even where a group or a battalion of brave men put up a resolute resistance there were always faint-hearted ones who gave way long before their position was hopeless.

The attack, which was on a wide front, was to go forward at dawn on the 30th August. On the left the 42/Division was moving on Riencourt, and on the right 1/Wellington had Frémincourt as their objective. Just before zero Major Sinel received information from the English troops that they would be unable to move for some little time. In accordance with instructions received from Brigade, 2/Auckland were thereupon held back, although the rest of the advance continued as arranged. The German artillery opened up at once, and a heavy barrage was put down on the sunken roads in which the Aucklanders had assembled. Many casualties occurred. Major Sinel and Major McClelland were both slightly wounded, but were able to carry on. Dr. Simcox, who was with the Battalion while Dr. Harpur was on leave, was severely wounded. Padre Dobson took over the aid post and superintended the care of the wounded through the rest of the fighting. The padre was one of the few Main Body men still surviving, and had had a long war experience. He was well known for his courage and sang-froid.

When at last the Battalion did advance, the enemy were

The Auckland Regiment

prepared for the move, and concentrated very heavy machine-gun fire on the advancing troops. Bancourt fell to the 6th Company, under Captain Moncrieff, a very brave and able soldier, who had left New Zealand as one of the sergeant-majors attached to the original Battalion of the Auckland Regiment. The Haurakis drew up in a long line, set their teeth and went straight for the village, which they took, very largely owing to the dashing leadership of Lieutenant Taylor. Further progress was difficult. On the ridge beyond, which ran astride of the Bancourt-Bertincourt road, were a number of Niessen huts very strongly held by the enemy. From here and from Riencourt, which was as yet untaken, a very heavy fire was poured in. On the open slope, bare of all cover, men went down in scores. Soon all was confusion. The majority simply lay flat and fired if any target presented itself. In one place a dry water-course running up the hill enabled some to creep forward and so obtain a precarious hold on the ridge. Half way up, a large chalk quarry gave cover for a number. Out on the left, which was now several hundred yards ahead of the 42/Division, the danger of a flanking attack by the Huns was a serious one. To meet any danger from this quarter the 3/Company were sent out to form a defensive flank. It was impossible to get further forward, but what ground had been gained was resolutely held against counter-attacks, that continued to develop throughout the day. Under cover of darkness the position was roughly organised, and some more ground occupied, while wounded, who could not be approached by daylight, were picked up and sent back.

At dawn next morning two enemy tanks came out and headed for our line. One reached the chalk quarry and skirted along the edge—a couple of yards only from a line of men who lay flat on their faces, scarcely daring to breathe. It was a terrible moment, and then the tank passed on, finally falling down a small bank, and sticking helplessly. Fighting through the day was heavy, until the fall of Riencourt took off the pressure from the flank. This made the enemy's position no longer tenable, and during the night of September 1st-2nd he

To Bapaume!

commenced to draw back. In a short while the withdrawal became a general retirement, which was followed up by the 2/Brigade. In this action 2/Auckland took 150 prisoners, 51 machine-guns and one tank. Their losses were heavy, over 350 being killed and wounded. Lieutenant Carter, who as signal corporal had done so well on the 15th September, 1916, was here mortally wounded. He was very well known in the Regiment, and was extremely popular. Lieutenant W. Hill, who also died of wounds, was another well-known figure who had been with the Battalion in the early days. Lieutenants Hall, McCreanor, Taylor and Abel were all brave and capable men, whose loss was a severe blow to the Battalion.

XXVIII

September

> "*Boots, belts, rifle and pack,*
> *All you'll need till you come back,*
> *All you'll doff when you lie down to sleep.*
> *All they'll take off when they bury you deep.*
> *Boots, belt, rifle and pack.*"
> —C. G. N. in "Anzac Book."

The first few days of September were spent by the 1/Brigade in resting and reorganising. 2/Auckland were in huts and bivouacs on the Bancourt battlefield. Their cookers were brought up and the men received back their overcoats. It can hardly be imagined what a comfort an overcoat is after living in the open without one for a fortnight. If a man rolls himself into a round ball, tucks one tail of the coat over his head and the other under his feet, and then stops up the chinks with his tunic, the amount of heat generated is quite surprising. A heavy downpour of rain flooded a number of bivvies, but apart from the discomfort caused by this, the time passed pleasantly and quietly enough.

Reinforcements joined up in such numbers that a man who was slightly wounded at Grévillers and rejoined after Bancourt felt himself a stranger. The new men were of good quality. Throughout the whole of the war the New Zealand standard of manhood was maintained in the most remarkable fashion—the difference in this respect between the Main Body and the very latest of the reinforcements being relatively small. Many of the men in each draft were just of age, and had been for years eagerly looking forward to the time when they would be able to follow their elder brothers overseas. A very excellent leaven was also provided by older men, who, long before the war, had been settled in positions of responsibility, and with whom the breaking up of home and business was a serious matter.

Colonel Allen rejoined on September 5th, his wound having been quite a slight one.

September

1/Auckland on the 3rd of September moved from outside Bapaume to the area between Bancourt and Fremicourt, from whence a day later they moved to Haplincourt, and then to Riencourt, where they stayed for the remainder of the rest period, drilling and working.

In the meanwhile the advance had gone well forward. The 2/Brigade followed the enemy closely through Haplincourt and Bertincourt to Ruyaulcourt, from where after further fighting the pursuit continued through Neuville-Bourganval and Metz-Couture past Havrincourt Wood, and so to the Hindenburg line, on which it was the intention of the enemy to make a resolute stand. The German line ran along the high ground from Gouzeaucourt Wood, through the villages of Trescault and Havrincourt, and included a portion of the old British line—African Trench—which was particularly well sited for defensive purposes. The Rifle Brigade were now in the line, and after carrying out an attack on the 12th were to be relieved by the 1/Brigade, who on the 11th commenced to move up in readiness for the change over. That night 1/Auckland bivouacked at Ytres and 2/Auckland between Haplincourt and Bertincourt. At dawn the 62/Division and the Rifle Brigade made a successful attack, and as the 1/Brigade marched up prisoners were coming back in numbers. Many of them were Jæger troops, whose green uniforms patched with leather were conspicuous amongst the more common field-greys. They were good men, and had fought with much determination. 2/Auckland, going into brigade reserve, took over some trenches, deep dug-outs and huts round the village of Metz, where they remained until relieved. Except for some shelling they had a very quiet time.

During the night, 1/Auckland relieved the 3/N.Z.R.B. in captured position east of Metz. Here they were heavily shelled, for the enemy, being now as he thought on a secure line, had his artillery in the old gun positions, and was shelling freely, using a good deal of "ground-shrapnel" and gas. This ground-shrapnel was a particularly objectionable form of frightfulness, which was fortunately only used to any great extent

The Auckland Regiment

during the last two or three months of the war. Up to this time the enemy had relied on the air-burst and the ordinary type of H.E., which buried itself some feet in the ground before exploding. Both types had obvious disadvantages. The first wasted much of its energy on the empty air, while the second was inevitably to a large extent smothered by the dead weight of earth which had to be thrown out. By fitting an exceedingly sensitive fuse to the H.E. shell a "ground-burst" was obtained. Every fragment of the shell thus became potentially destructive against troops advancing in the open. A well-placed barrage of these shells would have been as nearly impenetrable as anything of the sort could be.

Great numbers of dead Jægers were lying about in the captured line, and many more live ones were obviously assembling in the trenches opposite, with the idea no doubt of launching a counter-attack. Bombing raids were carried out to disorganise the enemy. They were very successful, and the parties inflicted severe losses on the enemy and managed to withdraw with very light casualties themselves. Later on in the afternoon the enemy attack took place. It was a strong one, and he succeeded in driving in the advanced posts. At midnight he attacked once more, using liquid fire, and, coming in both on flank and front, caused a further retirement of the posts back on to the main line.

On the 14th, the New Zealand Division was relieved, and the 1/Brigade marched back to the vicinity of Bapaume, behind which the whole of the Division was concentrated. The next fortnight was given up to rest, reorganisation and training, in preparation for the heavy fighting which was to take place in the next few weeks.

At this time there were few who imagined that the end was as close as it actually proved to be. Certainly it was evident that Germany was weakening fast. In a succession of great victories nearly all the ground lost in the disasters of the spring had been reoccupied. The submarine campaign was being more than held. American troops were pouring into France by the hundred thousand. But still, the winter was

September

close at hand—the enemy were back on strongly fortified positions; they still had enough war material and enough men to fight on for months, and it seemed to many that, although perhaps there was just a possibility of a quick decision, it was more probable that another winter and spring campaign would be necessary to carry the Allied arms to the Rhine.

Training was easy enough, and the men recuperated quickly in the good billets and pleasant surroundings. During this time Dr. Holland-Rose, of Cambridge University, the famous historian, gave a series of lectures on various historical subjects. These lectures were attended by hundreds, and the lecturer was very pleased with the attentive and intelligent hearing given to him. Lectures of this sort were the chief success of the educational scheme with the men in the field. Another feature of the work, which was carried on under extreme difficulties, was the divisional library, which had been commenced during the winter spent in the Ypres salient. This library, consisting of the best books in all departments of knowledge, was a rallying point for all the students of the Division.

The New Zealanders were sufficiently far back to be out of the range of gun fire, but at night Hun bombing 'planes were particularly active against Bapaume. The town was a most important centre of communications. Roads radiated from it in all directions, and a very great deal of traffic was continually passing through. In the old days, when the Division was in rest outside Bailleul, the night raiders had been located by searchlights and then heavily shelled by the anti-aircraft guns. A very fine pyrotechnic display was thus given for the benefit of all who cared to watch the proceedings; the raider dropped his bombs and then departed, trailing shrapnel bursts behind him. Anti-aircraft gunners and the searchlight people felt after the commotion had subsided that they had really done something toward winning the war, while the Hun, from his point of view, was just as satisfied—he had dropped his bombs, and they had burst with a loud noise. No one was hurt, and by morning the various participants were sleeping

The Auckland Regiment

the sleep of the just. Times, however, had changed, and the "strafing" of raiders had become a much more scientific business. As the drumming in the air grew louder, the throb of the German engine became more clearly discernible, and as the big Gotha approached the town the searchlights flashed out, and half-a-dozen dazzling beams crossed and recrossed each other in the darkness. At last the beams converge on the raider and hold him fast in a point of intense light. Then a British fighter that has been up on patrol flies up to within fifty feet of the blinded Hun, and rattles in a short burst of fire. In a few seconds the Gotha commences to fall. Streaks of smoke and flame burst from her. She is on fire, and falling fast. A thousand feet from the ground she tumbles out of the searchlight beams, and then in a sheet of her own flame crashes amongst the ruins of the town—her bombs exploding as they fall to earth. For a couple of miles round the infantry in all the camps have been looking on with eagerness, and the fall of the enemy raider is greeted with a cheer. Then the searchlights went out, the patrol machine took up its beat backward and forward along the railway line, and the spectators went back to rest.

One of the principal events of the rest period was an inspection of the Battalions, carried out by General Russell. Much trouble was taken by everyone to reach a very high degree of polish, 1/Auckland in particular being highly successful in this endeavour. "Spit and polish" presented certain difficulties, owing sometimes to the shortage of the requisite supplies, but enthusiastic company officers usually managed, by scouring the country, to obtain sufficient for the purpose. Equipment was "blancoed" with khaki blanco, and its life thereby shortened. Bayonets whose surfaces had been dulled by a chemical process in the course of manufacture, were furbished with emery paper. "Soldiers Friend" and brasso made all brasswork shine like fire. A battalion polished up in this fashion presented a very imposing sight. The British Army was the only one in Europe to maintain the tradition of polished brass on active service. All others—French, German, American,

September

Belgian, Italian and Portuguese—having adopted the dull metal. On a sunshiny day a battalion marching along a dusty road would, at a distance of a few hundred yards, be almost indistinguishable, when of a sudden a ray of sunlight would strike on all the shoulders swinging in unison, and a shimmer of shining brass ran like a line of flame from one end of the column to the other. This was an extraordinarily beautiful sight, especially against a background of green fields.

XXIX

Welsh Ridge—Crêvecœur—Rumilly —Le Quesnoy

The whole of the German line from Verdun to the sea was now endangered. They had lost all they had gained, and more; Lille was threatened by the British, and Metz by the French and Americans. Cambrai, defended by the great block of powerful fortifications known as the Hindenburg line, was the central buttress of the enemy position. If they could hold in the centre they would still have an opportunity of winning a breathing space. Cambrai became the storm centre, and practically the full force of the British Army was employed against it. While the New Zealanders had been resting, a very brilliant operation, carried out largely by Canadian troops, had broken through the main defences opposite the town. The decisive action was about to take place, and the New Zealand Division was brought up to co-operate with other troops on the right of the town itself. Running in an irregular line in front of Cambrai was the canalised river de l'Escaut, which, as it was nowhere fordable, presented a considerable obstacle to the advance. In some places it had already been crossed, but opposite the New Zealand sector it bent back in a deep loop, and an advance of several kilometres was necessary before the bridge-heads at Crêvecœur could be reached. The front line ran along the railway from Epehy to Marcoing. Immediately facing it was the wide flat-topped Welsh Ridge, which on the further side fell away steeply to the Vacquarie Valley—a dry watercourse on the other side. Across the valley a level plain stretched for a mile and a half to the Bonavis Ridge, which covered Crêvecœur itself. The aim of the New

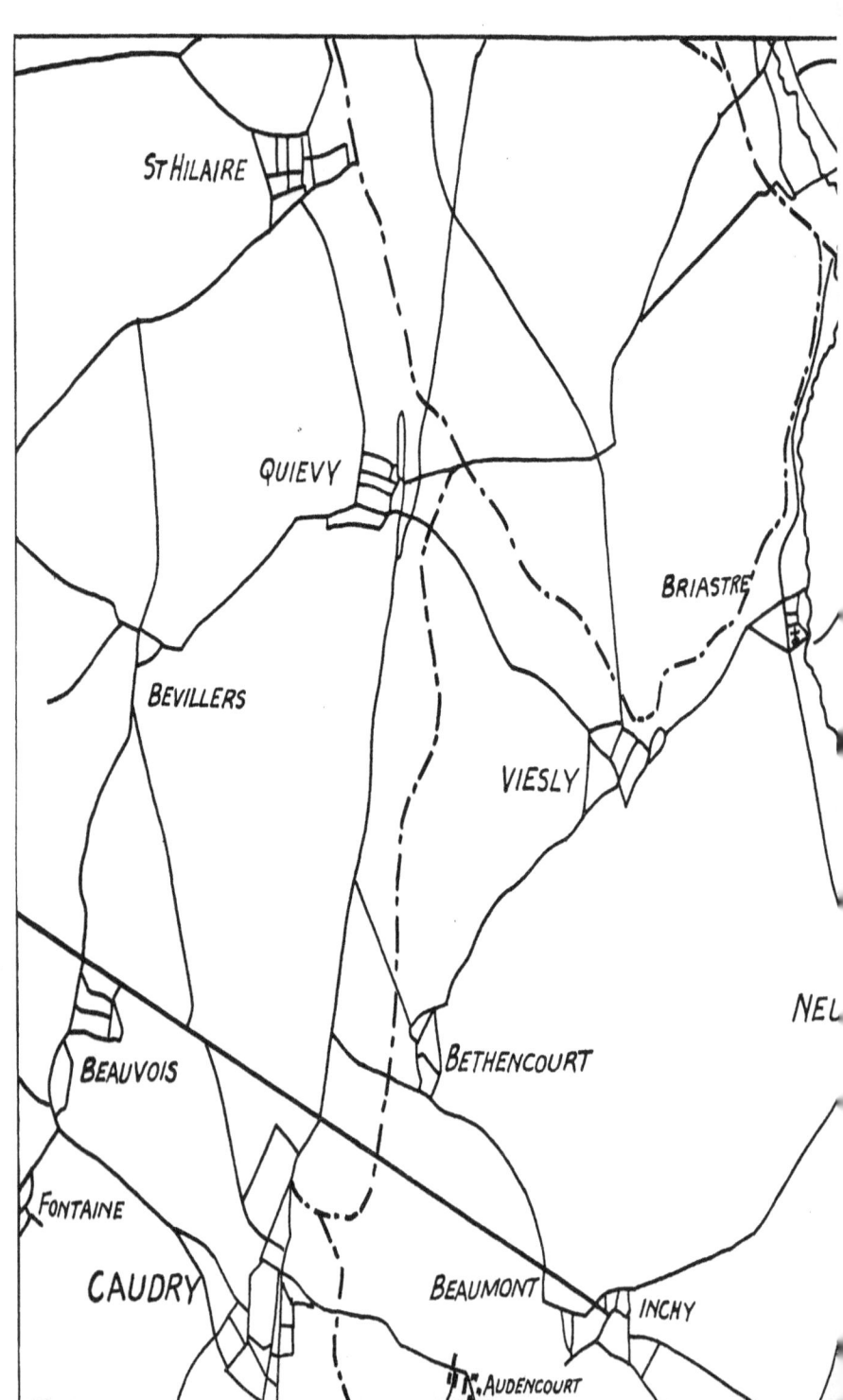

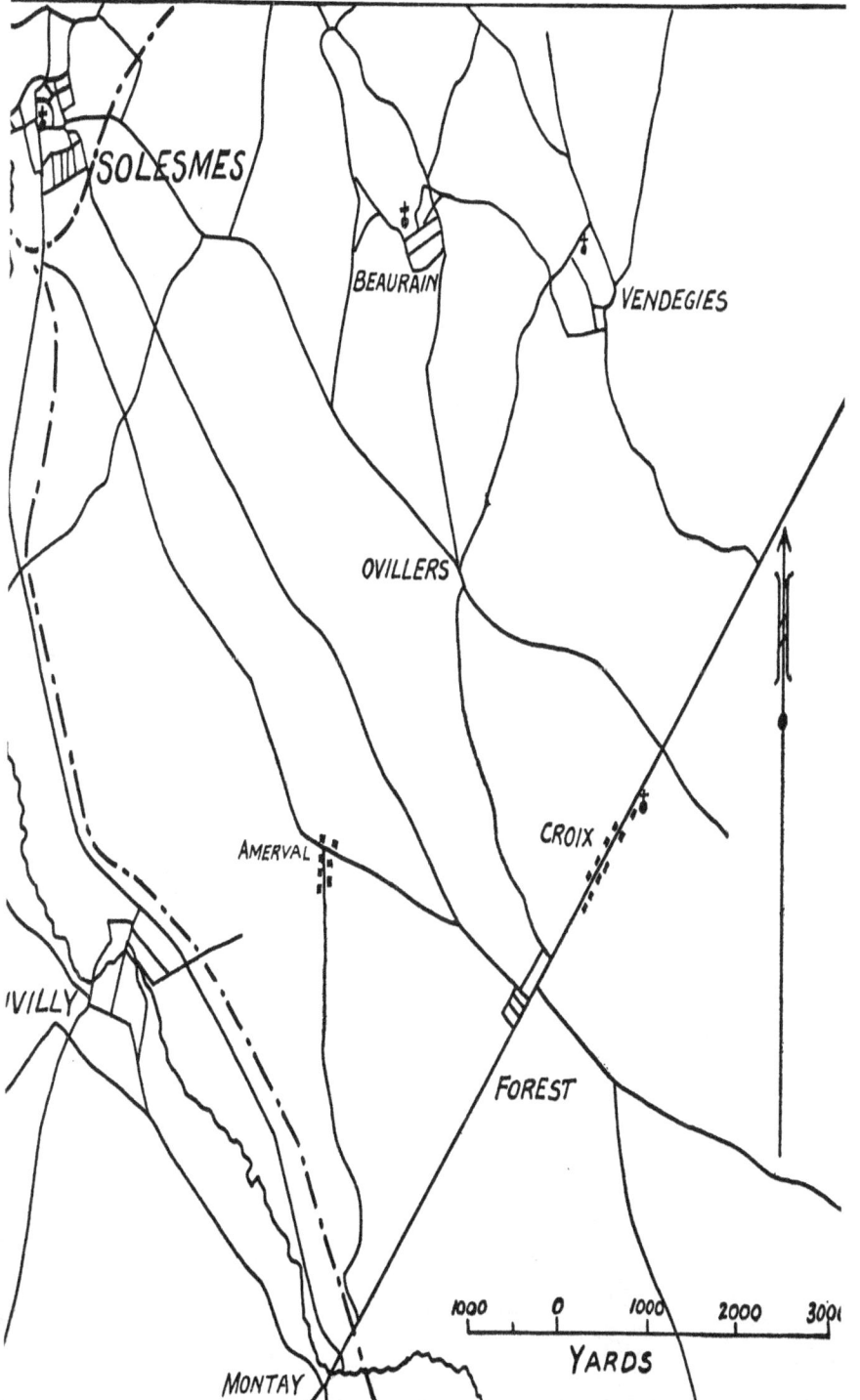

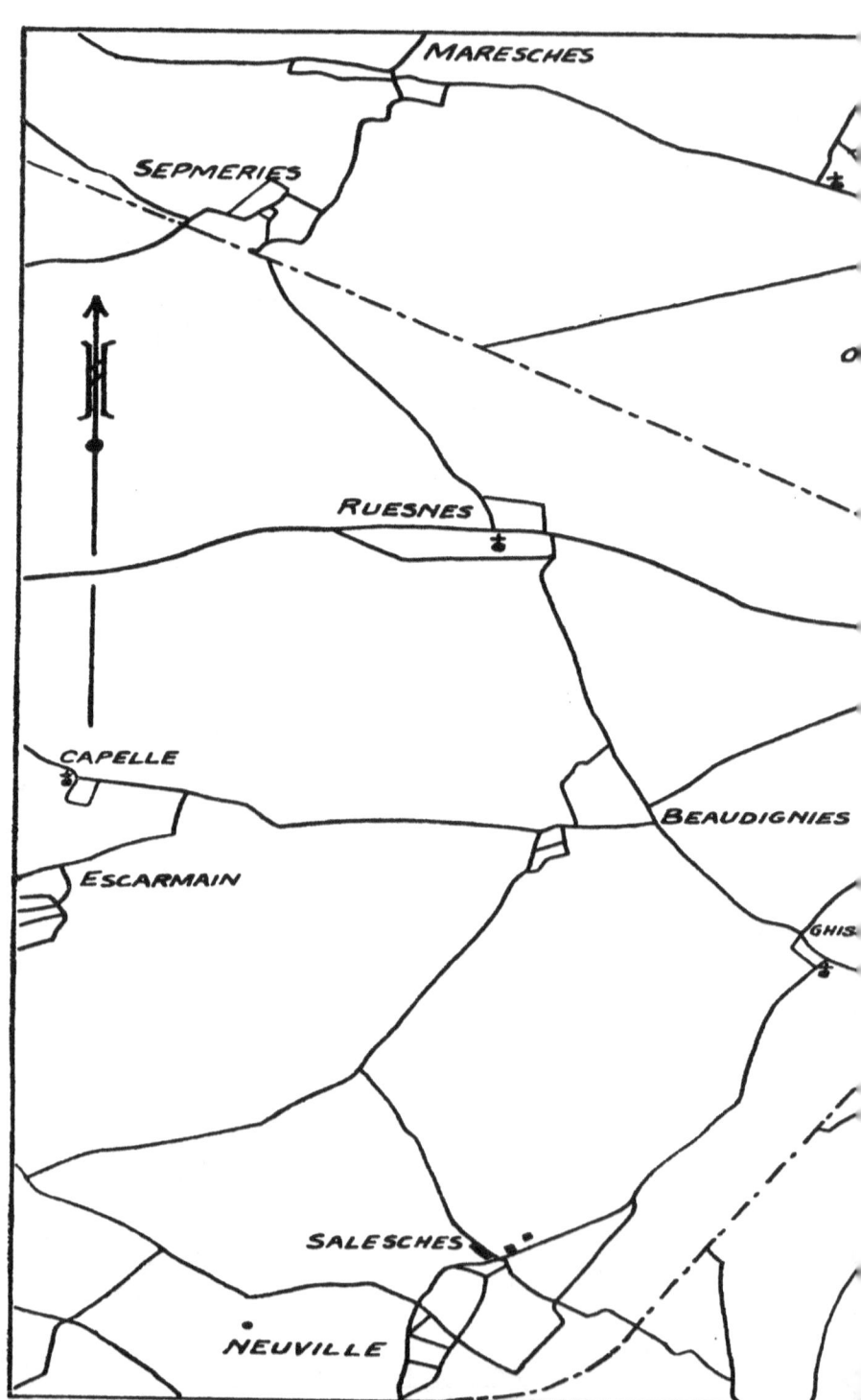

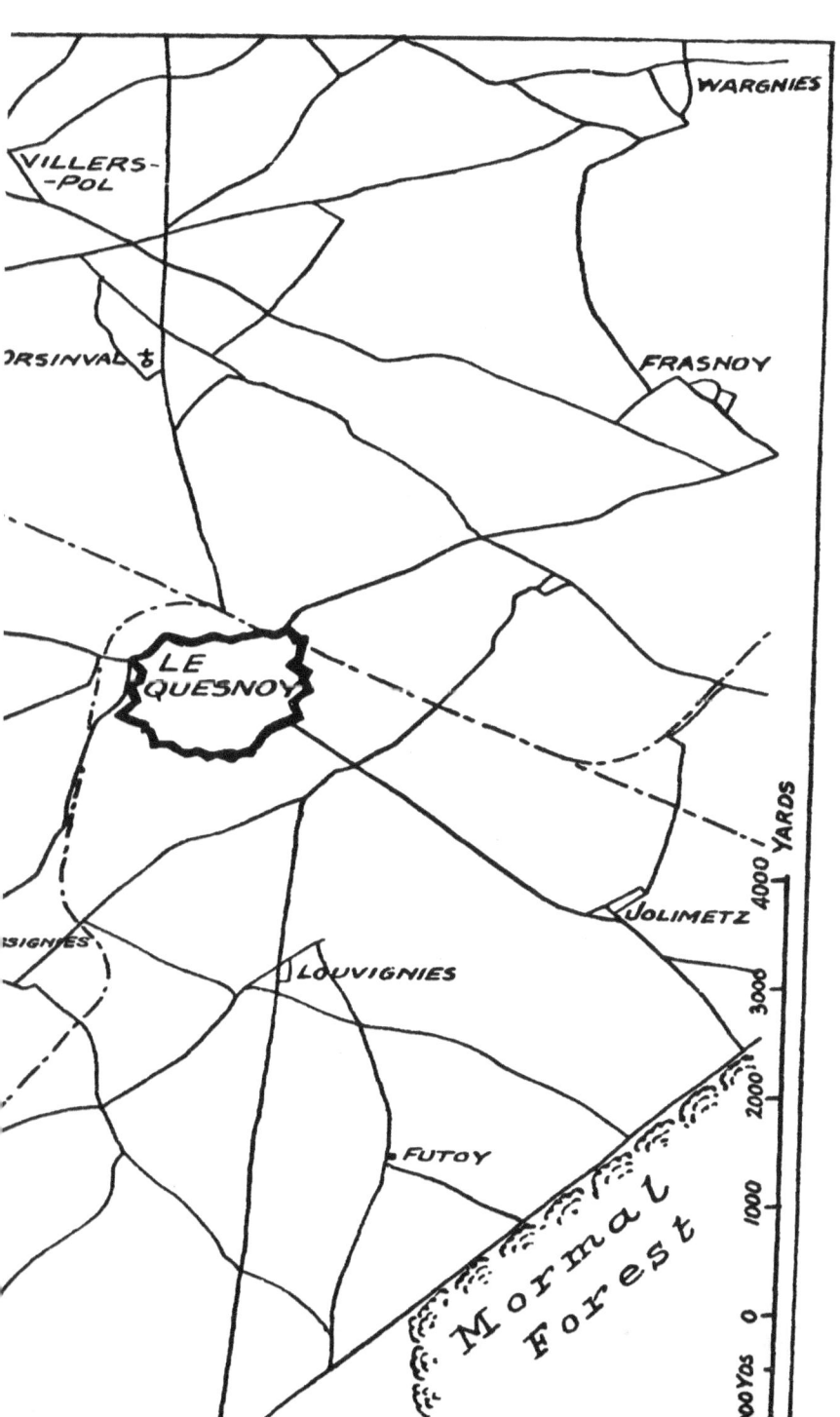

Welsh Ridge—Crêvecœur—Rumilly—Le Quesnoy

Zealand Division was to capture Welsh Ridge, Bonavis Ridge, secure the river crossings, and then, after taking Crêvecœur, to push forward and establish a line of posts on the high ground about the mill of Esnes and the hamlet of La Targette. The advance was to be made on a two brigade front, with the 2/Brigade on the right and the 1st on the left. On the 1st Brigade sector the Wellington Regiment were on the right and the Auckland on the left. It was hoped that the leading battalions—1/Auckland and 2/Wellington—would reach Bonavis Ridge, and that from there 1/Wellington would cross the river at Rue des Vignes, while 2/Auckland, crossing at Crêvecœur, would occupy the village and pass on to the high ground.

On the 28th of September the battalions moved by motorlorry from Bapaume to Neuville-Bourjonval. After a rather miserable day, and a difficult and tedious march, the assembly positions were reached, and final preparations were made in ample time. At zero, 3.30 a.m. on the morning of the 29th, the attack commenced under cover of darkness. What took place can hardly be described as a battle—it was more like a procession. Scarcely any resistance was offered, although the enemy were in considerable force, with the usual number of machine-guns in position. Some of his heavy artillery came into action, but the men were nearly all past the line of this barrage before it commenced to fall. A much more serious impediment than the enemy were the huge belts of wire which crossed the line of advance. These, with the normal difficulty of moving masses of men in the darkness, caused a certain confusion, and in some cases a certain divergence from the correct line of advance. By six o'clock the leading companies were crossing the Bonavis Ridge. No particular opposition was being offered by the enemy, and the troops, although a little mixed, were by no means disorganised. Having taken so much ground with such ease they were in the best of spirits, and quite capable of pushing forward to complete the task. Colonel Alderman, however, stopped the advance, not only of his own battalion, but also of 2/Auckland, who were in very close support, and were prepared to go through. Unfortu-

The Auckland Regiment

nately, Colonel Allen had been somewhat delayed, and when he reached the front found that the opportunity had passed, dawn having broken, and the enemy, having recovered from the first shock of the surprise, were commencing to make a determined resistance. Casualties had been ridiculously small compared with the results obtained. In the whole Regiment the only two platoons to lose at all heavily were two of the 6th Company of the 2nd Battalion, who, missing direction, finished up on the flank of 2/Wellington, and there in some buildings near Lateau Wood had some sharp fighting. No accurate list of captures was made, but the two Auckland Battalions between them took at least 15 guns of various calibres, beside very many machine-guns and numbers of prisoners. The ground gained was of the utmost value, and as the battle had gone well all along the line, Cambrai was more than half-encircled. The surprise attack in the darkness again proved a great success. That such an attack could be carried out showed that the Division had attained a high standard of training and morale.

The day passed quietly, and then during the night 1/Wellington and 2/Auckland received orders to cross the river early next morning and complete the operation. Preparations for the attack were much hindered by the darkness, which was particularly intense. Runners lost themselves, and the telephonic communications broke down. Colonel Allen, arriving at the headquarters of the 15/Company, found none of the company commanders present for the conference he had summoned. They did not arrive until 4 a.m., by which time it was too late to carry out the plan of attack exactly as at first intended. There was no time for the Battalion to concentrate, and in consequence each company had to move independently to its battle station.

The l'Escaut River, after running north-east for some miles, turned at Crèvecœur and ran due west for a considerable distance. To the south of the village 1/Wellington were to cross by the bridge from the Rue des Vignes, and were then to work up to the high ground by Lesdain. Right in the bend

Welsh Ridge—Crêvecœur—Rumilly—Le Quesnoy

of the river, by the Château de Revelon, was the crossing by which 2/Auckland were to enter Crêvecœur. Here, owing to the canalisation, there were two branches of the river to be crossed, and between them a flat, marshy island some hundred and fifty yards wide. Two bridges had thus to be crossed, and as it was most likely that they would be strongly held and swept by machine-gun fire it was necessary that the attack should be both strong and swift.

At four o'clock the enemy commenced to shell heavily, to break up, if possible, any concentration of troops that might be preparing for an advance. An hour later the 15/Company, under Captain Evans, M.C., an exceptionally fine officer, who had seen much service with the mounted troops and with the 4/Brigade, were moving forward under cover of darkness toward the bridge-head. At first everything went well. In the cold, wet, misty dawn the 15th crossed the stone bridge and occupied the island. The leading platoon led on across the second branch of the river, and commenced to establish themselves on the further side. Success seemed assured, as signs of demoralisation were plainly showing amongst the enemy. Many of their men were already running back. If the 3rd and 16th Companies arrived up to time the village would be taken. They did not come, and very soon the opportunity passed.

1/Wellington had missed their way in the darkness, and, wandering away to the right in the direction of Banteux, did not succeed in coming into action at all. The 3rd Company, feeling out to their right in an endeavour to keep touch, also lost direction, and, with the 16th Company, approached the Rue des Vignes bridge instead of the one at Crêvecœur. Rue des Vignes was strongly held by the enemy with numerous machine-guns. Major Sherson and Captain Stewart attacked at once, and after some stiff fighting, in which several casualties occurred, cleared the ground up to the river bank. It was impossible to cross, as the bridge itself was swept by the enemy machine-gun fire. Here Captain Stewart was wounded. As a corporal in the Wellington Battalion he had been one of the small band who held Chunuk Bair all through the terrible day

The Auckland Regiment

of August 8th, 1915. Promoted to commissioned rank, he had served through the campaigns in France and Flanders with 2/Auckland, and was universally recognised as one of the best fighting officers the Battalion ever had.

The 15th Company, in the meantime, were being very hard pressed. As soon as the enemy saw that there was no further development of the assault they took heart of grace, and commenced to counter-attack in force. They lost heavily from the Lewis gun fire which was poured into them, but nevertheless pressed hard on the platoon who were holding the outskirts of the village. This platoon was in a most dangerous position. Their retreat across the bridge was almost impossible, owing to the heavy fire directed upon it, while they were too few to hold their ground without reinforcements. Private Crichton here distinguished himself greatly. Twice he swam the river under heavy fire to take messages to company headquarters. The bridge itself was mined, and, to prevent the enemy blowing it up, Crichton cut the wires and not only that but removed the fuses from and then detached the mines from the bridge—a most daring piece of work. Orders were sent to the forward platoon to withdraw if possible. Some managed to do this by running the gauntlet of the machine-guns, others hid on the river-bank and got back after dark, while a few were captured. By this time part of the 6th Company, under Lieutenant Somers, had reinforced on the island. Their commander was hit as he crossed the bridge, and for some time the company was commanded by Sergeant Bishop. Fighting continued all the morning, and ended in a deadlock. Between the Huns and the Aucklanders was the bridge, which neither side could hope to pass in daylight. Crichton, although wounded in the foot, stayed with the company, and for the remainder of the day was helping the stretcher-bearers to clear the wounded. For his valour and devotion to duty he was awarded the Victoria Cross.

Colonel Allen, discovering the whereabouts of the 3rd and 6th Companies, withdrew them from the Rue des Vignes, with the idea of working them over a temporary bridge some little

Welsh Ridge—Crêvecœur—Rumilly—Le Quesnoy

distance to the left of the village. It was while engaged in reconnoitring the possibilities of a move in this direction that Major Sherson was killed. Sergeant-Major Roberts, who was with him, managed to return to Battalion Headquarters, and reported against any attempt being made in daylight, as a strong force of the enemy, well posted, were covering the bridge. Nothing further could be done, except later in the day to picket the Rue des Vignes bank of the river, to prevent the development of any turning movement the enemy might attempt if the crossing were left unguarded.

There was no hope now of taking Crêvecœur by frontal assault, and, in consequence, Brigade made arrangements for 1/Auckland and 2/Wellington to pass the river at Masnieres and encircle the village from the west. 2/Auckland were to be prepared to push patrols through the village as soon as the enemy showed signs of retiring. 1/Auckland crossed the Escaut by one of the temporary wooden bridges between Masnieres and Crêvecœur and took up a battle station facing due east toward Serranvillers, with 2/Wellington (who were to storm Crêvecœur) on the right. Troops of the 1/Division were to storm Rumilly, a powerfully-organised village on the left flank. Colonel Alderman disposed the battalion in depth. The 15th Company, commanded by Captain Daldy, and the 3rd, under Major Devereux, were to form the first line. If everything went well the 16th Company, under Lieutenant A. W. Gordon, was to pass to the front in the latter stages of the advance, and occupy the trench line which ran directly in front of Serranvillers, while the 6th Company, under Captain Forbes, was to remain in battalion reserve. The advance, as planned, was to penetrate to a depth of some 3500 yards along the plateau and the slope of the ridge, which ran in an easterly direction from Masnieres to Serranvillers, leaving Crêvecœur to the right rear. Stretching ahead, the country was open and treeless, destitute of all cover, except for several sunken roads which crossed the front parallel to the line of advance. Zero hour was fixed for 5.30 a.m., and a barrage moving forward a hundred yards every three minutes was to cover the advance.

The Auckland Regiment

Immediately the barrage opened the 15th and 3rd Companies moved, and quickly over-running the enemy outposts, advanced rapidly on the Crucifix Road, which they took with little loss, capturing 400 prisoners, beside 40 machine-guns. Nothing could illustrate better the low morale of the German army than that such a surrender should take place. Posted as these men were, they should have held their ground against many times the number they surrendered to. The best troops in the world can make no progress across the open against well-served machine-guns. Once past Crucifix Road, the opposition stiffened considerably, and the next two roads were only taken after severe fighting, in which Lieutenant Aickin distinguished himself. Three hundred more prisoners were captured, and many of the enemy were shot down as they endeavoured to retire back on the village.

On the left, owing to the failure of the English troops to carry Rumilly, the whole flank was completely in the air, and as counter-attacks now commenced to develop, both from Serranvillers and Rumilly, the position rapidly became serious. Captain Daldy formed a defensive flank, but his men were few and the line to be covered was a long one. Enemy fire was heavy, and from the left they had a perfect enfilade of the newly-won positions. It was a bitter thing to fall back, but obviously there was nothing else to be done. A new line was formed on the Crucifix Road, mainly through the efforts of Lieutenant Gordon, who set a very fine example, and this was held. Many men failed to get back and were killed, wounded, and a few even taken prisoners. Groups of men, cut off here and there, fought to the death rather than surrender. The flanking platoon of the 15th attacked by overwhelming numbers, defended itself heroically, and the whole line fought to the finish. Even when they were all dead the Huns feared for a long time to close in. On the Crucifix Road there was for a while much overcrowding, as not only were men coming in from the front, but also supports were moving up. Enemy artillery on the flank opened up and caused heavy losses. Riflemen and Lewis gunners lined the bank, and soon

Welsh Ridge—Crêvecœur—Rumilly—Le Quesnoy

checked the German attack. As soon as possible, reorganisation was commenced. The 6th Company held the line of the road, while the 3rd, 15th and 16th were disposed in depth in the rear. Owing to the exceptionally heavy losses, one company of 1/Wellington was placed at the disposal of the battalion, and later in the day they relived the 6th Company and held the front line until the relief. Crêvecœur had been taken by 2/Wellington, with some small assistance from 2/Auckland, who had pushed patrols through the village as soon as the pressure from the flank had caused the enemy to withdraw from the bridge-heads.

The next two days passed comparatively quietly, and there was no change in the general situation. There were occasional intense crashes of artillery fire, and twice on the morning of October 3rd the enemy put down a heavy barrage on the front line, but failed to follow up with the infantry attack that was expected. A report was at this time circulated to the effect that the enemy were evacuating their position, but a reconnoitring patrol established the fact that they were still holding in full strength.

1/Auckland had lost very heavily. When the Battalion was relieved the total strength, excluding Headquarters, was only 5 officers and 157 O.R.'s. the losses for the period, 28th September to October 4th, were:—

	Officers.	O.R.'s.
Killed	2	46
Wounded	10	249
Missing		53
Total	12	348

2/Auckland lost during the same period 4 officers and 18 O.R.'s killed, 6 officers and 112 O.R.'s wounded, and 17 O.R.'s missing.

For the next week the 1/Brigade, withdrawn from the line, lived comfortably in dug-outs of the Hindenburg line, resting and reorganising. The 2/Brigade and the Rifle Brigade carried on with the advance, and after a little stiff fighting between Serranvillers and Esnes the advance swept on for some ten miles through Fontaine-au-Pire and Beauvois, across the Cambrai-Le Cateau road, until, on October 9th, the advance guards were only a few thousand yards from the Selle River. Here the 1/Brigade took over, and with 1/Wellington and 2/Auckland in the van, advanced to the line of the river. No opposition was met with—the enemy everywhere retiring as our men established contact with them. As the Guards Division on the right had failed completely to make any forward movement, the flank was in considerable danger, but the Vickers machine-guns had no difficulty in breaking up the attack which was for a while threatened.

October 12th saw the whole Division relieved and concentrated round Beauvois and Fontaine. The week spent here was very pleasant. For the first time in six months men were living in real houses, that had been made into comfortable billets by the Huns. While in billets, the Prince of Wales passed through the area, and the 1/Brigade were lined up along the road with orders to cheer him spontaneously and heartily. It is very difficult to get New Zealanders to cheer at any time, and quite impossible to make them do so "by numbers," and so the attempt broke down most dismally.

East of the Selle River the advance had been continued, and Solesmes fell on the 20th of October, while on the evening of the same day the bridge-heads of the Ecaillon River were reached. Four days later the last ridge before Le Quesnoy was stormed, and here the advance rested for the next ten days. The main difficulty now was not the overcoming of the enemy defence, which was now breaking everywhere almost at a touch, but the increasing difficulty of getting supplies forward. From Hébuterne to Crêvecœur the advance had been made across a ruined and desolated country. As the enemy retreated they blew up the bridges, damaged every rail in the line, placed mines ingeniously fused so as to blow up perhaps weeks after, and, in short, did all that the wit of man could devise to hamper the pursuit that was pressing so close on their heels. As the railway track had everywhere to be

Welsh Ridge—Crêvecœur—Rumilly—Le Quesnoy

repaired, and, as even when this was done, delayed explosions were frequently occurring and causing damage at some critical point, it was not to be wondered at that a breathing space was necessary.

The 1/Brigade awaited the continuation of the advance in Solesmes, a manufacturing town that until the very last had been untouched by the war. It was the first place from which the enemy had not removed the civilian population. The French folk showed a great desire to bow and raise their hats to the New Zealanders, and in every way were most kind and obliging. Very polite people they were until a batch of prisoners were escorted back through the town. Then the "gamins" collected hastily from all quarters, after the fashion of small boys, and "barraged" the unhappy Huns with old tins and refuse of sundry sorts—a most pleasant diversion, when it is remembered that only a few days before the "kamarads" had been lording it about these very streets, and small boys who misbehaved were liable to summary castigation. Grown-ups did not throw tins, but indulged in facetious and candid remarks concerning the prisoners personal appearance, family history and probable future. French people can be most charmingly frank when the fit seizes them. One Hun officer was recognised, and with a howl of fury there was a general rush in his direction, and the infuriated mob commenced to beat him to death. Rescued with difficulty from their hands, a serious charge was at once laid against him.

It was now obvious that the end was very near. Bulgaria surrendered. Turkey collapsed utterly. Austria was granted an armistice that amounted to practically unconditional surrender. The whole of the German Western front was crumbling rapidly.

Just at this time, however, the New Zealand Division was more concerned over the rumour that they were to be given the "King's rest." This popular myth had been circulated in the Division ever since the first few weeks in Armentières. Whenever the troops had had a hard fight or a particularly trying trench spell, the old, old story was circulated, and every-

The Auckland Regiment

body cheered up at the prospect of "three months right back" in some place thickly populated with desirable mademoiselles, well supplied with estaminets, picture shows, pierrots, and chips and eggs. In this heaven there was to be neither sight, nor sound, nor smell of the unpleasant Hun. "Blighty" and Paris leave was to be abundant, and training was not to be severe. Of such stuff were dreams composed. After the long, hard advance, the rumour of the rest that was to come, after one more fight, was most inspiring.

In the meantime, however, there was the one more fight. Le Quesnoy, once one of the most important of the French border fortresses—a place that had been fortified by Vauban—was the objective of the Division. With the railway line passing through, it was still of very great importance, and was strongly held by the enemy.

The plan of attack was for the 1/Brigade to move on the left, and the Rifle Brigade on the right. 1/Auckland and battalions of the Rifle Brigade were to surround the town, and, if necessary, the Riflemen were to storm the place, while the remainder of the New Zealanders were to sweep forward in an easterly direction and penetrate as deeply as possible into the enemy position. 2/Auckland, for the first time in their history, were in brigade reserve. Colonel Allen went on leave, and Major Sinel came up to command the Battalion.

After a miserable night, the morning of November 4th broke fair and fine. At 5.45 a.m., fifteen minutes after zero, 1/Auckland moved off by platoons, with twenty-five yards interval between each, the 6th Company, under Major Dittmer, leading, followed by the 15th, under Captain McCarthy, Battalion Headquarters, the 3rd, under Captain Lang, and the 16th, under Captain Forbes.

While crossing the Ruesnes-Le Quesnoy road an enemy 'plane flew overhead, and soon after the Battalion was heavily shelled, but, fortunately, the resulting losses were very slight. Lining up on the Le Quesnoy-Orsinval road, with the 6th and 15th leading, the Aucklanders moved forward and took the hamlet of Ramponeau, capturing many prisoners, machine-

Welsh Ridge—Crêvecœur—Rumilly—Le Quesnoy

guns and field pieces. It was here that Peter Prendergast was mortally wounded. For a long while he had enjoyed a wonderful reputation with 1/Auckland, and prior to the advance was wearing the M.M. with a bar to it. His great ambition was to win the Victoria Cross, and on all occasions he was the foremost volunteer when any fighting was to be done. Several times he had been desperately wounded, but every time returned more hostile than before. A very poor parade-ground soldier, he was the despair of the Guards' school, to which he was once sent to learn the refinements of the military business. In the line, however, he was in the first class; and for desperate, reckless daring his reputation is equalled by very few who fought with the Auckland Regiment.

At Ramponeau, the Wellington Battalions passed through 1/Auckland, who wheeled to the right, and shortly after 10 a.m. linked up with the 2/N.Z.R.B., thus completing the encirclement of the town. Here they remained in position, guarding the approaches and preventing all egress while the Rifle Brigade stormed the outer defences. The inner wall was then breached by artillery fire, and an officer carried in a flag of truce and invited the enemy to surrender. They refused this and also a second summons dropped from an aeroplane. About seven in the evening the Rifle Brigade advanced with scaling ladders, and climbing the walls rushed into the town. Le Quesnoy was ours, and the New Zealanders had fought their last battle.

The Auckland Battalions bivouacked in Villerau, with the exception of the 16th Company, under Captain McFarland, which pushed forward and established posts in the Forêt de Mormal.

Next morning 1/Auckland were relieved, and went back to billets near Le Quesnoy, where they remained for some days, sight-seeing and cleaning up after the late departed but unlamented Hun. On the morning of November 11th the whole Division was relieved and commenced to move back for "the King's rest." As the Aucklanders approached Solesmes a message was given to the officers riding ahead. It

The Auckland Infantry Regiment

was the news of the signing of the armistice. So the end had come at last, and the King's rest would have to wait until the "guerre prochaine"—that sweet bye and bye, in which mademoiselle dated her promises. There was no delirious excitement—for one thing the news was more or less expected, and for another four years of fighting dulls the enthusiasms. But there was a deep sense of thankfulness. "Thank God the bloody business is over at last." And men commenced to talk about New Zealand, and Auckland Town, and home, without that "if" which for so many years had cast a shadow over all bright plans for the future.

XXX

Germany

News came that the New Zealand Division was to have the honour of forming part of the army of occupation, and that it was to prepare to move on foot and by train to Cologne, on the Rhine. Now this news was received with mixed feelings. Nearly all were agreed that such an excursion was most desirable, but all were of one mind that the best method of marching there was to go by train. New Zealanders, when put to it can march as far and as fast as most folk, but they have a rooted objection to doing more "foot-slogging" than is absolutely necessary. The idea of marching for the good of the health was never appreciated as much as it might have been, and the air always became thicker and of a more sulphurous taint when the line of march lay for some miles along the railway. The flesh is always weak, especially when the spirit is not willing. However, orders are orders, and the first part of the march until the German border was reached had to be done on "Shanks his mare." And really, once everyone settled down to it the march was the best of good fun. There was a most delightful novelty about everything. Every few miles almost was some famous town or interesting place. Bavai, Maubeuge, Namur, Charleroi, Liége, Tamines—where in 1914 the Huns shot 500 civilians in cold blood. Liége, with its forts not damaged so much as to be noticeable; Jemappes, and so finally through Verviers to the German border. Nearly every night the battalions were in fresh billets, sometimes good, sometimes the reverse—one night a railway station, the next a factory, then a huge château stripped of all its woodwork, and after that again a hospitable little place where nearly

The Auckland Regiment

everyone managed to secure a bed. One thing was always in evidence, and that was the joy and enthusiasm of the liberated people—French and Belgian—which in some places burst out into scenes of wild excitement. At Lobbes, the first town across the Belgian border, the "brave British heroes" had a wonderful reception. The population came out in mass. Small boys begged for the honour of carrying a rifle, the girls laughed and joked and blew kisses, madame wept for the joy of it, and monsieur with his hat off bowed solemnly to "monsieur le colonel" as he rode through at the head of his men. At Verviers the excitement was even more intense. Streets were placarded "Welcome, Tommy; we never doubted that you would come again." While the New Zealanders were not particularly flattered at being called "Tommy," yet they entered fully into the spirit of the thing. It is very pleasant to be made a fuss of—especially by a town-full of womenfolk—and a little flattery always goes down well, especially when you feel that you belong to the best regiment in the division, and that the division is that of New Zealand, one "tolerably well known in the war," to parody Danton.

Entraining at the little station of Herbesthal, just across the border, the battalions arrived at Ehrenfeld, a suburb of Cologne, about 9 a.m. on the morning of December 21st, and from here marched through Cologne, crossing the Rhine by the bridge of boats to Mulheim, and marching from there, 1/Auckland to Immigrath, and 2/Auckland to Berg Neukirchen. Here the main business was to be as impressive as possible, and in this the Aucklanders succeeded quite well. Guards were mounted with great state and ceremony, and the Germans appeared suitably impressed. It is probable, however, that the most lasting impression made by the New Zealanders was on the women and children. Children are the same all the world over; and brown-skinned "Abdul" who blackened "Mr. McKenzie's boots" in Cairo had many points in common with fair-haired little Fritz, who begged for chocolate in the streets of Cologne—and New Zealanders always have a soft spot for children. Elderly Huns, if by no means enthusiastic, were a

Germany

canny folk, and always took pains to be scrupulously polite. With the women the New Zealanders soon threatened to be as popular as they had been with madame and mademoiselle. Our men throughout the whole war displayed two qualities that made them much appreciated, whether as guests or as conquerors. In the first place, they never smashed the furniture just to show how pleased they were, and secondly, their mothers had taught them to be polite to women. Now such politeness is not perhaps the strongest point of the English Tommy. The average Frenchman, though exceedingly polite to you as a stranger, has only an elementary sense of the little courtesies toward women that the average New Zealander regards as the commonplace, while the Huns apparently regarded their female possessions as useful and sometimes ornamental chattels. If the further East one goes the less courtesy there is, then the Bolsheviks must thoroughly deserve all they have been getting the last three years. When "mein frau" and the frauleins found that the men in the slouch hats gave up seats in the tramcars, opened doors, placed chairs, and were not even above giving a hand to work the pump or do some little thing about the billet, they began to look on the "Diggers" with favourable eyes. Despite the strict orders against fraternisation, many men went to dances and other like social functions, and it was only the fact that demobilisation started quickly and proceeded rapidly that saved New Zealand the necessity of assimilating several German war-brides.

XXXI

Home

> "*Then there was shouting and laughing and weeping: and all the kings came to the shore, and they led away the heroes to their homes, and bewailed the valiant dead.*"
> "The Heroes," Kingsley.

The first draft of men left the Regiment on January 13th, led by Captain Tuck. As they marched away the bands played them off with "Boys of the Old Brigade," and they were cheered as they tramped on down the road that was leading them home. Very quickly now the Regiment melted away. Some came back on the *Horarata*, the first boat-load of fit men to return, and on a brilliant day steamed up past the yellow cliffs of Coromandel, past Tiri Lighthouse, and then up through the Rangitoto Channel, past North Head, and so up the Waitemata to the wharf and the immense multitude who thronged every pier, and street, and eminence that gave a view of the great transport as she slowly swung into her berth at the Railway Wharf. The long, long trail had at last led home.

One scene more, and the story of the Regiment is finished. The two Allens returned with many others of the Auckland Regiment on the *Waimana*. On the wharf they were welcomed by all the men of the Regiment who could get down. There were speeches and replies, a photograph taken with Red Diamond flags as a background, and then "Old Steve" and "Bob" went shoulder high up Queen Street.

APPENDIX A

Badges, Patches and Numbers

Owing to the scheme adopted in the formation of the original Auckland Battalion from the four existing regiments of infantry in the military district, and the companies thus formed retaining the names and badges of the original regiments from which they were drawn, four separate badges were used in each battalion of the Auckland Regiment. These were the 3rd (Auckland), 6th (Hauraki), 15th (North Auckland), and 16th (Waikato) regimental badges.

When 2/Auckland was formed, on the model of 1/Auckland, with the same companies, wearing the same badges, it was found necessary to devise some method of distinguishing the men of the two battalions. To do this the "patch" system was adopted. The colours of the Auckland Regiment were red and black, and the first battalion patch was a "red diamond on a black square," worn by 2/Auckland.

For some time 1/Auckland, as the original battalion, did not wear any patch, and rather gloried in the fact; but gradually, they too, fell into line, wearing the red and black in vertical strips—black, red and black.

When the 3/Auckland Battalion was formed they adopted the three vertical strip arrangement of colours, and wore them—red, black and red.

Patches were about two inches square, and worn on the back of the tunic an inch below the collar line.

For purposes of accuracy in returns every man on joining the N.Z.E.F. was given a distinctive number. The system first adopted was changed during the course of the war. When

The Auckland Regiment

the Expeditionary Force was formed it was divided up into various units, each one of which was given a separate number:—

Headquarters	1	Otago Infantry		8
Artillery	2	Otago Mounted Rifles		9
Medical Corps	3	Wellington Infantry		10
Engineers	4	Wellington Mounted Rifles		11
Army Service Corps	5	Auckland Infantry		12
Canterbury Infantry	6	Auckland Mounted Rifles		13
Canterbury Mounted Rifles	7			

The first man on the Auckland Roll was Lieutenant-Colonel Plugge—his number being 12/1. As the names were added, the numbers rose from 12/1 to 12/4000. For a considerable period the men joining the Battalion were all numbered 12/—. After the evacuation of Gallipoli, however, the system ceased to be satisfactory. First of all it was found to be necessary to draft a certain number of mounted men into the infantry. They came with their 13/— numbers. Next it was found that the most convenient system was to train reinforcements in New Zealand, and then to forward them to the Expeditionary Force, and not to particular units. It was found that if a man was given a 12/— number he was perhaps not needed with the Auckland Regiment, and so was sent elsewhere. So by degrees the "bar" system became utterly confused, and lost its original usefulness and distinction.

After the Ninth Reinforcements, numbers were given consecutively, without reference to the unit or arm of the service. Gradually the "straight" numbers swamped the "bars," and in the latter stages of the war a "bar" number was not frequently met with, and the possessor of it felt a reasonable pride in his distinction.

APPENDIX B

Chronology

1914

1. August 4—Declaration of War.
2. ,, 11—Alexandra Park opens and Auckland Battalion Formed.
3. September 1—March to Manurewa and Bivouac.
4. ,, 23—Farewell in the Domain.
5. ,, 23—Departure.
6. ,, 24—Return from North Cape.
7. October 11—Departure for Wellington.
8. ,, 16—Departure from Wellington.
9. ,, 22—Route March through Hobart.
10. ,, 28—Arrive at Albany.
11. November 1—Departure from Albany.
12. ,, 10—Cocos Islands and Sinking of the *Emden*.
13. ,, 14—Crossing the Line Ceremony.
14. ,, 15—Colombo.
15. ,, 30—Suez.
16. December 3—Alexandria.
17. ,, 4—Zeitoun Camp.
18. ,, 24—March through Cairo.

1915

19. January 26—Proceed to Ismalia and the Suez Canal.
20. February 26—Return to Cairo.
21. April 3—Riot in Cairo.
22. ,, 10—Embarked on *Lutzow* for Lemnos.
23. ,, 15—Mudros Harbour.
24. ,, 25—**Battle of the Landing**
25. May 8—**Battle of Krithia.**
26. ,, 20—Bivouac in Reserve Gully.
27. ,, 24—Armistice for Burial of Dead.
28. June 2—Quinn's Post.
29. ,, 5-6—First Raid at Quinn's.
30. ,, 7-8—Second Raid at Quinn's Post.
31. ,, 9—Local Reserve in Monash. Fourth Reinforcements join.
32. ,, 25-26—Courtenay's Post.
33. July 8—Local Reserve in Monash.
34. ,, 16—Courtenay's Post.
35. ,, 21—First Issue of Gas Helmets.
36. ,, 25—In Local Reserve.
37. August 2—Relieve in Quinn's Post.
38. ,, 5-6—Happy Valley.
39. ,, 7-12—**Battle of Chunuk Bair and of Suvla Bay.**

[267]

The Auckland Regiment

1916

40. August 12 to September 14—Rhododendron Spur.
41. September 15—Embark on *Osmanieh* for Lemnos.
42. October   8—Embark for Anzac.
43. November 27—Blizzard.
44. December 20—**Evacuation.**
45.   ,,   20–25—Lemnos.
46.   ,,   25—Embark on *Marsova* for Egypt.
47.   ,,   Arrive in Moascar Camp.
48. January 1 to April 5—Training at Moascar.
49. March   1—Formation of 2/Auckland Battalion.
50. April   5–6—1/Auckland embark on *Franconia* at Port Said for France.
51.   ,,   7–8—2/Auckland embark on *Ascania* at Alexandria for France.
52.   ,,   16—1/Auckland arrive at Morbecque.
53.   ,,   20—2/Auckland arrive at Rebecque.
54.   ,,   30—2/Auckland to Bleu.
55. May   9—1/Auckland to Estaires.
56.   ,,   12—1/Auckland to Armentières.
57.   ,,   13—1/Auckland to Port Egal Sector.
58.   ,,   14—2/Auckland to Willow Walk—Buterne Farm Sector.
59.   ,,   21—1/Auckland Relieved.
60.   ,,   22–23—2/Auckland Relieved.
61.   ,,   29—1/Auckland to Line.
62. June   1—2/Auckland to Line.
63.   ,,   2—Notice given by Germans of Jutland.
64.   ,,   7—2/Auckland to Billets.
65.   ,,   9—1/Auckland to Subsidiary Line.
66.   ,,   15—1/Auckland to Billets in Blue Blind Factory.
67.   ,,   20—2/Auckland to Houplines Sector.
68.   ,,   21—1/Auckland to Willow Walk—Buterne Farm—Epinette.
69. July   3—1/Auckland Raided in l'Epinette.
70.   ,,   4—1/Auckland Relieved and go to Subsidiary Line.
71.   ,,   8—2/Auckland Relieved and go out Subsidiary Line.
72.   ,,   15—1/Auckland to Line at Port Egal Sector
73.   ,,   16—2/Auckland to Line at Houplines.
74.   ,,   20—1/Auckland Raid
75.   ,,   25—2/Auckland to Billets.
76. August   5—1/Auckland to Subsidiary Line.
77.   ,,   6—1/Auckland to Trenches 74, 75, 76, 77.
78.   ,,   8—2/Auckland to Front Line at Houplines.
79.   ,,   12—3rd Company 2/Auckland Raid.
80.   ,,   16—1/Auckland Relieved and entrain at Steenwerck.
81.   ,,   18—2/Auckland entrain at Steenwerck for Ebblinghem.
82.   ,,   20—1/Auckland arrive at Neuville-Forceville.
83.   ,,   20—2/Auckland arrive at Allery.
84. September   2—1/Auckland arrive in Airaines Area.
85.   ,,   2—2/Auckland arrive at Riencourt.
86.   ,,   3—1/Auckland to Yseux-Belloy.
87.   ,,   3—2/Auckland to Picquigny.
88.   ,,   7—1/Auckland to Cardonette.
89.   ,,   7—2/Auckland to Cardonette.
90.   ,,   8—1 and 2/Auckland to Albert Area.
91.   ,,   10—2/Auckland to Mametz Wood.
92.   ,,   12—2/Auckland to Front Line by Thistle Dump.
93.   ,,   15—**2/Auckland Storm Switch Line.**
94.   ,,   15—1/Auckland move to Mametz Wood.

Appendix B

95.	September	16—1/Auckland to Front Line.
96.	,,	16—2/Auckland to Check Line.
97.	,,	18—1/Auckland move back to Check and Savoy Trenches.
98.	,,	18—2/Auckland go in to Flers Trench.
99.	,,	24-25—1/Auckland take over 750 yards by Factory Corner.
100.	,,	25—2/Auckland to Black Watch Area.
101.	,,	27—**1/Auckland Assault Gird Trench.**
102.	,,	28—1/Auckland back to Reserve.
103.	,,	28—2/Auckland to Gird Trench.
104.	October	1—2/Auckland Support 2/Canterbury in Assault.
105.	,,	3—2/Auckland proceed to Mametz.
106.	,,	4—1/Auckland Relieved to Pommers Redoubt.
107.	,,	7—1/Auckland proceed Albert to Airaines.
108.	,,	7—Pont Remy to Liercourt.

2/AUCKLAND IN ARMENTIÈRES.

109.	October	11—2/Auckland Pont Remy to Strazeele.
110.	,,	13—2/Auckland to Armentières.
111.	,,	14—2/Auckland to Front Line at Houplines.
112.	November	1—2/Auckland to Subsidiary Line.
113.	,,	3—2/Auckland 6th Company Raid.
114.	December	2—2/Auckland Houplines to Armentières.
115.	,,	2/Auckland to Billets at La Gorgue.
116.	,,	23—2/Auckland to Line in V.C. Sector.

1/AUCKLAND—OCTOBER TO DECEMBER.

117.	October	11—1/Auckland to Cæstre.
118.	,,	14—1/Auckland to Cordonniere Sector
119.	,,	25—1/Auckland to Front Line.
120.	November	4—1/Auckland to Support.
121.	,,	6—1/Auckland to Reserve.
122.	,,	8—1/Auckland to Support.
123.	,,	12—1/Auckland to Line Right Sub-sector.
124.	,,	24—1/Auckland to Support.
125.	,,	28—1/Auckland to Line Right Sub-sector.
126.	December	6—1/Auckland Strong Patrols go out.
127.	,,	6—1/Auckland to Support.
128.	,,	14—1/Auckland to Right Sub-sector.
129.	,,	21—1/Auckland have Impromptu Armistice.
130.	,,	23—1/Auckland Relieved by 2/Auckland.

1917
REORGANISATION OF BRIGADES—2/AUCKLAND TO 1/BRIGADE FROM JANUARY 1.

131.	January	8—1/Auckland to Tin Barn Avenue Sector.
132.	,,	8—2/Auckland to Estaires.
133.	,,	12—2/Auckland Relieve at Tin Barn.
134.	,,	20—1/Auckland Relieve at Tin Barn.
135.	,,	28—2/Auckland Relieve at Jay Post.
136.	February	8—1/Auckland to Estaires.
137.	,,	9—1/Auckland Relieve 2/Auckland.
138.	,,	21—**2/Auckland Raid at Fleurbaix.**
139.	,,	23—1/Brigade move to Romarin-Le Bizet Sector.
140.	,,	25—1/Auckland to Front Line at Despierre Farm.
141.	,,	25—2/Auckland Inspected by General Plumer.
142.	March	1—2/Auckland Relieve 1/Auckland.
143.	,,	9—1/Auckland Relieve 2/Auckland.
144.	,,	15—1/Auckland and 2/Auckland to Le Nieppe.

[269]

The Auckland Regiment

145.	March	18—1/Auckland to Aldershot Camp.
146.	,,	31—1/Auckland Relieve in Support at Ploegsteert.
147.	April	1—2/Auckland Relieve in Line at Hill 63.
148.	,,	6—1/Auckland Relieve North of Ashlane.
149.	,,	15—2/Auckland Relieve 1/Auckland Plus Douve Farm.
150.	,,	24—1/Auckland Relieve 2/Auckland.
151.	,,	27—1/Auckland to De Seule.
152.	,,	27—2/Auckland to De Seule.
153.	,,	30—1/Auckland to Aldershot Camp—2/Auckland to Neuve Eglise.
154.	May	4—1/Auckland Relieve 1/Wellington in the Line.
155.	,,	5—Back Areas and Neuve Eglise Shelled.
156.	,,	8—1/Auckland Relieved.
157.	,,	10—Brigade Relieved and proceed to Strazeele Area.
158.	,,	18—Brigade Horse Show.
159.	,,	18——1/Auckland and 2/Auckland entrain for St. Omer.
160.	,,	18—1/Auckland to Setques and 2/Auckland to Esquerdes.
161.	,,	18-30—Training for Battle of Messines.
162.	,,	31—1/Brigade move to Wallon-Capel Area
163.	June	1—1/Brigade to La Motte Area.
164.	,,	2—1/Brigade to De Seule Area.
165.	,,	3—1/Auckland to Hill 63.
166.	,,	3—2/Auckland to Divisional Offensive Front.
167.	,,	7—**Battle of Messines.**
168.	,,	9—1/Auckland and 2/Auckland to Kortypyp and Bulford.
169.	,,	18—1/Auckland to Front Line at Prowse Point.
170.	,,	22—1/Auckland Raid by Warneton.
171.	,,	23—2/Auckland Relieve 1/Auckland.
172.	,,	28—1/Auckland from Catacombs to De Seule.
173.	,,	30—1/Auckland to Bleu—2/Auckland to Steentje.
174.	July	1-19—Brigade in Training.
175.	,,	19—1/Auckland to Prowse Point—2/Auckland to Kortypyp.
176.	,,	30—2/Auckland Relieve 1/Auckland.
177.	,,	31—1/Auckland Raid at Warneton.
178.	August	3—1/Auckland and 2/Auckland to Canteen Corner.
179.	,,	17—2/Auckland to Line at La Basse Ville.
180.	,,	22—2/Auckland Relieve 1/Auckland.
181.	,,	25—1/Auckland and 2/Auckland move to Cæstre Area.
182.	,,	29—1/Auckland to Quesques—2/Auckland to Fromentelles.
183.	September	1-25—Training for Passchendaele.

4/BRIGADE—3/AUCKLAND.

184.		4/Brigade Formed.
185.	May	29—4/Brigade arrive at Le Havre.
186.	,,	31—4/Brigade arrive at Bailleul.
187.	June	7-10—3/Auckland on Working Parties from Hill 63.
188.	,,	11—3/Auckland to Front Line in Lys Sector.
189.	,,	14—3/Auckland Occupy Enemy Line.
190.	,,	15—3/Auckland to Pont Nieppe.
191.	,,	15-30—3/Auckland Working Parties.
192.	July	1-7—3/Auckland Working Parties from Brune Gaye.
193.	,,	8—3/Auckland go in Front Line at Le Touquet.
194.	,,	16—3/Auckland Relieved.
195.	,,	16-28—3/Auckland on Working Parties.
196.	,,	31—3/Auckland Relieved 3/Canterbury on Warnave Sector.

Appendix B

197.	August	8—3/Auckland Relieved and proceed to Brune Gaye.
198.	,,	16—3/Auckland to Front Line in Warnave Sector.
199.	,,	24—3/Auckland move to Brune Gaye.
200.	September	2—3/Auckland move to Le Waast.
201.	,,	14—Sir Douglas Haig's Review.
202.	,,	25—1, 2 and 3/Auckland leave Lumbres Area.
203.	,,	28-29—1, 2 and 3/Auckland arrive in Watou Area.
204.	October	1—1/Auckland move to Ypres North Billet Area.
205.	,,	1—2/Auckland to Old British Front Line.
206.	,,	1—3/Auckland to Old British Front Line.
207.	,,	2-3—1/Auckland and 2/Auckland to Front Line.
208.	,,	3-4—2/Auckland take Battle Station.
209.	,,	4—**Battle of Gravenstafel, Abraham Heights and Broodseinde.**
210.	,,	5—1/Auckland Relieved.
211.	,,	5—2/Auckland Relieved.
212.	,,	5-6—3/Auckland Relieved to Goldfish Chateau.
213.	,,	14-15—3/Auckland to Front Line at Belle Vue Spur.
214.	,,	18—3/Auckland to Support Abraham Heights.
215.	,,	19—1/Auckland to Front Line at Krön Prinz Farm.
216.	,,	19—2/Auckland to Support at Kansas Farm.
217.	,,	19—3/Auckland Relieved to Old British Front Line.
218.	,,	22—1/Auckland Relieved by Canadian Troops.
219.	,,	22—3/Auckland proceed Alquines.
220.	,,	23—2/Auckland Relieved by C.M.R.
221.	,,	24—1/Auckland proceed to Colomby.
222.	,,	26—2/Auckland proceed to Senninghem.
223.	November	12—3/Auckland entrain for Ypres.
224.	,,	15—1/Brigade entrain for Ypres and proceed to Micmac.
225.	,,	26—1/Auckland and 2/Auckland to Camps at Belgian Chateau.

1/AUCKLAND FROM NOVEMBER 26 TO MARCH 10.

226.	November	26—1/Auckland Working Parties from Belgian Chateau.
227.	December	10—Brigade Schools Open.

1918

228.	January	18—1/Auckland to Dickebusch Huts.
229.		
230.		26—1/Auckland to Reutel Sector Front Line.
231.	February	1—1/Auckland to Railway Wood and Halfway House.
232.	,,	8—1/Auckland to Front Line Broodseinde Sector.
233.	,,	14—1/Auckland to Walker Camp.
234.	,,	23—1/Auckland to Halifax Camp.
235.	March	10—1/Auckland proceed Rest Area at Staple.

2/AUCKLAND FROM NOVEMBER 26 TO MARCH 10.

	November	26—2/Auckland Working Parties from Belgian Chateau.
236.	January	17—2/Auckland move to Dickebusch Huts.
237.	,,	20—2/Auckland to Front Line at Cameron Covert.
238.	,,	20—2/Auckland to Support near Crucifix.
239.	February	1—2/Auckland to Front Line Reutel Sector.
240.	,,	7—2/Auckland Relieved, proceed to Ypres.
241.	,,	8—2/Auckland to West Farm Camp.
242.	March	9—2/Auckland to Montreal Camp.
243.	,,	10—2/Auckland by lorries to Zuypteene.

The Auckland Regiment

3/AUCKLAND FROM NOVEMBER 12.

244.	November	15—3/Auckland to Forrester Camp.
245.	„	14—3/Auckland to Front Line Nordemhoek Sector. Zillebeke.
246.	„	21—3/Auckland Relieved and proceed to Railway Dug-outs, Zillebeke.
247.	„	25—3/Auckland to Halfway House.
248.	December	1—3/Auckland to Howe Camp.
249.	„	5—3/Auckland to Walker Camp.
250.	„	15—3/Auckland to Front Line at Nordemhoek.
251.	„	22—3/Auckland Relieved and proceed to Railway Dug-outs.
252.	„	27—3/Auckland to Front Line at Nordemhoek Sub-sector.
253.	January	2—3/Auckland to Support Area, Halfway House.
254.	„	18—3/Brigade in Corps Reserve.
255.	February	8—3/Auckland become Auckland Works Battalion.
256.	March	24—1/Brigade leave Cassel Station for the Somme.
257.	„	25—1/Brigade detrain at Hangest-sur-Somme.
258.	„	26—**Battle of Mailly-Maillet.**
259.	„	
260.	„	28—1/Auckland Relieved.
261	„	30—**2/Auckland Storm La Signy Farm.**
262.	„	31—2/Auckland Relieved.
263.	April	2—1/Auckland go into Front Line.
264.	„	4—1/Auckland Relieved from Line.
265.	„	9—2/Auckland Relieved in Front Line at Waterloo Bridge.
266.	„	14—2/Auckland Relieved in Line.
267.	„	14—1/Auckland to Front Line at La Signy.
268.	„	17—1/Auckland Relieved to Purple Line.
296.	„	**24—**1/Auckland to Front Line at Hébuterne—2/Auckland to Support.
270.	„	30—1/Auckland to Support—2/Auckland to Front Line.
271.	May	6—1/Auckland to J 22—2/Auckland to Purple Line.
272.	„	13—1/Auckland to Front Line on Serre Road.
273.	„	13—2/Auckland in reserve at Colincamps.
274.	„	15—1/Auckland 15th Company Raid.
275.	„	18—1/Auckland Relieved—2/Auckland occupy Front Line.
276.	„	24—2/Auckland Relieved and proceed to St. Leger-Authie.
277.	„	24-31—1/Brigade in Reserve about Authie.
278.	June	1—1/Auckland in Front Line at Hébuterne.
279.	„	1—2/Auckland in Reserve at Sailly-au-Bois.
280.	„	6—1/Auckland Relieved and proceed to Tented Camp at Couin.
281.	„	6—2/Auckland to Vauchelles.
282.	July	1—1/Brigade take over Rossignol Wood Sector.
283.	„	1—1/Auckland take over Support at Gommecourt.
284.	„	1—2/Auckland Front Line at Rossignol Wood.
285.	„	9—1/Auckland to Reserve at Rossignol Farm.
286.	„	9—2/Auckland to Reserve in Hutted Camp, Coigneux.
287.	„	17—1/Auckland Front Line at Hébuterne.
288.	„	17—2/Auckland to Reserve at Sailly.
289.	„	25—1/Auckland Relieved—2/Auckland to Front Line.
290.	August	2—1/Auckland to Coigneux—2/Auckland to Chateau de la Haye.
291.	„	
292.	„	10—1/Auckland to Front Line at Rossignol Wood.

Appendix B

293.	August	10—2/Auckland in Support at Gommecourt.
294.	„	18—1/Auckland Relieved and go to Brigade Reserve.
295.	„	18—2/Auckland move up in Support.
296.	„	18—**2/Auckland Take Grevillers.**
297.	„	24—1/Auckland take over Line from 2/Auckland.
298.	„	29—2/Auckland Relieve 1/Auckland in front of Bapaume.
299.	„	30—**2/Auckland Take Bancourt.**
300.	September	1-2—1/Brigade go into Rest.
301.	„	11—1/Brigade move up to Front Line.
302.	„	12—1/Auckland Relieve in Front Line east of Metz.
303.	„	12—2/Auckland Relieve in Reserve at Metz.
304.	„	14—1/Brigade return to Bapaume.
305.	2 „	28—1/Auckland and 2/Auckland moved to Neuville-Bourjonval.
306.	„	29—**1/Brigade Attack Welsh Ridge.**
307.	„	30—**2/Auckland Attack Crêvecoeur.**
308.	October	1—**1/Auckland Attack towards Serranvillers.**
309.	„	3—1/Auckland Relieved.
310.	„	3-10—1/Brigade in Hindenburg Line Resting.
311.	„	12—New Zealand Division concentrated round Fontaine.
312.	November	4—**New Zealanders Storm Le Quesnoy.**
313.	„	11—Armistice Signed.
313.	December	21—Aucklanders Enter Cologne.
315.	January	14—Demobilisation of Auckland Regiment Begins.

r

APPENDIX C

Honours and Awards

The rank shown is the rank held at the time of award.

THE VICTORIA CROSS

No. 4/400—Sergt. SAMUEL FORSYTH, late N.Z. Engineers.
(Killed in action)

For most conspicuous bravery and devotion to duty in the attack on Grevillers, 24th August, 1918. On nearing the objective, his company came under heavy machine-gun fire. Through Sergeant Forsyth's dashing leadership and total disregard of danger, three machine-gun positions were rushed and the crews taken prisoners, before they could inflict any casualties on our troops. During the subsequent advance his company came under heavy fire from several machine-guns, two of which he located by a daring reconnaisance. In his endeavour to gain support from a tank he was wounded, but after having the wound bandaged he again got into touch with the tank, which, in the face of very heavy fire from machine-guns and anti-tank guns, he endeavoured to lead, with magnificent coolness, to a favourable position. The tank, however, was put out of action. Sergeant Forsyth then organised the tank crew and several of his men into a section, and led them to a position where the machine-guns could be outflanked. Always under heavy fire, he directed them into positions which brought about the retirement of the enemy and enabled the advance to continue. This gallant N.C.O. was at that moment killed by a sniper. From the moment of the attack to the time of his death, Sergeant Forsyth's courage and coolness, combined with great power of initiative, proved an invaluable incentive to all who were with him, and he undoubtedly saved many casualties among his comrades.

No. 24/1699--Sergt. REGINALD STANLEY JUDSON, D.C.M., M.M.

For most conspicuous bravery and devotion to duty, when in an attack on enemy positions south of Bapaume, on 26/8/18, he led a small bombing party under heavy fire, and captured an enemy machine-gun. He then proceeded up a sap alone, bombing three machine-gun crews before him. Jumping out of the trench, he ran ahead of the enemy. Then, standing on the parapet, he ordered the party—consisting of two officers and about ten men—to surrender. They instantly fired on him, but he threw a bomb and jumped down amongst them, killed two, put the rest to flight, and so captured two machine-guns. This prompt and gallant action not only saved many lives, but enabled the advance to continue unopposed.

No. 14/131—Private JAMES CRICHTON.

For most conspicuous bravery and devotion to duty at Crèvecœur, 30/9/18, when, although wounded in the foot, he continued with the advancing troops, despite difficult obstacles in canal and river. When his platoon was subsequently forced back by a counter-attack, he succeeded in carrying a message, which involved swimming a river and crossing an area swept by machine-gun fire, subsequently rejoining his platoon. Later, he undertook, on his own initiative, to save a bridge which had been mined, and though under close fire from machine-guns

Appendix C

and snipers, he succeeded in removing the charges, returning with the fuse and detonators. Though suffering from a painful wound, he displayed the highest degree of valour and devotion to duty.

COMPANION OF THE ORDER OF ST. MICHAEL AND ST. GEORGE (C.M.G.)

Lieut.-Col. Alderman W. W., D.S.O.
Lieut.-Col. Allen, S. S., D.S.O. (and Bar)
Major Dawson, T. H., C.B.E.
Colonel Plugge, A.
Lieut.-Col. Young, R., C.B., D.S.O., Legion d'Honneur (Croix de Chevalier)

COMPANION OF THE ORDER OF THE BRITISH EMPIRE (C.B.E.)

Major Dawson, T. H., C.M.G.
Major Watson, J. T.

BAR TO DISTINGUISHED SERVICE ORDER (D.S.O.)

Lieut.-Col. Allen, S. S., C.M.G., D.S.O.
Lieut.-Col. Allen, R. C., D.S.O.

DISTINGUISHED SERVICE ORDER (D.S.O.)

Lieut.-Col. Alderman, W. W., C.M.G.
Lieut.-Col. Allen, S. S., C.M.G.
Lieut.-Col. Allen, R. C.
Capt Ardagh, P. A., M.C. (N.Z.M.C.)
Lieut.-Col. Blair, D. B., M.C.
Major Duthie, N. A.
Major McClelland, C. H.
Major McKenzie, A. G.
Major Orr, E. H.
Major Sinel, W. C.
Capt. Vercoe, H. R.

OFFICER OF THE ORDER OF THE BRITISH EMPIRE (O.B.E.)

Major Westmacott, H. H. S.

MEMBER OF THE ORDER OF THE BRITISH EMPIRE (M.B.E.)

Capt. Booth, C. H.
Lieut. Quartley, A. G.
Capt. Wood, R. W. F.
Capt. Mewett, J. E. H., M.C.

BAR TO MILITARY CROSS (M.C.)

Capt. Coates, J. G., M.C.
Capt. Evans, J., M.C.
Lieut. Gordon, A. W., M.C.
Capt Gray, W. P., M.C.

MILITARY CROSS (M.C.)

Capt. Addison, A. S. (N.Z.M.C.)
2nd Lieut. Aitken, W. P.
Capt. Ardagh, P. A., D.S.O. (N.Z.M.C.)
Lieut. Blampied, M.
Lieut. Carter, J. C.
Lieut. Clark, S. O.
Capt. Coates, J. G.
2nd Lieut. Collins-Morgan, C. E. (Killed in action)
Lieut. Cooper, A. C. (Killed in action)
Lieut. Cousins, P. S.
Capt. Devereux, G. de B. (Killed in action)
Lieut. Dittmer, G.

The Auckland Regiment

MILITARY CROSS (M.C.)—Continued

Rev. Dobson, C. J. H.
Lieut Duigan, D. F.
Capt. Evans, J.
Capt. Forbes, A. M.
Lieut. Garroway, R.
Lieut. Gordon, A. W.
Lieut. Gray, W. P.
2nd Lieut. Greenwood, J. H., M.M.
Lieut. Hally, C.
  (Killed in action)
2nd Lieut. Hill, W. J. R.
  (Died of wounds)
Lieut. Holland, G. H.
  (Killed in action)
Capt. Hubbard, A. C.
  (Killed in action)
2nd Lieut. Jack, A. D.
2nd Lieut. Jones, J. A.
Lieut. King, H. L.
Lieut. Lang, F. W.
Lieut. Lang, W. R.
2nd Lieut. Le Petit, N. V.
2nd Lieut. Mackay, W. C.
Lieut. Metcalf, L. W.
Capt. Mewett, J. E. H., M.B.E.

2nd Lieut. Miller, H.
Capt. Morpeth, R. N.
Lieut. Moncrief, E. G.
2nd Lieut. McAdam, H. M.
Lieut. McFarland, R. D.
Lieut. McKenzie, F. E.
Capt. Napier, W. E. L.
Capt. Nelson, A. D. (N.Z.M.C.)
Lieut. O'Gorman, F. R.
Lieut. Oxenham, C.
Lieut. Porritt, E. A.
Lieut. Seaward, C. F.
Lieut. Seddon, S. T.
Lieut. Senior, C. H. A.
  (Since Deceased)
Lieut. Stewart, F.
Lieut. Taylor, J. A.
Lieut. Tilsley, R., D.C.M.
Lieut. Tuck, G. A.
Lieut. Vause, H.
Lieut. Vickerman, K. L.
Lieut. Walker, D. J. B.
Capt. Wallingford, J. A.
Capt. Watson, W.
2nd Lieut. Woodward, W. J.

DISTINGUISHED CONDUCT MEDAL (D.C.M.)

32495 Sgt. Alexander, C. S.
42881 S.S.M. Bates, W.
12/4137 Sgt. Black, T., M.S.M.
12/1555 Q.M.S. Birnie, G.
26783 Sgt. Brewer, J. H., M.M.
12/3569 Pte. Brown, W. G., M.M.
18758 Sgt. Buckthought, N. W.
11375 Sgt. Buckworth, C. G.
24/1635 Sgt. Cusack, J.
32945 C.S.M. Evans, J. H.
28121 L.-Cpl. Ford, G. C.
  (Killed in action)
12/1627 Sgt. Frew, J. (Francis)
  (Killed in action)
12/577 C.S.M. Gordon, T. J.
12/3356 Sgt. Hewlett, T. W.
12/566 Sgt. Hill, J. L.
12/3062 Pte. Johnson, H. A.
14272 Sgt. Jordan, E. W.
24/1699 Sgt. Judson, R. S., V.C., M.M.
18890 Sgt. Lloyd, L. J.
12/4051 Cpl. Mahoney, W. F.

12/1725 C.S.M. Moss, E. S.
12/3398 Pte. McClennan, A.
12/4045 Sgt. McCreanor, J.
  (Killed in action)
12/1783 Cpl. McKenzie, K.
10250 Sgt. O'Brien, J. L.
12/3449 Sgt. Proctor, W. A.
18583 Sgt. Randell, W. E.
12/1015 Cpl. Reid, W. J.
12/3795 Sgt. Robinson, S.
26932 Pte. Speakman, J. B.
12/1799 Cpl. Spencer, W. H.
12/257 R.S.M. Stichbury, W. S.
24076 Cpl. Stuart, G. L.
23/1213 Sgt. Taylor, J. A.
12/1062 Pte. Tempany, G. A.
  Sgt. Tilsley, R., M.C.
12/878 Sgt. Tribe, L.
12/1006 Sgt. Waterson, D.C.
12/1020 Cpl. Watson, F. W.
  (Killed in action)
14513 Pte. Webster, A. S.
34458 Pte. Wilson, J. H.

BAR TO MILITARY MEDAL (M.M.)

26596 Sgt. Dowsing, C. E., M.M.
12/540 Cpl. Fraser, J. McJ., M.M.
  (Killed in action)
10236 Pte. Kelsall, E., M.M.
12/2790 Sgt. Muir, A. H., M.M.
12/3761 Sgt. McLeod, J. D., M.M.

12/617 Pte. Porter, C. W., M.M.
7/2414 Sgt. Prendergast, P., M.M
  (Killed in action)
14479 Pte. Quinn, C., M.M.
23/2289 Sgt. Thomas, L., M.M.
20460 Pte. Turley, J. T., M.M.

Appendix C

MILITARY MEDAL (M.M.)

10089	Pte. Alexander, J.	12/1933	Cpl. Crowhurst, S. A.
14212	Pte. Allom, W. H.		(Killed in action)
28643	Pte. Andrews, B.	12/3603	Sgt. Cuthbertson, W. J.
12/2632	Sgt. Andrews, W. T.		(Died since discharge)
28313	Pte. Annand, D. B.	38879	Pte. Curry, C. J. H.
	(Killed in action)	33849	Cpl. Dacre, L. M.
28316	Pte. Arthur, L. C.	12/1185	Sgt. Davidson, D.
13/3000	Pte. Ashwin, L. F.	23305	Pte. Davis, J. S.
11382	Cpl. Bain, J. H.	11432	Pte. Dawson, J. R.
12/3245	Sgt. Baker, H.	12/2268	L.-Cpl. Dean, E. J.
5/650a	Cpl. Baker, J. F.	12/2995	Cpl. De Luen, F.
13/542	Sgt. Balle, J. T.		(Killed in action)
35476	Sgt. Barr, J. P.	42301	Pte. Denize, H. V.
30742	Pte. Bartle, J. R.	23/1613	L.-Cpl. Dewar, O. B.
23952	Pte. Bath, A. F. F.	47414	Pte. Donghi, H. A.
12/2947	Cpl. Beehre, H. M.	12/530	Pte. Downie, H. C.
	(Killed in action)	26576	Sgt. Dowsing, C. E.
12/2950	Pte. Biddick, J. H.	12334	Pte. Edwards, C.
30908	Pte. Bishop, J.	1/624	Pte. Fairweather, S.
11367	Sgt. Bishop, T. A.	12/1994	Pte. Faithfull, W. H.
23958	Pte. Bishoprick, A. E.	12/3012	Pte. Finnerty, J.
12/3254	Sgt. Black, D. C.	31407	L.-Cpl. Flavell, R. H.
59856	Cpl. Black, C. A.	52403	Pte. Flowerday, H. N.
11387	Sgt. Bradley, J. H.	12/3321	Pte. Forrest, T. F.
12/1567	Sgt. Brady, A. T.	12/104	Sgt. Fox, E. V.
38336	L.-Cpl. Bray, C.	12/540	Pte. Fraser, J. McI.
26783	Pte. Brewer, J. H., D.C.M.	12/2700	Sgt. Fraser, J. R.
6/3259	Cpl. Brierley, W.	26827	Cpl. Freshney, J. B.
12/3263	Pte. Bright, W. G.	23827	Pte. Gates, F. G.
12/3268	Sgt. Brown, E. B.		(Since deceased)
12/1905	Sgt. Brunton, N. T.	25226	Pte. Gawler, S. R.
12/3272	Pte. Bullen, R. H.	10/3264	L.-Cpl. Giles, S.
3/483	L.-Cpl. Burton, O. E.	12/3328	L.-Cpl. Gill, A. M.
	Medaille d'Honneur	12/2710	L.-Cpl. Gillespie, L. W.
12/914	Sgt. Calame, P. E.	12/2711	Sgt. Gilmore, W. B.
12/1576	Sgt. Cameron, K. E.	1/639 & 12/2540	L.-Cpl. Girven, E.
20297	Pte. Cameron, R.	11458	Pte. Glasscock, W. D.
36408	Pte. Campbell, K.	31625	L.-Cpl. Glogloski, E. W.
13/2542	L.-Cpl. Campion, D. A.	12/116	Cpl. Goulden, H. H.
	(Killed in action)	20335	Pte. Griffin, A.
12/1911	Cpl. Carter, C. R.	14101	Col. Griffiths, C. C.
	(Killed in action)	14418	Pte. Grundy, H. R.
21209	Pte. Chitty, T. W.	12/627	Sgt. Gunn, F.
48621	Pte. Church, D. M.	54357	Pte. Gunn, J.
12/1589	Pte. Clarke, N.	55306	Pte. Guthrie, R. A.
38664	Pte. Cochran, H. R.	12/3662	Sgt. Guy, T. F.
25197	Pte. Cole-Baker, D. P. G.	35637	Pte. Hadfield, R. H.
	(Killed in action)	35354	Pte. Halvorsen, G.
12/2983	Pte. Coppell, R. W.	12/3348	Pte. Hansen, J. T.
12/2252	Sgt. Coulam, F.	23308	Cpl. Harding, R. W.
	(Died since discharge)	23/1659	Sgt. Hart, R. G.
12/2674	Pte. Couch, C. A.	12/755	Sgt. Hastie, G.
32822	Cpl. Cowie, R.	60116	Pte. Havill, J.
12/528	Sgt. Cox, A. B.	38693	Col. Hay, A. C.
34330	Pte. Coxhead, S. M.	14261	Pte. Hinchco, A.
12/73	Sgt. Crawford, E. H.		(Died of wounds)
31957	Pte. Crawford, T. H.	12/3050	Pte. Howe, A. J. H.
55585	Pte. Cray, D.	12/2333	Sgt. Howe, D. W.
		12/3051	Pte. Howie, W. J.

The Auckland Regiment
MILITARY MEDAL (M.M.)—Continued

52325	Pte. Hunter, E. J.		12/602	Sgt. McQueen, A. A.
12/3055	Sgt. Inch, V. W.		34409	Pte. Naden, F. N.
11482	Pte. Jackson, F.		27139	Pte. Nankervis, W. H.
10/3608	Pte. Jamieson, R.			(Killed in action)
30813	Pte. Jaques, P.		60180	Pte. Neal, H. R.
14/44a	Pte. Johnson, A. R.		25571	Cpl. North, L. G.
12/3062	Pte. Johnson, H. A. D.C.M.		12/204	L.-Cpl. Oldham, W. A.
			28403	Sgt. O'Regan. P. J.
38401	Pte. Jones, E. J.		12/3119	Pte. Owen, J.
24/1699	Sgt. Judson, R. S., V.C., D.C.M.			(Killed in action)
			42186	Sgt. Paddy, W. C.
10236	Pte. Kelsall, E.		21083	Pte. Parsons, J.
32023	Pte. Land, I. G.		12/3121	L.-Cpl. Patton, H. L.
12/2755	Pte. Lauder, A.			(Killed in action)
24394	Pte. Leo., E. M.		25/800	L.-Cpl. Paynter, L. H.
12/3075	L.-Cpl. Leigh, T. J.		30844	Pte. Pegler, S. P.
12/2015	Sgt. Lessels, D.		12/2925	Cpl. Pethybridge, W. T.
12/1699	Pte. Lewin, C.		12/617	Pte. Porter, C. W.
12/3387	Sgt. Lock, S. G. S.		7/2414	Cpl. Prendergast, P.
14284	L.-Cpl. Looker, W. L.			(Killed in action)
12/3709	Pte. Livsey, R.		14478	L.-Cpl. Preston, W. E.
24094	Pte. Luff, E.		30843	L.-Cpl. Price, W. V.
12/906 & 23/1437	Pte. Manning, F. E.		23/1728	Pte. Prince, A. T.
44756	Pte. Martin, A.		14479	Pte. Quinn, C.
40341	Pte. Mateer, F. E.		12/4078	Pte. Ray, K.
23/1731	Cpl. Maynard, L. R.		10418	Sgt. Rees, E. T.
44768	L.-Cpl. Mead, A. D.		12/2926	Sgt. Rice, S. D.
11498	Pte. Menzies, A.		21333	Pte. Richardson, J. F.
12/3727	Pte. Middlemiss, W. P.		32065	Pte. Richter, O. G. C.
12/3729	Pte. Miller, D.		12/276	C.S.M. Roberts, C. P.
14460	Pte. Miller, O. McL.		12/3458	Cpl. Robertson, J. F.
12/2392	Cpl. Mitchell, G. G.		14483	Pte. Robinson, F. M.
13/2347	L.-Cpl. Moffat, L. P.		13810	Pte. Robinson, G.
5/436	Cpl. Moffitt, J. E.		12/626	Cpl. Robinson, N. M.
14291	L.-Cpl. Molesworth, C.E.N.		14/62	Sgt. Rogers, J. H.
11502	L.-Cpl. Moody, F. H.		27141	Cpl. Roper, G. J.
12/3737	L.-Cpl. Moon, W. H.		12/2828	Sgt. Rossiter, C.
31680	Pte. Moore, K. S.		33141	Sgt. Rowe, A. N.
	(Killed in action)		12/625	Sgt. Ruff, J. A. P.
21306	Cpl. Morgan, L. O.		28796	Pte. Rufford, A.
12/4061	Sgt. Morris, H. M.		28371	Pte. Russell, H. F.
12/2790	Sgt. Muir, A. H.		14487	Pte. Ryan, F. L.
47911	Pte. MacKay, W. J.		14488	Cpl. Ryder, C. A.
12/2047	Pte. McBeath, C.		12/3805	Sgt. Sage, A. H.
25604	Cpl. McCorquodale, D. A.		13/2366	Pte. Searle, E.
14470	Pte. McCoskrie, C. O.			(Killed in action)
10/2445	Pte. McCullagh, J. W.		12/2832	L.-Cpl. Shaw, W. R.
12/2052	Pte. McDivett, R.		23266	Pte. Sheahan, J.
	(Killed in action)		42417	Pte Simons, L. W.
47917	Pte. McDonald, C. G.		25326	Cpl. Slater, G.
12/3756	Sgt. McGowan, E. A.		7/2427	Cpl. Smillie, J.
12/3110	L.-Cpl. McIntosh, C.		52477	Pte. Smith, E. H.
	(Killed in action)		24/1822	L.-Cpl. Smith, E. M.
12/4231	Sgt. McKechnie, J.		7/2425	Pte. Smith, R. R.
12/1736	Pte. McKenzie, E. G.		12/1799	Pte. Spittle, C.
1/721 & 13/2223	Sgt. McKenzie, N.A.		12/850	Sgt. Squires, B. C.
64713	Pte. McLean, T. A.		12/3481	Pte. Stacey, E. E.
25289	Cpl. McMahon, P. R.		33954	Cpl. Steward, A. de B.
12/1305	Cpl. McMillan, N.		44795	Pte. Stirling, N. D.

Appendix C

MILITARY MEDAL (M.M.)—Continued

42227	Pte. Stokes, A.		26946	Pte. Watkins, L.
14502	Pte. Stow, J. C.		12/3862	Sgt. Watson, S. V.
19185	Pte. Sutherland, H.		40401	Pte. Webb, M.
22291	C.S.M. Sutton, W.		25976	Sgt. Welch, J.
12/3164	L.-Cpl. Taaffe, J. T. B.		12/3505	L.-Cpl. White, C. J.
24/1555	Sgt. Tarbutt, L. O. S.		16028	Pte. Whitelaw, L. A.
56047	Pte. Taylor, E.		12/3193	Pte. Whitehouse, C. H.
23/2289	Sgt. Thomas, L.			(Killed in action)
33973	Pte. Tilby, W. H.		13/3091	Pte. Wilkie, R. A.
16982	Pte. Todd, W.		12/3159	Cpl. Williams, S. G.
12/2862	Pte. Torrens, W. J.		14519	Sgt. Williams, W. E.
12/1811	Pte. Tribe, L. R.		29119	Cpl. Wills, E. J.
12/4285	Pte. Troughear, A.			(Died of wounds)
12/912	Sgt. Trotter, W. J. R.		12/4122	Cpl. Winkley, J. R.
33659	Cpl. Tuck, H. J.		10976	Pte. Wotherspoon, P.
11371	Sgt. Turley, C. E.		38472	L.-Cpl. Wilson, A. J. K.
20460	Pte. Turley, J. T.		28608	Cpl. Wilson, C. R.
12/3495	Pte. Turnbull, L.		12/3520	Pte. Wright, J. D.
14508	Pte. Underwood, H.		12/669	Pte. Yorke, C. D.
55001	Pte. Watkins, H. T.		12/3025	Pte. Young, A.

MERITORIOUS SERVICE MEDAL (M.S.M.)

12/516	S.S.M. Bethell, J. G.		12/982	Sgt. Mawhinney, W.
12/4137	Cpl. Black, T., D.C.M.		12/2398	Sgt. Morris, B. J.
12/2893	R.Q.M.S. Child, C.		12/603	Pte. McGovern, J. J.
26814	C.Q.M.S. Dimery, S.		23/977	Sgt.-Maj. McKenzie, J. H.
18/808	L.-Cpl. Forrest, S. V.		15/170	Pte. Narborough, R. B.
12/361	S.-Sgt. Goulden, R. T.		24/1813	Pte. Scott, H.
12/2724	Cpl. Harding, F. S.		12/3151	Cpl. Seatter, J. I.
12/2611	S.-Maj. Harris, C. V. N.		1/763 & 11542	Sgt. Selbie, D. W.
12/137	R.Q.M.S. Hatt, A. R.		12/3834	Sgt. Steele, J.
12/1008	S.-Sgt. Hodge, H. S.		4/137a	S.-Sgt. Thompson, A. E.
12/931	Sgt. Jones, T.		12/886	Sgt.-Maj. Thompson, A. S.
12/399	Sgt. Logan, D. M.			(Killed in action)

MENTIONED IN DESPATCHES

	Lt.-Col. Alderman, W. W. C.M.G., D.S.O. (2)		Rev. Dobson, C. J. H., M.C.
	Lt.-Col. Allen, R. C., D.S.O. (3)		Capt. Dinneen, J. D. (Died of wounds)
	Lt.-Col. Allen, S. S., C.M.G., D.S.O. (4)		Major Duthie, N. A., D.S.O. (2)
	Sgt. Andrews, W. T., M.M.		2nd Lieut. Ellis, F. A.
	Capt. Ardagh, P. A., D.S.O., M.C. (N.Z.M.C.)		Lieut. Ellisdon, F. J. H.
13/524	Sgt. Balle, J. T., M.M.		Capt. Evans, J., M.C. (and Bar)
	Lt.-Col. Blair, D. B. D.S.O., M.C. (2)		2nd Lieut. Farrell, J. F.
	Lieut. Bond, A. J.		2nd Lieut. Fitchett, W. B.
12/2650	Sgt. Boyd, T.	12/2695	Sgt. Finlayson, L.
	Brig.-Gen. Brown, C. H. J. D.S.O. (2). (Killed in action)	20319	Pte. Flynn, J. A.
		12/1627	Sgt. Frew, J. (Francis) (Killed in action)
63822	Pte. Campbell, A.	11450	C.Q.M.S. Frost, L. H.
	Lieut. Carter, J. C.	12/361	S.-Sgt. Goulden, R. T., M.S.M.
12/528	Sgt. Cox, A. B., M.M.		Major Grant, S. A. (Died of wounds)
12/1185	Sgt. Davidson, D., M.M.		Capt. Grainger, M. O.
	Major Dawson, T. H., C.M.G., C.B.E. (2)		Capt. Gray, W. P., M.C. (and Bar)

The Auckland Regiment

MENTIONED IN DESPATCHES—*Continued*

	2nd Lieut. Greenwood, J. H. M.C., M.M.
33883	Sgt. Hume, R. G.
40323	Pte. Hurley, F. (Died of wounds)
	Lieut. Holland, G. H., M.C. (Killed in action)
12/3055	Sgt. Inch, V. W.
8/3652	S.-Sgt. Keegan, H. C.
	2nd Lieut. Lorie, A.
12/280	Cpl. Lippiatt, G. E. R.
12/3709	Pte. Livsey, R., M.M.
12/1710	Pte. Maroni, C. J.
12/2398	Sgt. Morris, B. J., M.S.M.
12/413	2nd Lieut. Melville, J. A. (Died of sickness)
12/3217	Capt. McGregor, A. G.
12/3758	S.-Sgt. McInnes, W.
13/102	Pte. McGill, J. C.
	Major McFarland, R. D., M.C.
	Lt.-Col. McKenzie, A. G., D.S.O.
	Major McClelland, C. H., D.S.O.
65001	Pte. Narbey, A. A.
12/606	Pte. Noakes, E. L.
	Major Orr, E. H., D.S.O.
	Col. Plugge, A., C.M.G. (2)
	Sgt. Randell, W. E., D.C.M.
30089	Cpl. Ramsey, W. P., Croix de Guerre (Belgium)
	Lieut. Reid, W. J., D.C.M.
	Capt. Seddon, S. T., M.C.
	Major Sinel, W. C., D.S.O.
	Capt. Speedy, A. P.
12/1799	Cpl. Spencer, W. H., D.C.M.
12/178	L.-Cpl. Stacey, D. E.
5/1338	Pte. Sloan, M.
12/267	Bugler Treacher, D. R. (Killed in action)
	2nd Lieut. Todd, N. T.
12/2500	S.-Sgt. Turner, W. J.
	Capt. Tuck, G. A., M.C.
	2nd Lieut. Thompson, A. S. M.S.M.
	Lieut. Tilsley, R., M.C., D.C.M.
12/1062	Cpl. Tempany, G. A., D.C.M.
	Capt. Vercoe, H. R., D.S.O.
	2nd Lieut. Watson, F. W., D.C.M.
	Lieut. Worley, R. P.
	2nd Lieut. Wylie, L. T., Belgian Croix de Guerre
12/3862	C.Q.M.S. Watson, S. V.
	Lt.-Col. Young, R., C.B., D.S.O., Legion d'Honneur (Croix de Chevalier) (5)

The names of the following were brought to the notice of the Secretary of State for War for valuable services at Home towards the successful conduct of the war:—

Major Beamish, F. E.
Major Dawson, T. H., C.M.G., C.B.E. (2)
Major Watson, J. T., C.B.E.
Captain Wood, R. W. F., M.B.E. (2)

MERITORIOUS SERVICE CERTIFICATE

12/164   W.O. I McCarthy, H. R.

Foreign Decorations

MEDAILLE MILITAIRE (FRENCH)

12/2263   Pte. Davies, J.

CROIX DE GUERRE (FRENCH)

6/3358	Pte. Harris, W. J.	12/3171	Sgt. Tombs, H. G.
25157	Pte. Moynihan, D. (Killed in action)		Major West, F. L.-G.
11330	Sgt. McGregor, J. L. (Died of wounds)	12/3159	Cpl. Williams, S. G.

MEDAILLE D'HONNEUR (FRENCH)

3/483   Sgt. Burton, O. E., M.M.

Appendix C

CROIX DE GUERRE (BELGIAN)

	Lieut. Nicholls, G. H.	12/3135	Cpl. Ramsey, A. N.
30845	Pte. Pegler, M. D.	18862	Sgt. Sinel, K.
	(Killed in action)	10/3796	Sgt. Wylie, L. T.

SERBIAN GOLD MEDAL

12/470 Pte. Gault, A. (Died of wounds)

SERBIAN SILVER MEDAL

12/606 Pte. Noakes, E. L.

SERBIAN SILVER STAR (2nd Class)

12/525 Sgt. Conlan, F. J.

MEDAILLE BARBATIE SI CREDENTIA (ITALIAN)

12/3264 Pte. Brinsden, N. P.

APPENDIX D

*"Greater love hath no man than this, that
a man lay down his life for his friends."*
—St. John, xv., 14.

*"In Flanders fields the poppies blow
Between the crosses, row on row,
That mark our place; and in the sky
The larks, still bravely singing, fly,
Scarce heard amid the guns below.
We are the Dead. Short days ago
We lived, felt dawn, saw sunset glow,
Loved, and were loved; and now we lie
In Flanders fields."*
—John McCrea.

Casualty Totals of Killed, Died of Wounds and Disease

	Officers.	N.C.O.'s and Men.
AUCKLAND BATTALION—		
Gallipoli Campaign	19	410
FIRST AUCKLAND—		
France and Flanders	32	792
Died in New Zealand	1	37
SECOND AUCKLAND—		
France and Flanders	47	750
Died in New Zealand	3	37
THIRD AUCKLAND—		
France and Flanders	9	183
Died in New Zealand	—	5
AUCKLAND REGIMENT (Overseas)—		
Unclassified		8
Died in New Zealand		18
	111	2242

About one-sixth of all the men who served with the Regiment lost their lives.

Appendix D

Officers, N.C.O.'s and Men of the Auckland Regiment killed in action, died of wounds or disease during the Gallipoli Campaign

Officers

12/686	Lieutenant	Allen, H. G.	Anzac	25/4/15
12/1875	Lieutenant	Aldridge, A. G.	At Sea	10/8/15
12/26	Major	Bayly, R. H. R.	Anzac	20/5/15
12/688	Lieutenant	Baddeley, H. S.	Anzac	25/4/15
12/8	Lieutenant	Carpenter, D. R.	Anzac	6–10/5/15
12/1600	Lieutenant	Corbett, J. M.	Anzac	8/6/15
12/683	Lieutenant	Dodson, F. H.	Anzac	25/4/15
12/1026	Lieutenant	Frater, R. A.	At Sea	30/4/15
12/296	Lieutenant	Flower, W. E. F.	Anzac	25/4/15
15/131	Major	Grant, S. A.	At Sea	11/8/15
12/1853	Major	Hume, A. G.	Anzac	10/8/15
12/917	Lieutenant	Mooney, R.	Anzac	10/8/15
12/1075	Lieutenant	Morgan, H.	Anzac	6–10/5/15
12/1492	Lieutenant	Richardson, H. G.	Anzac	25/4/15
12/503	Lieutenant	Reid, S. G. T.	Anzac	6–10/5/15
12/32	Lieutenant	Screaton, T. G. N.	Anzac	6–10/5/15
12/4	Lieutenant	Steadman, N.	Anzac	6–10/5/15
12/1795	Lieutenant	Simpson, W. S.	Anzac	31/5/15
12/2	Major	Stuckey, F.	Anzac	25/4/15

N.C.O.'s and Men

12/299	Private	Ardern, F. R.	Anzac	25/4/15
12/10	L.-Corporal	Adams, T. F.	Anzac	25/4/15
12/1002	Private	Angove, E.	Anzac	8/5/15
12/14	Private	Anker, A.	At Sea	9/6/15
12/1872	Private	Abbott, W. J.	Anzac	8/8/15
12/677	Private	Adams, W. H.	Anzac	8/8/15
12/1878	Private	Andrews, E.	Anzac	8/8/15
12/1136	Private	Adams, G. J.	19th Gen. Hosp.	27/8/15
12/1829	Private	Armstrong, J. T.	Anzac	19/11/15
12/1542b	Private	Anderson, W. E.	Anzac	25/4/15
12/673	Private	Anderson, H. R.	Anzac	8/5/15
12/297	Private	Anderson, H. K.	At Sea	21/5/15
12/300	Private	Appleton, C.	Anzac	8/5/15
12/2212	Private	Billing, C. V.	Anzac	8/8/15
12/1561	Private	Borthwick, A.	Anzac	8/8/15
12/1907	Private	Bullock, W. A. T.	Anzac	8/8/15
12/959	Private	Bond, A.	Anzac	25/4/15
12/30	L.-Corporal	Bigwood, P.	Lemnos	23/4/15
12/1563	Private	Boyce, C. H.	15th Gen. Hosp.	3/5/15
12/301	Sergeant	Bruce, H. J.	At Sea	27/4/15
12/500	Private	Baillie, D. S.	At Sea	3/5/15
12/1569	Private	Brown, N.	At Sea	11/5/15
12/510	Sergeant	Begg, K.	Anzac	25/4/15
12/698	Private	Bell, S. A.	Anzac	8/5/15
12/1156	Private	Boud, W. P.	Anzac	25/4/15
12/509	Bugler	Boreham, A. C.	Anzac	25/4/15
12/43	Private	Brown, G. M.	Anzac	8/5/15
12/694	Sergeant	Burbush, D. G.	Anzac	25/4/15
12/304	Corporal	Bradley, J. F.	Anzac	17/5/15
12/501	Private	Billings, C. B.	Anzac	16/6/15
12/497	Private	Booth, E. N.	Anzac	7/6/15
12/1568	Private	Brown, J. McN.	Anzac	8/6/15

The Auckland Regiment

12/702	Private	Burns, H. J.	Anzac	29/6/15
12/1565	Private	Bradbury, E. E.	Anzac	25/4/15
12/1147	Private	Bell, A. O.	Anzac	8/8/15
12/962	Private	Black, A. H.	Anzac	8/8/15
12/20	Private	Barnard, H.	Anzac	12/8/15
12/1880	Private	Ballantine, A. G.	At Sea	13/8/15
12/953	Sergeant	Brown, H. W. B.	Anzac	8/8/15
12/1148	Private	Bell, R. J.	Anzac	25/4/15
12/1572	Private	Bunn, H.	At Sea	25/9/15
12/2228	Private	Burton, A. R.	At Sea	12/8/15
12/705	Private	Burgess, T. H.	Constantinople	25/9/15
12/2652	Private	Bradley, W.	At Sea	19/11/15
12/2206	Private	Baine, F. B.	Anzac	8/8/15
12/311	Private	Baker, R. J.	Anzac	25/4/15
12/1547	Private	Bard, A.	Anzac	25/4/15
12/699	Private	Barnett, L. M.	Anzac	25/4/15
12/314	Private	Black, W.	Anzac	25/4/15
12/1532	Private	Bailey, H.	Anzac	25/4/15
12/1849	Private	Cox, G.	Anzac	8/5/15
12/66	Corporal	Corlett, A. S.	Anzac	16/5/15
12/520	Private	Carlton, W.	Anzac	6/5/15
12/64	Private	Cook, E. J. M.	Anzac	28/4/15
12/1585	Private	Carter, W. M.	Anzac	8/5/15
12/707	Private	Clark, L. G.	Anzac	8/5/15
12/526	Private	Cameron, H.	Anzac	8/5/15
12/1000	Private	Craig, R.	Anzac	25/4/15
12/26a	Private	Cuthbertson, J.	Anzac	8/5/15
12/1919	Private	Clegg, W. H.	At Sea	19/6/15
12/328	Private	Cooper, J.	England	24/6/15
12/1603	Private	Currie, W. S.	At Sea	9/8/15
12/719	Private	Capstick, R. J.	Anzac	8/8/15
12/2543	Private	Cooke, A.	Anzac	8/8/15
12/1172	Private	Charlesworth,A.J.W.	Anzac	25/4/15
12/941	Private	Cornwall, J. M.	Anzac	25/4/15
12/711	Private	Cowdrey, A. C.	Anzac	25/4/15
12/709	Private	Couston, G.	Anzac	25/4/15
12/1594	Private	Colbourne, E. J.	Anzac	8/5/15
12/50	Private	Cairnie, G. J. B.	Anzac	5/6/15
12/1581	Private	Campbell, S. R.	Anzac	25/4/15
12/2237	Private	Carswell, H.	Anzac	8/8/15
12/874	Private	Charteris, M. M.	Anzac	25/4/15
12/1590	Private	Clark, L. H.	Anzac	8/8/15
12/1593	Private	Cole, W. E.	Anzac	25/4/15
12/63	Sergeant	Commons, K. W.	Anzac	8/5/15
12/713	Bugler	Cooke, N. D.	Anzac	8/5/15
12/524	Private	Coster, J. P.	Anzac	5/6/15
12/70	Private	Cowper, R.	Anzac	8/5/15
12/75	Private	Crutcher, G.	Anzac	25/4/15
12/710	Private	Cox, E. W.	Anzac	25/4/15
12/126	Private	Cardno, R. W.	Anzac	8/8/15
12/2264	Private	Davies, R. S.	Anzac	8/8/15
12/729	Private	Denyer, B. C.	Anzac	8/5/15
12/1188	Private	De Andrad, A. M.	Anzac	8/5/15
12/1064	Private	Dawson, P. A.	Anzac	8/5/15
12/1080	Sergeant	Davis, T. M.	At Sea	14/5/15
12/724	Private	Devonside, G. R.	Anzac	8/5/15
12/182	Private	Donovan, T.	Anzac	5/5/15
12/723	Private	Drewet, O. H.	Anzac	8/5/15
12/1193	Private	Douds, J.	Anzac	25/4/15
12/728	Private	Dove, J. J. C.	Anzac	25/4/15

The Auckland Regiment

12/1048	Sergeant	Cohen, E. H. M. (Drummond)	Anzac	10/8/15
12/341	Private	Dunphy, R.	Anzac	25/4/15
12/969	Private	Dutton, J. H.	Anzac	8/8/15
12/973	Private	Donelly, R. E.	Anzac	8/8/15
12/2272	L.-Corporal	Devereaux, P. J.	Anzac	10/8/15
12/1949	Private	Elsmore, F. J.	Anzac	8/8/15
12/535	Private	Enwright, F. B.	1st Aus. Gen. Hos.	28/5/15
12/345	Private	Ensor, H. G. H.	Anzac	30/4/15
12/93	Private	England, B. F.	Anzac	25/4/15
12/731	Private	Eades, J. W.	Anzac	25/4/15
12/1200	Private	Enersen, J. C.	Anzac	8/5/15
12/734	Private	Feather, F.	Egypt	11/4/15
12/99	Private	Fisher, W. T.	At Sea	10/5/15
12/103	L.-Corporal	Fothergill, F. A.	Anzac	8/5/15
12/542	Corporal	Frew, A.	Anzac	10/8/15
12/2294	Private	Fraser, A. J.	Anzac	8/8/15
12/107	Private	Frank, W. S.	Anzac	25/4/15
12/353	L.-Corporal	Furze, H. C.	Anzac	25/4/15
12/1962	Private	Greenslade, W.	Anzac	8/8/15
12/747	Private	Guy, R.	15th Gen. Hosp.	8/5/15
12/1214	Private	Gibb, W. J.	Anzac	25/4/15
12/746	Bugler	Gillander, F. N.	Anzac	8/5/15
12/743	L.-Corporal	Gillanders, T. A.	Anzac	25/4/15
12/744	Corporal	Grimwade, L. R.	Anzac	25/4/15
12/1635	Private	Gibbons, F.	Anzac	5/6/15
12/1109	Private	Guillaume, E. J.	At Sea	15/6/15
12/742	Corporal	Grant, C.	15th Gen. Hosp.	1/7/15
12/1643	Private	Gore, J. H.	Anzac	8/5/15
12/1084	Private	Griffiths, W. J.	19th Gen. Hosp.	18/8/15
12/1955	Private	Gardner, W. N.	Anzac	8/8/15
12/1637	Corporal	Giles, R.	Anzac	8/8/15
12/1967	Private	Grundy, H. V.	Anzac	8/8/15
12/1024	Private	Gardiner, R. D.	21st Gen. Hosp.	28/8/15
12/113	Private	Gilkes, G. C.	Lemnos	23/8/15
12/1957	Private	Gibson, J. B.	At Sea	5/9/15
12/544	Private	George, J. G.	At Sea	13/8/15
12/1956	Private	Gemming, T. J.	Anzac	8/8/15
12/1964	Private	Gregory, J.	Anzac	8/8/15
12/1423	Private	Griffin, F. L.	Anzac	25/4/15
14/31a	Private	Grierson, W. A.	Anzac	8/5/15
12/966	Private	Griffin, W.	Anzac	8/8/15
12/947	Private	Hewett, D. S.	Egypt	20/3/15
12/136	Private	Huggett, M.	Anzac	28/4/15
12/1678	Private	Huxtable, J. B.	Egypt	1/6/15
12/307	Private	Hargreaves, R.	Anzac	25/4/15
12/763	Private	Hartland, W. E.	Anzac	25/4/15
12/1071	Private	Harwood, A.	Anzac	5/5/15
12/762	Corporal	Haycock, F. E.	Anzac	25/4/15
12/130	Private	Heald, S. H.	Anzac	8/5/15
12/100	Corporal	Hutchinson, B.A.C.	Anzac	30/5/15
12/370	Private	Harold, E. L.	Egypt	15/6/15
12/1425	Private	Harp, J. A.	Anzac	5/6/15
12/672	Private	Hurley, J.	Anzac	4/6/15
12/1437	Private	Howe, H. J.	At Sea	6/6/15
12/367	Private	Hally, C. J.	At Sea	26/7/15
12/2324	Sergeant	Hay, V. J.	Anzac	8/8/15
12/925	Private	Houston, J. L.	Anzac	8/8/15
12/1675a	Private	Hunter, A.	Anzac	8/8/15
12/364	Private	Hutchinson, W. G.	Anzac	8/8/15

The Auckland Regiment

12/766	L.-Corporal	Haybittle, A. R.	Anzac	13/8/15
12/1976	Private	Harvey, M. T.	At Sea	5/9/15
12/377	Private	Hamilton, W. F.	Anzac	8/8/15
12/1653	Private	Harker, J. W.	Malta	19/8/15
12/372	Private	Harvey, R. M.	Anzac	8/8/15
14/41a	Private	Harding, H.	Anzac	25/4/15
12/368	Private	Harrison, W. L.	Anzac	25/4/15
12/751	Private	Hayward, T. W.	Anzac	25/4/15
12/1428	Private	Heastman, J. E.	Anzac	8/8/15
12/749	Sergt.-Maj.	Hobbs, J. B.	Anzac	25/4/15
12/363	Sergeant	Howie, A. J. D.	Anzac	25/4/15
12/991	Private	Hawkins, R A.	Anzac	5/6/15
12/298	Private	Isaacs, T.	Egypt	18/3/16
12/1681	Private	James, E. W.	Anzac	8/5/15
12/1684	Private	Johnson, J. M.	Anzac	5/6/15
12/772	Private	Jemmett, H. J.	At Sea	9/6/15
12/2342	Private	Jeffery, E. J.	1st Aus. Gen. Hos.	12/8/15
12/773	Private	Jensen, L.	Anzac	8/8/15
12/1999	Private	Jones, G. A.	Anzac	8/8/15
12/1996	Private	Jackson, F. C.	Anzac	8/8/15
12/1442	Private	Jessol, G.	Anzac	8/8/15
12/1014	Private	Jack, E. R.	Anzac	5/9/15
12/370	Corporal	Jackson, J. G.	At Sea	11/11/15
12/1998	Private	Johansen, C. O.	Anzac	8/8/15
12/915	Private	Jones, E. H.	Anzac	8/5/15
12/25	Private	Kittelty, W. L.	Anzac	8/8/15
12/2361	Private	Knight, E. W.	Anzac	8/8/15
12/774	Corporal	Kemp, W. D.	Anzac	13/8/15
12/389	Private	Kitto, J. V.	Anzac	8/5/15
12/1009	L.-Corporal	Keyes, H. F.	Anzac	25/4/15
12/1693	Corporal	Kibblewhite, L.	At Sea	11/5/15
12/1452	Private	Law, A. J.	Anzac	8/8/15
12/2365	Private	Legge, C. S.	Anzac	10/8/15
12/149	Sergeant	Lambert, R. W.	Anzac	25/4/15
12/783	Corporal	Lane, D. B.	Anzac	25/4/15
12/394	Private	Lowry, S. T. A.	Anzac	8/5/15
12/1135	Sergt.-Maj.	Leech, J. D. L.	Anzac	19/5/15
12/2167	Private	Lornie, A. P.	Anzac	5/6/15
12/2171	Private	Le Gallais, L.	Anzac	23/7/15
12/1696	Private	Lawson, A. J.	Anzac	8/8/15
12/1073	Private	Lawson, P.	Anzac	8/8/15
12/1697	Private	Lee, E.	Anzac	8/8/15
12/2555	Corporal	Lloyd, G. J.	Anzac	8/8/15
12/2020	Private	Lowther, W. G.	Anzac	8/8/15
12/1451	Private	Lambert, J.	Anzac	8/6/15
8/593	Private	Langley, H.	Anzac	25/4/15
12/1533	Private	Leeming, G.	Anzac	25/4/15
12/148	Private	Lambert, E.	Anzac	5/6/15
12/952	Private	Lawrence, E. B. J.	Anzac	25/4/15
12/1985	Private	Mill, E. S.	Anzac	8/8/15
12/981	Private	Meehan, F. J.	Egypt	5/5/15
12/978	Private	Mills, J. H.	At Sea	9/5/15
12/417	Private	Munro, R. A.	Egypt	22/5/15
12/177	Private	Moeki, W.	Anzac	25/4/15
12/159	L.-Corporal	Macfarlane, G. R.	Anzac	5/5/15
12/793	Corporal	Munro, N. H.	Anzac	8/5/15
12/799	Private	Morten, R. F.	At Sea	10/6/15
12/1705	Private	Mahoney, U. J.	Anzac	8/6/15
12/415	Private	Morrison, J. A.	Anzac	25/4/15
12/2035	Private	Miller, A.	At Sea	10/8/15

Appendix D

12/2032	Private	Merrick, J. J.	Malta	24/8/15
12/2544	Private	Masterman, G. F.	Anzac	8/8/15
12/2414	Private	Mackandry, W. P.	Anzac	8/8/15
12/545	Private	Moore, R. A.	At Sea	13/8/15
12/1703	Private	Madigan, J. F. J.	Anzac	8/6/15
12/800	Private	Martin, A.	Anzac	25/4/15
12/599	Private	Matthews, C. A.	Anzac	25/4/15
12/418	Private	May, C. W.	Anzac	25/4/15
12/174	Private	Midgley, P. L.	Anzac	8/5/15
12/1717	Private	Millar, J. G.	Anzac	8/6/15
2/1721a	Private	Moreland, J.	Anzac	8/8/15
12/402	Private	Manning, L.	Anzac	25/4/15
12/1055	Private	Meekan, S.	Anzac	25/4/15
12/1039	Private	Morpeth, M.	Anzac	25/4/15
12/2402	Private	Mould, A. V.	Anzac	8/8/15
12/1709	Private	Mardell, F. W.	San Stefano	1/5/15
12/1746	Private	McLeod, F. J.	Anzac	8/5/15
12/1702	Private	McKay, D. G.	At Sea	14/3/15
12/1479	Private	McQuillan, W. A.	Egypt	7/5/15
12/1734	Private	McIndoe, A.	Egypt	21/5/15
12/1740	Private	McLaren, E. A.	Anzac	8/5/15
12/194	Private	McMillan, R.	Anzac	8/5/15
12/806	Private	McDowell, H.	Anzac	8/5/15
12/410	Private	McGinley, F.	Anzac	8/5/15
12/1735	Private	McKenna, G. W.	Anzac	8/5/15
12/2061	Private	McLennan, D. A.	Lemnos	13/8/15
12/2417	Private	McKinnon, K.	Anzac	8/8/15
12/2023	Private	McKay, H. S.	Anzac	14/8/15
12/2419	Private	McLaren, G.	Anzac	8/8/15
12/821	Private	McRae, D.	England	20/10/15
12/2773	Corporal	McLean, R. F.	Egypt	26/11/15
12/1728	Private	McCarthy, H.	Anzac	8/6/15
12/903	Private	McMaster, H.	Anzac	8/5/15
12/1472	Private	McGrath, L. P.	Anzac	8/5/15
12/411	Private	McLean, E. T.	Anzac	8/5/15
12/1116	Private	Nears, E.	Egypt	10/5/15
12/423	Private	Newman, E. J.	Egypt	15/5/15
12/197	Private	Neighbour, E. W.	Anzac	8/5/15
12/1752	Private	Nethey, W. H.	Anzac	8/5/15
12/2065	Private	Needham, F. H.	Anzac	8/6/15
12/203	Corporal	O'Donnell, J.	Anzac	25/4/15
12/1482	Private	Ogilvie, P.	Anzac	25/4/15
12/208	Private	Osborne, C. W.	Lemnos	15/5/15
12/2072	Private	Olsen, J. H.	Anzac	8/8/15
12/1755	Private	O'Grady, J.	Anzac	25/4/15
12/819	Private	Onion, D. G.	Anzac	25/4/15
12/2077	Private	Parkinson, T.	Anzac	8/8/15
12/1768	Private	Polglase, H. T.	Anzac	25/4/15
12/828	Private	Philson, W. N.	Anzac	25/4/15
12/110	Sergt.-Maj.	Partridge, J. E.	At Sea	4/5/15
12/826	Private	Patterson, A.	Anzac	22/5/15
12/842	Corporal	Petersen, J. G.	Anzac	25/4/15
12/950	Corporal	Passmore, R.	Anzac	25/4/15
12/1764	Private	Pevreal, A. J.	At Sea	10/6/15
12/1485	Private	Pearcy, W. E.	Anzac	8/6/15
12/789	Private	Pearce, H.	Anzac	26/6/15
12/1762	Private	Pearce, H.	Egypt	17/8/15
12/1859	Private	Paul, H. S.	Anzac	8/8/15
12/1021	Private	Pirritt, G.	Anzac	8/8/15
12/2446	Private	Pritt, H. C.	Anzac	8/8/15

The Auckland Regiment

12/2433	Private	Parkin, H.	Anzac	8/8/15
12/830	Private	Paine, F. A.	Anzac	25/4/15
12/213	Private	Parker, J. J.	Anzac	5/6/15
12/834	Private	Paterson, J. G.	Anzac	25/4/15
12/437	Private	Pavitt, A.	Anzac	8/5/15
12/835	Private	Pearmain, W. J.	Anzac	25/4/15
12/121	Sergeant	Pearse, R. P.	Anzac	25/4/15
2/1765a	Private	Pfundt, B.	Anzac	25/4/15
12/52	Private	Primrose, W. S.	Anzac	25/4/15
12/837	Private	Procter, H.	Anzac	5/6/15
12/220	Private	Porter, G.	Anzac	—
12/615	Private	Price, T. W.	Anzac	8/5/15
12/2093	Private	Quane, R. A.	Anzac	8/8/15
12/1784	Private	Rushbrook, E. E.	Anzac	8/8/15
12/2103	Private	Rodgers, D.	Anzac	8/8/15
12/227	Private	Randrup, H. B.	Anzac	8/5/15
12/913	Private	Ramsay, G. S.	Anzac	8/5/15
12/852	Private	Reading, H.	Anzac	25/4/15
12/128	Sergt.-Maj.	Rogers, J.	Anzac	25/4/15
12/974	Private	Rice, E. T.	Anzac	6/6/15
12/2451	Sergeant	Riley, W. C.	Anzac	8/8/15
12/2452	Private	Rist, J. H.	Anzac	8/8/15
12/844	Private	Ross, F. G.	Anzac	8/5/15
12/234	Private	Roberts, M. R.	Anzac	8/5/15
12/854	Private	Rutland, G. L.	Anzac	25/4/15
12/446	Private	Runciman, J.	Anzac	25/4/15
12/1782	Private	Robinson, H. S.	Anzac	31/1/16
12/2121	Private	Snowden, T.	Anzac	8/8/15
12/1131	Private	Scott, F.	Anzac	8/5/15
12/859	Private	Sittauer, C.	Anzac	28/4/15
12/861	Private	Sircombe, R. W.	Anzac	25/4/15
12/1788	Private	Sanders, A. F.	Anzac	25/4/15
12/910	Private	Strongman, W. J.	Anzac	8/5/15
12/1501	Private	Sheppherd, E. F.	Anzac	8/5/15
12/1797	Private	Dooling, C. (Smith)	At Sea	20/6/15
12/635	Private	Sanford, H. R.	Anzac	6/7/15
12/858	Private	Stewart, D.	Egypt	27/7/15
12/1800	Private	Stevens, D.	1st Aus. Gen. Hos.	2/8/15
12/919	Corporal	Savory, C.	Anzac	8/5/15
12/2129	Private	Sutherland, J. S.	Lemnos	2/8/15
12/464	Private	Selwyn, H.	At Sea	10/8/15
12/2471	Sergt.-Maj.	Sinton, C. B.	Anzac	8/8/15
12/2110	L.-Corporal	Sheffield, P. F. J.	Anzac	10/8/15
12/2475	Private	Smith, H.	Anzac	8/8/15
12/2111	Private	Sherratt, A.	Anzac	8/8/15
12/463	Private	Skellern, S. E.	Anzac	8/8/15
12/218	Sergeant	Spence, J. McK.	Anzac	16/11/15
12/2474	Private	Smith, H. W.	England	8/12/15
12/2115	Private	Simpson, F. J.	Anzac	8/8/15
12/1866	Private	Shearer, P.	Anzac	8/5/15
12/1512	Private	Stewart, C. E.	Anzac	8/6/15
12/462	Private	Scott, J. A.	Anzac	25/4/15
12/245	Private	Shaw, L. H.	Anzac	8/5/15
12/162	Private	Small, J. W.	Anzac	25/4/15
12/499	L.-Corporal	Standen, R. E.	Anzac	25/4/15
12/471	Private	Sutton, A. S.	Anzac	25/4/15
12/968	Private	Shergold, S.	Anzac	8/8/15
12/260	Private	Taylor, W. P.	Anzac	9/8/15
12/1814	Private	Turvey, C.	Anzac	8/8/15
12/1061	Private	Talbot, C. J.	Anzac	25/4/15

Appendix D

12/885	Private	Tawse, A.	Anzac	8/5/15
12/262	Private	Thomas, D. J.	Anzac	8/5/15
12/647	Corporal	Telfer, J. V.	Anzac	8/8/15
12/2137	Private	Tracey, J.	At Sea	9/8/15
12/2499	Private	Trivers, L. S.	Anzac	12/8/15
12/1520	Private	Troup, J. A.	Anzac	17/9/15
12/261	Private	Temperley, C. K.	Malta	3/9/15
12/2490	Private	Thomson, J.	Anzac	8/8/15
12/945	Private	Thoreson, C. H.	Anzac	25/4/15
12/475	Private	Ticklepenny, A. C.	Anzac	25/4/15
12/267	Bugler	Treacher, D. R.	Anzac	8/6/15
12/887	Private	Turner, N.	Anzac	25/4/15
12/473	Private	Tuke, H. L.	At Sea	7/6/15
12/653	Private	Underwood, W. P.	Anzac	8/8/15
12/1447	Private	Valentine, S. H.	Anzac	3/6/15
12/2502	Private	Vickery, C.	Anzac	10/8/15
12/480	Private	Wilson, C.	Anzac	8/8/15
12/483	Private	Watson, R.	At Sea	26/4/15
12/1837	Private	Wilson, W. McD.	Egypt	7/5/15
12/289	Corporal	Willis, W. B. de L.	Egypt	12/5/15
12/1527	Private	Williams, F. J.	Anzac	28/4/15
12/491	Private	Wild, R. N.	Anzac	10/5/15
12/484	Private	Williams, J. N.	Anzac	25/4/15
12/1826	Private	Warner, W. H.	Anzac	8/5/15
12/1074	Private	Williams, G.	Egypt	9/6/15
12/697	Private	Webb, W. W.	Anzac	2/6/15
12/274	Private	Williams, H.	Anzac	4/6/15
12/1830	Private	Whitson, T. H.	Anzac	8/6/15
12/1832	Private	Williams, J.	15th Gen.	6/5/15
12/2147	Private	Walsh, P. C.	Egypt	30/7/15
12/2515	Private	Williams, A. E.	3rd Aust. Gen.	11/8/15
12/2148	Private	Ward, A. E.	Anzac	8/8/15
12/1114	Private	Warden, C. A.	Anzac	8/8/15
12/1838	Private	Wise, W.	Anzac	8/8/15
12/2151	Private	Wills, E. G.	Anzac	8/8/15
12/1827	Private	Watson, E. A.	N.Z. Gen. Hosp.	10/9/15
12/2146	Private	Walsh, N. H.	Lemnos	2/9/15
12/154	Private	Westaway, W. R.	At Sea	23/10/15
12/666	Sergeant	Wells, W. S.	Anzac	19/11/15
12/1820	Private	Wadsworth, A. C.	Anzac	25/4/15
12/146	Private	Walker, T. W.	Anzac	8/5/15
12/1822	Private	Walsh, J.	Anzac	8/5/15
12/489	Private	Wilson, T. S.	Anzac	25/4/15
12/2161	Private	Wrobleske, F. W.	Anzac	8/8/15
12/2162	Private	Wyllie, J. B.	Anzac	8/8/15
12/897	Sergeant	Warwick, J. W.	Anzac	25/4/15
12/899	Private	Watson, H. Y.	Anzac	25/4/15
12/279	Private	West, A. J. J.	Anzac	25/4/15
12/479	L.-Corporal	Wyrall, C. M.	Anzac	8/5/15
12/1529	Private	Yorke, A.	Anzac	8/8/15
12/1528	Private	Yeats, A.	Anzac	25/4/15
12/892	Private	Young, N. S.	Anzac	17/8/15
12/894	Sergeant	Young, C. E. L.	Anzac	—

The Auckland Regiment

Officers, N.C.O.'s and Men of 1/Auckland killed in action, died of wounds or disease during the campaigns in France and Flanders

Officers

6/1446a	2nd Lieut.	Allan, J.	France	27/3/18
18214	2nd Lieut.	Brambley, P. R.	France	28/2/17
12/2618	2nd Lieut.	Brumby, H. R.	France	1/10/16
12/59	Lieutenant	Coates, R. E. O.	France	7/6/17
10/35	Lieutenant	Cobb, J. W.	France	7/6/17
	Captain	Dinneen, J. D.	France	1/10/16
		Mentioned in Despatches		
12/1190	Major	Devereux, G. de B.		1/10/18
12/2281	Lieutenant	Ellisdon, F. J. H.	France	26/9/16
		Mentioned in Despatches		
26/1549	Lieutenant	Hair, H. G.	France	26/3/18
12/373	Captain	Holland, G. H.	France	17/12/18
		M.C., and Mentioned in Despatches		
23/345	2nd Lieut.	Herzog, J. J. C.	France	15/5/18
12/2185	2nd Lieut.	Issacs, H. C.	France	4/10/17
12/2613	2nd Lieut.	Jackson, A. B.	France	29/8/18
12/3526	2nd Lieut.	Jacka, F. C.	France	30/8/18
12/2021	2nd Lieut.	Lury, G. H.	France	29/8/18
27689	Lieutenant	Lynch, C.	France	1/8/17
10/1295	2nd Lieut.	Morgan, C.	France	5/10/17
13/2001	Major	Mahan, A.	France	4/10/17
18899	2nd Lieut.	Morpeth, A.	France	2/10/17
22550	2nd Lieut.	McRoberts, E. O.	France	4/10/17
5/519	2nd Lieut.	McGovern, J.	France	1/10/18
33098	Captain	McCarthy, J. C.	France	4/11/18
12/4305	2nd Lieut.	McCormick, W. R.	France	7/6/17
12/2904	Captain	Parry, E. C.	France	6/10/17
3/1186	2nd Lieut.	Petrie, A. J.	France	18/4/18
12/3121	2nd Lieut.	Patton, H. L.	France	27/8/18
25147	2nd Lieut.	Rose, E.	France	4/10/17
32542	2nd Lieut.	Russell, N. R.	France	26/3/18
12/3822	2nd Lieut.	Simpson, F. R.	France	4/12/16
22540	2nd Lieut.	Smith, E. C.	France	3/6/17
12/2616	2nd Lieut.	Wilson, F. R.	France	19/9/16
14726	2nd Lieut.	White, K.	France	4/10/17

N.C.O.'s and Men

12/1543a	Private	Armstrong, T. C.	France	7/6/16
12/2930	Private	Aldridge, R. B.	France	3/7/16
12/1544	Private	Avery, C. C.	France	30/9/16
12/2545	L.-Corporal	Abbott, K. F.	France	26/9/16
12/2932	Private	Alley, D. C.	France	27/9/16
12/2929	Private	Aldred, J. R.	France	30/9/16
22745	Private	Aitcheson, R.	France	7/6/17
12/3238	Private	Anderson, J.	France	7/6/17
12/678	Private	Atkinson, J.	France	29/7/17
35233	Private	Appelbe, A.	France	4/10/17
14366	Private	Ashby, G. F.	France	22/10/17
14547	Private	Anderson, J.	France	26/3/18
42731	Private	Absolum, N. W. L.	France	26/3/18
42011	L.-Corporal	Ashworth, H. O.	France	25/8/18

Appendix D

46255	Private	Alsop, W. H.	France	22/7/18
61169	Private	Ayton, J. B.	France	1/10/18
63805	Private	Anderson, J.	France	4/10/18
28313	L.-Corporal	Annand, D. B.	France	1/10/18
70627	Private	Armitage, H. R.	France	24/10/18
12/1545	Private	Baillie, J. R.	France	3/7/16
12/880	Private	Barrington, A. J.	France	3/7/16
12/2952	Private	Billing, B.	France	3/7/16
12/1901	Private	Bridges, H. G. deR.	France	3/7/16
12/2969	Private	Butterworth, R.	France	3/7/16
12/1891	Private	Bourke, P. W.	France	19/7/16
12/2957	Private	Bradley, T. G.	France	9/8/16
12/1549	Private	Barron, R.	France	16/9/16
12/3942	Private	Blair, H.	France	26/9/16
12/2958	Private	Brennan, L. J.	France	26/9/16
12/2643	Corporal	Bennetts, N.	France	28/9/16
12/2651	Private	Boyd, W. E.	France	28/9/16
12/2656	Private	Brodie, C. C.	France	28/9/16
23335	Private	Baker, V. H.	France	5/10/16
12/2949	Private	Bennett, J. R.	France	27/9/16
23/2550	Private	Butcher, A. T.	France	30/9/16
23339	Private	Bovett, F.	France	28/9/16
23338	Private	Bennett, O. H.	France	30/9/16
12/2963	Private	Booth, B. B.	England	11/10/16
10073	Private	Bailey, H. I.	France	28/2/17
25178	Private	Bilton, J.	France	28/2/17
21176	Private	Barker, R.	France	3/6/17
21192	L.-Corporal	Board, C.	France	7/6/17
28664	Private	Brodie, J.	France	7/6/17
12/2655	Private	Brigham, C.	France	3/6/17
12/2219	Private	Bloxham, S. E.	France	7/6/17
31577	Private	Bain, R. D.	France	7/6/17
21172	Private	Bailey, A. W.	France	7/6/17
14379	Private	Brewer, H. A.	France	7/6/17
11383	Private	Baker, K.	France	7/6/17
11808	Private	Brophy, J. M.	France	8/6/17
30739	Private	Butterworth, H. B.	France	9/6/17
31933	Private	Beresford, L. L.	France	7/6/17
12/1155	Corporal	Bollard, E. A.	France	23/6/17
33810	Private	Bailey, R.	France	29/6/17
12/1574	Sergeant	Byers, J. S.	France	7/6/17
12/2955	Sergeant	Blucher, C. T.	France	4/10/17
14217	Private	Beaton, R.	France	4/10/17
21200	Private	Burke, P.	France	4/10/17
42034	Private	Burnett, P.	France	4/10/17
14380	Private	Brockelsby, L.	France	24/6/17
12/2635	Private	Baldwin, E. H.	France	20/8/17
42028	Private	Brown, C. C.	France	8/8/17
44679	Private	Brier, H. H.	France	21/8/17
42274	Private	Browne, P. W.	France	4/10/17
14384	Private	Burrows, H. E.	France	4/10/17
28653	Private	Beaumont, A. G. R.	France	4/10/17
12/1899	Private	Brickdale, J. B.	France	4/10/17
33812	Private	Baldwin, S. H.	France	21/10/17
46274	Private	Blaymires, W. J.	France	16/10/17
56221	Private	Burrow, W. J.	France	31/8/18
52129	Private	Bennett, J. A.	France	28/1/18
11223	Private	Biggs, N.	France	28/1/18
48442	Private	Brunton, A. R.	France	1/2/18
12/517	Private	Broderick, H. A.	France	31/7/17

The Auckland Regiment

44826	Private	Burnard, H. G.	France	28/3/18
44692	Private	Baker, W. T.	France	4/10/17
15093	Private	Bagnall, L. J.	France	26/3/18
56530	Private	Baird, W. S.	France	26/3/18
12/2639	Sergeant	Bater, R. N.	France	26/3/18
56234	Private	Bentley, J. R.	France	26/3/18
52034	Private	Bonstead, S.	France	26/3/18
14378	Private	Brennan, S.	France	26/3/18
24459	Private	Burdett, W.	France	3/4/18
30732	Private	Barton, P. G.	France	4/10/17
26773	Private	Bell, P.	France	4/10/17
12/2920	Corporal	Brenan, E. L.	France	4/10/17
12/2947	Sergeant	Beehre, H. M., M.M.	France	17/4/18
60053	Private	Barry, G.	France	20/4/18
12/3247	Private	Baildon, W.	France	24/8/18
12/4143	Sergeant	Brownlie, S. G.	France	7/6/18
54809	Private	Beer, F. W.	France	20/7/18
56545	Private	Bowler, T.	France	10/9/18
48440	Private	Browne, A. H. M.	France	14/9/18
54817	Private	Boggs, J.	France	29/9/18
30729	L.-Corporal	Byrne, G. J.	France	29/9/18
61186	Private	Blatch, E. A.	France	1/10/18
46222	Private	Brown, C. R.	France	1/10/18
74156	Private	Burton, R. C.	France	2/10/18
56231	Private	Bowring, V. K.	France	30/9/18
70079	Private	Boler, A. L.	France	1/10/18
71714	Private	Bowgen, V. G.	France	2/10/18
63814	Private	Bathurst, J. E.	France	1/10/18
44824	Private	Bycroft, G. R.	France	1/10/18
12/2970	L.-Corporal	Campbell, D. B.	France	13/6/16
12/2665	Private	Clark, F. H.	France	2/7/16
12/1169	L.-Corporal	Carter, C. H.	France	3/7/16
12/1914	Private	Christiansen, C. E.	France	10/7/16
12/330	C.S.M.	Cowan, J. J.	France	16/7/16
12/2546	Corporal	Clerk, E. J.	France	21/7/16
12/2670	Private	Coomer, P.	France	20/9/16
12/2677	L.-Corporal	Cox, L.	France	21/9/16
12/2661	Private	Carew, D. W.	France	17/9/16
12/1936	Private	Cussons, T. R.	No. 1 Aust. Gen.	22/9/16
12/3965	Private	Cranwell, A.M.	France	25/9/16
12/3278	Private	Cash, E. A.	France	27/9/16
23345	Private	Clemson, T.	France	27/9/16
12/2256	Sergeant	Crawford, S. H.	France	28/9/16
11409	Private	Claridge, M. L.	France	7/10/16
12/2984	Private	Coulthard, J.	France	4/10/16
12/2183	Private	Clark, F.	France	12/10/16
14031	Private	Casey, T.	France	3/11/16
16534	Private	Chuck, W. J.	France	28/2/17
12/2971	Private	Campbell, F.	France	4/3/17
12/3288	Private	Croft, A.	England	9/3/17
26804	L.-Corporal	Cumberworth, W. R.	France	28/3/17
10999	Private	Cleary, P. J.	France	5/5/17
30748	Private	Carson, W. F.	France	8/6/17
14225	Private	Cameron, C. V.	France	8/6/17
28321	Private	Charles, E. C.	France	7/6/17
12/3208	Private	Cowper, A.	England	18/6/17
26799	Private	Cowie, D.	France	20/6/17
24340	Private	Chamberlain, M.	France	23/6/17
26790	Private	Canham, H. A.	France	19/6/17
5/220	Private	Campbell, R. G.	France	27/6/17

[292]

Appendix D

14389	Private	Caldwell, J.	France	4/10/17
12/2679	Private	Cranston, F.	France	2/10/17
25671	Private	Campbell, A.	France	4/10/17
12/2232	L.-Corporal	Carlton, E.	France	29/7/17
12/1933	Sergeant	Crowhurst, S., M.M.	France	21/8/17
42283	Private	Carmichael, J.	France	4/10/17
31953	Private	Coleman, C.	France	12/10/17
40509	Private	Cantell, E. V.	France	4/10/17
36771	Sergeant	Campbell, E. G.	France	4/10/17
14393	Private	Clark, N. McC.	France	5/10/17
44702	Private	Clark, W.	France	23/10/17
30755	Private	Cleave, J. P.	France	30/10/17
12/193	Private	Craswell, P. W.	France	4/10/17
29671	Private	Cox, J.	France	4/10/17
26564	Private	Coleman, A. de S.	France	21/6/17
14229	Private	Clark, R. H.	France	23/6/17
41273	Private	Capstick, W. G.	France	26–27/3/18
30716	Private	Crawford, T.	France	4/10/17
52148	Private	Carpenter, W. J.	France	27/3/18
53643	Private	Christie, M.	France	27/3/18
52152	Private	Clanachan, W.	France	27/3/18
49694	Private	Cavalier, V.	France	31/3/18
60080	Private	Crowhurst, F. E.	France	20/4/18
47862	Private	Cox, C.	France	26/3/18
28579	Corporal	Chapman, S. G.	France	26/3/18
68513	Private	Cain, J. J.	France	16/8/18
40516	Private	Cooper, E. J.	France	16/8/18
54834	Private	Chalmers, W. J.	France	25/8/18
52010	Private	Carthy, T. P.	France	21/7/18
51557	Private	Cowan, P. M.	France	20/7/18
48457	Private	Costar, R. E.	France	13/9/18
42290	Private	Clark, G. C. L.	France	13/9/18
55585	Private	Craig, D.	France	29/9/18
46117	Corporal	Clarke, L. H.	France	25–26/8/18
62014	Private	Campbell, R. W.	France	28/8/18
49767	Private	Coffey, M. J.	France	28/8/18
24093	Private	Corbett, W. T.	France	30/8/18
52954	Private	Clark, A.	France	30/8/18
18624	Private	Cottle, D. C.	France	3/10/18
56250	Private	Cawkwell, T. M.	France	13/10/18
26787	Sergeant	Cammell, A. M.	France	1/10/18
14231	Private	Crawford, A. M.	France	1/10/18
62024	Private	Crosbie, J. C.	France	1/10/18
67960	Private	Cornish, W. A.	France	4/11/18
12/1851	Private	Driffill, W. C. H.	France	18/5/16
12/2987	Private	Daking, C.	France	3/7/16
12/2684	Corporal	Davitt, A. W.	France	3/7/16
12/2996	Corporal	Dixon, A. L.	France	3/7/16
7/2380	Private	Divan, G.	France	16/9/16
23355	Private	Davis, R. E.	France	26/9/16
12/994	Private	Dixon, I. N.	France	26/9/16
12/3307	Private	Drummond, W.	France	26/9/16
12/336	Sergeant	Dynes, F. R.	France	26/9/16
12/829	Sergeant	Dunlop, J.	France	28/9/16
12/727	Private	Dunn. J. A.	France	28/9/16
12/1614	Private	Donald, R. H.	France	5/5/17
14405	Private	Donahoe, E. J.	France	4/6/17
13744	Private	Doole, W. J.	France	9/6/17
31616	Private	Duigan, J.	France	7/6/17
12/2688	Corporal	Dunton, A.	France	7/6/17

The Auckland Regiment

31968	Private	Dunwoodie, W. D.	France	23/6/17
40526	Private	Dodd, J.	France	7/8/17
42308	Private	Drummey, J.	France	4/10/17
12/1613	Private	Dinsdale, J.	France	4/10/17
14595	Private	Dumbell, H. C.	France	23/6/17
12/2687	Sergeant	Drummond, A. E.	France	4/10/17
12/3299	Private	Donaghy, F.	France	6/10/17
31974	Private	Davy, A. C.	France	26/3/18
51698	Private	Deed, G. H. J.	France	26/3/18
12/2995	Sergeant	De Luen, F., M.M.	France	26/3/18
42307	Private	Doyle, J.	France	4/10/17
49074	Private	Dawes, J.	France	27/3/18
42058	Private	Drake, F. G.	France	27/3/18
59622	Private	Dickson, M. S.	France	28/9/18
38361	Private	Diggs, H. J. E.	France	30/8/18
18211	Private	Dewar, D.	France	1/10/18
16536	L.-Corporal	Duane, C.	France	1/10/18
63835	Private	Dew, A. G.	France	1/10/18
44457	Private	Durnett, A. B.	France	1/10/18
68698	Private	Dickinson, J.	France	1/10/18
65015	Private	Dalton, A. J.	France	1/10/18
12/3001	Private	East, A. F.	France	3/7/16
12/1853	Private	Egerton, W. A.	France	3/7/16
11014	Private	Evans, A. W.	France	16/9/16
12/3004	Private	Edwards, S.	France	17/9/16
23307	Private	Ellen, W. H.	France	27/9/16
12/3007	Private	Ewan, R.	France	5/10/16
12/2549	Private	Evans, W. A.	France	28/9/16
25220	Private	Edwards, S. G.	France	30/7/17
31618	Private	Evans, J. E.	France	26/7/17
24/1650	Private	Edmett, E. G.	France	7/6/17
12/2280	L.-Corporal	Ellis, W.	France	9/10/17
48629	Private	Edmondson, T.	France	28/3/18
38368	Private	Ellison, J.	France	26-27/3/18
41969	Private	Edwards, H. J.	France	26/3/18
42312	Private	Elmbranch, J. F.	France	4/10/17
31980	Private	Eastwood, F. J.	Germany	24/6/17
12/3628	Corporal	Edmonds, J. F.	France	4/11/18
60092	Private	Evitt, C. F.	France	23/7/18
12/3015	Private	Freeman, O. V.	France	16/5/16
12/2698	Private	Ford, W. A.	France	25/9/16
12/1620	Private	Fegan, W. R.	France	25/9/16
12/2701	Private	French, W. H.	France	27/9/16
12/2295	Private	Fredriksen, F.	France	28/9/16
12/2694	T.-Corporal	Farrow, J.	France	26/9/16
15082	Private	Fenton, A. F.	France	14/2/17
11447	Private	Ferguson, R. A.	France	12/3/17
12/1627	Sergeant	Frew, J., D.C.M. (Francis)	France	26/7/17
31620	Private	Fisher, A. V.	France	29/7/17
31983	Private	Fraser, D. E.	France	4/10/17
28332	Private	Fountaine, H. R.	France	4/10/17
12/2695	L.-Corporal	Finlayson, L. (Ment. in Despatches)	France	7/10/17
14603	Private	Farch, J.	France	23/6/17
15099	Private	Fenwick, H. G.	France	11/10/17
35161	Private	Foster, H. H.	France	19/10/17
51710	Private	Faulkner, E.	France	20/10/17
42070	Private	Finnerty, J. T.	France	22/10/17
14247	L.-Corporal	Flanagan, J. F.	France	22/10/17

Appendix D

12/735	Private	Fish, A. G.	France	1/2/18
12/1952	Private	Frogbrook, E. B.	France	30/11/17
28703	Private	Fleury, W.	France	4/10/17
28331	Private	Finlayson, J. L.	France	4/10/17
38681	Private	Fothergill, F. J.	France	27/3/18
68522	Private	Farquhar, G.	France	15/8/18
12/540	Corporal	Fraser, J. M. (M.M. and Bar)	France	16/8/18
48481	Private	Fletcher, R.	France	4/6/18
42316	Private	France, H.	France	26/3/18
42071	Private	Fitness, A.	France	1/10/18
28708	Private	Frith, S. G.	France	1/10/18
71617	Private	Follett, H. L. C.	France	4/11/18
12/3533 } 6/2351	Private	George, R.	France	1/7/16
12/3020	Private	Gambling, E. W.	France	3/7/16
11453	Private	Genge, B.	France	26/9/16
12/550	Private	Gardner, W.	France	27/9/16
12/470	Private	Gault, A.	France	26/9/16
25230	Private	Grant, D.	France	19/12/16
12/3022	Private	Geary, W.	France	30/9/16
31627	Private	Grant, H.	France	18/5/17
11459	Private	Gough, F. E.	France	8/6/17
11024	Private	Granger, C. M.	France	7/6/17
12/3026	Private	Godfrey, H.	France	7/6/17
12/3023	Corporal	Gilroy, N.	France	7/6/17
30798	Private	Gorcum, W.	France	19/6/17
14416	L.-Corporal	Goodwin, W.	France	4/10/17
38377	Private	Gould, A. D.	France	4/10/17
12/3025	Private	Goodall, J. C.	France	10/10/17
12/1959	Corporal	Goodall, J. R.	France	4/10/17
30785	Private	Goodwin, E. H.	France	4/10/17
56590	Private	Green, L. A.	France	28–29/11/17
52415	Private	Groves, S. T. J.	France	26–27/3/18
46332	Private	George, B. R.	France	26/3/18
13751	L.-Corporal	Gould, W. A.	France	4/10/17
31988	Private	Gadd, H.	France	27/3/18
63863	Private	Gwynne, J. H.	France	4/4/18
40311	L.-Corporal	Greene, J. G.	France	16/8/18
70393	Private	Gavin, T.	France	22/7/18
52191	Private	Gates, R.	France	20/7/18
18789	Private	Grainger, W. H.	France	23/7/18
70270	Private	Goodwin, W. H.	France	1/10/18
31631	Private	Grubb, O. U.	France	1/10/18
31628	L.-Corporal	Gray, G. P.	France	26/3/18
65017	Private	Graves, E.	France	8/10/18
71741	Private	Gough, J.	France	1/10/18
14421	Private	Grandy, R.	France	4/11/18
67973	Private	Gregory, P. W.	France	1/10/18
61259	Private	Gibbs, W. J.	France	1/10/18
12/2533	Private	Hardley, G. E.	France	16/5/16
12/3041	Private	Harrow, R. M.	France	23/6/16
12/2742	L.-Corporal	Howe, C. T. C.	France	1/7/16
12/564	Private	Heywood, H. L.	France	23/6/16
12/3053	Corporal	Hunter, F. V.	France	29/6/16
12/3341	Private	Hall, G.	France	4/7/16
12/122	T.-Sergeant	Hand, W. J.	France	2/7/16
12/588	L.-Corporal	Harding, J. J.	France	3/7/16
12/3040	Private	Harris, W. J.	France	3/7/16
12/1079	Private	Hennesy, P.	France	3/7/16

The Auckland Regiment

12/555	Private	Hill, W. G.	France	3/7/16
12/3362	Private	Houston, H. E.	France	3/7/16
12/1972	Private	Hanna, R. G.	France	9/8/16
12/3036	Private	Hall, A. J.	France	16/9/16
12/2732	Corporal	Heatley, E.	France	16/9/16
12/2319	Private	Harrison, C. R.	France	17/9/16
11467	Private	Hogg, W. A. A.	France	23/9/16
12/1993	Private	Hurley, T. R.	France	27/9/16
12/2327	Private	Herdman, J. G.	France	27/9/16
12/4019	Private	Hulme, F. E.	France	27/9/16
12/2315a	Private	Hamilton, C.	France	28/9/16
12/2731	Private	Heard, H.	France	25/9/16
13020	Private	Hickey, E.	France	28/9/16
12/2722	Private	Halliday, A.	France	14/10/16
12/3052	Private	Huckin, A.	France	30/9/16
12/3038	Private	Hamilton, H.	France	26/9/16
28342	Private	Hill, W.	France	7/6/17
25246	Private	Hutson, G. H.	France	7/6/17
14260	Private	Haylock, E.	France	8/6/17
12/4000	Corporal	Hall, G. S.	France	7/6/17
32001	Private	Harvey, T.	France	7/6/17
12/2738	Private	Hodder, V. J.	France	7/6/17
5/285	Sergeant	Hulme, G.	France	22/6/17
28885	Private	Holland, F. A.	England	6/9/17
39659	Private	Hayes, R.	France	29/7/17
17/79	Private	Hansen, H. C.	France	25/8/17
12/1978	Corporal	Hawkins, J. H.	France	4/10/17
38699	Private	Hill, L.	France	4/10/17
12/2741	Private	Hourston, A.	France	4/10/17
12/3042	Private	Hayward, L. B.	France	7/10/17
12/758	Private	Hayward, R. H.	France	23/6/17
31636	Private	Hamley, R.	France	6/10/17
47193	Private	Hahu, L. L.	France	23/10/17
40565	Private	Henderson, L. A.	France	22/10/17
12/4014	Private	Holm, J. W.	France	4/10/17
19144	Private	Hodges, S. H.	France	4/10/17
28724	Private	Hogan, W.	France	23/6/17
14430	Corporal	Hughes, N.	France	23/6/17
52201	Private	Hamilton, A. F.	France	26–27/3/1
31125	Private	Hansen, I. R.	France	26–27/3/1
14261	Private	Hinchco, A., M.M.	France	27/3/18
40316	Private	Hill, T. M.	France	26/3/18
39660	Private	Hothersall, E. J.	France	3/4/18
27280	Private	Halliday, J.	France	27/3/18
56977	Private	Henry, C. E.	France	15/8/18
60127	Private	Hutchinson, R.	France	15/8/18
62698	Private	Heap, J. R.	France	24/8/18
40568	Private	Holland, J. J.	France	24/7/18
38381	Private	Hamilton, R. J.	France	2/10/18
42329	Private	Henderson, W. J.	France	29/9/18
60122	Private	Hodgson, L.	France	25/8/18
70481	Private	Haynes, D. S.	France	25–26/8/1
46350	Private	Hunt, A. B.	France	25–26/8/1
59907	Private	Hill, R.	France	1/10/18
40555	Private	Hamilton, C. R.	France	1/10/18
70281	Private	Heffron, W. T.	France	4/11/18
12397	Private	Hart, G. W.	France	1/10/18
60113	Private	Hare, H. D.	France	1/10/18
59293	Private	Hartley, J.	France	23/10/18
63871	Private	Hennesy, M.	France	1/10/18

Appendix D

12/3056	Private	Irvine, T.	France	26/9/16
5/1266a, 10/1266	Private	Ilbert, G. A.	France	28/2/17
40328	Private	Ingram, W. R.	France	4/10/17
12/2347	Private	Johanson, H.	France	3/7/16
12/4204	Private	Johnson, J.	France	17/9/16
12/3371	Private	Jones, L. K.	France	25/9/16
8/1266, 23309	Private	Tilyard, F. G. (Jackson)	France	27/9/16
12/387	Private	Jolley, A.	France	28/9/16
12/2924	Corporal	Johnson, D. W.	France	25/9/16
10126	Private	Jaques, W. T.	France	20/9/16
14268	Private	Jesson, H.	France	28/2/17
30814	Private	Jackson, P. H.	France	11/6/17
29638	Private	Johnson, F. T.	France	25/7/17
25255	Private	Johanson, E. H.	France	4/10/17
42112	Private	Jamieson, E. H. A.	France	4/10/17
26854	L.-Corporal	Jones, W. R.	France	4/10/17
12/3063	Corporal	Johnston, R. H.	France	5/10/17
18807	Private	Jacobs, W. N.	France	4/10/17
32007	Private	Jones, L. M.	France	4/10/17
60132	Private	James, C. R.	France	30/3/18
38399	Private	Jenkin, F. J.	France	28/8/18
38402	Private	Jones, J. H.	France	3/10/18
59911	Private	Judd, E. S.	France	1/10/18
49090	Private	Jones, T. F.	France	1/10/18
7/2559	Private	Kelly, F. J.	France	23/9/16
23392	Private	Kelly, M.	France	9/11/16
12/2553	L.-Corporal	Kemp, A. M.	France	13/2/17
29902	Private	Keam, S. J.	France	7/6/17
26858	Private	Knilands, R.	France	7/6/17
22491	Private	Kingdon, F.	France	23/6/17
12/3701	Private	Kilburn, D. A.	France	4/10/17
28348	Private	King, R. J.	France	4/10/17
38716	Private	Kettle, J. J.	France	4/10/17
12/3066	L.-Corporal	Kelly, J.	France	5/5/18
22523	Sergeant	Keesing, T. A.	France	1/10/18
56614	Private	Keeley, W. F.	France	1/10/18
23/1420	Private	Knapp, J. E. H.	France	1/10/18
71811	Private	Kennedy, R. T.	France	4/11/18
16761	Private	King, W. E.	3rd N.Z. Gen. Hos.	14/12/18
40335	Private	Kemp, L. G.	France	4/10/17
11493	Private	Libeau, A. G.	France	17/9/16
12/2756	Private	Law, A.	France	2/10/16
12/4212	Private	Lee, A. H.	France	28/9/16
12/2764	Private	Lunn, W.	France	28/9/16
14444	Private	Leslie, J. H.	France	16/11/16
12/3083	Private	Leewell, J.	France	30/9/16
14441	Private	Lawrence, R.	Germany	10/12/16
14443	Private	Leckie, J. G.	France	28/2/17
16563	Private	Lodge, F.	France	28/2/17
20174	Private	Lawrence, L. G.	France	23/6/17
12/4215	L.-Corporal	Lincoln, R	France	23/6/17
30821	Private	Long, J. W.	France	4/10/17
12/2011	Private	Leatt, J.	France	4/10/17
57102	Private	Large, H. H.	France	23/12/17
14208	Private	Lynds, G. B.	France	23/6/17
38840	Corporal	Larnach, M. J.	France	26–27/3/18
32520	Private	Laurence, P.	France	4/10/17
23401	Private	Lissaman, A. D.	France	30/3/18

The Auckland Regiment

No.	Rank	Name	Place	Date
13771	Private	Laird, C. W.	France	2/4/18
28742	Corporal	Lupton, F.	France	18/4/18
12/785	Sergeant	Linton, A. W.	France	14/8/18
58893	Private	Leitch, P.	France	27/8/18
38414	L.-Corporal	Lilley, C. W. A.	France	1/10/18
56621	Sergeant	Lamont, J.	France	1/10/18
39068	Sergeant	Liggins, W. J.	France	1/10/18
12/3084	Private	Mack, C.	France	3/7/16
12/3432	Private	Muir, J. D.	France	3/7/16
12/1038	Private	Murphy, V.	France	3/7/16
12/3431	Private	Mounce, C. L.	France	15/7/16
5/407a	Private	Mangan, J.	England	31/7/16
12/2390	Private	Milne, R. N.	France	16/9/16
12/2897	L.-Corporal	Matthews, G. W.	France	19/9/16
12/1722	L.-Corporal	Morris, H. B.	France	28/9/16
12/2393	Private	Mold, W. E.	France	23/9/16
12/3418	Private	Meachem, G. C.	France	25/9/16
12/2027	L.-Corporal	Matthews, A. E.	France	28/9/16
12/2375	Corporal	Marriner, P. D.	France	29/9/16
12/3102	Private	Macintosh, J.	France	27/4/16
12/1724	Private	Morrison, D.	France	16/9/16
12/3713	Private	Macintosh, J. S.	France	19/9/16
25729	Private	Moir, D. R.	France	6/6/17
18830	Private	Moran, P. O. P.	France	7/6/17
11503	Private	Morrison, R. T.	France	7/6/17
26892	Private	Mulvihill, J. L.	France	7/6/17
14035	Private	Matheson, G. G.	France	7/6/17
12/3430	L.-Corporal	Morris, L. A.	France	25/7/17
14658	Private	Morgan, J.	France	21/6/17
12/3925	Private	Montgomery, H.	France	31/7/17
31684	Private	Morrison, J.	France	24/8/17
14289	Private	Midford, W. G.	France	4/10/17
21294	Private	Medwell, T.	France	4/10/17
14653	Private	Martin, H.	France	15/10/17
31674	Private	Martin, F. M.	France	23/6/17
46371	Private	Meaney, A. W.	France	22/10/17
18825	Private	Marshall, E. J.	France	31/7/17
12/2770	L.-Corporal	Mackenzie, B. B.	France	30/9/16
14285	L.-Corporal	Mackenzie, J. S.	France	26/3/18
12/2406	Private	Murland, W.	France	4/10/17
32532	Private	Menzies, W. G.	France	26-27/3/18
34403	Private	Murphy, T.	France	26-27/3/18
24029	Private	Maxwell, T. H.	France	27/3/18
31691	L.-Corporal	Mackay, N.	France	27/3/18
52355	Private	Morton, J. C.	France	19/4/18
51573	Private	Martin, H. S.	France	30/3/18
31680	Private	Moore, K. S., M.M.	France	27/3/18
34407	Private	Mapp, R.	France	30/4/18
54926	Private	Munro, H. J.	France	27/3/18
34473	Private	Munro, J. C.	France	16/8/18
43741	Private	Mogford, B.	France	22/7/18
53597	Private	Morris, G. A.	France	18/4/18
10081	Corporal	Matthews, E. N.	France	28/8/18
44299	Private	Matthews, D. M.	France	13/9/18
25157	Corporal	Moynihan, D.	France	13/9/18
28746	Private	Mann, W. G. P.	France	19/9/18
60154	Private	Mann, E. F.	France	25-26/8/18
60158	Private	Matthews, L. T.	France	30/8/18
68003	Private	Miller, J. P.	France	1/10/18
54546	Private	Meyer, F. J.	France	29/9/18

Appendix D

74021	Private	Meagher, T. M.	France	1/10/18
60167	Private	Morton, R. F.	France	1/10/18
48658	Private	Matchett, L.	France	1/10/18
40595	Private	Marvin, W. S.	France	1/10/18
63906	Private	Morris, E. R.	France	6/10/18
76061	Private	Mason, T. A. J.	France	4/11/18
74112	Private	Murphy, F. J.	France	4/11/18
24/844	L.-Corporal	Murray, E.	France	4/12/18
54919	Private	Moan, W. J.	France	1/10/18
12/2776	Private	McNeil, R. E.	France	3/7/16
12/2046	Private	McAlpine, L.	France	8/7/16
12/4234	Private	McLean, K.	France	23/7/16
12/3098	Private	McCarthny, S. C.	France	18/8/16
5/979a	Private	McCarthy, W. E.	France	23/9/16
12/3400	Private	McHaffie, G. H.	France	25/9/16
12/3411	Private	McRae, T. McK.	France	26/9/16
12/3100	Private	McKay, J. C.	France	27/9/16
12/1727	Private	McAllister, D. J.	France	28/9/16
12/2416	Private	McKillop, H. A.	France	6/10/16
12/3104	Private	McMillan, L.	France	30/9/16
12/3107	Private	McMillan, W. A.	France	30/9/16
12/4043	Private	McCarthy, P.	France	28/2/17
19163	Private	McArthur, J. A.	France	7/6/17
14307	Private	McMahon, J.	England	13/6/17
12/2052	Private	McDivitt, R., M.M.	France	25/7/17
30825	Private	McCammon, F. J.	France	4/10/17
18838	Private	McKinstrey, J. L.	France	4/10/17
12/2060	Sergeant	McLean, D.	France	6/10/17
43377	Private	McKenzie, K.	France	12/1/18
48553	Private	McNeish, W.	France	28/11/17
26653	Private	McCoid, J.	France	26-27/3/18
41246	Private	McCready, W. L.	France	4/10/17
12/3110	L.-Corporal	McIntosh, C., M.M.	France	20/4/18
56334	Private	McLaren, H.	France	26/3/18
46374	Private	McAnally, S. C.	France	27/3/18
32045	Private	McClean, W. A.	France	16/8/18
56330	Private	McLachlan, D.	France	20/7/18
10377	Private	McNeight, W. G.	France	1/10/18
28763	Private	McGrath, V.	France	1/10/18
60976	Private	McNamara, D.	France	1/10/18
12/2797	Private	Newton. F. J.	France	3/7/16
12/3111	Private	Neels, F. A.	France	15/8/16
12/2800	Private	Noble, E.	France	15/8/16
12/2586	Private	Norling, A.	France	16/9/16
12/2795	Private	Neve, C. D.	England	21/11/16
19093	Private	Nolan, C.	France	23/6/17
21312	Private	Nelson, B.	France	31/7/17
38435	Private	Noble, A.	France	23/8/17
27139	Private	Nankervis,W., M.M.	France	22/10/17
12/2796	Corporal	Newman, R. C.	France	11/5/18
70325	Private	Nott, T. C.	France	15/8/18
61363	Private	Nobel, J. W.	France	26/8/18
44946	Sergeant	Davis, E. A. (Neilsen)	France	1/10/18
46775	Private	Nightingale, E.	France	4/10/18
12/4236	Private	Nancekivell, J.	France	26/9/16
12/3117	Private	O'Donnell, P.	France	3/7/16
14313	Private	O'Buglien, E. R.	France	7/6/17
12/3116	Corporal	O'Donnell, J.	France	2/11/16
42383	Private	Osborne, R. B.	France	22/10/17

[299]

The Auckland Regiment

12/2427	Private	Osborne, J.	France	4/10/17
29681	Private	O'Neill, P.	France	18/10/17
21316	Private	Orchard, C. J.	France	26–27/3/18
12/3119	Private	Owen, J.	France	5/4/18
24/1769	Private	Orr, G.	France	28/8/18
65905	Private	O'Connor, H.	France	29/8/18
12/2823	Private	Powell, G. M.	France	6/6/16
12/3124	Private	Perkins, W. R.	France	21/6/16
12/3439	Private	Pappin, W. J.	France	7/7/16
12/3122	Private	Pearce, R. J.	France	6/8/16
12/1860	Private	Pratt, S. E.	France	9/8/16
12/439	Sergeant	Pemberton, S.	France	17/9/16
12/2814	Private	Parker, L. F.	France	2/10/16
12/2073	Private	Page, H. J.	France	26/9/16
11720	Private	Powell, V. J.	France	26/9/16
12/2075	Private	Parker, A.	France	28/9/16
12/2437	Private	Payne, E. W.	France	28/9/16
12/2821	Private	Phillips, R.	France	28/9/16
11532	Private	Porter, S.	France	2/10/16
12/838	Private	Page, W. J.	France	5/10/16
11719	Private	Parkinson, F.	France	26/9/16
12/2080	Private	Perkins, S. R. B.	France	26/9/16
18846	Private	Palmer, G.	France	25/3/17
14319	Private	Peppercorn, R. S.	France	23/6/17
28404	Private	Palmer, A.	France	24/6/17
14678	Private	Pussell, W.	France	7/10/17
28367	Private	Payton, C.	France	4/10/17
14320	Corporal	Pepperell, F.	France	4/10/17
38738	Private	Paddison, H. A.	France	8/10/17
14861	Private	Powley, C. H.	France	4/10/17
12/2811	Sergeant	Paine, F. J. W.	France	6/10/17
44782	Private	Paige, C. H.	France	4/10/17
19172	Private	Palmer, J. D.	France	27/3/18
13800	Private	Pilcher, C. S.	France	26–27/3/18
44775	Private	Pratt, C. E.	France	26–27/3/18
42395	Private	Pope, E. T.	France	4/10/17
63926	Private	Petty, G. H. J.	France	16/5/18
44778	Private	Prior, A.	France	31/8/18
34425	Private	Parsons, W. C.	France	28/9/18
40362	Private	Purdie, D.	France	1/10/18
45551	L.-Corporal	Peckham, H.	France	1/10/18
31703	L.-Corporal	Phillips, P. W.	France	1/10/18
7/2414	Sergeant	Prendergast, P. (M.M. and Bar)	France	2/10/18
63923	Private	Parker, R. F. W.	France	7/10/18
50608	Private	Purdy, A. W.	France	4/11/18
47197	Private	Paul, C. W.	France	15/12/18
33602	Private	Poad, W. L.	France	1/10/18
23314	L.-Corporal	Quinlan, G. A.	France	26/3/18
51776	Private	Quinlan, T. M.	France	28/4/18
46388	Private	Quinlan, G. T. F.	France	4/10/17
12/3456	Private	Rhodes, W. E.	France	8/6/16
12/1093	Private	Russell, G. E.	France	5/7/16
12/3148	Private	Russell, L.	France	3/7/16
12/3140	Private	Riddle, J.	France	30/9/16
12/624	Private	Reinhardt, C.	France	28/2/17
26919	Private	Robbins, W. D.	France	5/5/17
10109	Private	Roe, A. H.	France	7/6/17
12/2559	Sergeant	Rowe, H. J.	France	7/6/17
25310	Private	Read, W. P.	France	7/6/17

Appendix D

23934	Private	Robertson, D. A.	France	7/6/17
42402	Private	Robinson, N. R.	France	4/10/17
23432	L.-Corporal	Rice, J.	France	4/10/17
40365	Private	Rhodes, W. J.	France	4/10/17
25377	Private	Robinson, V. W.	Germany	25/6/17
12/845	L.-Corporal	Rowe, T. E.	France	4/10/17
30857	Private	Rawlinson, P. J.	France	18/10/17
12/3798	Private	Roger, A. S.	England	24/10/17
14329	Private	Russell, H.	France	23/6/17
40638	Private	Robinson, J. J.	France	26–27/3/18
34432	Private	Ross, A.	France	26–27/3/18
42397	Private	Reid, A.	France	4/10/17
23431	Private	Reid, S.	France	27/3/18
38748	Private	Reid, H. E. G.	France	29/3/18
63419	Private	Roach, G. J.	France	18/5/18
40366	Private	Rowell, A. E.	France	28/6/18
46488	Private	Robb, D. T.	France	31/8/18
49745	Private	Ramsey, A. H.	France	27/8/18
53715	Private	Round, T. L.	France	30/8/18
34429	L.-Corporal	Reynolds, A. E.	France	1/10/18
52467	Private	Rice, W. J.	France	1/10/18
63939	Private	Rogers, S. C. W.	France	29/9/18
59988	Private	Roger, D.	France	2/10/18
63940	Private	Rossiter, L.	France	1/10/18
56080	Private	Roberts, G. F.	France	14/10/18
12/3150	Private	Ryan, J.	France	1/6/16
12/3465	Private	Rule, A. G.	France	28/9/16
12/3136	Private	Ravenhill, P.	France	26/9/16
52051	Private	Ryan, L. J.	France	1/10/18
12/2835	Private	Schumacher, E. N. R.	France	3/7/16
12/2898	Private	Shaw, G. E.	France	3/7/16
12/1097	Private	Sing, A.	France	3/7/16
12/4090	Private	Smith, C. M.	France	3/7/16
12/2124	Private	Stoodley, J. W.	France	19/7/16
12/2844	Private	Simpson, R. O.	France	26/9/16
12/3472	Private	Sargant, L.	France	26/9/16
12/2470	L.-Corporal	Simpson, R.	France	27/9/16
12/3154	Corporal	Smith, C. C.	France	28/9/16
12/2472	Private	Skinner, H.	France	28/9/16
12/636	Private	Stancliffe, T.	France	26/9/16
12/4092	Private	Stanaway, C.	France	26/9/16
12/1513	Private	Swallow, E. G.	France	28/9/16
12/2852	Private	Snowden, I.	France	13/12/16
12/867	Private	Scown, R.	France	17/9/16
12/2120	Corporal	Smith, J. R.	France	26/9/16
12/251	Private	Smith, J. B.	France	23/4/17
12/2106	Private	Scanlon, J.	France	8/5/17
12/468	Sergeant	Salmon, A. L.	Franec	7/6/17
26923	Private	Sellars, G. M. V.	France	7/6/17
18865	Private	Smith, J. J. F.	France	7/6/17
11124	Private	Shortt, B. F.	France	7/6/17
14334	Private	Simmonds, W. H. R.	France	7/6/17
19180	Private	Shaw, J. E. T.	France	7/6/17
12/3153	Private	Shelton, W. W.	France	12/7/17
12/1511	L.-Corporal	Stephenson, G. F.	France	26/7/17
22504	Private	Styles, F.	France	8/6/17
12/3480	Private	Smith, W.	France	23/6/17
42223	Private	Slater, G.	France	4/10/17
18860	Private	Sadler, J.	France	31/7/17
12/4085	Private	Seaton, W.	France	4/10/17

The Auckland Regiment

30870	Private	Shirtcliffe, J. A.	France	4/10/17
26970	L.-Corporal	Smith, W. S.	France	4/10/17
30867	Private	Somerville, R. McG.	France	4/10/17
32080	Private	Stokes, C. H.	France	5/10/17
48686	Private	Storey, C. O.	France	28/10/17
12/2847	Private	Sloan, D.	France	23/6/17
26928	Private	Slade, F.	France	3/10/17
42218	Private	Syme, C.	France	20/10/17
56365	Private	Scott, E. A.	France	28/3/18
12/3818	Private	Sharp, R. G.	France	26–27/3/18
54989	Private	Sinton, J.	France	26–27/3/18
12/4279	Sergeant	Stewart, A.	France	26–27/3/18
33192	Corporal	Swan, D. G.	France	26–27/3/18
34447	Private	Sherlock, A. C.	France	4/10/17
47606	Private	Stanton, A. L.	France	26/3/18
31742	L.-Corporal	Sutherland, A. R.	France	26/3/18
12/243	Corporal	Scott, A. T.	France	26/3/18
28808	Private	Shaw, W. J.	France	15/5/18
44790	Private	Scott, A. E.	France	1/10/18
31444	Private	Stayte, J. W.	France	1/10/18
65191	Private	Skirving, M. R.	France	1/10/18
44876	Private	Smith, C.	France	26/3/18
28816	Private	Stanaway, A.	Switzerland	3/11/18
33965	Private	Saunders, W.	France	1/10/18
12/881	Private	Thomason, A.	France	19/9/16
12/4110	Private	Tremain, C.W. H.	France	26/9/16
12/2625	Corporal	Taylor, A. E.	France	28/9/16
12/3167	Private	Taylor, S. A. R.	France	28/9/16
10076	L.-Corporal	Taylor, J. C.	France	13/12/16
24083	Private	Thomson, J.	Germany	3/11/16
20941	Private	Totton, B. K.	France	8/6/17
12/3166	L.-Corporal	Taylor, F. C.	France	7/6/17
12/1810	Private	Trigg, J.	France	10/7/17
32089	Private	Thomson, A. McG.	France	22/6/17
40395	Private	Tavinor, H. G.	France	4/10/17
42425	L.-Corporal	Thayer, H. R.	France	4/10/17
47610	Private	Torr, F. J.	France	24/10/17
26943	L.-Corporal	Thompson, W.	France	26/1/18
26013	Corporal	Thompson, R. W.	France	26/3/18
49754	Private	Thomson, B. H. B.	France	26/3/18
31766	L.-Corporal	Tilsley, W. A.	France	28/3/18
47256	Private	Tole, J.	France	23/4/18
48584	Private	Tattersall, T. N.	France	26/3/18
56681	Private	Trainer, F. H.	France	30/9/18
34456	Private	Taylor, S. T.	France	26/3/18
12/1514	Sergeant	Taylor, A.	France	27/8/18
31748	Private	Trembath, G. H.	France	1/10/18
12/2133	L.-Corporal	Thompson, J. H.	France	4/11/18
70361	Private	Trail, R.	France	1/10/18
12/3176	Private	Urwin, W. E.	France	3/7/16
12/650	Private	Underwood, F. P.	France	2/10/16
12/3177	Private	Vause, W. E.	France	3/7/16
12/2143	Private	Voigt, F. E. P.	France	25/9/16
12/3497	Private	Valentine, G.	France	26/9/16
10118	Private	Vicars, R.	France	7/6/17
12941	Private	Vickery, H. S.	France	9/6/17
12/2865	Private	Vendt, A.	France	20/6/17
11558	Private	Vercoe, E. H.	France	4/10/17
12/2512	L.-Corporal	Whitburn, A. J.	France	16/5/16
12/1842	L.-Corporal	Worth, N.	France	17/5/16

Appendix D

Number	Rank	Name	Country	Date
12/3504	Private	Wheeler, F. J.	France	5/7/16
12/3181	L.-Corporal	Wagener, W. E.	France	3/7/16
12/3192	Private	White, W. H. H.	France	3/7/16
12/1526	Private	Wilcox, H. O.	France	3/7/16
12/2870	Private	Wade, W. J.	France	25/7/16
12/2518	Private	Wilson, W.	France	4/7/16
12/2872	Private	Walker, C. L.	France	16/9/16
10117	Private	Warman, P. W.	France	16/9/16
12/284	Private	Whitburn, H.	France	16/9/16
12/2883	Private	Wild, A. C.	France	17/9/16
12/3857	Private	Wallbank, A. H.	France	27/9/16
23467	Private	Wright, H.	France	27/9/16
12/2155	Private	Whitmore, F. G.	France	28/9/16
12/3185	L.-Corporal	Watchorn, J. F.	France	28/9/16
12/2876	Private	Weatherley, F. W.	France	27/9/16
23466	Private	Woods, W. H.	France	11/10/16
12/954	Private	Wright, G. C.	France	26/9/16
12/2882	Private	Whittington, A. N.	France	17/9/16
12/1828	Private	Watson, W.	France	25/3/17
12/2884	Sergeant	Wilkinson, C. T.	France	21/4/17
28387	Private	Winstone, W. H.	France	7/6/17
12/4293	Private	Webster, T. C.	France	28/2/17
18877	Private	Welham, R.	France	11/6/17
19196	Private	Walsh, J.	France	7/6/17
12/2149	Private	Warren, A. W.	France	7/6/17
18122	Private	Waugh, C.	France	7/6/17
12/3519	L.-Corporal	Wright, J. C.	France	7/6/17
12/3193	Private	Whitehouse, C. H.	France	8/6/17
24090	Private	Williams, L. G.	France	7/6/17
22294	Private	Ward, C. B.	France	23/6/17
12/2881	Private	Welsh, W.	France	5/10/17
24495	Private	Wells, H.	France	4/10/17
14893	Corporal	West, H. J.	France	4/10/17
28836	Private	Ward, J. F.	France	4/10/17
12/2145	Private	Walker, A. L.	France	4/10/17
12/273	Private	Walding, A.	France	22/10/17
42251	Private	Whiting, A.	France	22/10/17
40426	Private	Woodall, A. D.	France	22/10/17
12/2522	Sergeant	Wouldes, G. C.	France	22/10/17
12/3858	L.-Corporal	Wallis, F. D.	France	23/10/17
40404	Private	White, E. R.	France	4/10/17
12/3499	Private	Waller, A. E.	France	6/3/18
12/478	Private	Webb, W. W.	England	7/12/17
31752	Private	Warin, G. A.	France	4/10/17
28259	L.-Corporal	Wilson, H. L.	France	26/3/18
23460	L.-Corporal	Wasley, A. S.	France	4/10/17
28837	Private	Warren, H. J.	France	26–27/3/18
51798	Private	Walker, J. J.	England	11/4/18
31755	Private	White, A. E.	France	16/4/18
35134	Sergeant	Wallace, J. G.	France	15/5/18
14345	L.-Corporal	Wood, J.	France	15/5/18
64181	Private	Walton, W. E.	France	19/7/18
47613	Private	Wilton, S.	France	3/6/18
59778	Private	Willis, F. W.	France	20/7/18
54673	Private	Ward, S. L.	France	25/8/18
32110	L.-Corporal	White, E. P.	France	1/10/18
60244	Private	Widdows, R. E.	France	1/10/18
63465	Private	Wilson, R.	France	1/10/18
44883	Private	Williams, R.	France	1/10/18
12/663	Private	Williams, F. H.	France	1/10/18

The Auckland Regiment

34466	Private	Wright, E. W.	France	1/10/18
46421	Private	Wright, H.	France	1/10/18
64685	Private	Wallacê, G. M.	France	1/10/18
12/2593	L.-Corporal	Yeats, D. D. M.	France	22/10/16
12/3204	Private	Yorston, T. M.	France	30/9/16
51812	Private	Youngman, R. J.	France	27/3/18

Deaths in New Zealand—1/Auckland

Officers

14040	2nd Lieut.	Twining, H. A.	10/11/18

N.C.O.'s and Men

28314	L.-Corporal	Arundel, Ralph Victor	20/11/19
15897	Private	Ardern, Chas. Joseph	about 12/3/20
11429	Private	Christian, Jas. Sherman	10/11/19
36411	Private	Callaghan, Stewart	9/7/19
14230	L.-Corporal	Crapp, Harry	21/6/20
12/28	Private	Campbell, Colin Mitchell	3/8/18
38346	Private	Chapman, George	25/2/19
29897	Private	Dunford, Thomas	13/8/18
45487	Private	Deeble, Wm.	9/11/18
59872	Private	Doherty, Wm. Fredk.	24/8/20
12/1051	Corporal	Eames, Joseph	4/6/19
12/2292	Private	Forster, Robson Cameron	17/10/19
31624	Private	Furniss, Wm.	12/11/18
32274	Private	Gooding, Walter Edwin	29/3/19
12/2712	Private	Glasgow, George	27/4/20
12/1424	L.-Corporal	Griffiths, Ernest	17/11/18
14257	Private	Gamble, Albert	7/2/20
12/3674	Private	Henderson, Harry Leonard	3/11/18
52225	Private	King, Edward	10/7/20
12/1858	Private	Knox, Patrick Christopher	10/11/18
7/2558	Private	Kelly, Wm. Patrick	15/11/19
34388	Private	Lord, Wm. Jasper	26/3/20
23311	Private	May, Ernest Chas.	4/12/18
31087	Private	Murray, John Hugh	15/8/20
12/2374	Private	Marriner, Chas. C.	15/9/19
12/1731	Sergeant	McGill, Fred	18/11/18
12/2778	Corporal	McVicar, Arthur	13/9/19
32050	Private	Oldfield, John	10/11/20
42202	Private	Reach, Claude Edward	23/8/19
12/248	Private	Sibbit, Frank	19/11/18
38762	W.O. II	Smith, Jas. Readshaw	10/7/19
12/4093	Private	Stanley, Herbert Andrew	30/11/18
30876	Private	Shanley, Reginald John	21/11/18
20459	Private	Tulley, Joseph Walter	2/1/19
12/1523	Private	Waring, Edward	25/11/18
18883	Private	Wooster, Frank Rupert	27/1/19
24468	Private	Wren, John Wm.	15/12/18

Appendix D

Officers, N.C.O.'s and Men of 2/Auckland killed in action, died of wounds or disease during the campaigns in France and Flanders

Officers

12/294	Captain	Algie, C. S.	France	21/7/16
12/3216	Captain	Armstrong, G. C.W.	France	15/9/16
14349	2nd Lieut.	Ancell, E. G.	France	19/10/16
24304	Lieutenant	Allen, J. C.	France	19/10/17
22519	2nd Lieut.	Abel, A. H.	France	1/9/18
10270	2nd Lieut.	Bremner, A. D.	France	15/9/16
12/703	2nd Lieut.	Baxter, R. T.	France	30/7/17
15/14	Brig.-Gen. (D.S.O.	Brown, C. H. J. Three times mentioned in Despatches)	France	7/6/17
19088	2nd Lieut.	Cutler, C. J. K.	France	4/11/16
12/321	2nd Lieut.	Cooper, A. C., M.C.	France	7/6/17
25988	2nd Lieut.	Craig, E. A.	France	5/10/17
41180	Lieutenant	Cox, W. J.	France	27/3/18
12/1911	2nd Lieut.	Carter, C. R., M.M.	France	18/9/18
12/2620	2nd Lieut.	Dagg, J. S.	France	15/9/16
25992	2nd Lieut.	Ellis, E. G.	France	4/10/17
10/338	2nd Lieut.	Foss, S. J. B.	France	24/9/16
12/2601	T.-Captain	Foster, F. R.	France	8/6/17
12/2610	2nd Lieut.	Goodwin, R.	France	1/10/16
18905	2nd Lieut.	Grimwade, E. N.	France	1/8/17
12/2337	Captain	Hunter, J. F. K.	France	15/9/16
12/3672	Captain	Hatrick, J. G.	France	2/10/16
12/3343	2nd Lieut.	Hall, H. F.	France	9/6/17
14347	Captain	Hubbard, A. C., M.C.	France	4/10/17
12/3342	2nd Lieut.	Hall, G. S.	France	30/8/18
12/2567	2nd Lieut.	Hill, W. J. R., M.C.	France	5/9/18
12/1984	2nd Lieut.	Hickman, C.	France	12/11/18
23035	2nd Lieut.	Halley, C., M.C.	—	—
22513	Captain	King, H. W.	France	21/2/17
35642	2nd Lieut.	Laidlaw, A. F.	France	27/3/18
4/499	2nd Lieut.	Mulgan, W. R.	France	29/9/18
12/3759	2nd Lieut.	McLean, R. D.	France	15/9/16
12/160	Lieutenant	McKenzie, J.	France	22/2/17
12/2623	Captain	McArthur, A. K.	France	30/3/18
12/4045	2nd Lieut.	McCreanor, J. (D.C.M.)	France	1/9/18
12/48	2nd Lieut.	Page, G. D.	France	6/10/16
19085	Lieutenant	Pitt, E. S.	France	12/10/17
24298	2nd Lieut.	Richards, W. P.	France	7/10/17
12/4512	2nd Lieut.	Sheridan, G. B.	France	15/9/16
10275	Lieutenant	Scott, V. R. S.	France	4/10/17
7/1323	2nd Lieut.	Shaw, L. J.	France	29/9/18
27812	Major	Sherson, E.	France	30/9/18
12/250	2nd Lieut.	Slade, D. G.	France	30/9/18
44955	2nd Lieut.	Somers, R. B. L.	France	30/9/18
18896	Lieutenant	Thomas, W. A.	France	2/2/17
12/3843	Lt. (T.-Capt.)	Thomas, F.	France	4/10/17
23/1213	2nd Lieut.	Taylor, J. A. (D.C.M.)	France	31/8/18
33087	2nd Lieut.	Webster, G.	France	24/8/18

The Auckland Regiment
N.C.O.'s and Men

18742	Private	Allan, H. A.	France	21/2/17
12/3543	Private	Austen, C. H.	France	11/6/16
12/3906	Private	Armitage, W.	France	30/6/16
12/3540	Private	Andrews, W.	France	23/7/16
12/292	Sergeant	Adams, J. T.	France	15/9/16
12/3541	Corporal	Armitage, J. H.	France	17/9/16
24/1584	Private	Anderson, J.	France	20/9/16
24/1583	Private	Armstrong, W.	France	20/9/16
13/2994	Private	Adams, L.	France	15/9/16
10284	Private	Ahier, W. R.	France	6/5/17
18741	Private	Akersten, H. S.	France	8/6/17
12957	Private	Allcock, W.	Germany	21/2/17
13/2290	Private	Almond, J. R.	France	21/2/17
31571	Private	Amey, D. F.	France	7/6/17
31573	Private	Andrew, C. F. B.	France	27/6/17
23940	L.-Corporal	Alison, C. F.	France	7/6/17
23/1541	Private	Atkinson, C. C.	France	4/10/17
24323	Corporal	Ashton, N.	France	4/10/17
25426	L.-Corporal	Allison, H. J.	France	3/10/17
34304	Private	Aitken, A. H.	France	4/10/17
11378	Private	Anderson, H. R. R.	France	30/3/18
38105	Private	Anderson, P. L.	France	24/8/18
38643	Private	Ansenne, H. M.	France	30/3/18
60046	Private	Armstrong, C. P.	France	30/8/18
12/3240	Private	Appleyard, W. J.	France	27/3/18
12/3274	Private	Brown, G. W.	France	19/5/16
23/1542	Pte. (T.-Cpl.)	Babb, A. P. T.	France	5/6/16
12/3231	Sergeant	Brookfield, A. G. P.	France	23/6/16
12/3950	Private	Bryson, C.	France	29/6/16
12/3553	Corporal	Bennett, R. M.	France	15/9/16
12/4139	Private	Boyd, H. R.	France	15/9/16
12/3269	Private	Budd, A. E.	France	20/9/16
24/1588	Private	Ball, H. J.	France	21/9/16
7/752	Private	Buchanan, R.	France	22/9/16
12/3563	Private	Bright, C.	France	23/9/16
11394	Private	Braithwaite, W. H.	France	27/9/16
12/3546	Private	Bailey, W. V.	France	15/9/16
12/3557	Private	Blair, H. N.	England	19/10/16
23953	Private	Begbie, A. J.	France	15/9/16
12/3251	L.-Corporal	Bertelsen, C.	France	15/9/16
12/4147	Private	Bush, H. W.	France	15/9/16
12/3565	Private	Brown, D.	France	15/9/16
12/4523	L.-Corporal	Bak. C. M. G.	France	15/9/16
12/3571	L.-Corporal	Butler, M. R.	France	21/9/16
23954	Private	Bennett, C. E.	France	21/2/17
12/3259	Sergeant	Boyne, H. W.	France	21/2/17
24484	Private	Brown, H. V.	France	7/6/17
12/3953	Corporal	Burrows, I. H.	France	9/6/17
30746	Private	Brett, J.	France	8/6/17
11816	Private	Bean, N.	France	21/2/17
25449	Private	Breed, H. A.	France	21/2/17
14385	Private	Butler, E. A. O.	France	21/2/17
12/3253	Private	Birch, L.	France	20/6/17
18750	Private	Bennett, C. H.	France	7/6/17
14369	Private	Bates, R.	France	21/2/17
24/1589	Private	Ball, L.	France	4/10/17
44680	Private	Bond, E.	France	4/10/17
23/1571	Private	Britton, J. F.	France	4/10/17

Appendix D

26784	Private	Brown, A. N.	France	4/10/17
12/4521	Private	Bowles, P. McL.	France	7/6/17
23/1548	Private	Barton, C.	France	7/6/17
38653	Private	Bolger, J. J.	France	4/10/17
24/1602	L.-Corporal	Brogan, F.	France	8/10/17
51676	Private	Bateman, N. C.	France	1/2/18
49063	Private	Baverstock, H.	France	27/2/18
48614	Private	Barlow, J. R.	France	27/3/18
31942	Private	Bluett, C.	France	27/3/18
40498	Private	Braidwood, J.	France	22/12/17
28655	Private	Belcher, G.	France	30/3/18
38335	L.-Corporal	Bowyer, A. H. O.	France	1/4/18
28648	Private	Ballard, W. J.	France	30/3/18
48613	Private	Barton, F. E.	France	30/3/18
12/948	Sergeant	Brown, J. D.	France	11/4/18
12/3558	Private	Bolton, W. H.	France	17/4/18
45461	Private	Bethell, R.	France	31/3/18
25453	Private	Bunn, E.	Switzerland	7/7/18
23/2152	Private	Blake, G.	France	24/8/18
25175	Private	Babe, H. W.	France	24/8/18
31808	Private	Barnes, W. G.	France	24/8/18
61992	Private	Beswick, F.	France	24/8/18
47567	Private	Bird, S.	France	9/5/18
54813	Private	Bishop, W. N. C.	France	23/5/18
53467	Private	Brittain, F. M.	France	31/8/18
27769	L.-Corporal	Bartosh, J. L.	France	30/8/18
12/3273	Private	Burrill, R. J.	France	30/8/18
63811	Private	Balsom, W. A.	France	1/9/18
10709	Sergeant	Bowdery, A. T.	France	1/9/18
24/1600	Sergeant	Bowman, T. W.	France	30/9/18
68508	Private	Brewer, W.	France	30/9/18
74146	Private	Bartlett, C. F.	France	30/9/18
74012	Private	Burr, C. H.	France	29/9/18
40291	L.-Corporal	Bischoff, G. T.	France	1/10/18
10/2087	Corporal	Burrell, A. F.	France	1/10/18
12/1599	Private	Corda, A.	France	6/6/16
12/3290	T.-Sergeant	Chalis, V. E.	France	23/6/16
12/2672	Private	Cooper, H. G.	France	22/7/16
12/523	Private	Cowley, R. H.	France	13/9/16
12/3284	Private	Cockfield, H.	France	15/9/16
12/3960	Private	Collins, M.	France	15/9/16
12/3961	Private	Collins, R. H.	France	15/9/16
24/1622	T.-Sergeant	Curtis, E. C.	France	15/9/16
12/4153	Private	Catton, J.	France	21/9/16
13/2285	Sergeant	Cowan, W. H.	France	15/9/16
23969	Private	Cantlay, C. F.	France	31/10/16
12/3524	Private	Chitty, F. E.	France	15/9/16
12/3229	L.-Corporal	Claridge, A. W.	France	15/9/16
22501	Private	Clarke, W.	France	18/1/17
12/3282	L.-Corporal	Clark, J. B.	France	31/1/17
11418	Private	Cullen, T.	France	5/2/17
19124	Private	Clarke, H.	Germany	21/2/17
12/901	Private	Costello, P. J.	France	11/5/17
24/1611	Corporal	Campbell, W. A.	France	7/6/17
26791	Private	Carleton, A. H.	France	7/6/17
21210	Private	Churchill, H. G. S.	France	7/6/17
11171	Private	Cockroft, O.	France	7/6/17
23/1584	Private	Chapman, W. J.	France	9/6/17
12/1582	Private	Carey, S.	France	21/2/17
21207	Private	Carr, A.	France	21/2/17

[307]

The Auckland Regiment

19118	Private	Clarke, A. R.	France	21/2/17
20972	Private	Crahart, W. J.	France	7/6/17
28671	Private	Cammick, C. A.	France	7/6/17
8/3216	Private	Clarken, P.	France	1/8/17
23/1587	L.-Corporal	Choat, S. W.	France	4/10/17
12/2253	Corporal	Couper, J. R.	France	4/10/17
26805	Private	Curry, W.	France	7/6/17
28681	Private	Coulthard, R.	France	17/8/17
12/3920	Sergeant	Clark, E. M.	France	4/10/17
20973	Private	Crosby, M.	France	3/2/18
25197	Private	Cole-Baker, D. P. G. (M.M.)	France	4/10/17
31599	Private	Collins, L. E.	France	1/12/17
13/2027	Private	Corrigan, M.	France	30/3/18
38353	L.-Corporal	Cork, H. R.	France	28/3/18
11404	Private	Cafferty, J.	France	29/3/18
21216	Corporal	Cole, D. C.	France	4/10/17
23/1582	Private	Casar, J. R.	France	31/3/18
52163	Private	Crompton, F.	France	24/8/18
12/1184	L.-Corporal	Crisp, F. G.	France	2/5/18
36418	Private	Clark, S.	France	30/8/18
25/854	Private	Clements, H. L.	France	30/8/18
62502	Private	Campbell, R. J.	France	31/8/18
31051	Private	Corbett, T. J.	France	2/9/18
68691	Private	Crimins, C.	France	1/9/18
60070	Private	Codlin, A. D.	France	1/9/18
13/2542	C.S.M.	Campion, D. A. (M.M.)	France	29/9/18
68511	Private	Corkhill, T. A.	France	1/9/18
18767	Private	Crook, E.	France	31/8/18
35512	Private	Cameron, J. S.	France	30/9/18
74080	Private	Carter, H. N.	France	30/9/18
73314	Private	Cunningham, A. E.	France	30/9/18
12/3583	Sergeant	Chitty, H. L.	France	30/9/18
40435	Private	Comrie, P. H.	France	1/10/18
70251	Private	Crowley, T. G.	France	17/10/18
46288	Private	Campbell, T.	England	13/10/18
23/2553	Private	Claridge, S. T.	France	16/11/18
42053	L.-Corporal	Cullen, J. H.	France	16/2/18
24/1641	Private	Dickson, C. F.	France	28/7/16
12/3293	Sergeant	Davies, M.	France	15/9/16
12/3976	L.-Corporal	Dean, R. E.	France	15/9/16
12/3618	Private	Doyle, J. J.	France	15/9/16
8/3237	Private	Dawson, F. B.	France	21/9/16
12/3983	Private	Duff, C. J.	France	21/2/17
12333	Private	Duley, M. G.	France	21/2/17
12/3623	Private	Dunn, J. C.	France	25/3/17
12/3613	Private	Devereaux, J. P.	France	24/3/17
12/3298	Corporal	Doidge, E. B.	France	21/2/17
12/3223	Corporal	Durham, N.	England	1/6/17
12/3973	Private	Davis, C. E.	France	7/6/17
10329	Private	Dodds, T. N.	France	7/6/17
26577	Private	Dowsing, R. J.	France	7/6/17
21225	Private	Davidson, C. K.	France	7/6/17
11005	Private	Day, F.	France	7/6/17
12/1937	Private	Danderson, J.	France	21/2/17
12147	Private	Dann, J.	France	4/10/17
5/579	Private	Dearsley, W.	France	4/10/17
26815	Private	Diprose, F. D.	France	21/10/17
25209	Private	Dexter, A.	France	27/3/18

[308]

Appendix D

38673	Private	Douglas, R. G.	France	30/11/17
45481	Private	Devitt, J.	France	30/3/18
12/2991	Private	Dickson, H. A.	France	30/3/18
28688	Private	Danrell, S. I.	France	31/3/18
12156	Sergeant	Dustow, E. A.	France	24/8/18
70453	Private	Davies, S.	France	30/8/18
53483	Private	Dick, W. B.	France	31/8/18
40531	Private	Dyer, W.	France	31/8/18
41761	Private	Davis, H.	France	29/9/18
12/3309	L.-Corporal	Duffy, P.	France	24/10/18
6/4029	Private	Elder, J.	France	15/9/16
8/3252	Private	Evenson, H. E.	France	15/9/16
23992	Private	Elliott, A. T.	France	21/2/17
21235	Private	Ernest, T.	France	8/6/17
12368	Private	Evans, A. J.	Germany	25/2/17
49076	Private	Edwards, J. A.	France	1/9/18
46320	Private	Ellis, R. C.	France	30/9/18
24/2525	Private	Faire, C. S.	France	15/9/16
13/2433	Private	Finlayson, M. I.	France	15/9/16
12/3645	Private	Furniss, H. J.	France	15/9/16
12/3318	Sergeant	Field, H. J.	France	23/9/16
12/3317	L.-Corporal	Ferguson, F.	France	20/9/16
12997	Private	Fitton, W. J.	France	1/11/16
12/3636	Private	Ferrett, S. C.	France	15/9/16
12/3314	Corporal	Farbrother, D. J. C.	France	21/2/17
31623	Private	Fox, C.	France	5/5/17
21244	Private	Flaxman, R.	France	6/6/17
18783	Private	Fletcher, G. H.	France	7/6/17
18782	Private	Fiedler, O.	France	21/2/17
24003	Private	Foy, J. M.	France	21/2/17
33863	Private	Faithfull, C. B.	France	31/7/17
52400	Private	Fenton, J. G.	France	27/3/18
60098	Private	Forrest, E. A.	France	27/3/18
12375	Corporal	Franke, A.	France	30/3/18
48630	Private	Fairweather, W. F.	France	28/3/18
25285	Sergeant	Forbes, W. R.	France	4/4/18
63847	Private	Feierabend, P. H.	France	13/4/18
28868	Private	Faithfull, W. McC.	France	2/5/18
49079	Private	Fulton, S.	France	29/3/18
52180	Private	Farrelly, B.	France	30/8/18
12/1629	Private	Futter, J.	France	30/8/18
42313	Private	Fisher, J. B.	France	4/9/18
25496	Private	Fesche, H. A. M. F.	France	31/8/18
28121	L.-Corporal	Ford, G. C., D.C.M.	France	1/9/18
12/3013	Private	Fitzpatrick, J. A.	France	4/10/17
12/3656	Private	Gray, H. C.	France	19/5/16
17/64	Corporal	Gardner, J.	France	9/7/16
12/3647	Private	Garnsworthy, W.	France	15/9/16
13/2322	Private	Glasgow, W. N.	France	15/9/16
23/1647	Private	Gracie, A.	France	15/9/16
12/356	Private	Gibbons, E. E.	France	9/10/16
21253	Private	Graham, R.	France	18/1/17
24/1661	Private	Gallaugher, H.	France	21/2/17
12/3996	Private	Green, A.	France	21/2/17
18792	Private	Greer, S.	France	17/3/17
24007	Private	Graham, C. H.	France	15/3/17
18888	Private	Gebbie, N. W. T.	France	17/4/17
25509	Private	Godfrey, E. D.	France	17/4/17
24008	Private	Green, C. N.	France	9/6/17
31990	Private	Glessing, J. P. H.	France	4/6/17

The Auckland Regiment

18786	Private	Gebbie, H. A.	France	7/6/17
30788	Private	Gregory, A. F.	France	23/6/17
18904	Corporal	Grant, A. N.	France	31/7/17
42318	Private	Galloway, F. A.	France	4/10/17
26756	Private	Goer, C. A.	France	4/10/17
18790	Corporal	Gribble, L. J.	France	4/10/17
30795	Private	Gill, A. W. T.	France	7/6/17
32513	Sergeant	Gallagher, D.	France	4/10/17
20316	Private	Garrett, S.	France	13/10/17
56589	Private	Garmonsway, H. G.	France	27/3/18
48634	Private	Gill, B.	France	30/3/18
12/3031	Private	Gribble, L. G.	France	4/10/17
33875	Private	Gribble, A.	France	5/5/18
68602	Private	Garlick, A.	France	29/9/18
52198	Private	Grey, F. R.	France	30/9/18
49705	Private	Gray, R. W.	France	16/9/18
73249	Private	Glen, P.	France	1/10/18
33872	Private	Giles, W. H.	France	4/10/17
12/549	Sergeant	Granger, J. H.	France	20/9/16
13/1050	Private	Hylton, T.	France	29/6/16
12/4534	Private	Henderson, H.	France	30/6/16
12/3681	Private	Hobson, T. W.	France	7/7/16
13/2814	Private	Hunter, O.	France	7/7/16
12/3665	Private	Hamilton, C. E.	2nd Lon. Gen. Hos.	21/8/16
23/2194	Private	Hair, P. R. M.	France	15/8/16
12/3683	Sergeant	Hogan, G. R.	France	15/9/16
10/3277	Private	Haig, J.	France	15/9/16
12/4190	Private	Hedley, W. T.	France	15/9/16
24/1684	Corporal	Heron, E. B.	France	15/9/16
11472	Private	Hughes, J. F.	France	15/9/16
24/1553	C.S.M.	Hunter, R. W.	France	15/9/16
12/4185	Private	Hardwick, H. T.	France	30/9/16
12/4021	Private	Hynes, A. L.	France	15/9/16
23/1673	Private	Hoare, T. P.	France	20/9/16
23/1681	Private	Horsman, A.W. C.	France	15/9/16
18805	Private	Huyton, R. T.	France	31/1/17
24014	Private	Haynes, W. R.	France	21/2/17
12/3684	Private	Hooker, A. L.	France	21/2/17
18794	Private	Hall, J.	France	7/4/17
12/4001	Private	Hanlon, T. P.	France	5/5/17
26/1552	Sergeant	Hirst, S. L. B.	France	9/6/17
28722	Private	Herk, T. S.	France	4/6/17
26835	Private	Healey, M.	France	5/6/17
22458	Private	Hammerell, H.	France	7/6/17
21260	Private	Harrison, A.	France	7/6/17
26845	Private	Hood, G. H.	France	7/6/17
18797	Private	Hardwick, W. A.	France	7/6/17
14264	Private	Heaton, W.	France	21/2/17
18801	Private	Hopewell, V.	France	21/2/17
12/4012	Corporal	Hinchmore, A.	France	1/8/17
12/2728	Corporal	Hastie, J. M.	France	4/10/17
11790	C.Q.M.S.	Hodge, R. E. K.	France	5/2/18
12/4536	Private	Hooper, R.	France	27/3/18
38695	Private	Harley, R. L.	France	4/10/17
12/3888	Private	Hayhoe, J. P.	France	30/3/18
40564	Private	Hedlund, A. K.	France	30/3/18
12546	Private	Hill, J. McC.	France	30/3/18
24016	Private	Hunter, D.	France	30/3/18
56592	Private	Hartland, J. L.	France	31/3/18
40318	Private	Hall, R.	France	4/10/17

Appendix D

38673	Private	Douglas, R. G.	France	30/11/17
45481	Private	Devitt, J.	France	30/3/18
12/2991	Private	Dickson, H. A.	France	30/3/18
28688	Private	Danrell, S. I.	France	31/3/18
12156	Sergeant	Dustow, E. A.	France	24/8/18
70453	Private	Davies, S.	France	30/8/18
53483	Private	Dick, W. B.	France	31/8/18
40531	Private	Dyer, W.	France	31/8/18
41761	Private	Davis, H.	France	29/9/18
12/3309	L.-Corporal	Duffy, P.	France	24/10/18
6/4029	Private	Elder, J.	France	15/9/16
8/3252	Private	Evenson, H. E.	France	15/9/16
23992	Private	Elliott, A. T.	France	21/2/17
21235	Private	Ernest, T.	France	8/6/17
12368	Private	Evans, A. J.	Germany	25/2/17
49076	Private	Edwards, J. A.	France	1/9/18
46320	Private	Ellis, R. C.	France	30/9/18
24/2525	Private	Faire, C. S.	France	15/9/16
13/2433	Private	Finlayson, M. I.	France	15/9/16
12/3645	Private	Furniss, H. J.	France	15/9/16
12/3318	Sergeant	Field, H. J.	France	23/9/16
12/3317	L.-Corporal	Ferguson, F.	France	20/9/16
12997	Private	Fitton, W. J.	France	1/11/16
12/3636	Private	Ferrett, S. C.	France	15/9/16
12/3314	Corporal	Farbrother, D. J. C.	France	21/2/17
31623	Private	Fox, C.	France	5/5/17
21244	Private	Flaxman, R.	France	6/6/17
18783	Private	Fletcher, G. H.	France	7/6/17
18782	Private	Fiedler, O.	France	21/2/17
24003	Private	Foy, J. M.	France	21/2/17
33863	Private	Faithfull, C. B.	France	31/7/17
52400	Private	Fenton, J. G.	France	27/3/18
60098	Private	Forrest, E. A.	France	27/3/18
12375	Corporal	Franke, A.	France	30/3/18
48630	Private	Fairweather, W. F.	France	28/3/18
25285	Sergeant	Forbes, W. R.	France	4/4/18
63847	Private	Feierabend, P. H.	France	13/4/18
28868	Private	Faithfull, W. McC.	France	2/5/18
49079	Private	Fulton, S.	France	29/3/18
52180	Private	Farrelly, B.	France	30/8/18
12/1629	Private	Futter, J.	France	30/8/18
42313	Private	Fisher, J. B.	France	4/9/18
25496	Private	Fesche, H. A. M. F.	France	31/8/18
28121	L.-Corporal	Ford, G. C., D.C.M.	France	1/9/18
12/3013	Private	Fitzpatrick, J. A.	France	4/10/17
12/3656	Private	Gray, H. C.	France	19/5/16
17/64	Corporal	Gardner, J.	France	9/7/16
12/3647	Private	Garnsworthy, W.	France	15/9/16
13/2322	Private	Glasgow, W. N.	France	15/9/16
23/1647	Private	Gracie, A.	France	15/9/16
12/356	Private	Gibbons, E. E.	France	9/10/16
21253	Private	Graham, R.	France	18/1/17
24/1661	Private	Gallaugher, H.	France	21/2/17
12/3996	Private	Green, A.	France	21/2/17
18792	Private	Greer, S.	France	17/3/17
24007	Private	Graham, C. H.	France	15/3/17
18888	Private	Gebbie, N. W. T.	France	17/4/17
25509	Private	Godfrey, E. D.	France	17/4/17
24008	Private	Green, C. N.	France	9/6/17
31990	Private	Glessing, J. P. H.	France	4/6/17

[309]

Appendix D

30948	Private	Hogg, T.	France	27/3/18
62203	Private	Harris, A. S.	France	24/8/18
61282	Private	Hughes, R. A. J.	France	1/5/18
12/2720	Private	Haines, A.	France	30/8/18
17/83	Private	Hayes, P. F.	France	30/8/18
61280	Private	Harris, R. J.	France	26/8/18
40323	Private	Hurley, F.	France	1/9/18
		(Ment. in Despatches)		
18800	Private	Heney, W.	France	31/8/18
30941	Private	Holton, F. C.	France	1/9/18
12/748	Private	Howie, J. L.	France	1/9/18
74036	Private	Hall, R. M.	France	30/9/18
27642	L.-Corporal	Horner, W.	France	30/9/18
24/1679	Private	Hawkes, R. E.	France	30/8/18
30367	Private	Hardwick, W.	France	31/1/18
18799	Private	Harvey, J. D.	France	27/6/17
12/4537	Private	Jackson, G.	France	15/9/16
23/1702	Private	Johnston, J.	France	20/9/16
11483	Private	Jesson, E. H.	France	15/9/16
13028	Private	Jennings, N. W.	France	7/6/17
18809	Private	Jones, D. J.	France	21/2/17
24/1696	Private	Johnston, R.	France	21/2/17
42340	Private	Johnson, R.	France	4/10/17
40574	Private	Jones, L. H.	France	4/10/17
28344	Private	Janvier, A. R.	France	4/10/17
25/1763	L.-Corporal	Joyce, I.	France	28/8/18
12/2350	Private	Johnston, C.	France	1/9/18
57583	Private	Jones, H. H.	France	4/11/18
31663	Private	Knox, A.	France	2/8/17
12/4029	Private	Kay, O. A.	France	15/9/16
12/388	Private	Killgour, G. W.	France	15/9/16
24/1700	Private	Kearney, J.	France	15/9/16
18813	Private	King, A. J.	France	4/1/17
31661	Private	Kirk, J.	France	17/5/17
18811	Private	Kelly, H. C.	France	7/6/17
31657	Private	Kendon, H. S.	France	7/6/17
12/1103	C.S.M.	Keven, J. H.	France	7/6/17
27650	Private	Kelly, J.	France	7/6/17
33893	Private	Kay, J.	France	4/10/17
25888	Private	Kearney, W.	France	7/6/17
40577	Private	Kell, F. A.	France	27/3/18
44740	Private	Kelly, S. H.	France	27/3/18
25/1769	Private	King, A. W.	France	4/10/17
49908	Private	Kinimont, D. A.	France	29/12/17
60138	Private	Kelsall, G. H.	France	30/3/18
30817	Private	Knapping, C. J.	France	30/3/18
46355	L.-Corporal	Kane, J. E. A.	France	30/8/18
28347	Private	King, P.	France	1/9/18
42347	L.-Corporal	King, P. T.	France	1/9/18
59920	Private	Knight, W. D.	France	1/9/18
35118	Private	Knyvett, C. E. A. V.	France	25/1/18
12/3698	Private	Keefe, A. H.	France	4/6/16
12/4041	T.-L.-Cpl.	Lockley, B. A.	France	24/6/16
12/4037	Private	Lemon, D.	France	25/6/16
25/773	Private	Leith, W. A.	France	9/7/16
24/1568	L.-Corporal	Long, S. R.	France	7/7/16
13/924	Private	Laugesen, T. C.	France	5/9/16
12/575	Private	Lambert, B. S.	France	13/9/16
23/478	Private	Lane, H. A.	France	15/9/16
12/3384	Sergeant	Lee, W. A.	France	18/9/16

The Auckland Regiment

12418	Private	Laurensen. E.	France	9/10/16
14449	Private	Lippiatt, W. E.	France	9/11/16
28745	Private	Liddington, T. L.	France	21/4/17
18817	Private	Lippiatt, C.	France	5/5/17
24021	Private	Langston, W. F.	France	21/2/17
12/4036	Private	Lawford, H. W.	France	22/2/17
7/863	Corporal	Lane, M. M.	France	7/6/17
10099	Private	Linney, N.	France	7/6/17
12/3392	Private	Lowther, J.	France	9/6/17
42129	Private	Leaf, R. W.	France	1/8/17
43178	Private	Lilewall, F.	France	1/8/17
21028	Private	Lakey, P.	France	21/2/17
12/4042	Private	Lofthouse, H.	France	21/2/17
12/3381	C.S.M.	Lamont, W. A.	France	4/10/17
10041	Corporal	Langford, A. J.	France	4/10/17
23397	Private	Lang, A.	France	4/10/17
30822	Private	Leather, G. A.	France	4/10/17
40338	Private	Lang, W.	France	27/3/18
63354	Private	Leen, J. E.	France	10/4/18
18816	Private	Lilley, J. T.	France	25/8/18
31670	Private	Lupton, J.	France	24/8/18
63357	Private	Linton, J. C.	France	4/5/18
26866	Private	Lovelock, J. F.	France	30/8/18
60148	Private	Long, P. E.	France	31/8/18
25371	Private	Lees, H. F.	France	1/9/18
14446	Sergeant	Lovatt, A. J.	France	2/10/18
70305	Private	Lyons, P.	France	4/11/18
36462	Private	Long, A. W.	France	24/8/18
46235	Corporal	Lyall, W. C.	France	11/10/18
12/3722	Private	Mayes, G. H.	France	30/6/16
12/3732	Corporal	Mills, A. E.	France	7/7/16
12/4054	Private	Masefield.W. H. S.	France	14/7/16
10103	Private	Milnes, T.	France	14/9/16
12/4540	Private	Martin, J. W.	France	15/9/16
12/3721	Private	Massicks, E. J.	France	15/9/16
12/4063	Private	Mowat, J.	France	2/10/16
12/3745	Private	Mumford, L. G.	France	17/9/16
12425	Private	Martin, A. E.	France	26/9/16
12/3422	Private	Metcalfe, M. C.	France	29/9/16
12/3714	Private	Machean, K.	France	2/10/16
12/4055	Private	Masefield, K. H.	France	3/10/16
13/2860	Private	Moyle, C. S.	France	9/11/16
10980	Private	Moreton, J. E.	France	24/11/16
12/3723	T.-Corporal	Mearing, C. H.	France	15/9/16
21297	Private	Messenger, F.	France	26/2/17
21299	Private	Miller, J. J.	France	15/3/17
12/3724	Private	Medland, B.	France	15/9/16
22505	Private	Martin, E.	France	6/6/17
30036	Private	Maddock, S.	France	7/6/17
12/4053	Private	Marx, E. H.	France	7/6/17
12/3736	Private	Moore, J. W.	France	9/6/17
26870	Private	Mackay, G. J.	France	11/7/17
31679	Private	Mitchell, H.	France	7/6/17
24278	Private	Morris, J. C.	France	26/6/17
12/3711	Private	Mace, W. H. C.	France	21/2/17
11370	Corporal	Madill, A. R.	France	21/2/17
24030	L.-Corporal	Monstedt, J. A.	France	31/7/17
28751	Private	Munce, K. I.	France	3/10/17
13061	Private	Mitchell, D. W.	France	7/10/17
42157	Private	Maunsell, P. H.	France	4/10/17

Appendix D

42152	Private	May, J. G.	France	21/10/17
28761	Private	Murphy, S.	France	4/10/17
33920	Private	Monaghan, J.	France	27/3/18
52449	Private	Matuschka, H. D.	England	25/1/18
48661	Private	Martin, R. E.	France	30/3/18
45534	Private	Meadway, E. L.	France	30/3/18
38419	Sergeant	Motherwell, J. P.	France	27/3/18
48659	Private	Matthewson, H. H.	France	1/4/18
24/1757	Private	Morris, H.	France	4/10/17
14296	Private	Murphy, G. A.	France	2/4/18
12/3421	Corporal	Mettam, F. J.	France	6/4/18
38299	Private	Miller, E. D.	France	4/10/17
51760	Private	Morton, C. J.	France	6/5/18
2/1868	Private	Morell, H. V.	France	23/5/18
51960	Corporal	Moffat, J. B.	France	30/8/18
48871	Private	Mansbridge, S.	France	24/8/18
41835	Private	Marsh, H. C.	France	24/8/18
52447	Private	Marsh, E. C. H.	France	2/9/18
57108	Private	Mackenzie, J.	France	1/9/18
34106	Private	Mullin, D. F.	France	30/9/18
28356	Corporal	Murray, H. E.	France	30/9/18
14451	Private	Machell, H. R.	France	29/9/18
26885	Private	Mincher, O. A.	France	15/11/18
33906	Corporal	Mansfield, A. B.	France	30/9/18
70309	Private	Malavey, M. H.	France	11/10/18
73332	Private	Mackie, A. C.	England	19/12/18
43789	Private	Marshall, W.	France	14/1/18
54916	Private	Meduis, P.	France	18/2/18
44755	Private	Mason, E. E.	France	7/10/17
12/3397	Private	McArthur, M.	France	25/6/16
8/3328	Private	McEwan, J.	France	30/6/16
12/3755	Private	McDowell, W. H. R.	France	15/9/16
10/3335	Private	McDougal, J.	France	15/9/16
5/249	Private	MacDonald, E. J.	France	20/9/16
24039	Private	McLeod, C. F.	France	16/9/16
12/3109	Private	McNickle, M.	France	15/9/16
24038	Private	McKenzie, F. J.	France	1/3/17
10/3021	Private	McNiven, C. A.	France	15/9/16
14669	L.-Corporal	McLean, J.	France	1/5/17
26873	Private	McIsaac, A.	France	7/6/17
32040	Private	McKee, A. B.	France	4/6/17
17/223	Private	McAulay, C.	France	7/6/17
18839	Private	McLean, D.	France	7/6/17
32037	Private	McMullen, A.	France	7/6/17
24041	Private	McPhee, J.	France	7/6/17
26876	Private	McMeikan, J.	France	21/2/17
13/517	Private	McKenzie, A.	France	27/6/17
42836	Private	McElroy, G.	France	1/8/17
21288	Private	McLean, N. W.	France	21/2/17
13/3055	Sergeant	McCabe, G. L.	France	21/2/17
11506	L.-Corporal	McConnell, E. J.	France	1/8/17
10710	Private	McDougall, R. F.	France	4/10/17
38432	Private	McLean, O. A.	France	4/10/17
49781	Private	McKenzie, H.	France	18/10/17
30834	Private	McGowan, W. J.	France	21/10/17
38733	Private	McQuillan, B.	France	5/12/17
46376	Private	McConaughy, F. E.	France	30/3/18
42139	Private	McDermott, B. P.	France	30/3/18
49913	Private	McGinnis, J. A.	France	30/3/18
33205	L.-Corporal	MacShane, C. E.	France	4/4/18

The Auckland Regiment

26872	Private	McDonald, H. C.	France	30/3/18
60171	Private	McBride, C.	France	26/7/18
54568	Private	McLay, P.	France	31/3/18
12/3753	Corporal	McConnell, C. D.	England	15/5/18
39084	Private	McGill, D. A.	France	1/9/18
12/2777	Private	McRae, D. A.	France	1/9/18
36655	Private	McGregor, J.	France	29/9/18
73270	Private	McIntosh, H.	France	30/9/18
24035	Private	McDonald, E. A.	France	21/2/17
40612	Private	McPherson, R. C.	France	30/3/18
8/2091	Private	Nelson, A. T.	France	2/10/16
25570	Private	Nicolson, A. S.	France	21/2/17
13/3061	L.-Corporal	Nelson, H. P.	France	7/6/17
18841	Private	North, E.	France	9/6/17
18842	Private	North, W. H.	France	7/6/17
18438	Private	Norman, A. H.	France	7/6/17
23/1766	Sergeant	Nicholson, G.	France	12/4/18
64331	Private	Nelson, W. H.	France	1/9/18
59958	Private	Northwood, H. J.	France	30/9/18
12/2807	Private	O'Sullivan, E. M.	France	30/9/16
12/2804	Private	O'Hanlon, W.	France	21/2/17
12/3772	Private	O'Meara, W. J.	France	11/6/17
26967	Private	Orr, R. C.	France	21/2/17
30841	Private	Olney, A. C.	France	24/6/17
24046	Private	Osborne, C.	France	12/10/17
26966	Private	Orr, J. W.	France	4/10/17
21318	Private	Owens, S. J.	France	4/10/17
49736	Private	O'Keefe, P.	France	30/3/18
70327	Private	Oldale, H. E.	France	12/10/18
61370	Private	O'Neil, J. A.	France	20/9/18
12/3129	Private	Preece, P. J.	France	13/7/16
12/3781	Private	Phillipson, E. C.	France	24/7/16
23/2255	Private	Partridge, E. S.	France	13/9/16
23/1780	Private	Pivott, E.	France	18/9/16
13/2360	Corporal	Peart, A. C.	France	15/9/16
23/2258	Private	Perry, R. G.	France	15/9/16
10/3703	Private	Peters, W.	France	15/9/16
11/1213	Private	Philps, F.	France	15/9/16
13/2893	Corporal	Pirrit, J. A.	Franec	15/9/16
12/3448	Private	Prince, W. A.	France	15/9/16
12/3785	Private	Pirie, R. S.	France	21/9/16
23/2262	Private	Poole, O. C.	France	1/10/16
12/3445	Private	Postlewaight, C. A.	France	15/9/16
24050	Private	Pountney. E.	France	3/10/16
12/2812	Private	Palmer, F. K.	France	21/11/16
12/4073	Private	Pountney, W. R.	France	15/9/16
12/3128	Private	Price, T.	France	19/2/17
11528	Private	Peterson, F. N.	France	22/2/17
31706	Private	Prickett, J. W.	France	7/5/17
12/1769	Private	Porter, J. V.	France	4/6/17
12/3778	Private	Pemberton, A. W.	France	7/6/17
17820	Private	Preston, A.	France	7/6/17
12/3784	Private	Pierce, N. J.	France	21/2/17
12/3774	Private	Page, T.	France	1/8/17
31699	Private	Pengally, R.	France	2/8/17
24095	Private	Pile. C. E.	France	21/2/17
13/2886	Private	Pentelow, F.	France	21/2/17
24051	Private	Price, S.	France	21/2/17
10424	Private	Peterson, A.	France	21/2/17
12/3447	Corporal	Poulton, H. J. D.	France	7/6/17

Appendix D

28791	Private	Poulsen, L. P.	France	15/8/17
12/832	Sergeant	Pardoe, H.	France	4/10/17
31702	Private	Perrin, J. H.	France	4/10/17
38740	Private	Parker, W.	France	4/10/17
48563	Private	Pavitt, R.	France	30/3/18
54701	Private	Phillips, F.	France	27/8/18
25584	Private	Phillips, J. H.	France	1/9/18
30845	L.-Corporal	Pegler, M. D.	France	30/9/18
		Croix de Guerre (Belgian)		
35126	Private	Phillips, H.	England	16/9/18
10/3377	Private	Rider, H. F.	France	28/6/16
12/4083	Private	Robertson, D.	France	19/7/16
12/621	Private	Ridgers, A.	France	21/9/16
12/2450	C.S.M.	Richardson, M. H.	France	15/9/16
13/3071	Private	Rogers, W .E.	France	15/11/16
12/3799	Private	Ronaldson, R.	France	21/2/17
12/928	Sergeant	Robertson, W.	Germany	21/2/17
20426	Private	Ross, B.	France	8/6/17
10052	L.-Corporal	Redditt, A.	France	4/6/17
26691	Private	Rowlands, V.	France	4/6/17
10108	Private	Richdale, J. C.	France	7/6/17
22286	Private	Rudd, A. M.	France	24/6/17
14484	Private	Russo, J.	France	29/7/17
12/3795	C.S.M.	Robinson, S.	France	31/7/17
28799	Private	Romeo, J. M.	France	31/7/17
38446	Private	Russell, D. A.	France	3/10/17
26914	Private	Reid, R. A.	France	6/10/17
24/1794	Private	Riley, M.	France	7/10/17
35176	L.-Corporal	Raine, P.	France	5/10/17
18858	Private	Rowe, J. C.	France	5/10/17
26920	Private	Rose, W. McI.	France	4/10/17
39105	Private	Ryan, T. P.	France	2/4/18
28801	L.-Corporal	Robertson, E. H.	France	24/10/17
25/809	Private	Raw, W. J.	Germany	31/8/17
12/3790	L.-Corporal	Ravlich, J.	France	29/3/18
12/3804	L.-Corporal	Rutter, W. A.	France	30/3/18
5/11041a	Private	Rousham, R. N.	France	28/6/18
28203	Private	Rowlands, F. J.	France	23/8/18
33952	Private	Roberts, A. T.	France	30/8/18
49114	Private	Rankin, A. W.	France	1/9/18
60207	Private	Rose, W.	France	1/9/18
45556	Private	Reynolds, C. H.	France	30/9/18
12/3147	Sergeant	Russell, E.	France	30/9/18
14864	Private	Raynor, J.	France	7/11/18
58487	Private	Rowse, R. J.	France	5/10/18
67578	Private	Robertson, J. N.	France	11/10/18
12/3832	Private	Stockman, J.	France	4/6/16
12/2895	Private	Simpson, R. H. M.	France	19/9/16
12/2463	Private	Satchwell, K.	France	15/9/16
12/3474	Private	Seal, R.	France	15/9/16
12/3815	Private	Sellwood, W. E.	France	15/9/16
12/3812	Private	Scott, G. T.	France	15/9/16
13/2369	Private	Scott, R. H. V.	France	15/9/16
12/3824	Private	Smith, F. G.	France	15/9/16
12/3484	Private	Stewart, C.	France	15/9/16
23/1806	Private	Sherman, A.	France	19/9/16
12/4096	Private	Stevenson, J. W.	France	15/9/16
12/256	Sergeant	Stewart, G. Mc.	France	30/9/16
11545	Private	Snodgrass, W. A.	France	2/10/16
12/4280	Private	Stewart, G. J.	France	15/9/16

The Auckland Regiment

24/1814	Private	Scott, H. B.	France	22/11/16
12/2478	Private	Spence, J.	France	15/9/16
12/3839	L.-Corporal	Stewart, L. P.	France	5/1/17
12/3836	Private	Stevens, H. S.	England	15/2/17
14497	Private	Small, B. H.	France	21/2/17
25609	Private	Smith, W. W.	France	21/2/17
12/4276	Private	Starkey, L. E.	France	15/9/16
26009	Private	Scott, O.	France	4/6/17
30875	Private	Slade, H. A.	France	7/6/17
11548	Private	Smeed, N.	France	7/6/17
12/943	Private	Smith, J.	France	7/6/17
20443	Private	Stephenson, J. H.	France	7/6/17
24070	Private	Smith, L. F.	France	21/2/17
24075	Private	Storey, F.	France	21/2/17
31729	Private	Smith, R.	France	7/6/17
14491	Private	Sadler, S. J.	France	7/6/17
26969	Corporal	Southgate, H.	France	21/2/17
12/633	L.-Corporal	Sullivan, T. G.	France	21/2/17
20436	Private	Smith, E. A. F.	France	8/6/17
24/1804	Private	Sanderson, A. R.	France	4/10/17
12/3471	Private	Sanderson, S. J.	France	4/10/17
24063	Private	Sanderson, W.	France	4/10/17
24073	Private	Steers, O.	France	4/10/17
12/2836	L.-Corporal	Seed, G. J.	France	27/3/18
28805	Private	Schenk, F. L.	France	29/3/18
13/2366	Private	Searle, E., M.M.	France	20/1/18
28806	Private	Scott, A. R.	France	27/3/18
31440	Private	Shepherd, V. A.	France	27/3/18
28809	Private	Simms, F.	France	1/4/18
49753	Private	Scott, W. J.	France	11/4/18
61426	Private	Shead, E. W.	France	11/4/18
6/4148	Private	Steele, W. H.	England	26/4/18
48683	Private	Smith, V. J.	France	30/3/18
57156	Private	Scullin, F.	France	27/3/18
24064	Private	Sanderson, R.	France	30/3/18
61416	Private	Shaw, A.	France	7/5/18
63946	Private	Shanahan, T.	France	23/5/18
63679	Private	Scotton, D. V.	France	24/8/18
10389	Private	Shannon, A. F. M.	France	24/8/18
52484	Private	Speight, L. V.	France	31/8/18
22291	C.S.M.	Sutton, W., M.M.	France	2/9/18
63220	Private	Scott, W.	France	3/9/18
22373	Private	Shadwell, W.	France	1/9/18
40689	Corporal	Sharp, H. H.	France	1/9/18
59996	Private	Smith, H.	France	1/9/18
49749	Private	Smith, J. L.	France	1/9/18
49120	Private	Strong, T. W.	France	1/9/18
47253	Private	Stewart, J. S.	France	24/8/18
49125	Private	Small, H. E.	France	31/8/18
33961	Private	Sargent, G. E.	France	1/10/18
62647	Private	Sherman, F.	France	29/9/18
22290	Private	Simm, T.	France	29/9/18
70549	Private	Smethurst, W. E.	France	11/10/18
45564	Private	Stacey, W.	France	11/10/18
25/1211	Private	Timmins, W.	France	16/9/16
12/3846	Private	Tobin, G. H. W.	France	15/9/16
12/4109	Private	Trainer, C. E.	France	15/9/16
24080	Private	Thompson, M.	France	2/10/16
12/3849	Private	Trotman, H. L.	France	2/10/16
12/4284	Private	Tromans, W.	France	25/10/16

[316]

Appendix D

24764	Private	Thodey, F. D.	France	3/10/16
26944	Private	Trevarthen, A. G.	France	21/2/17
21350	Private	Tarlin, C. V.	Germany	22/2/17
10064	Private	Thomson, R. L.	France	5/6/17
25617	Private	Tomlinson, W. F.	France	21/2/17
12/3493	Private	Thomas, V. C.	France	7/6/17
12512	Private	Thomson, J. E.	France	1/8/17
12/4287	Private	Tutty, H. B.	France	4/10/17
12/2131	Sergeant	Terry, F.	France	4/10/17
33971	L.-Corporal	Thompson, G. C.	France	27/3/18
28007	Private	Taylor, C. B.	France	30/3/18
47201	Private	Thorpe, W. H. A.	France	30/8/18
31746	Private	Thurgood, G. F. L.	France	1/9/18
64386	Private	Triphook, C. E.	France	1/9/18
32092	Private	Tolme, D.	France	13/9/18
30879	Private	Turner, S. S.	France	30/9/18
60228	L.-Corporal	Tipper, J.	France	8/2/18
31446	Private	Taffard, E. E.	France	1/10/18
38459	Private	Thorburn, G. K.	France	30/3/18
24085	Private	Veart, A. E.	France	6/12/16
24/1558	Corporal	Vause, S.	France	13/6/17
45579	Private	Vickers, H.	France	30/3/18
46251	Private	Voysey, W. D.	France	5/9/18
12/3856	Private	Wallace, W.	France	30/5/16
12/3861	Private	Watkins, R. A.	France	23/7/16
13/2953	Private	Windsor, H. M.	France	14/9/16
12/3880	L.-Corporal	Wright, J. H.	France	14/9/16
24/1849	L.-Corporal	Waller, L. J.	France	15/9/16
11142	Private	Weir, J. W.	France	15/9/16
13/2952	Private	Wilkinson, E. L.	France	15/9/16
12/3515	Private	Wilson, J.	France	15/9/16
3/2383	Private	Wagstaff, A. A.	France	17/9/16
12/2562	Private	Wilson, A. J.	France	28/9/16
24/1860	Private	Wiggins, H. A.	France	15/9/16
12309	Private	Wilson, J. L.	France	2/10/16
21358	Private	Wall, R.	France	29/1/17
12/3870	Private	Whiterod, A. J.	France	7/5/17
20469	Private	Wallace, N.	France	7/6/17
21360	Private	Watt, W. J.	France	7/6/17
12/3510	Private	Wiedenbohm, G.	France	7/6/17
23/2304	Private	Williams, W. H.	France	8/6/17
28844	Private	Williams, J. E.	France	9/6/17
23/1880	Private	Wilson, H. F.	France	7/6/17
24/1866	Private	Williamson, H. J.	France	21/2/17
12306	Private	Walker, A. H.	France	1/8/17
25624	Private	Webb, R. B.	France	21/2/17
2/298	Private	White, J.	France	21/2/17
38780	Private	Wight, K. E.	France	31/7/17
18901	L.-Corporal	Williams, W. R.	France	31/7/17
30883	Private	Watkins, F. T.	France	7/6/17
12/3516	Corporal	Wood, E. H.	France	12/10/17
12/3506	Sergeant	Whitfield, I.	France	4/10/17
14518	Corporal	White, R.	France	4/10/17
5/527	Sergeant	Wilson, A. W.	France	4/10/17
31758	Corporal	Worner, G. W.	France	4/10/17
26955	Private	Wood, P. D.	France	10/11/17
17949	Private	Winyard, T. H.	France	1/12/17
12/3865	Private	Wells, F. B. A.	France	29/3/18
46153	Private	Willis, T. W.	France	8/4/18
49131	Private	Walker, W.	France	30/3/18

The Auckland Regiment

38473	Private	Wilson, H. T.	France	17/4/18
24087	Private	Watkins, W. A.	England	25/4/18
54998	Private	Walsh, J. E.	France	30/3/18
38462	Private	Walker, E. T. L.	France	30/3/18
29528	Private	Watts, J. C. R.	France	30/3/18
56388	Private	White, A. McG.	France	28/3/18
32916	Private	Walsh, T. P.	France	27/7/18
56694	Private	Wakefield, S. H.	France	31/3/18
56690	Private	Wallace, G.	France	23/5/18
52516	Private	Wall, R. F. W.	France	30/8/18
30893	Corporal	Wilson, J. A.	France	24/8/18
63801	Private	Weisert, G. E.	France	2/9/18
70377	Private	Wells, B. A.	France	4/9/18
60246	Private	Williams, J. G.	France	1/9/18
42445	Private	Withers, R. C.	France	1/9/18
21366	Private	Wolfe, S.	France	1/9/18
12/4554	Sergeant	Willshaw, S.	France	6/9/18
65025	Private	Woolley, S.	France	31/8/18
64399	Private	Wilson, A. W.	France	26/9/18
70367	Private	Wallis, C. M.	France	11/10/18
47259	Private	Whitley, S.	France	11/10/18
70609	Private	Watson, R. J.	France	30/9/18
63985	Private	Wilson, J. A.	France	29/9/18
31001	Corporal	White, A. B.	France	30/9/18
38471	Private	Williams, S. E.	France	24/8/18
52522	L.-Corporal	Whiteley, T. B. W.	France	11/10/18
31004	L.-Corporal	Woodgate, C. E.	France	20/11/17
13/967	Private	Wallen, L. L.	France	15/9/16
13/978	Private	Young, W. F.	France	15/7/16
12/3521	Private	Yaag, A.	England	23/2/17
12/3523	L.-Corporal	Young, W. J.	France	21/2/17
13/585	Private	Yorke, O.	France	21/2/17
51585	Private	Young, D. L.	France	27/3/18
60040	Private	Young, D.	France	24/8/18
33994	Corporal	Younie, L.	France	1/9/18
23468	Private	Zimmerman, F. X.	France	30/3/18

Deaths in New Zealand—2/Auckland

Officers

10069	2nd Lieut.	Johnston, Wm. Eli	20/1/18
12/3214	Captain	Kirker, Douglas Russell	1/12/18
12/2905	Captain	Senior, Chas. Hastings Alex.	27/10/18

N.C.O.'s and Men

33826	Private	Budd, Michael	1/5/20
4/1025	Private	Brogan, Wilfred Augustus	30/7/19
12/4145	Private	Bumpus, Gerald Wm.	18/2/20
12/3956	Private	Chiplin, Thomas Walter	18/11/19
12/2603	C.Q.M.S.	Cuthbertson, Wm. Jas.	22/4/20
31614	Private	Devine, Hugh Albert	9/11/18
12/4169	Private	Eades, Walter Harold	25/4/19
12/3643	Private	Fraser, Robert Lyle H.	30/8/20
21247	L.-Corporal	Freem, Thomas B.	24/5/20
69345	Private	Gaskin, Arthur Robert	16/5/19
12/1418	Private	Goodall, Wm. Henry	15/2/20
12/3024	Private	Good, Stewart A.	5/6/19

Appendix D

40550	Private	Grupen, Wm. Fredk.	14/11/18
70165	Private	Guild, Thomas	7/7/20
51724	Private	Henderson, Thos. George Wilkie	23/9/19
40573	Private	Johnston, David	20/7/18
24/205	Corporal	Kelly, Alfred Joseph	28/9/20
26863	Private	Lee, John Henry	17/11/18
28743	Private	Lye, Ernest Victor	19/11/18
46377	Private	McIntyre, Shirreffs	30/12/19
44861	Private	McKinlay, Wm.	11/11/18
40611	Private	McNeil, George Walker	9/11/18
12/2062	Private	McSweeney, Edmund	11/11/18
28777	Private	O'Dea, Jack Andrew	24/10/17
13/2885	Private	Parkinson, Arthur Edward	27/5/19
10106	Private	Pointon, Joseph Ebenezer	18/5/19
23/902	Private	Ryan, Edward Thomas	10/12/18
26936	Private	Stilton, Harold John	10/11/18
12/3485	Sergeant	Stone, John Henry	13/11/18
12/4099	Private	Stowell, Hector Arthur	23/11/18
12/3489	Private	Swanson, Arthur	18/11/18
24493	Private	Tuckey, John Wm. H.	20/1/21
12/2864	Private	Twohey, Arthur Paul	4/10/20
21357	Private	Vercoe, Norman Edmond	5/6/19
23/1860	Private	Walker, Theodore	2/11/18
12/390	Private	Warin, Kenneth Cranley	18/11/18
75907	Private	Woods, Chas, Paul Pittman	8/10/19

Officers, N.C.O.'s and Men of 3/Auckland killed in action, died of wounds or disease during the campaigns in France and Flanders

Officers

13/125	Captain	Ruddock, W. D.	France	13/6/17
12/1416	Captain	Gillet, L. H.	France	2/10/17
11/65	Lieutenant	Jickell, H. N.	France	19/10/17
23/2507	Lieutenant	Richardson, H. D.	France	5/10/17
8/1495	2nd Lieut.	Hare, F.	France	2/8/17
12/886	2nd Lieut.	Thompson, A. S.	France	4/8/17

M.S.M. Mentioned in Despatches

30111	2nd Lieut.	Hall, H. J.	France	4/10/17
22525	2nd Lieut.	Milnes, H. A. E.	France	4/10/17
12/2556	2nd Lieut.	Lorie, A.	France	28/12/17

Mentioned in Despatches

N.C.O.'s and Men

51630	Private	Abbott, C.	France	20/10/17
28574	Corporal	Anderson, D.	France	4-5/10/17
34325	Private	Baillie, T. D.	France	4/10/17
34317	Private	Baker, G.	France	4/10/17
52361	Private	Baker, W. L. V.	France	12/10/17
36535	Private	Barrett, J.	France	4/10/17
27170	Corporal	Bedford, W. C.	England	22/9/17
30899	Private	Bennett, F.	France	13/6/17
48316	Private	Billett, C.	France	28/12/17
44689	Private	Boden, A. J.	France	1/1/18
42027	Private	Boyd, W. L.	France	13/12/17
39651	Private	Butt, H. M.	France	8/6/17

The Auckland Regiment

34345	Private	Bryden, W. C.	France	13/6/17
25772	Private	Brameld, H.	France	14/7/17
40503	Private	Brookbanks, H. H.	France	17/8/17
33827	Private	Briddock, T. J.	France	30/6/17
18091	Private	Brown, J.	France	13/7/17
33809	{L.-Corporal {T.-Corporal	Brown, K. R.	France	16/10/17
34316	Private	Brooks, H. W.	France	30/12/17
48761	Private	Browne, E.	France	21/12/17
42271	Private	Brace, J. D.	France	19/10/18
10074	Private	Buchanan, P. K.	France	14/7/17
13418	Private	Burnett, H.	France	4/10/17
42279	Private	Burnside, G. H.	France	15/10/17
51553	Private	Burr, C. W.	France	16/10/17
22768	Private	Callaghan, H. W.	France	13/6/17
32811	Private	Caldwell, G.	France	11/6/17
32826	Private	Carson, A.	France	15/12/17
34471	Private	Carson, W.	France	2/7/17
42287	Private	Chambers, F. W.	France	17/10/17
33693	Private	Chisnall, J.	France	4/10/17
51692	Private	Cousins, J.	France	22/11/17
33833	Private	Cowie, A. G.	France	15/10/17
34337	Private	Cooke, W. J.	France	6/10/17
39170	Private	Collings, B. C.	France	3/10/17
32302	Private	Crook, H.	—	27/12/17
33839	Private	Cosgrave, S. L.	France	19/10/17
38494	Private	Craig, J. E.	France	14/6/17
12/2678	Private	Craig, D. G.	France	13/6/17
28988	Private	Cunningham, P.	France	13/6/17
31610	Private	Darrach, R. S.	France	28/12/17
34339	L.-Corporal	Davis, L. S.	France	4/10/17
31233	L.-Corporal	Dawson, S.	France	28/12/17
35108	L.-Corporal	De Bakker, H.	France	28/12/17
56259	Private	Deller, L. C.	France	11/1/18
48467	Private	Dickin, H. G.	France	20/11/17
33023	Corporal	Donovan, D. J.	France	4/10/17
12/3620	Private	Drew, J. P.	France	17/6/17
5/685	Private	Evans, E.	France	25/10/17
40308	Private	Eyre, C. R.	France	6/8/17
30356	Private	Flett, J. P.	France	7/10/17
35634	Private	Follett, W. R.	France	25/10/17
28584	L.-Sergeant	Francis, S. P. E.	France	16/6/17
33345	Private	Free, T. W.	France	10/12/17
30932	L.-Corporal	Gardner, E. C.	France	15/10/17
51714	Private	Gemmell, J.	France	21/11/17
32844	Private	Giles, F. A.	France	13/6/17
34599	Private	Gow, C.	France	4/10/17
25694	Private	Gray, J.	France	10/7/17
12/2308	Private	Green J.	France	13/6/17
11463	Private	Guinness, C. G.	France	19/10/17
25857	Private	Gumbley, C. R.	France	12/10/17
52416	Private	Guignier, P. P.	France	23/11/17
44722	Private	Hadfield, S.	France	4/10/17
34364	Private	Halliday, J. J.	France	2/7/17
42323	Private	Hamblin, E. J.	France	4/10/17
30947	Private	Hamill, C. P.	France	13/6/17
20998	Private	Hamilton, P.	France	15/10/17
25862	Private	Hansen, W. R.	France	4/10/17
23/1413	Private	Hatte, A. H.	France	19/10/17
32006	Private	Henderson, W. H.	France	4/10/17

[320]

Appendix D

12/3675	L.-Corporal	Henderson, W.	France	30/10/17
48641	Private	Hill, C. R.	France	28/12/17
28588	Sergeant	Holbeche, V. A. E.	France	18/10/17
55214	Private	Howe, H. B.	France	28/12/17
30803	Private	Horscroft, C. A.	France	4/10/17
12/3236	Sergeant	Hoe, S. R.	France	8/6/17
34376	Private	Ireland, J.	France	13/6/17
23/1913	C.S.M. W.O. II	Jackson, C. P. M.	France	5/10/17
12/768	C.Q.M.S.	Jamieson, L.	France	16/11/17
54886	Private	Johnson, A. J.	France	31/12/17
26628	Private	Jones, A. S.	France	18/10/17
45521	Private	Kelleher, D. F	France	17/10/17
56616	Private	King, J. F.	France	22/11/17
30954	Private	King, S. E.	France	15/7/17
31662	Private	Knight, C. W.	France	28/12/17
4977	Private	Krohn, C. M.	France	12/10/17
29034	Private	Large, H.	France	4/10/17
47194	Private	Lawry, W. J.	France	18/10/17
34475	Corporal	Livingstone, A.	France	4/10/17
28590	Sergeant	Lord, E. J.	France	4/10/17
26/838	Private	Lye, W. L. H.	France	22/10/17
11330	L.-Sergeant	MacGregor, J. L.	France	19/10/17
20927	Sergeant	MacLean, K. C.	France	4/10/17
33923	Private	McCabe, B. A.	France	18/10/17
30446	Private	McClymont, C.	France	4/10/17
36470	Private	McConnach, A.	France	7/1/18
34402	Private	McGuire, J.	France	30/11/17
36877	Private	McKenzie, K. J.	France	29/7/17
10/892	Private	McLeod, W.	France	18/10/18
39669	Private	McLeigh, G. W.	France	3/7/17
13793	Private	McPherson, J.	France	4/10/17
47233	Private	Macalister, R.	France	28/12/17
52446	Private	Magee, J.	France	2/9/18
36464	Private	Mahoney, G. R.	France	4/10/17
35119	Sergeant	Maine, W. F.	France	4/10/17
13703	Sergeant	Minifie, A.	France	8/7/17
38423	Private	Middleton, G. E.	France	2/10/17
36466	Private	Middleton, J.	France	14/6/17
32031	Private	Mortimer, R.	France	15/6/17
33902	L.-Corporal	Moffitt, C. A.	France	26/11/17
20197	Private	Muldoon, H. B.	France	10/7/17
33750	Private	Murphy, J. P.	France	4/8/17
31136	Private	Negus, C. W.	France	12/10/17
40614	Private	Nelson, C. A.	France	19/11/17
54944	Private	Nelson, C. E.	France	23/11/17
33755	Private	Newlove, L. C.	France	4/10/17
34492	Private	Nevitt, H.	France	28/12/17
40620	Private	Niccol, N. S.	France	28/12/17
39670	Private	Nicolai, W.	France	9/6/17
29059	L.-Corporal	Noblett, J.	France	15/10/17
12/3118	L.-Corporal	O'Neill, H. A.	France	4/10/17
18573	Private	Partridge, J.	France	3/10/17
29068	Private	Parry, F. Q.	France	19/11/17
12/2817	Private	Paton, J. A	France	4/10/17
35125	Private	Petrie, G. C. V.	France	9/6/17
31432	Private	Plaisted, E. A.	France	12/10/17
18849	Private	Pollard, N. F.	France	22/12/17
40636	Private	Poynton, M.	France	20/11/17
32052	Private	Presnell, F. P.	France	10/7/17

The Auckland Regiment

49740	Private	Quinton, E. J.	France	30/12/17
42396	Private	Radford, W.	France	18/10/17
53713	Private	Roberts, A. J.	France	28/11/17
33951	Private	Robinson, F. D.	France	4/10/17
34434	Private	Rudd, T.	France	28/12/17
34439	Private	Sanderson, A.	France	16/11/17
28545	Private	Scott, R. M.	France	10/8/17
35223	Private	Scott, T. A.	France	11/7/17
40647	Private	Seaton, J. F.	France	4/10/17
36368	Sergeant	Sinclair, W.	France	3/10/17
36494	Private	Simpson, F. L.	France	4/10/17
35225	Private	Spargo, W. J.	France	28/12/17
54985	Private	Stevens, A. R.	France	23/11/17
32243	Private	Stevenson, J.	France	5/7/17
42422	Private	Sutcliffe, B.	France	30/12/17
36891	Private	Sutherland, F. V	France	15/6/17
25/240	Sergeant	Sullivan, E. F.	France	14/6/17
30990	Private	Taylor, A. J.	France	13/6/17
42428	Private	Tims, A.	France	5/10/17
40393	Private	Toomey, N. E. J.	France	19/10/17
23/936	Private	Tosh, W. McK. L.	France	6/8/17
30882	Private	Wall, H. J.	France	28/12/17
42434	Private	Walker, J. G.	France	7/12/17
10/2788	T.-Sergeant	Warrington, H. F.	France	4/10/17
31008	Private	Wells, F.	France	8/6/17
51584	Private	Whitehorn, W. K. Croix de Guerre	France	15/10/17
29119	Corporal	Wills, E. J., M.M.	France	5/10/17
29116	Private	Willan, G.	France	28/12/17
40420	Private	Wilson, W. H.	France	28/12/17
44815	Private	Windsor, A. H.	France	18/12/17
10934	Private	Wilson, H.	France	23/6/17
16034	Private	Woods, R.	France	4/10/17
34467	Private	Younie, T.	France	7/10/17

Deaths in New Zealand—3/Auckland

39652	Private	Chetham, Howard Franklin	1/11/18
26617	Private	Henderson, Percy B.	15/11/18
12/2379	Private	Martin, Wm. Patrick	26/6/20
12/4223	Private	Morrison, George Wm.	20/11/18
39569	Private	Walton, Alfred Hardy	15/11/18

Auckland Regiment

12/2273	Private	Dickey, W.	England	1/6/16
33859	Private	Edmunds, C. L.	France	4/10/17
46335	L.-Corporal	Godley, W. P.	France	3/4/18
51732	Private	Hutchinson, T.	England	28/6/18
59925	Private	Lusby, W.	France	1/3/18
21117	Private	Thomas, G. H.	France	12/10/17
63980	Private	Whitaker, A.	France	15/4/18
42443	Private	Wilson, G. McF.	France	16/8/17

Battalions not given for above.

Deaths in New Zealand—Unclassified

12/556	Private	Bickerton, Chas, Frederick	6/11/18
12/2569	Private	Chitty, Albert Ernest	13/1/18
46852	Private	Coad, Wm. Ernest	27/11/18
12/3316	L.-Corporal	Ferguson, Edwin John Alex.	21/11/18

Appendix D

12/1963	Private	Greensides, Ernest	24/11/18
12/359	Private	Gemming, Thos. Alfred	26/4/17
12/756	Private	Henderson, Henry	8/3/20
52202	Private	Hamilton, George	17/11/18
12/933	Private	Long, Alfred Eric St. George	8/7/19
48982	Private	Moore, Edward	3/7/20
12/2049	Private	McConkey, Thomas Alfred	23/12/15
12/2078	Private	Paufai, Hono	6/11/18
12/2467	Private	Shepherd, Frederick W.	26/12/18
12/1499	Private	Shannon, Leslie Richard	9/1/16
12/2591	Corporal	Troward, Thomas Albany	21/5/18
12/1831	Private	Whittle, Thomas	6/11/18
12/2029	Private	Yeend, Henry Wm.	10/1/17

In list of deaths the word France includes Belgium.

"*Their memory endureth for ever.*"

"*To you from failing hands we throw
The torch. Be yours to lift it high.
If ye break faith with us who die,
We shall not sleep, though poppies grow
On Flanders fields.*"
—John McCrea.

"O Lord, since first the blood of Abel cried to Thee from the ground that drank it, this earth of Thine has been defiled with the blood of man shed by his brother's hand, and the centuries sob with the ceaseless horror of war. Ever the pride of kings and the covetousness of the strong have driven peaceful nations to slaughter. Ever the songs of the past and the pomp of armies have been used to inflame the passions of the people. Our spirit cries out to Thee in revolt against it, and we know that our righteous anger is answered by Thy holy wrath.

"Break Thou the spell of the enchantments that make the nations drunk with the lust of battle and draw them on as willing tools of death. Grant us a quiet and steadfast mind when our own nation clamours for vengeance or aggression. Strengthen our sense of justice and our regard for the equal worth of other peoples and races. Grant to the rulers of nations faith in the possibility of peace through justice, and grant to the common people a new and stern enthusiasm for the cause of peace. Bless our soldiers and sailors for their swift obedience and their willingness to answer to the call of duty, but inspire them none the less with a hatred of war, and may they never for love of private glory or advancement provoke its coming. May our young men still rejoice to die for their country with the valour of their fathers, but teach our age nobler methods of matching our strength and more effective ways of giving our life for the flag.

"O Thou strong Father of all nations, draw all Thy great family together with an increasing sense of our common blood and destiny, that peace may come on earth at last, and Thy sun may shed its light rejoicing on a holy brotherhood of peoples."

—Walter Rauschenbusch

www.ingramcontent.com/pod-product-compliance
Lightning Source LLC
Chambersburg PA
CBHW021828220426
43663CB00005B/162